NEGIMA! 32

Ken Akamatsu

TRANSLATED AND ADAPTED BY
Alethea Nibley and Athena Nibley

LETTERING AND RETOUCH BY
Scott O. Brown

KC
KODANSHA
COMICS

A Kodansha Comics Trade Paperback Original

Negima! volume 32 copyright © 2010 Ken Akamatsu
English translation copyright © 2011 Ken Akamatsu

Published in the United States by Kodansha Comics, an imprint of Kodansha USA Publishing, LLC, New York.

Publication rights for this English edition arranged through Kodansha Ltd., Tokyo.

First published in Japan in 2010 by Kodansha Ltd., Tokyo, as *Maho sensei Negima!*, volume 32.

ISBN 978-1-935-42959-3

Printed in the United States of America.

www.kodanshacomics.com

9 8 7 6 5 4 3 2 1

Translator/Adapter: Alethea Nibley and Athena Nibley
Lettering: Scott O. Brown

Honorifics Explained

Throughout the Kodansha Comics books, you will find Japanese honorifics left intact in the translations. For those not familiar with how the Japanese use honorifics and, more important, how they differ from American honorifics, we present this brief overview.

Politeness has always been a critical facet of Japanese culture. Ever since the feudal era, when Japan was a highly stratified society, use of honorifics—which can be defined as polite speech that indicates relationship or status—has played an essential role in the Japanese language. When addressing someone in Japanese, an honorific usually takes the form of a suffix attached to one's name (example: "Asuna-san"), is used as a title at the end of one's name, or appears in place of the name itself (example: "Negi-sensei," or simply "Sensei!").

Honorifics can be expressions of respect or endearment. In the context of manga and anime, honorifics give insight into the nature of the relationship between characters. Many English translations leave out these important honorifics and therefore distort the feel of the original Japanese. Because Japanese honorifics contain nuances that English honorifics lack, it is our policy at Kodansha Comics not to translate them. Here, instead, is a guide to some of the honorifics you may encounter in Kodansha Comics.

-san: This is the most common honorific and is equivalent to Mr., Miss, Ms., or Mrs. It is the all-purpose honorific and can be used in any situation where politeness is required.

-sama: This is one level higher than "-san" and is used to confer great respect.

-dono: This comes from the word "tono," which means "lord." It is an even higher level than "-sama" and confers utmost respect.

-kun: This suffix is used at the end of boys' names to express familiarity or endearment. It is also sometimes used by men

among friends, or when addressing someone younger or of a lower station.

chan: This is used to express endearment, mostly toward girls. It is also used for little boys, pets, and even among lovers. It gives a sense of childish cuteness.

Bōzu: This is an informal way to refer to a boy, similar to the English terms "kid" and "squirt."

Sempai/Senpai: This title suggests that the addressee is one's senior in a group or organization. It is most often used in a school setting, where underclassmen refer to their upperclassmen as "sempai." It can also be used in the workplace, such as when a newer employee addresses an employee who has seniority in the company.

Kohai: This is the opposite of "sempai" and is used toward underclassmen in school or newcomers in the workplace. It connotes that the addressee is of a lower station.

Sensei: Literally meaning "one who has come before," this title is used for teachers, doctors, or masters of any profession or art.

-[blank]: This is usually forgotten in these lists, but it is perhaps the most significant difference between Japanese and English. The lack of honorific means that the speaker has permission to address the person in a very intimate way. Usually, only family, spouses, or very close friends have this kind of permission. Known as yobisute, it can be gratifying when someone who has earned the intimacy starts to call one by one's name without an honorific. But when that intimacy hasn't been earned, it can be very insulting.

A word from the author

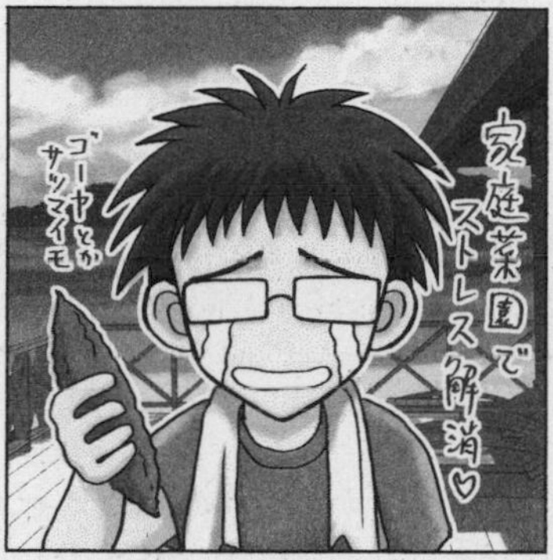
I RELIEVE STRESS WITH MY HOME VEGETABLE GARDEN ♥
家庭菜園でストレス解消♡
ゴーヤとかサツマイモ
GROWING GŌYA MELONS AND SWEET POTATOES.

Now presenting Negima! volume 32.

At last, the Magical World Arc is getting into the final battle with Fate! Before that...there still are a lot of things to do. Like make the final preparations, and get ready mentally. That's pretty much what this volume is about (laugh).

Ken Akamatsu's home page address*
http://www.ailove.net/

*Please note the webpage is in Japanese.

Ken Akamatsu

NEGIMA!

MAGISTER NEGI MAGI

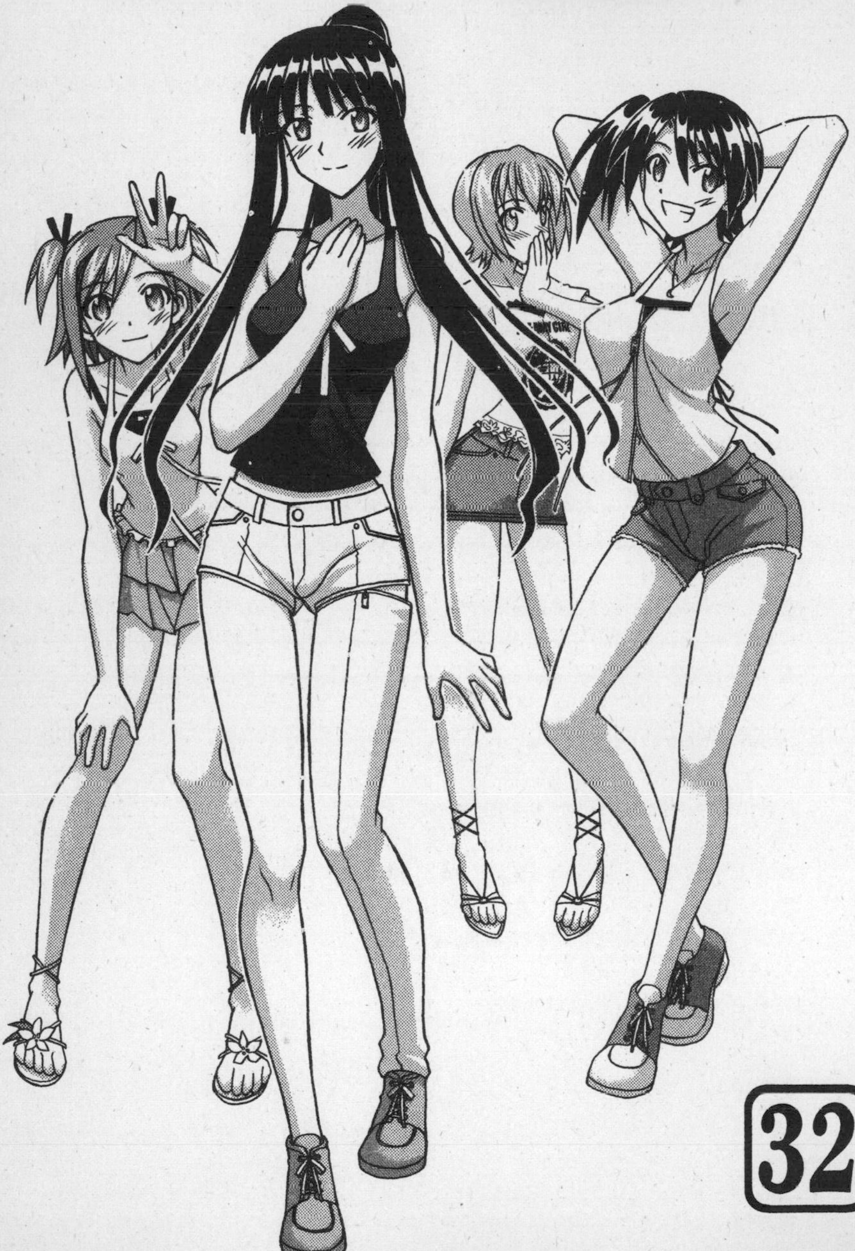

32

CONTENTS

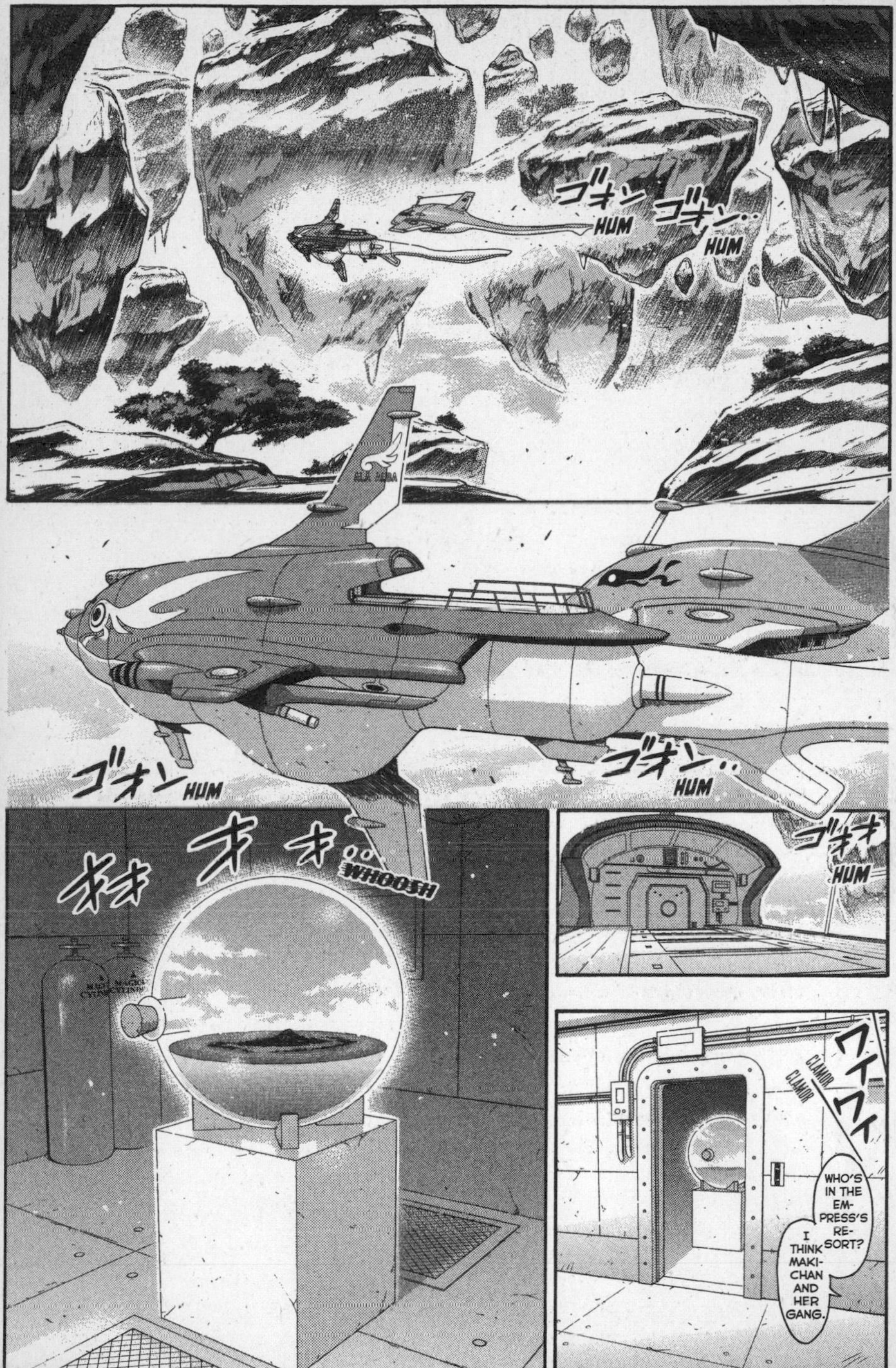
ゴオン‥
HUM
ゴオン
HUM
ゴオン‥
HUM
ゴオン
HUM
ゴオォ
HUM
ワイワイ
CLAMOR CLAMOR
WHO'S IN THE EMPRESS'S RESORT?
I THINK MAKI-CHAN AND HER GANG.
ォォ オォ‥
WHOOSH

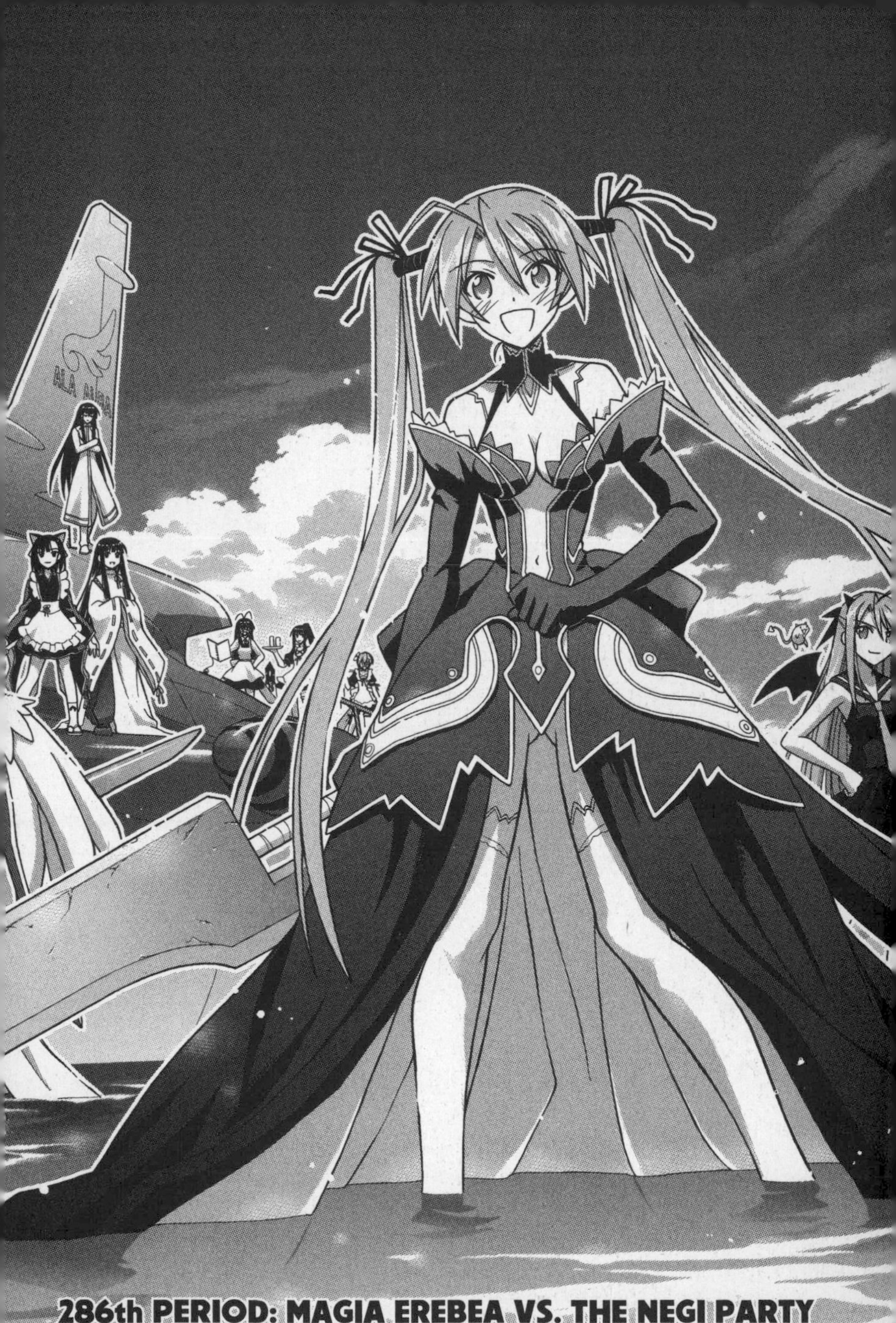

286th PERIOD: MAGIA EREBEA VS. THE NEGI PARTY

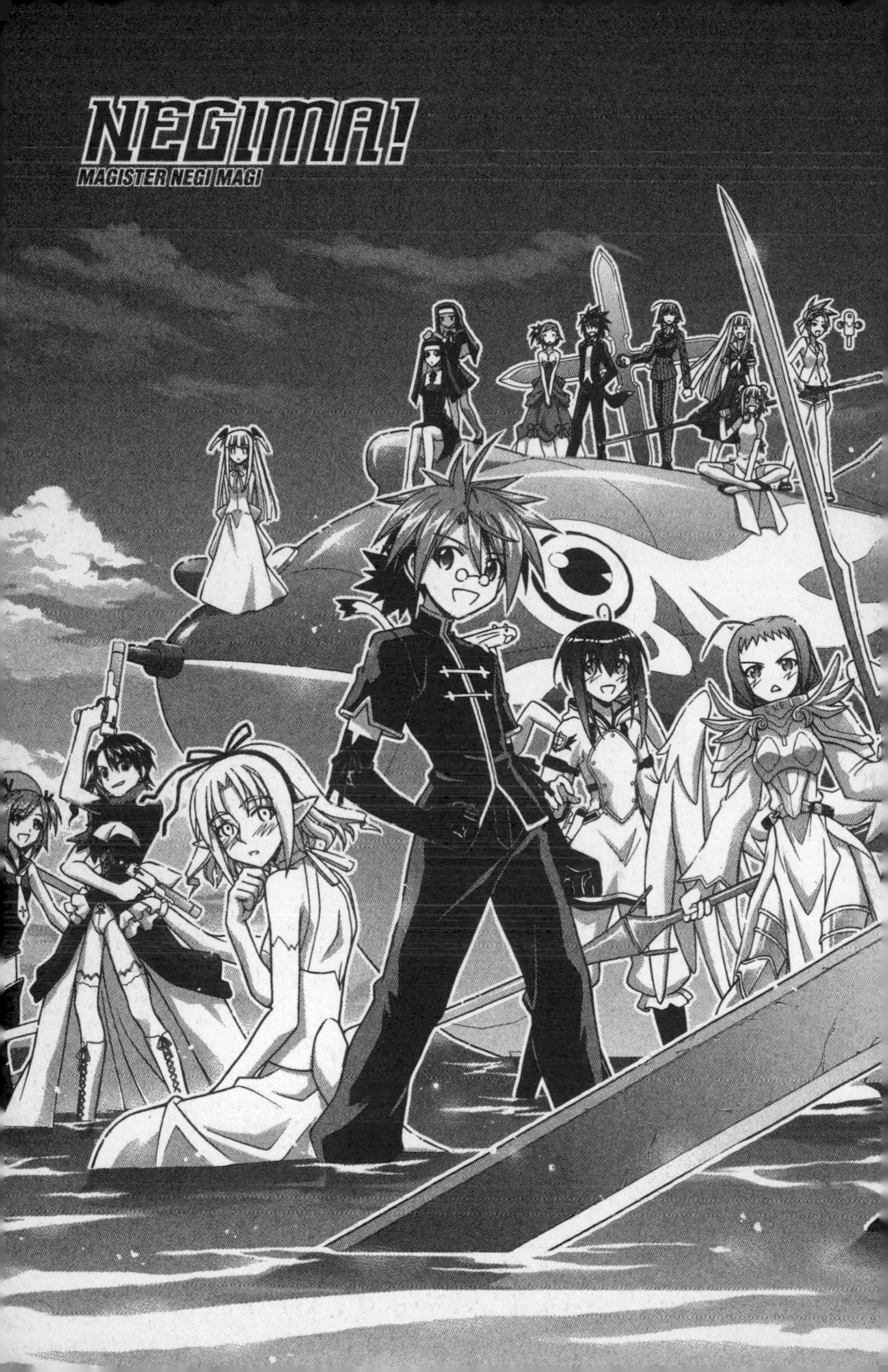
NEGIMA!
MAGISTER NEGI MAGI

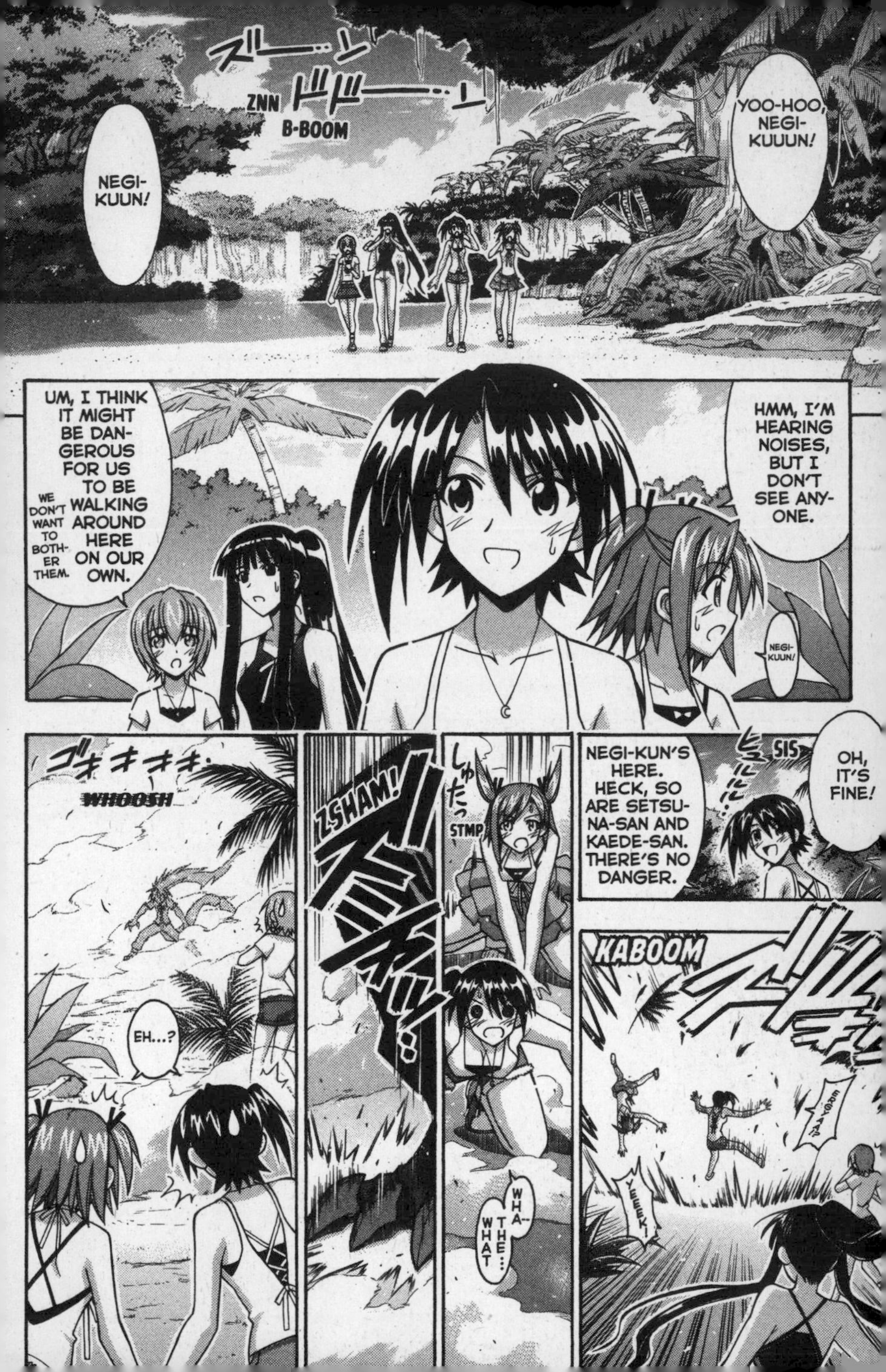
YOO-HOO, NEGI-KUUUN!
ZNN
B-BOOM
NEGI-KUUN!
HMM, I'M HEARING NOISES, BUT I DON'T SEE ANYONE.
NEGI-KUUN!
UM, I THINK IT MIGHT BE DANGEROUS FOR US TO BE WALKING AROUND HERE ON OUR OWN.
WE DON'T WANT TO BOTHER THEM.
OH, IT'S FINE!
SIS
NEGI-KUN'S HERE. HECK, SO ARE SETSUNA-SAN AND KAEDE-SAN. THERE'S NO DANGER.
KABOOM
YEEEK!
STMP
ZSHAM!
WHA- WHAT THE...
WHOOSH
EH...?

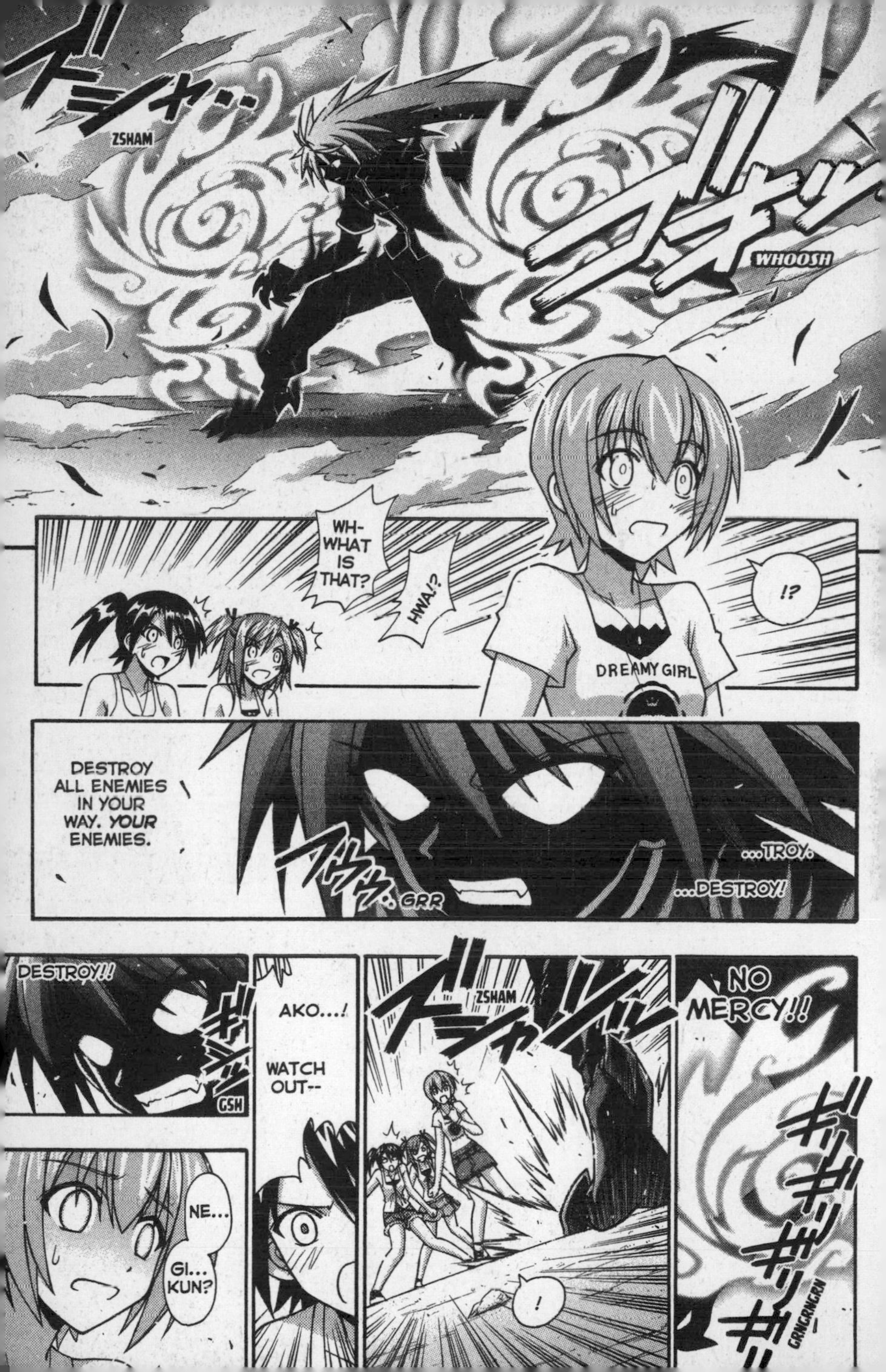
WHOOSH
ZSHAM
!?
WH-WHAT IS THAT?
HWA!?
DREAMY GIRL
...TROY.
...DESTROY!
GRR
DESTROY ALL ENEMIES IN YOUR WAY. YOUR ENEMIES.
NO MERCY!!
GRNGRNGRN
ZSHAM
!
AKO...!
WATCH OUT--
DESTROY!!
GSH
NE...
GI... KUN?

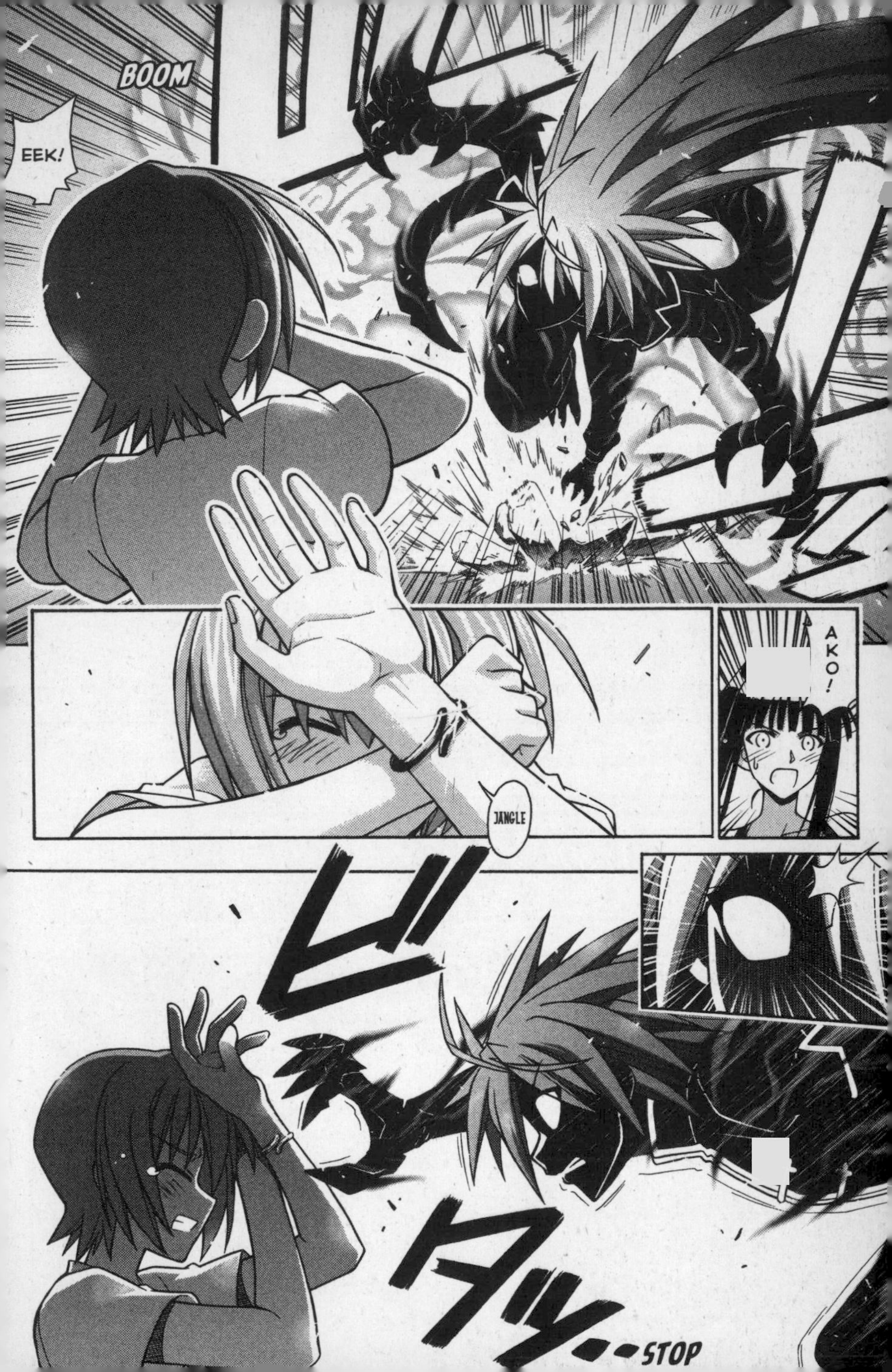
BOOM
EEK!
AKO!
JANGLE
STOP

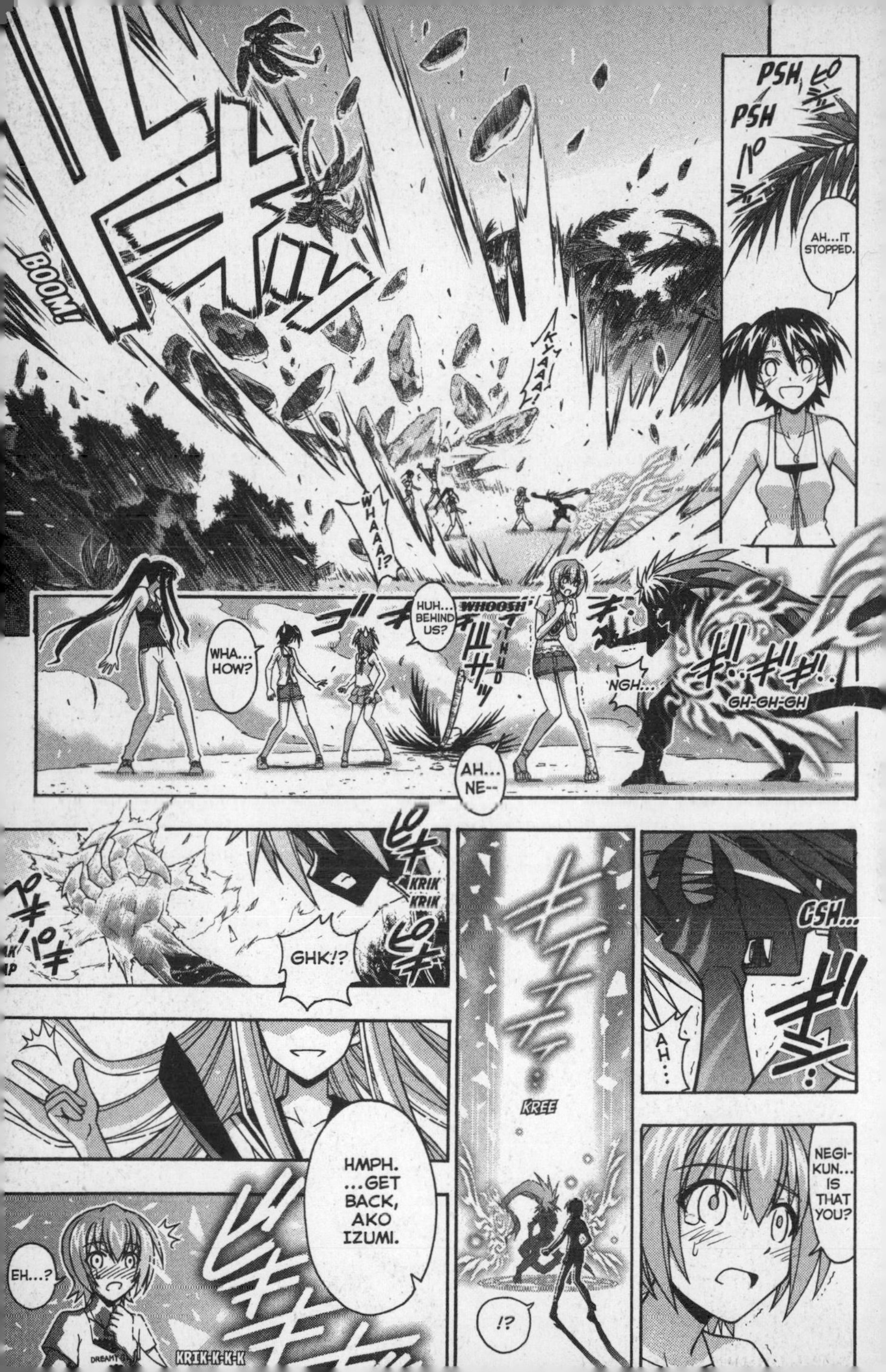

PSH
PSH
AH...IT STOPPED.
BOOM!
KYAAAA!
WHAAAA!?
GH-GH-GH
'NGH...
WHOOSH
THUD
AH... NE--
HUH... BEHIND US?
WHA... HOW?
GSH...
AH...
NEGI-KUN... IS THAT YOU?
KREE
!?
KRIK
KRIK
GHK!?
HMPH. ...GET BACK, AKO IZUMI.
EH...?
KRIK-K-K-K

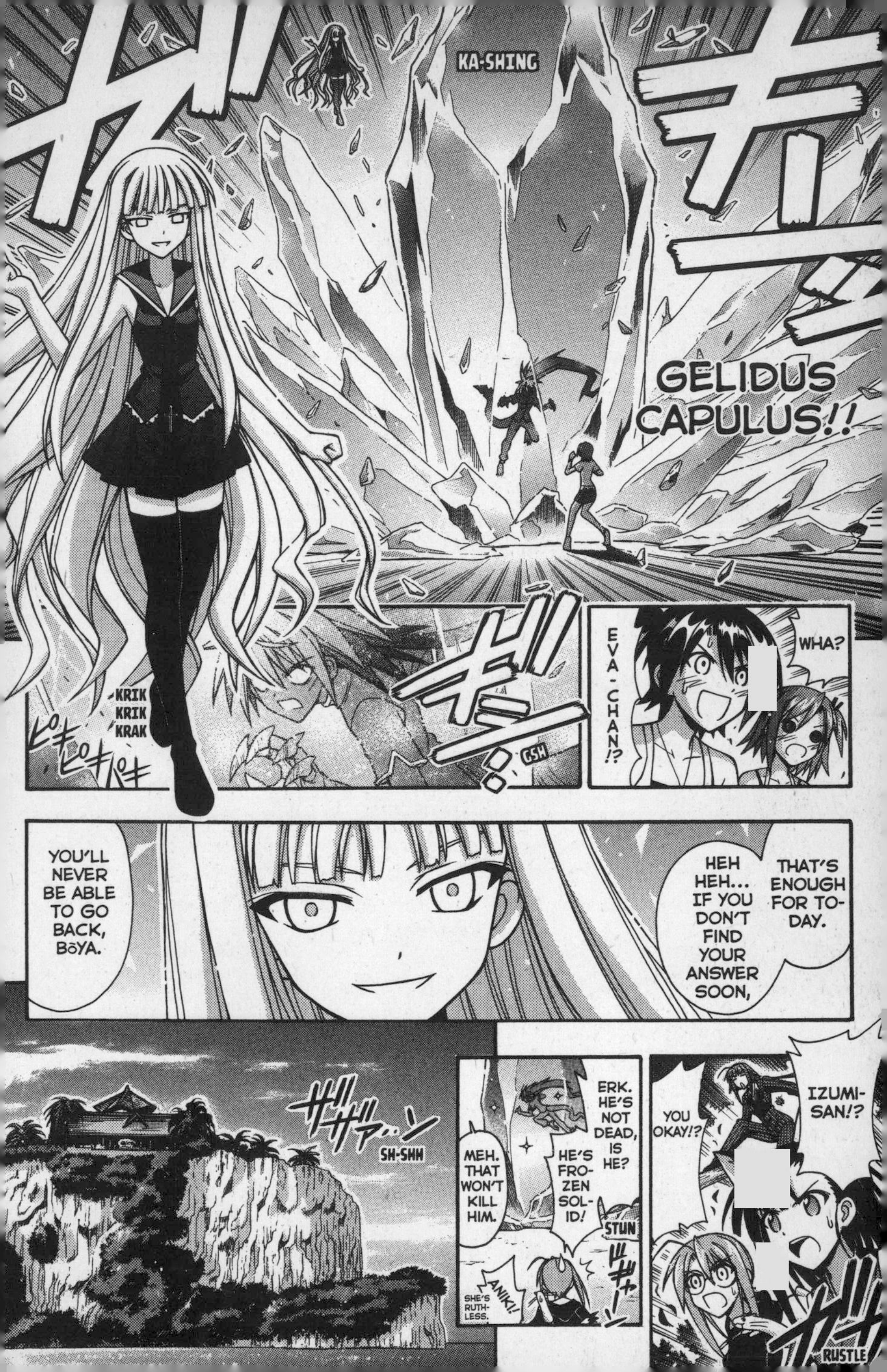
KA-SHING
GELIDUS CAPULUS!!
WHA?
EVA-CHAN!?
GSH
KRIK KRIK KRAK
THAT'S ENOUGH FOR TO-DAY.
HEH HEH... IF YOU DON'T FIND YOUR ANSWER SOON,
YOU'LL NEVER BE ABLE TO GO BACK, BōYA.
IZUMI-SAN!?
YOU OKAY!?
RUSTLE
ERK. HE'S NOT DEAD, IS HE?
HE'S FRO-ZEN SOL-ID!
MEH. THAT WON'T KILL HIM.
STUN
ANIKI!!
SHE'S RUTH-LESS.
SH-SHH

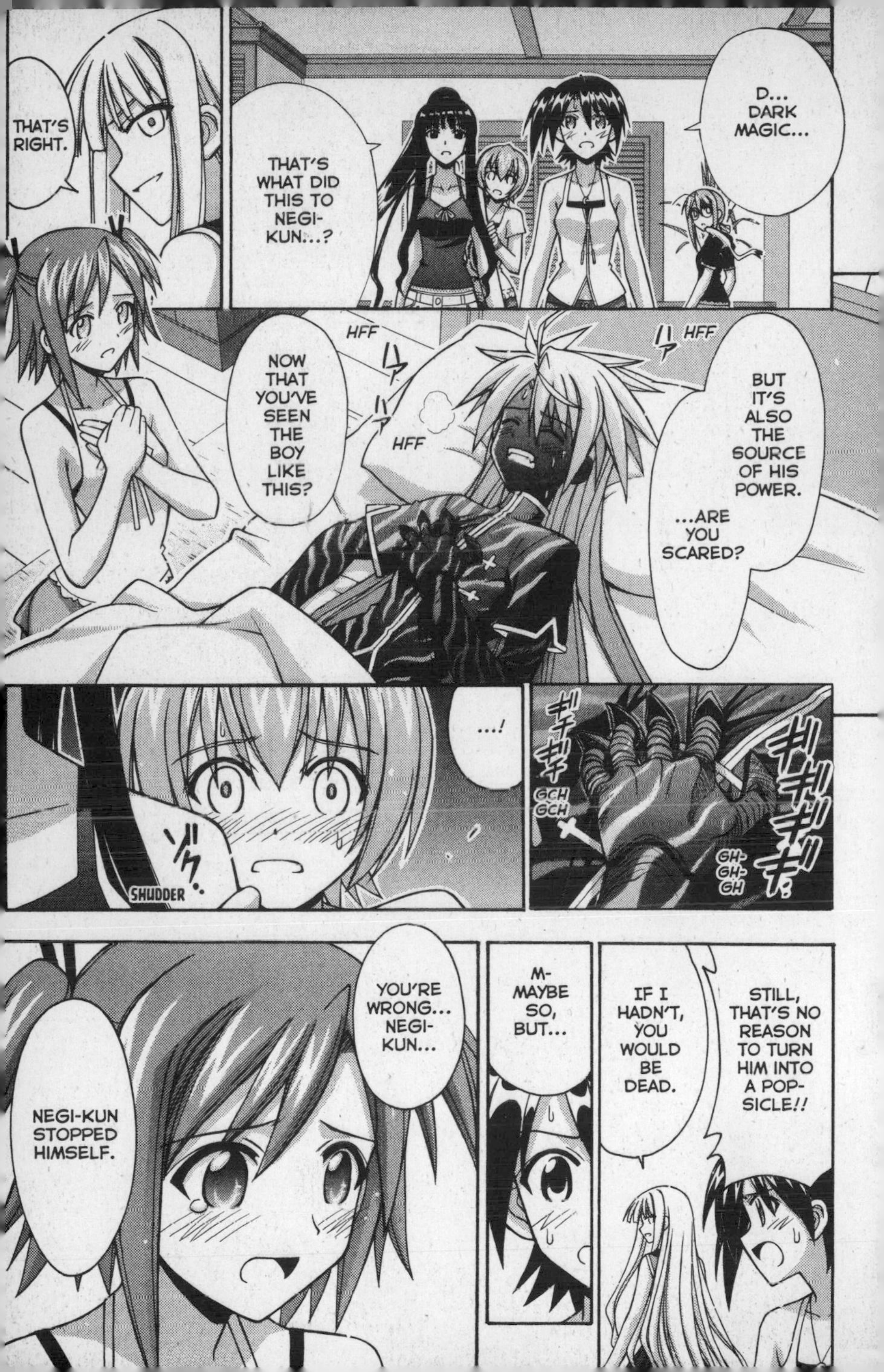

D... DARK MAGIC...
THAT'S WHAT DID THIS TO NEGI-KUN...?
THAT'S RIGHT.
HFF
BUT IT'S ALSO THE SOURCE OF HIS POWER.
...ARE YOU SCARED?
HFF
HFF
NOW THAT YOU'VE SEEN THE BOY LIKE THIS?
GH-GH-GH
GCH GCH
...!
SHUDDER
STILL, THAT'S NO REASON TO TURN HIM INTO A POP-SICLE!!
IF I HADN'T, YOU WOULD BE DEAD.
M-MAYBE SO, BUT...
YOU'RE WRONG... NEGI-KUN...
NEGI-KUN STOPPED HIMSELF.

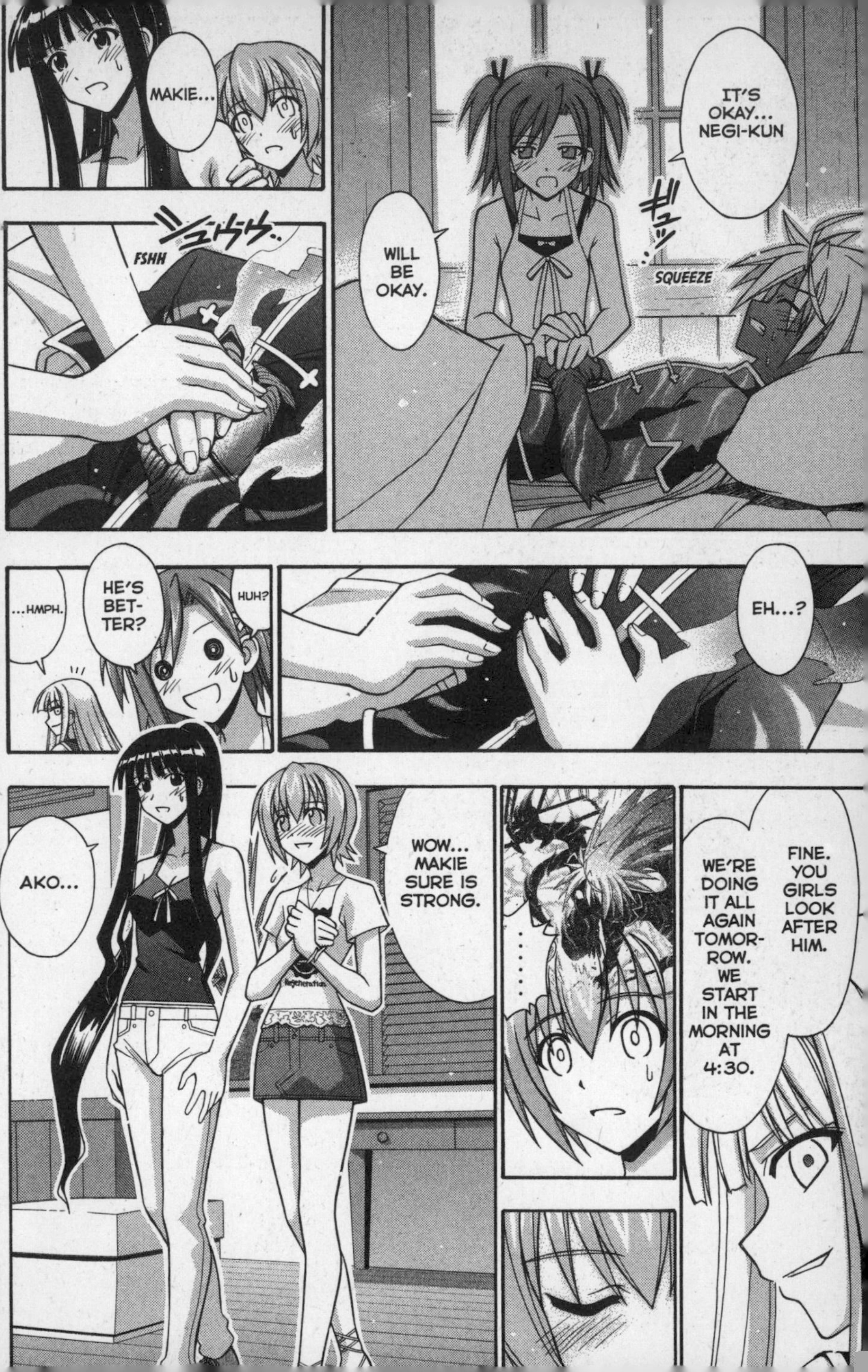
IT'S OKAY... NEGI-KUN
SQUEEZE
WILL BE OKAY.
MAKIE...
FSHH
EH...?
HUH?
HE'S BET-TER?
...HMPH.
FINE. YOU GIRLS LOOK AFTER HIM.
WE'RE DOING IT ALL AGAIN TOMOR-ROW. WE START IN THE MORNING AT 4:30.
......
WOW... MAKIE SURE IS STRONG.
AKO...

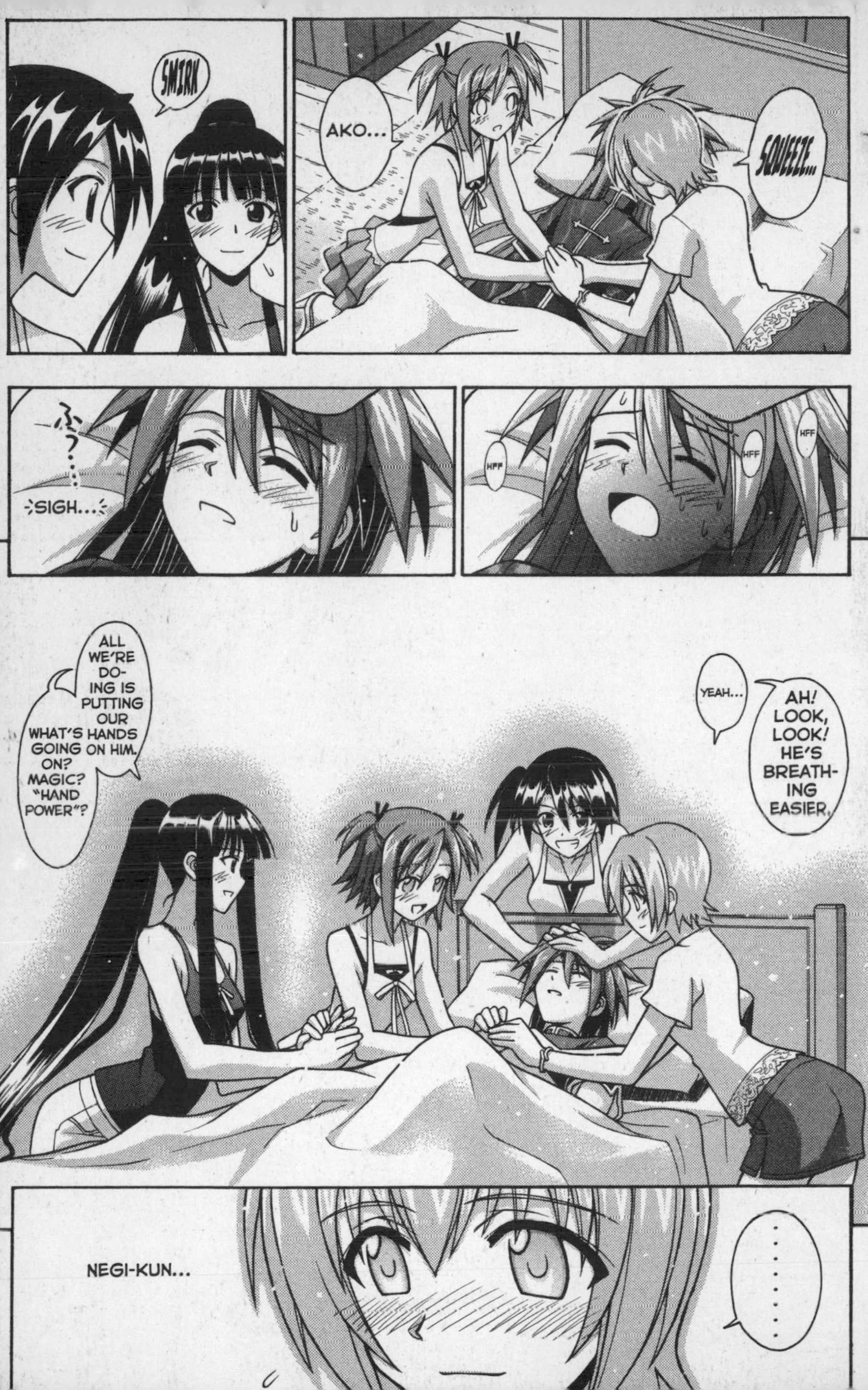
SQUEEZE...
AKO...
SMIRK
HFF
HFF
HFF
ふう…
SIGH...
AH! LOOK, LOOK! HE'S BREATHING EASIER.
YEAH...
ALL WE'RE DOING IS PUTTING OUR HANDS ON HIM.
WHAT'S GOING ON? MAGIC? "HAND POWER"?
......
NEGI-KUN...

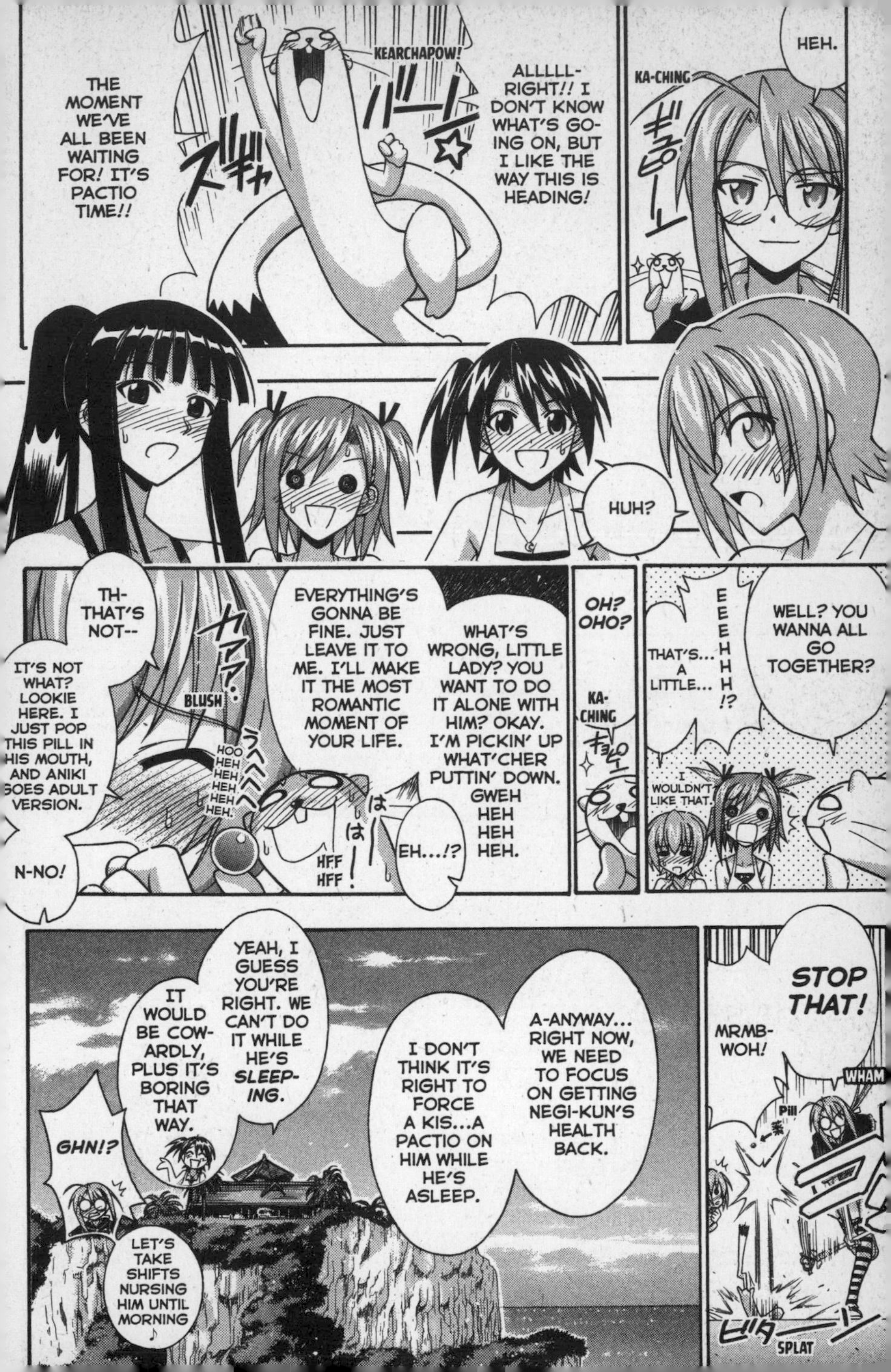
HEH.
KA-CHING
ALLLLL-RIGHT!! I DON'T KNOW WHAT'S GO-ING ON, BUT I LIKE THE WAY THIS IS HEADING!
KEARCHAPOW!
THE MOMENT WE'VE ALL BEEN WAITING FOR! IT'S PACTIO TIME!!
HUH?
WELL? YOU WANNA ALL GO TOGETHER?
EEEEHHH!?
THAT'S... A LITTLE...
I WOULDN'T LIKE THAT.
OH? OHO?
KA-CHING
WHAT'S WRONG, LITTLE LADY? YOU WANT TO DO IT ALONE WITH HIM? OKAY. I'M PICKIN' UP WHAT'CHER PUTTIN' DOWN. GWEH HEH HEH HEH.
EVERYTHING'S GONNA BE FINE. JUST LEAVE IT TO ME. I'LL MAKE IT THE MOST ROMANTIC MOMENT OF YOUR LIFE.
TH-THAT'S NOT--
BLUSH
IT'S NOT WHAT? LOOKIE HERE. I JUST POP THIS PILL IN HIS MOUTH, AND ANIKI GOES ADULT VERSION.
HOO HEH HEH HEH HEH HEH.
EH...!?
HFF HFF
N-NO!
STOP THAT!
MRMB-WOH!
WHAM
SPLAT
A-ANYWAY... RIGHT NOW, WE NEED TO FOCUS ON GETTING NEGI-KUN'S HEALTH BACK.
I DON'T THINK IT'S RIGHT TO FORCE A KIS...A PACTIO ON HIM WHILE HE'S ASLEEP.
YEAH, I GUESS YOU'RE RIGHT. WE CAN'T DO IT WHILE HE'S SLEEPING.
IT WOULD BE COW-ARDLY, PLUS IT'S BORING THAT WAY.
GHN!?
LET'S TAKE SHIFTS NURSING HIM UNTIL MORNING ♪

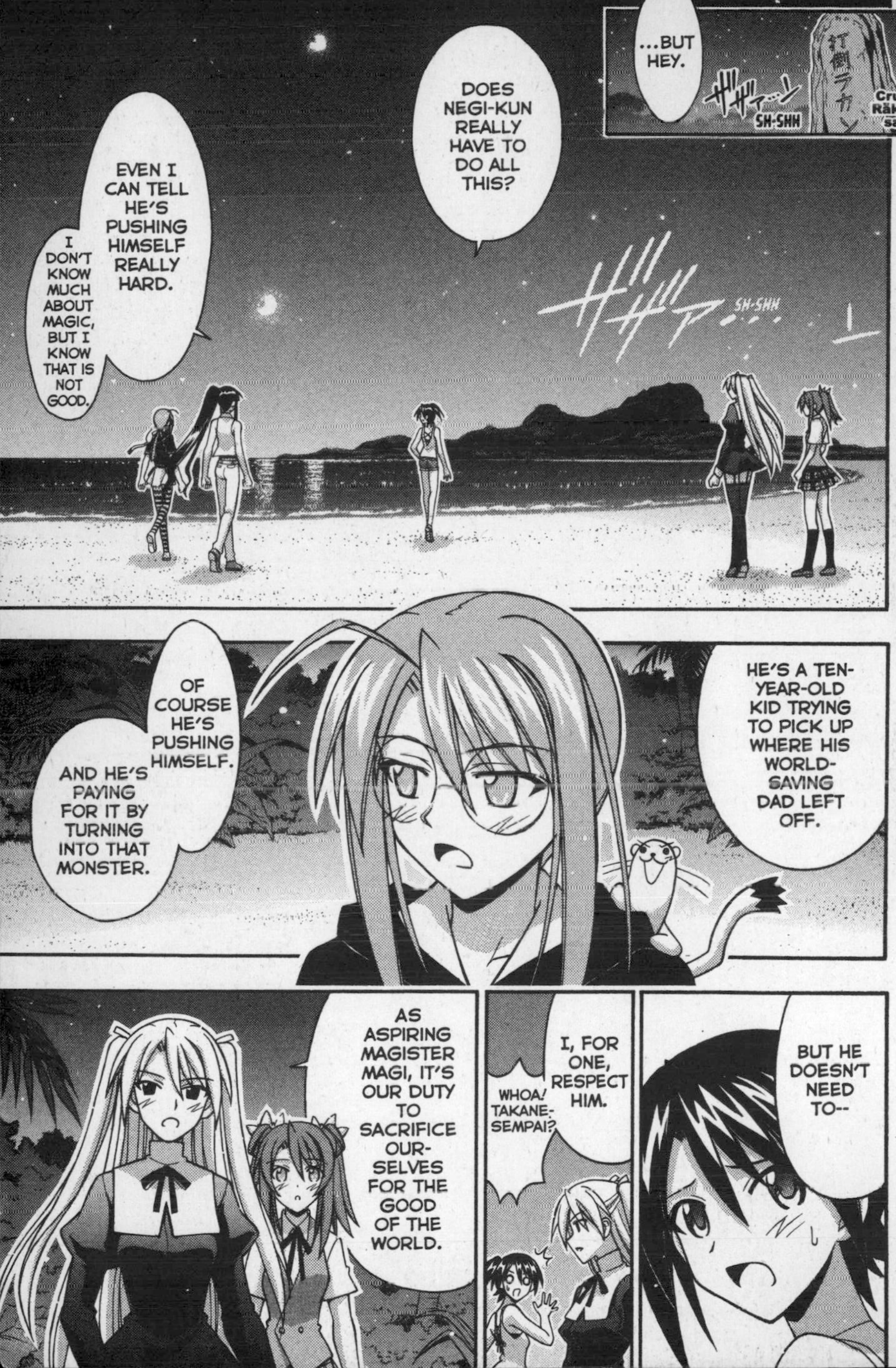

...BUT HEY.
SH-SHH
DOES NEGI-KUN REALLY HAVE TO DO ALL THIS?
EVEN I CAN TELL HE'S PUSHING HIMSELF REALLY HARD.
I DON'T KNOW MUCH ABOUT MAGIC, BUT I KNOW THAT IS NOT GOOD.
SH-SHH
HE'S A TEN-YEAR-OLD KID TRYING TO PICK UP WHERE HIS WORLD-SAVING DAD LEFT OFF.
OF COURSE HE'S PUSHING HIMSELF.
AND HE'S PAYING FOR IT BY TURNING INTO THAT MONSTER.
BUT HE DOESN'T NEED TO--
I, FOR ONE, RESPECT HIM.
WHOA! TAKANE-SEMPAI?
AS ASPIRING MAGISTER MAGI, IT'S OUR DUTY TO SACRIFICE OUR-SELVES FOR THE GOOD OF THE WORLD.

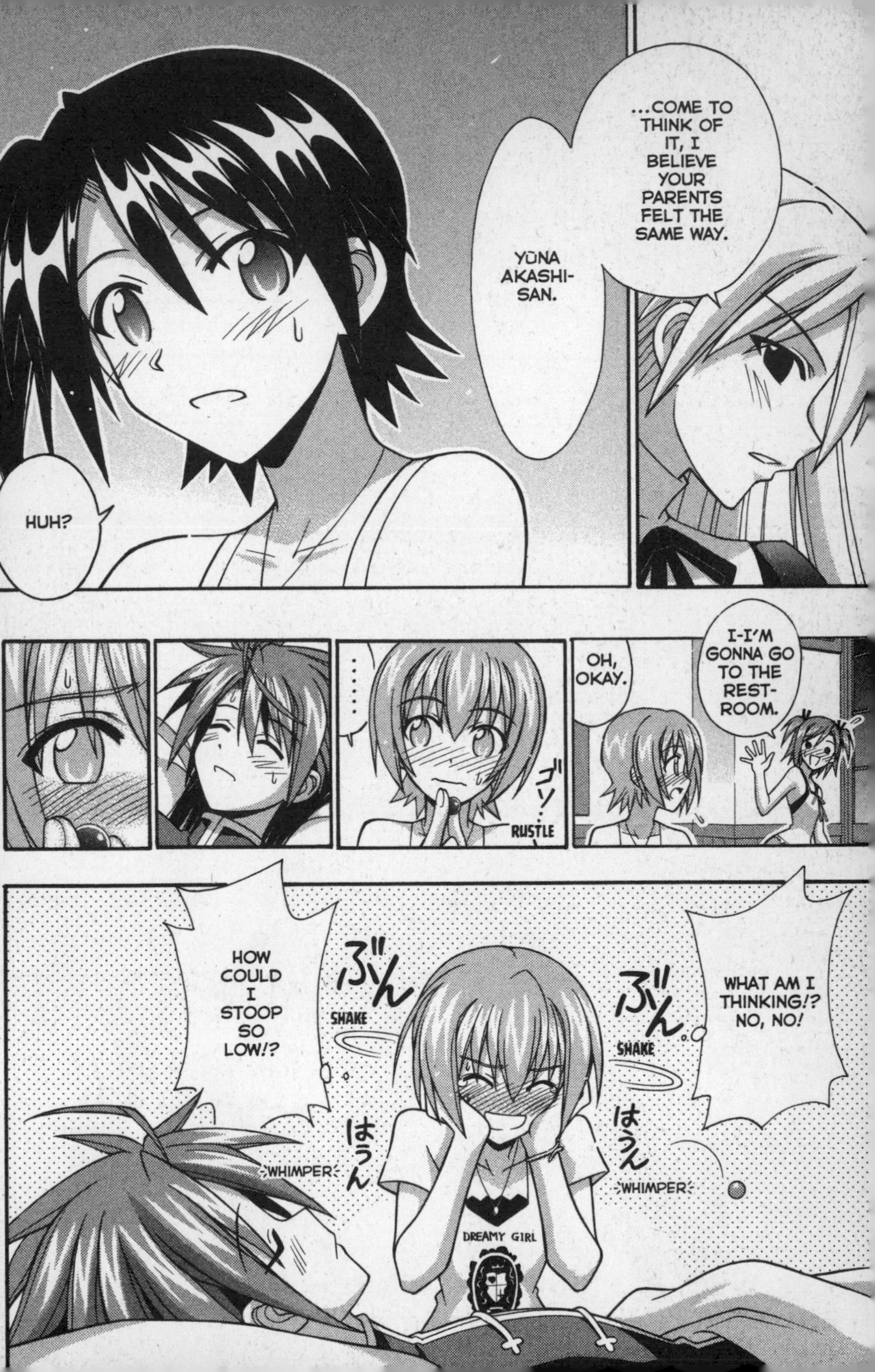
...COME TO THINK OF IT, I BELIEVE YOUR PARENTS FELT THE SAME WAY.
YŪNA AKASHI-SAN.
HUH?
I-I'M GONNA GO TO THE REST-ROOM.
OH, OKAY.
......
ゴソ…
RUSTLE
WHAT AM I THINKING!? NO, NO!
ぶん
SHAKE
はうん
WHIMPER
ぶん
SHAKE
HOW COULD I STOOP SO LOW!?
はうん
WHIMPER
DREAMY GIRL

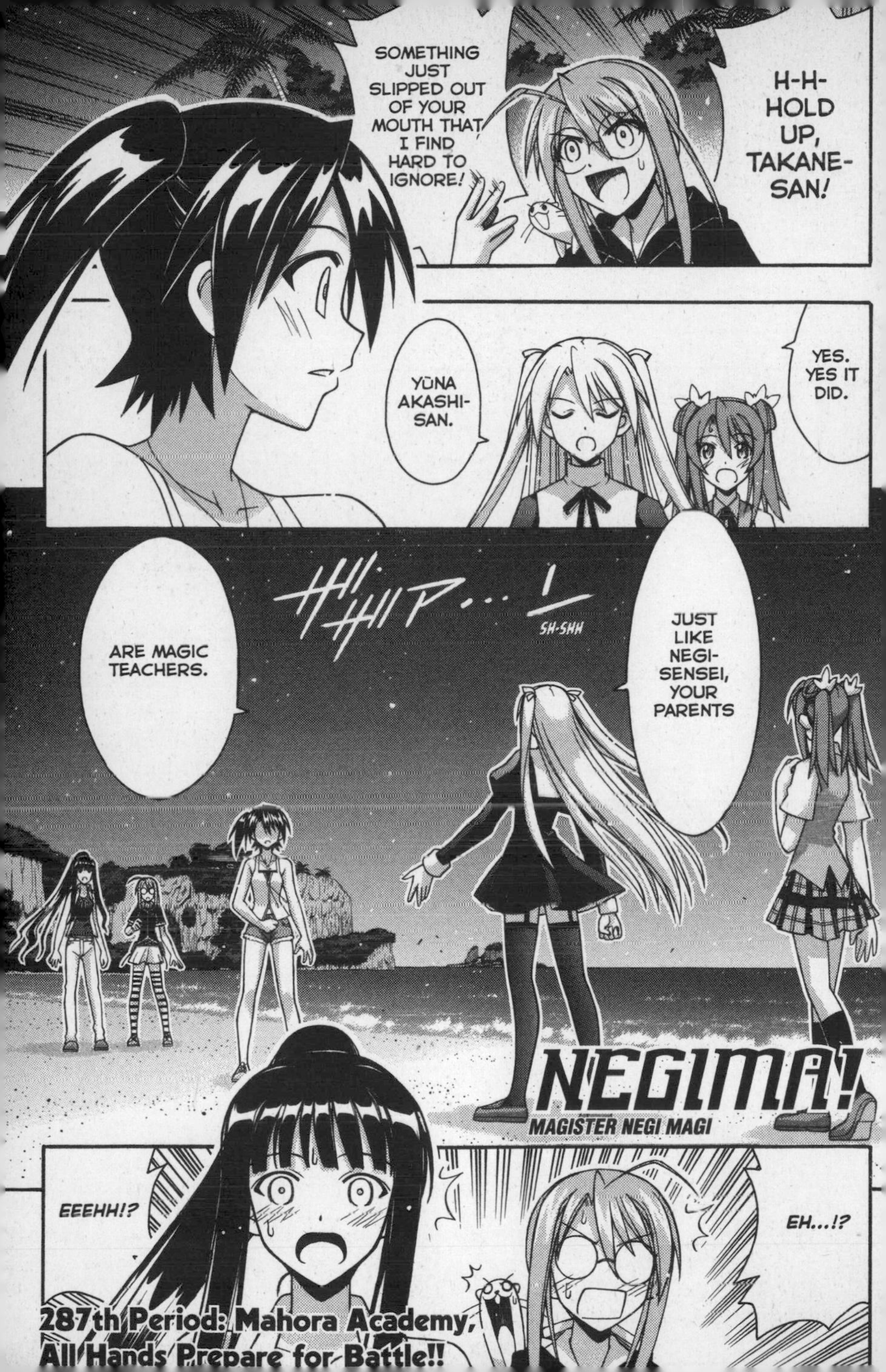
H-H-HOLD UP, TAKANE-SAN!
SOMETHING JUST SLIPPED OUT OF YOUR MOUTH THAT I FIND HARD TO IGNORE!
YES. YES IT DID.
YŪNA AKASHI-SAN.
JUST LIKE NEGI-SENSEI, YOUR PARENTS
SH-SHH
ARE MAGIC TEACHERS.
NEGIMA!
MAGISTER NEGI MAGI
EH...!?
EEEHH!?
287th Period: Mahora Academy, All Hands Prepare for Battle!!

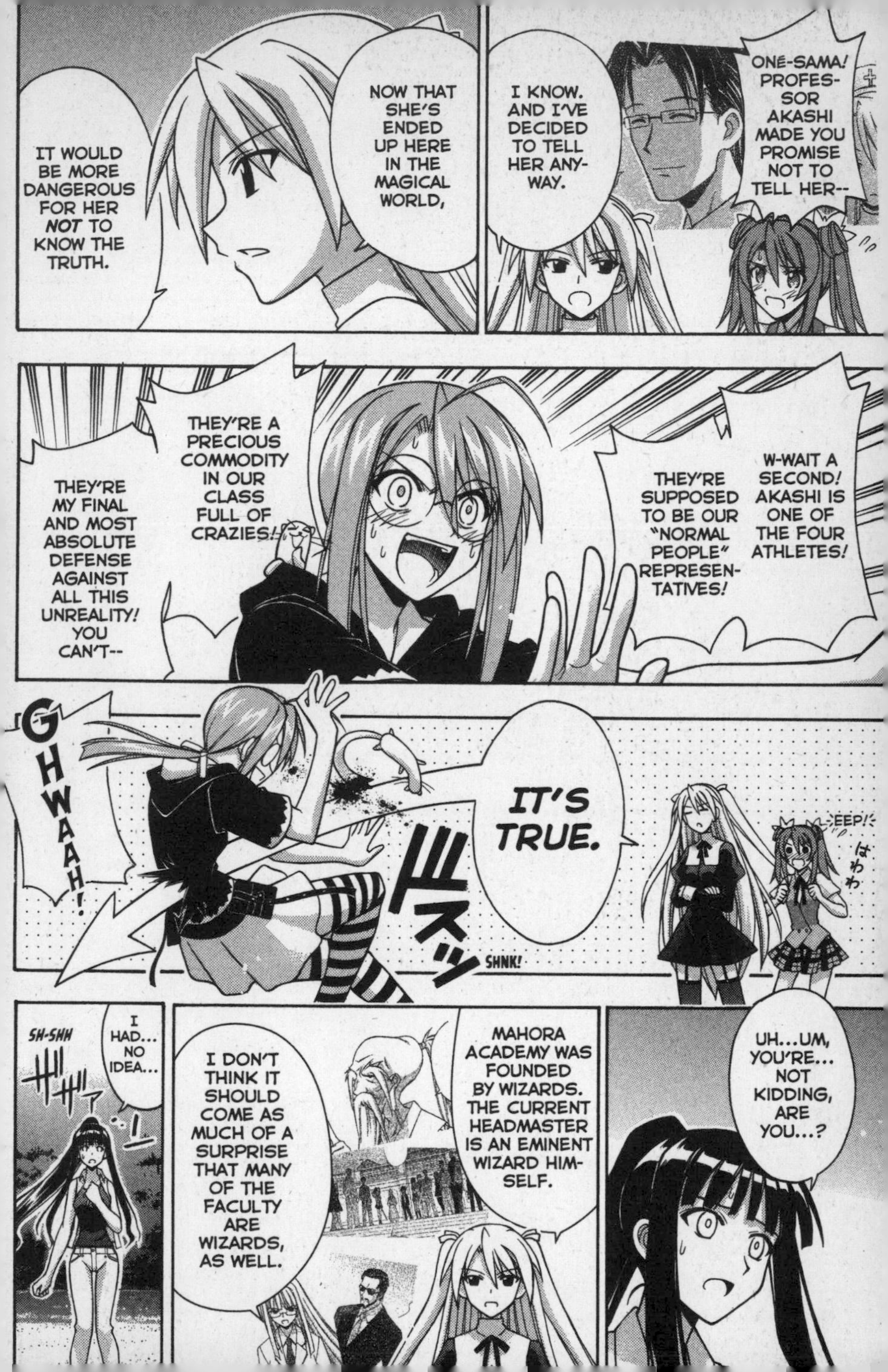
ONE-SAMA! PROFESSOR AKASHI MADE YOU PROMISE NOT TO TELL HER--
I KNOW. AND I'VE DECIDED TO TELL HER ANYWAY.
NOW THAT SHE'S ENDED UP HERE IN THE MAGICAL WORLD,
IT WOULD BE MORE DANGEROUS FOR HER *NOT* TO KNOW THE TRUTH.
W-WAIT A SECOND! AKASHI IS ONE OF THE FOUR ATHLETES!
THEY'RE SUPPOSED TO BE OUR "NORMAL PEOPLE" REPRESENTATIVES!
THEY'RE A PRECIOUS COMMODITY IN OUR CLASS FULL OF CRAZIES!
THEY'RE MY FINAL AND MOST ABSOLUTE DEFENSE AGAINST ALL THIS UNREALITY! YOU CAN'T--
EEP!
はわわ
IT'S TRUE.
ドスッ
SHNK!
GHWAAH!
UH...UM, YOU'RE... NOT KIDDING, ARE YOU...?
MAHORA ACADEMY WAS FOUNDED BY WIZARDS. THE CURRENT HEADMASTER IS AN EMINENT WIZARD HIMSELF.
I DON'T THINK IT SHOULD COME AS MUCH OF A SURPRISE THAT MANY OF THE FACULTY ARE WIZARDS, AS WELL.
I HAD... NO IDEA...
SH-SHH
ザザァ

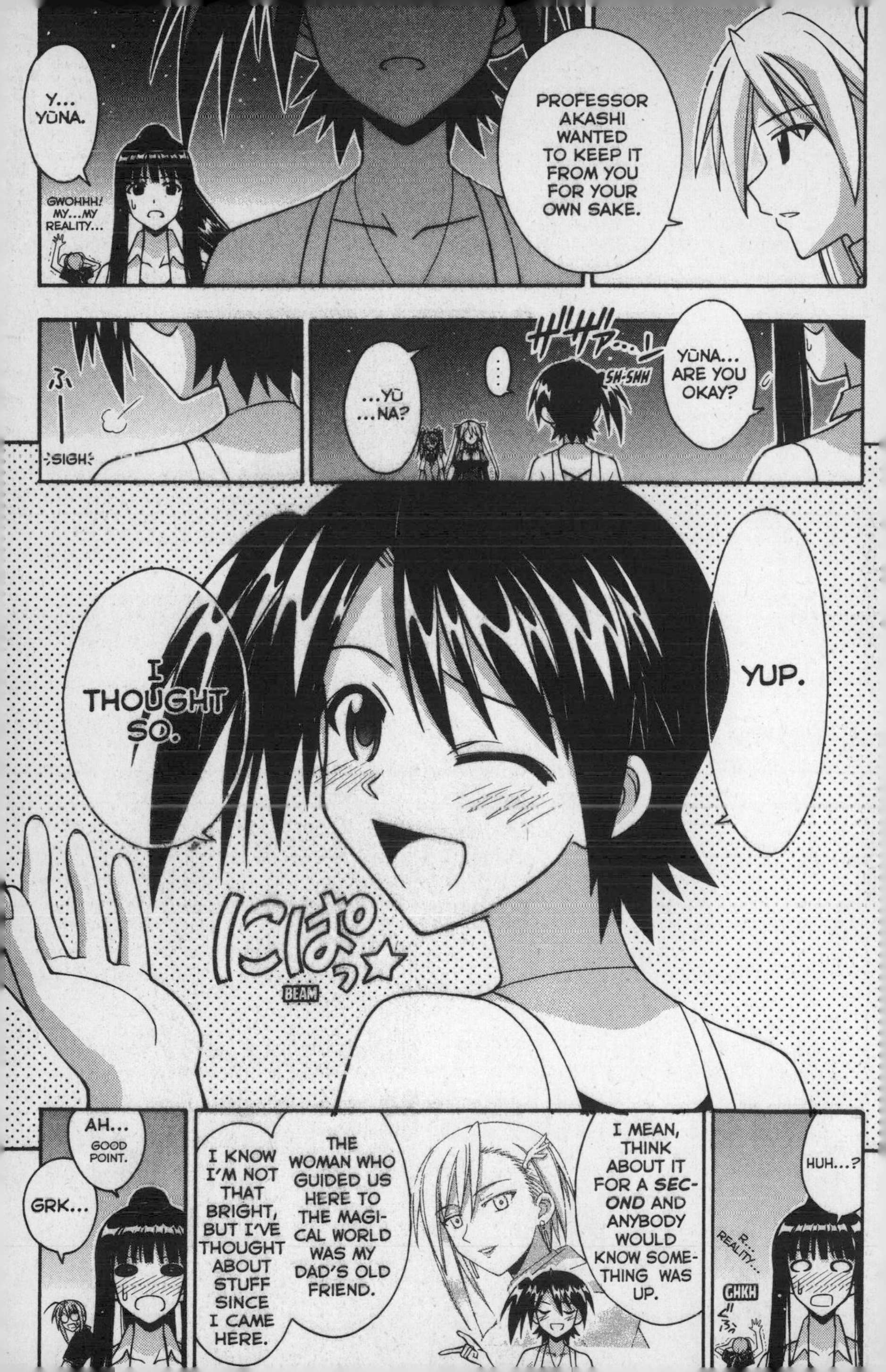
PROFESSOR AKASHI WANTED TO KEEP IT FROM YOU FOR YOUR OWN SAKE.
Y... YŪNA.
GWOHHH! MY...MY REALITY...
YŪNA... ARE YOU OKAY?
ザザァ…!
SH-SHH
...
...YŪ ...NA?
ふー
-SIGH-
YUP.
I THOUGHT SO.
にぱっ☆
BEAM
HUH...?
R... REALITY...
GHKH
I MEAN, THINK ABOUT IT FOR A SECOND AND ANYBODY WOULD KNOW SOMETHING WAS UP.
THE WOMAN WHO GUIDED US HERE TO THE MAGICAL WORLD WAS MY DAD'S OLD FRIEND.
I KNOW I'M NOT THAT BRIGHT, BUT I'VE THOUGHT ABOUT STUFF SINCE I CAME HERE.
AH... GOOD POINT.
GRK...

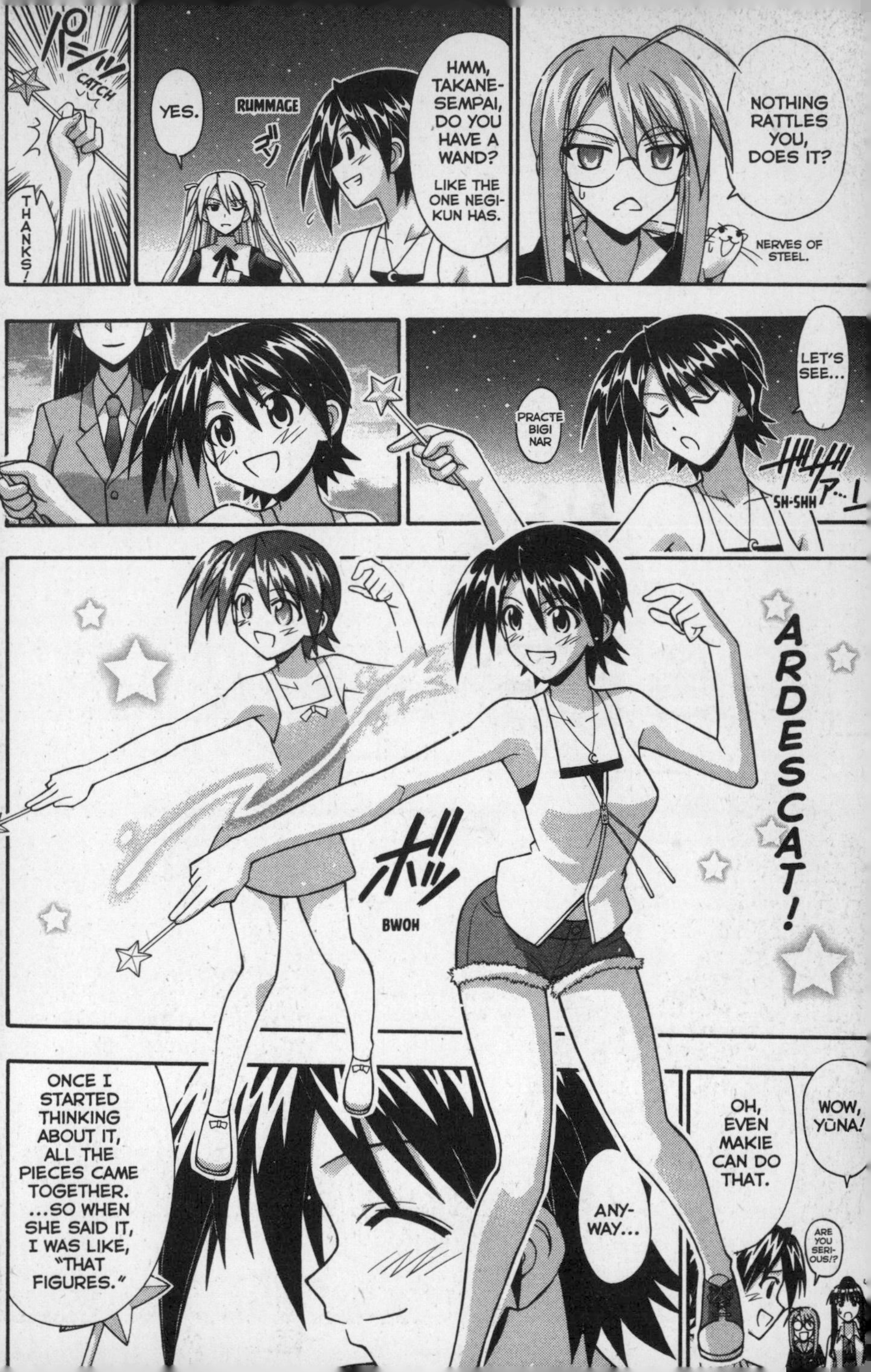
NOTHING RATTLES YOU, DOES IT?
NERVES OF STEEL.
HMM, TAKANE-SEMPAI, DO YOU HAVE A WAND?
LIKE THE ONE NEGI-KUN HAS.
RUMMAGE
YES.
CATCH
THANKS!
LET'S SEE...
PRACTE BIGI NAR
SH-SHH
ARDESCAT!
BWOH
WOW, YŪNA!
OH, EVEN MAKIE CAN DO THAT.
ARE YOU SERI-OUS!?
ANY-WAY...
ONCE I STARTED THINKING ABOUT IT, ALL THE PIECES CAME TOGETHER. ...SO WHEN SHE SAID IT, I WAS LIKE, "THAT FIGURES."

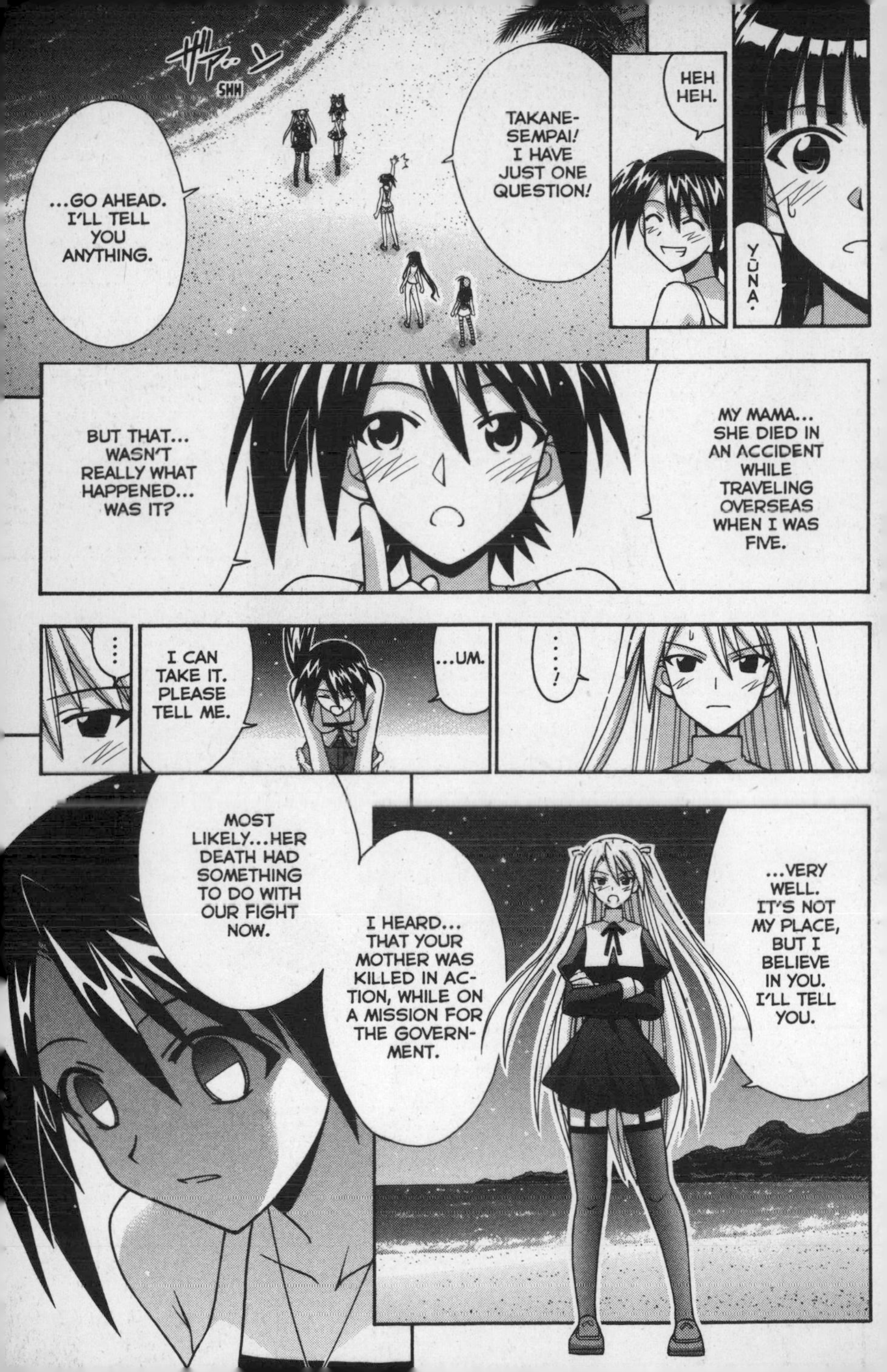
YŪNA.
HEH HEH.
TAKANE-SEMPAI! I HAVE JUST ONE QUESTION!
SHH
...GO AHEAD. I'LL TELL YOU ANYTHING.
MY MAMA... SHE DIED IN AN ACCIDENT WHILE TRAVELING OVERSEAS WHEN I WAS FIVE.
BUT THAT... WASN'T REALLY WHAT HAPPENED... WAS IT?
...?!
...UM.
I CAN TAKE IT. PLEASE TELL ME.
....
...VERY WELL. IT'S NOT MY PLACE, BUT I BELIEVE IN YOU. I'LL TELL YOU.
I HEARD... THAT YOUR MOTHER WAS KILLED IN ACTION, WHILE ON A MISSION FOR THE GOVERNMENT.
MOST LIKELY...HER DEATH HAD SOMETHING TO DO WITH OUR FIGHT NOW.

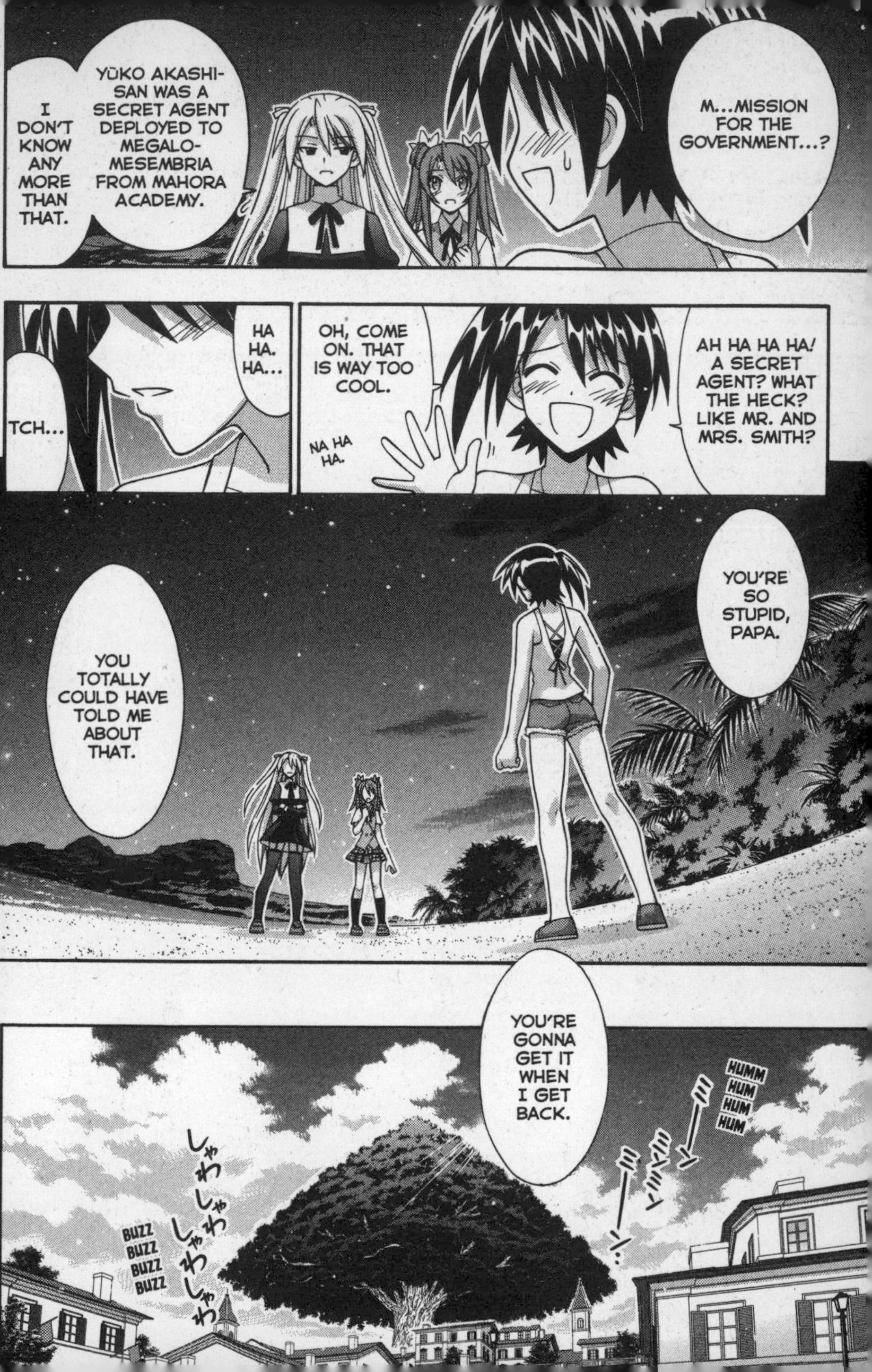
M...MISSION FOR THE GOVERNMENT...?
YŪKO AKASHI-SAN WAS A SECRET AGENT DEPLOYED TO MEGALO-MESEMBRIA FROM MAHORA ACADEMY.
I DON'T KNOW ANY MORE THAN THAT.
AH HA HA HA! A SECRET AGENT? WHAT THE HECK? LIKE MR. AND MRS. SMITH?
OH, COME ON. THAT IS WAY TOO COOL.
NA HA HA.
HA HA. HA...
TCH...
YOU'RE SO STUPID, PAPA.
YOU TOTALLY COULD HAVE TOLD ME ABOUT THAT.
YOU'RE GONNA GET IT WHEN I GET BACK.
HUMM HUM HUM HUM
しゃわしゃわしゃわしゃわ
BUZZ BUZZ BUZZ BUZZ

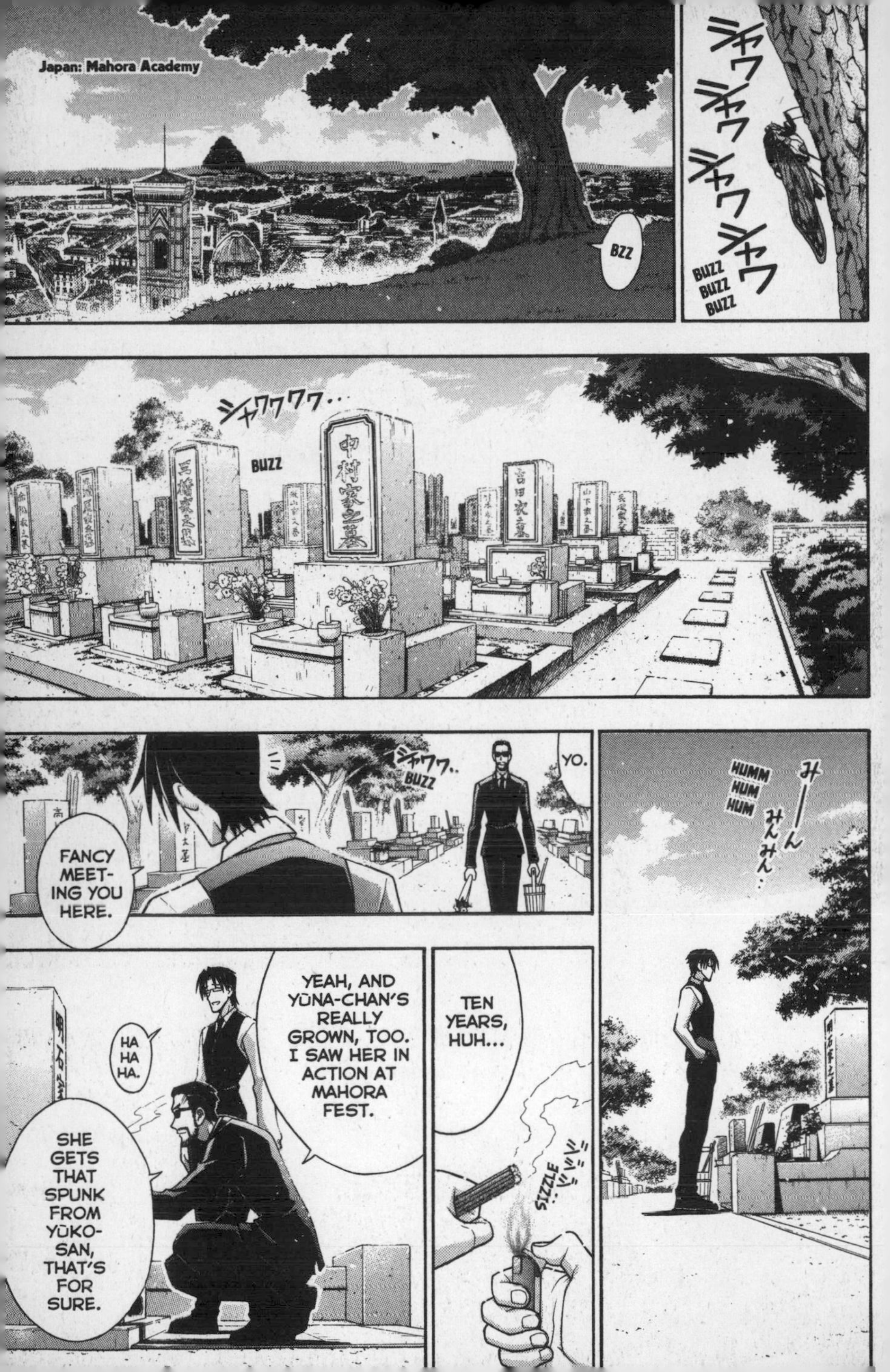

シャワ
シャワ
シャワシャワ
BUZZ
BUZZ
BUZZ
Japan: Mahora Academy
BZZ
シャワワワワ…
BUZZ
中村家之墓
HUMM
HUM
HUM
みーん
みんみん…
YO.
シャワワ..
BUZZ
FANCY MEETING YOU HERE.
TEN YEARS, HUH…
ジジ
SIZZLE
YEAH, AND YŪNA-CHAN'S REALLY GROWN, TOO. I SAW HER IN ACTION AT MAHORA FEST.
HA HA HA.
SHE GETS THAT SPUNK FROM YŪKO-SAN, THAT'S FOR SURE.

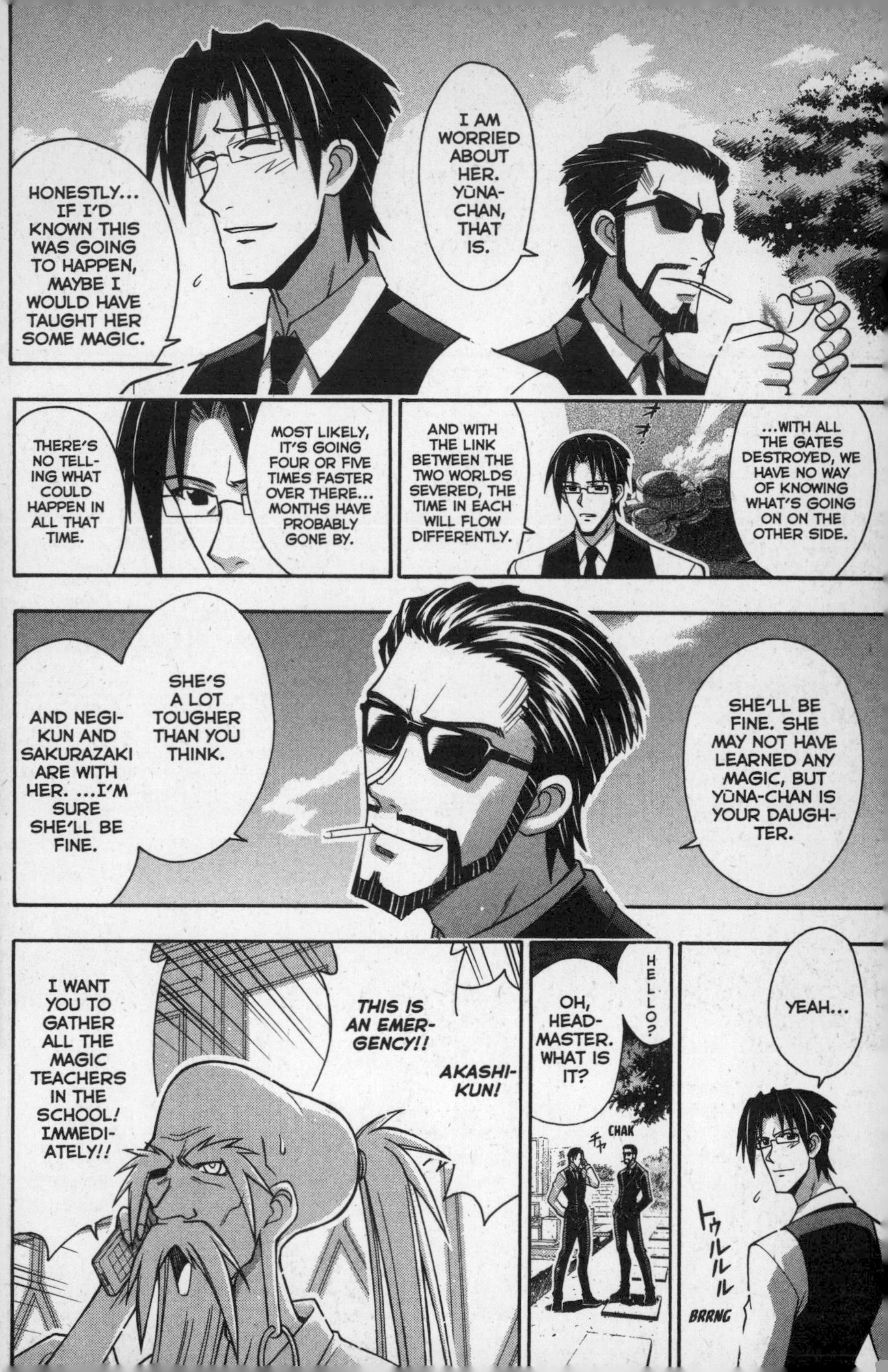
I AM WORRIED ABOUT HER. YŪNA-CHAN, THAT IS.
HONESTLY... IF I'D KNOWN THIS WAS GOING TO HAPPEN, MAYBE I WOULD HAVE TAUGHT HER SOME MAGIC.
...WITH ALL THE GATES DESTROYED, WE HAVE NO WAY OF KNOWING WHAT'S GOING ON ON THE OTHER SIDE.
AND WITH THE LINK BETWEEN THE TWO WORLDS SEVERED, THE TIME IN EACH WILL FLOW DIFFERENTLY.
MOST LIKELY, IT'S GOING FOUR OR FIVE TIMES FASTER OVER THERE... MONTHS HAVE PROBABLY GONE BY.
THERE'S NO TELLING WHAT COULD HAPPEN IN ALL THAT TIME.
SHE'LL BE FINE. SHE MAY NOT HAVE LEARNED ANY MAGIC, BUT YŪNA-CHAN IS YOUR DAUGHTER.
SHE'S A LOT TOUGHER THAN YOU THINK.
AND NEGI-KUN AND SAKURAZAKI ARE WITH HER. ...I'M SURE SHE'LL BE FINE.
YEAH...
トゥルルル
BRRNG
HELLO?
OH, HEADMASTER. WHAT IS IT?
CHAK
AKASHI-KUN!
THIS IS AN EMERGENCY!!
I WANT YOU TO GATHER ALL THE MAGIC TEACHERS IN THE SCHOOL! IMMEDIATELY!!

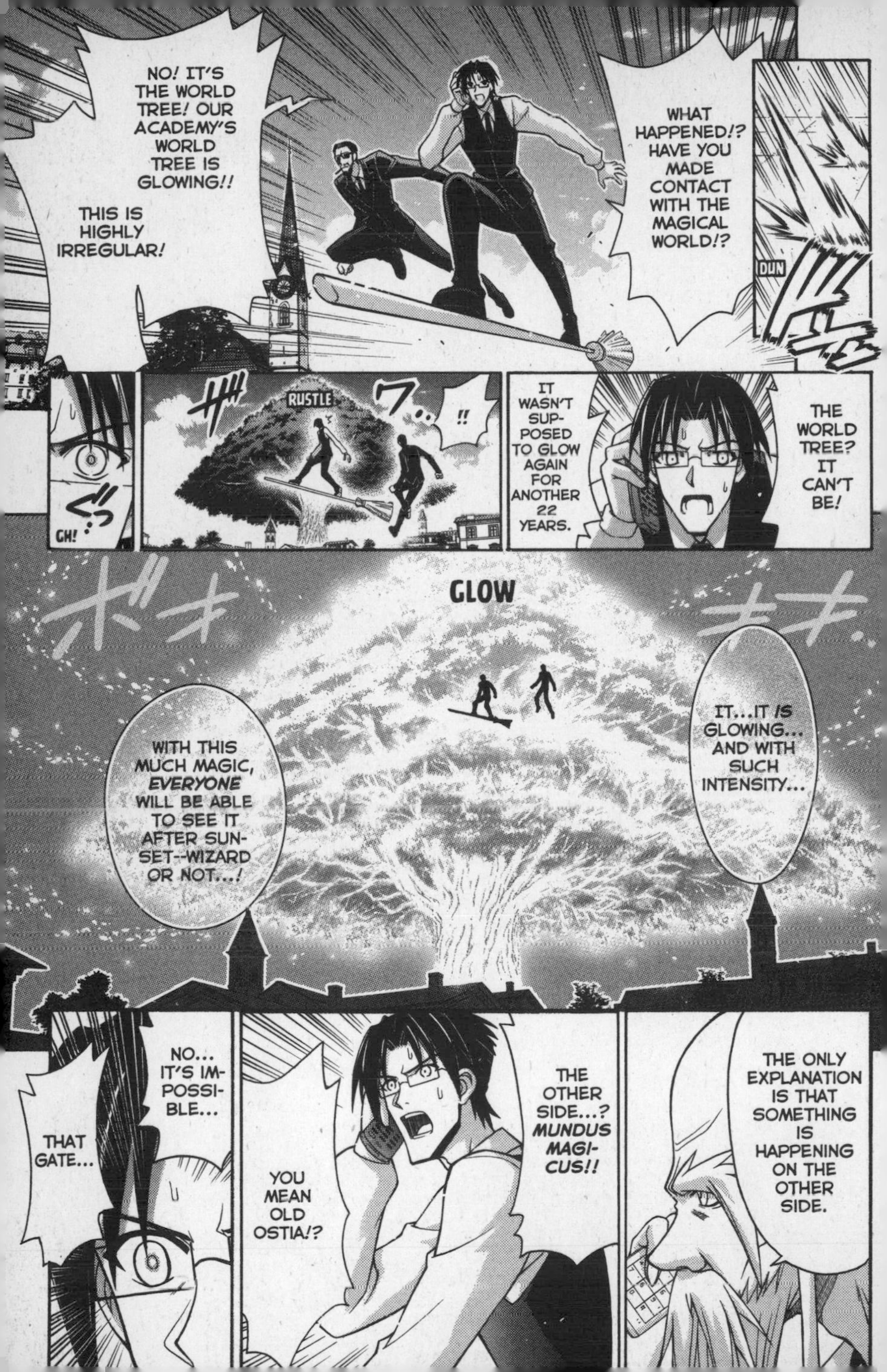
DUN
WHAT HAPPENED!? HAVE YOU MADE CONTACT WITH THE MAGICAL WORLD!?
NO! IT'S THE WORLD TREE! OUR ACADEMY'S WORLD TREE IS GLOWING!!
THIS IS HIGHLY IRREGULAR!
THE WORLD TREE? IT CAN'T BE!
IT WASN'T SUP-POSED TO GLOW AGAIN FOR ANOTHER 22 YEARS.
!!
RUSTLE
GH!
GLOW
IT...IT *IS* GLOWING... AND WITH SUCH INTENSITY...
WITH THIS MUCH MAGIC, ***EVERYONE*** WILL BE ABLE TO SEE IT AFTER SUN-SET--WIZARD OR NOT...!
THE ONLY EXPLANATION IS THAT SOMETHING IS HAPPENING ON THE OTHER SIDE.
THE OTHER SIDE...? ***MUNDUS MAGI-CUS!!***
YOU MEAN OLD OSTIA!?
NO... IT'S IM-POSSI-BLE...
THAT GATE...

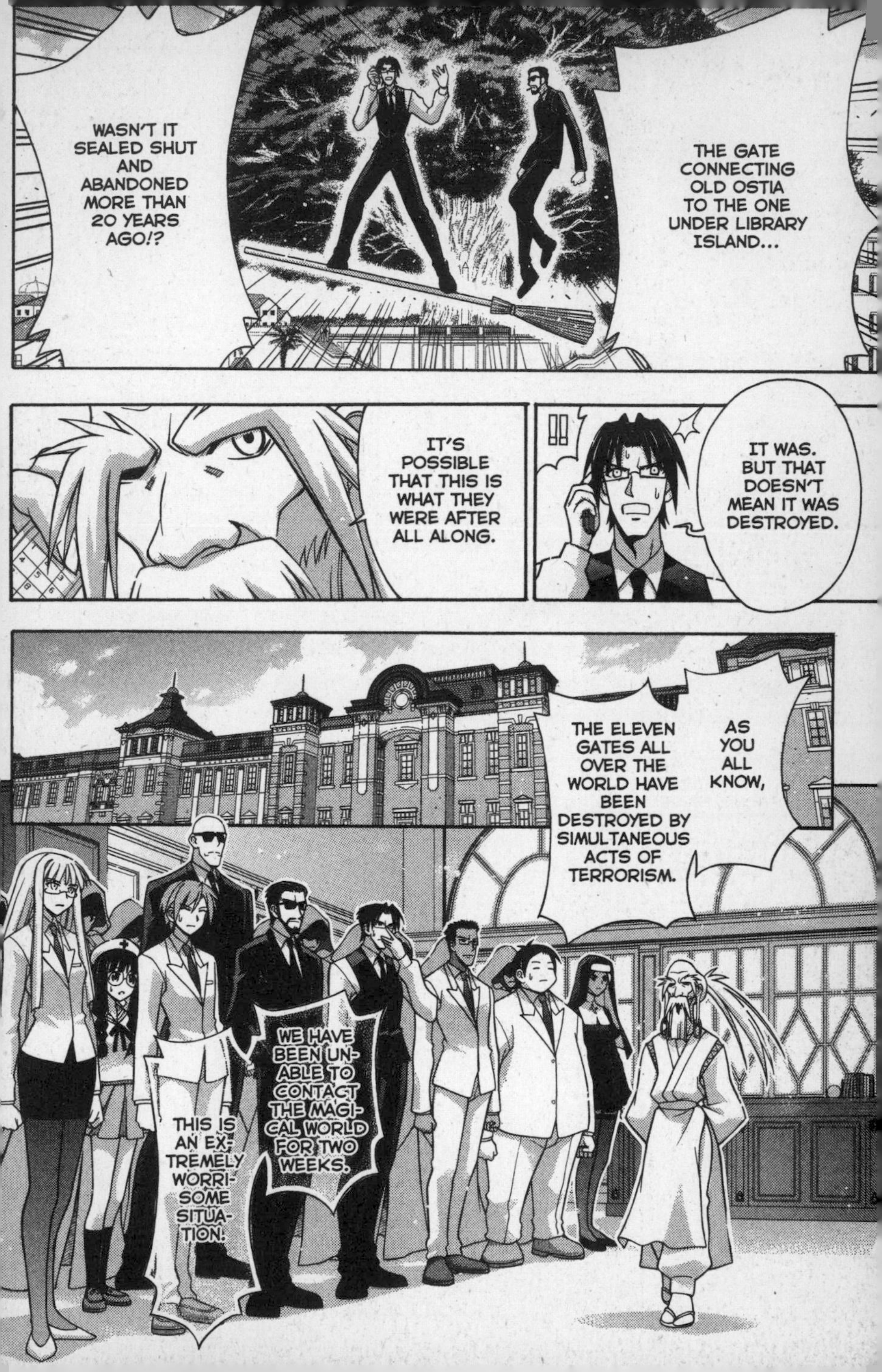
THE GATE CONNECTING OLD OSTIA TO THE ONE UNDER LIBRARY ISLAND...
WASN'T IT SEALED SHUT AND ABANDONED MORE THAN 20 YEARS AGO!?
!!
IT WAS. BUT THAT DOESN'T MEAN IT WAS DESTROYED.
IT'S POSSIBLE THAT THIS IS WHAT THEY WERE AFTER ALL ALONG.
AS YOU ALL KNOW,
THE ELEVEN GATES ALL OVER THE WORLD HAVE BEEN DESTROYED BY SIMULTANEOUS ACTS OF TERRORISM.
WE HAVE BEEN UNABLE TO CONTACT THE MAGICAL WORLD FOR TWO WEEKS.
THIS IS AN EXTREMELY WORRISOME SITUATION.

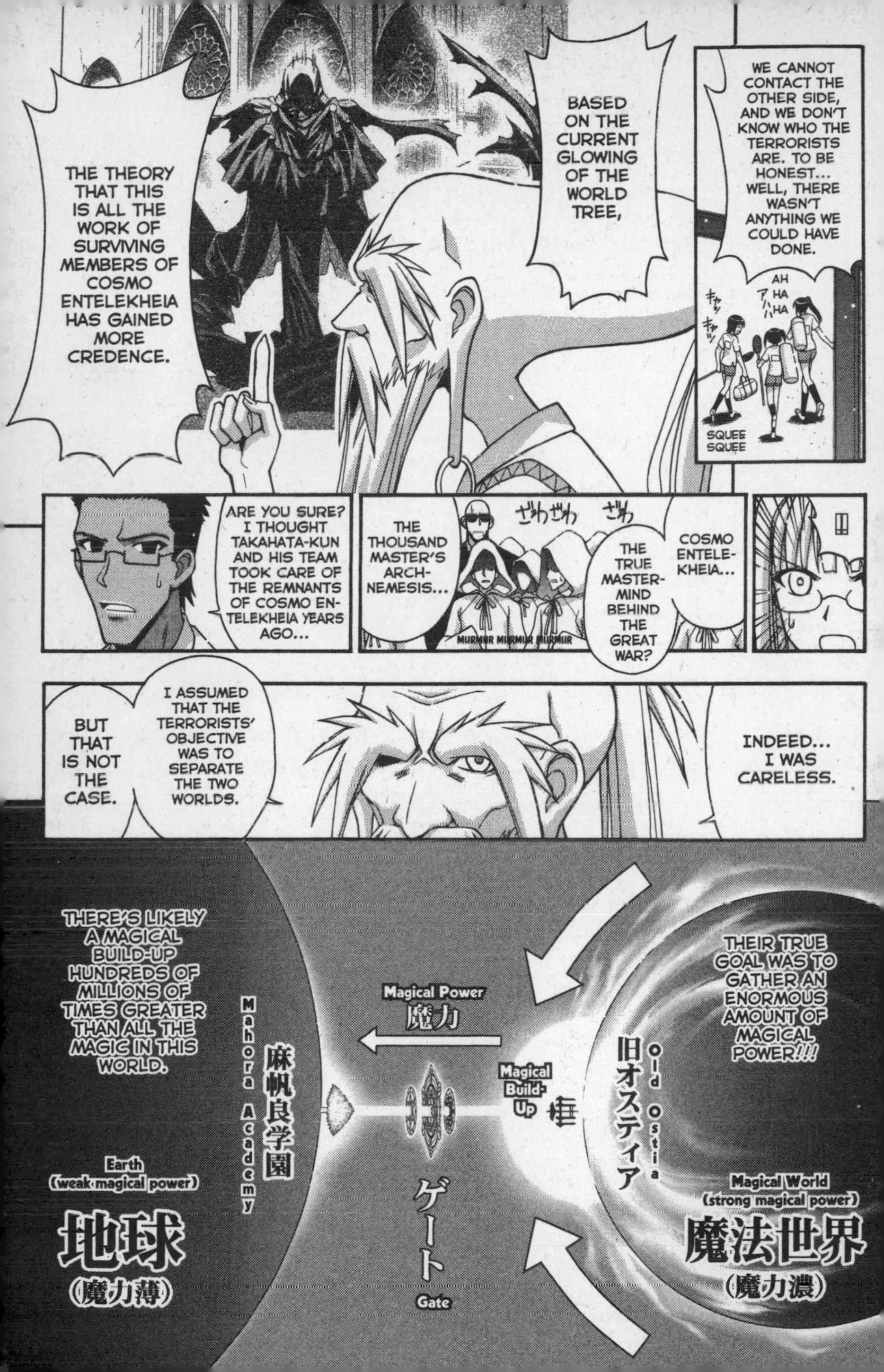

WE CANNOT CONTACT THE OTHER SIDE, AND WE DON'T KNOW WHO THE TERRORISTS ARE. TO BE HONEST... WELL, THERE WASN'T ANYTHING WE COULD HAVE DONE.
AH HA HA
アハハ
キャッ キャッ
SQUEE SQUEE
BASED ON THE CURRENT GLOWING OF THE WORLD TREE,
THE THEORY THAT THIS IS ALL THE WORK OF SURVIVING MEMBERS OF COSMO ENTELEKHEIA HAS GAINED MORE CREDENCE.
!!
COSMO ENTELE-KHEIA...
THE TRUE MASTER-MIND BEHIND THE GREAT WAR?
ざわざわ ざわ
THE THOUSAND MASTER'S ARCH-NEMESIS...
MURMUR MURMUR MURMUR
ARE YOU SURE? I THOUGHT TAKAHATA-KUN AND HIS TEAM TOOK CARE OF THE REMNANTS OF COSMO EN-TELEKHEIA YEARS AGO...
INDEED... I WAS CARELESS.
I ASSUMED THAT THE TERRORISTS' OBJECTIVE WAS TO SEPARATE THE TWO WORLDS.
BUT THAT IS NOT THE CASE.
THEIR TRUE GOAL WAS TO GATHER AN ENORMOUS AMOUNT OF MAGICAL POWER!!!
Magical World (strong magical power)
魔法世界
(魔力濃)
Old Ostia
旧オスティア
Magical Build-Up
蓄
Magical Power
魔力
ゲート
Gate
Mahora Academy
麻帆良学園
THERE'S LIKELY A MAGICAL BUILD-UP HUNDREDS OF MILLIONS OF TIMES GREATER THAN ALL THE MAGIC IN THIS WORLD.
Earth (weak magical power)
地球
(魔力薄)

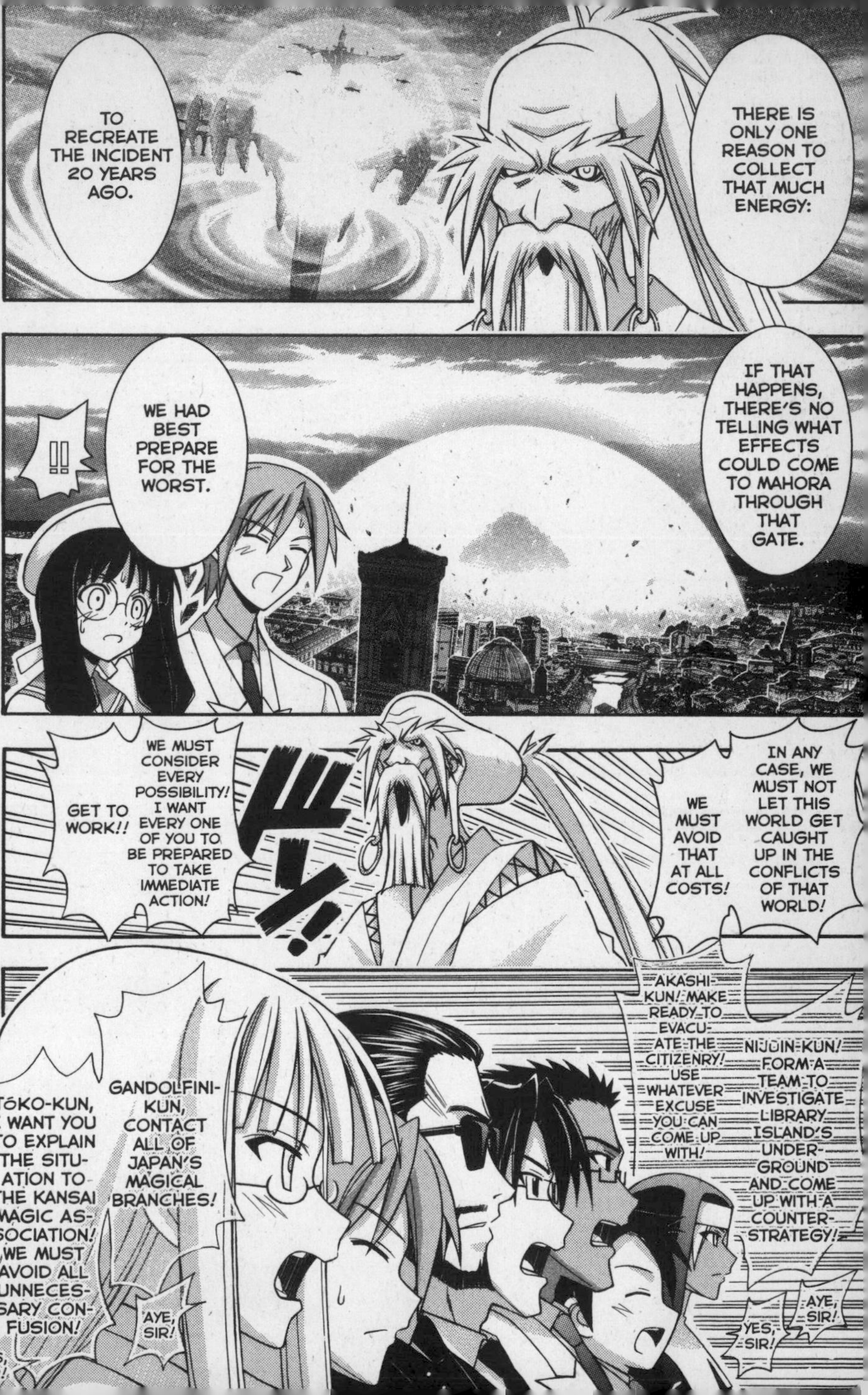
THERE IS ONLY ONE REASON TO COLLECT THAT MUCH ENERGY:
TO RECREATE THE INCIDENT 20 YEARS AGO.
IF THAT HAPPENS, THERE'S NO TELLING WHAT EFFECTS COULD COME TO MAHORA THROUGH THAT GATE.
WE HAD BEST PREPARE FOR THE WORST.
!!
IN ANY CASE, WE MUST NOT LET THIS WORLD GET CAUGHT UP IN THE CONFLICTS OF THAT WORLD!
WE MUST AVOID THAT AT ALL COSTS!
WE MUST CONSIDER EVERY POSSIBILITY! I WANT EVERY ONE OF YOU TO BE PREPARED TO TAKE IMMEDIATE ACTION!
GET TO WORK!!
NIJUIN-KUN! FORM A TEAM TO INVESTIGATE LIBRARY ISLAND'S UNDERGROUND AND COME UP WITH A COUNTER-STRATEGY!
AKASHI-KUN! MAKE READY TO EVACUATE THE CITIZENRY! USE WHATEVER EXCUSE YOU CAN COME UP WITH!
GANDOLFINI-KUN, CONTACT ALL OF JAPAN'S MAGICAL BRANCHES!
TŌKO-KUN, I WANT YOU TO EXPLAIN THE SITUATION TO THE KANSAI MAGIC ASSOCIATION! WE MUST AVOID ALL UNNECESSARY CONFUSION!
AYE, SIR!
YES, SIR!
AYE, SIR!
YES, SIR!

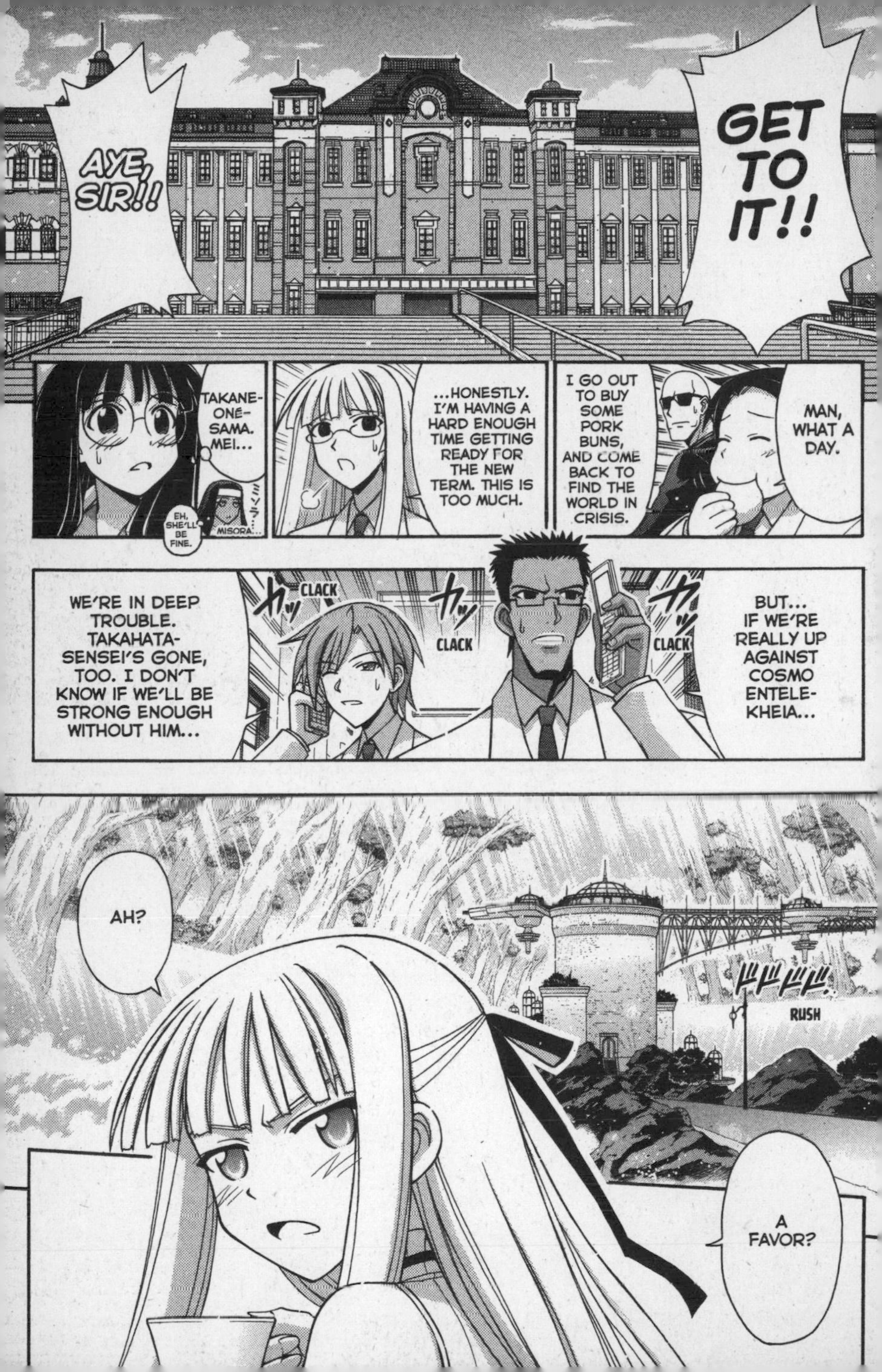
GET TO IT!!
AYE, SIR!!
MAN, WHAT A DAY.
I GO OUT TO BUY SOME PORK BUNS, AND COME BACK TO FIND THE WORLD IN CRISIS.
...HONESTLY. I'M HAVING A HARD ENOUGH TIME GETTING READY FOR THE NEW TERM. THIS IS TOO MUCH.
TAKANE-ONE-SAMA. MEI...
MISORA...
EH, SHE'LL BE FINE.
BUT... IF WE'RE REALLY UP AGAINST COSMO ENTELE-KHEIA...
CLACK
CLACK
CLACK
WE'RE IN DEEP TROUBLE. TAKAHATA-SENSEI'S GONE, TOO. I DON'T KNOW IF WE'LL BE STRONG ENOUGH WITHOUT HIM...
A FAVOR?
RUSH
AH?

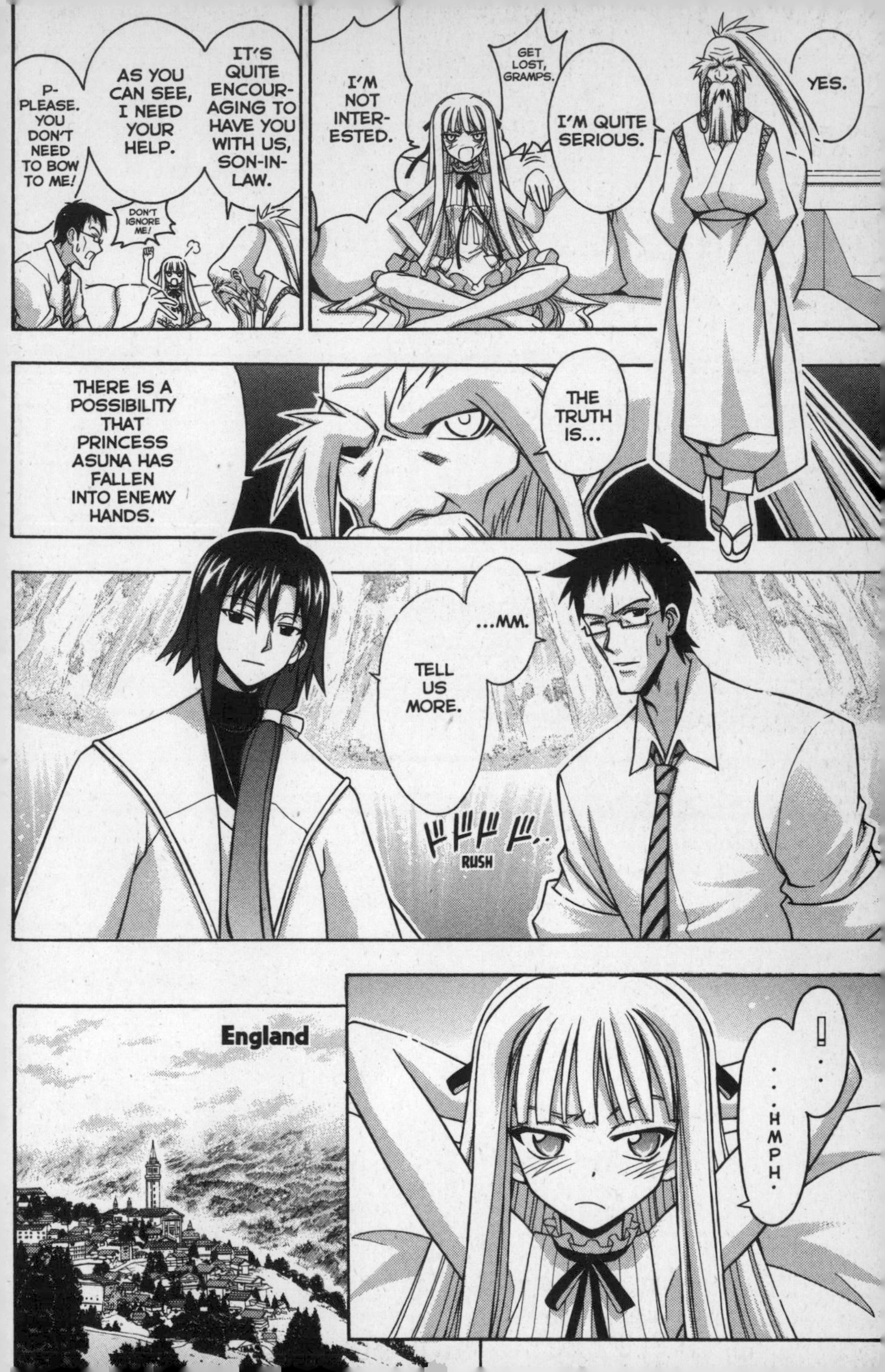
YES.
I'M QUITE SERIOUS.
GET LOST, GRAMPS.
I'M NOT INTERESTED.
IT'S QUITE ENCOURAGING TO HAVE YOU WITH US, SON-IN-LAW.
AS YOU CAN SEE, I NEED YOUR HELP.
DON'T IGNORE ME!
P-PLEASE. YOU DON'T NEED TO BOW TO ME!
THE TRUTH IS...
THERE IS A POSSIBILITY THAT PRINCESS ASUNA HAS FALLEN INTO ENEMY HANDS.
...MM.
TELL US MORE.
ドドドド
RUSH
!
...HMPH.
England

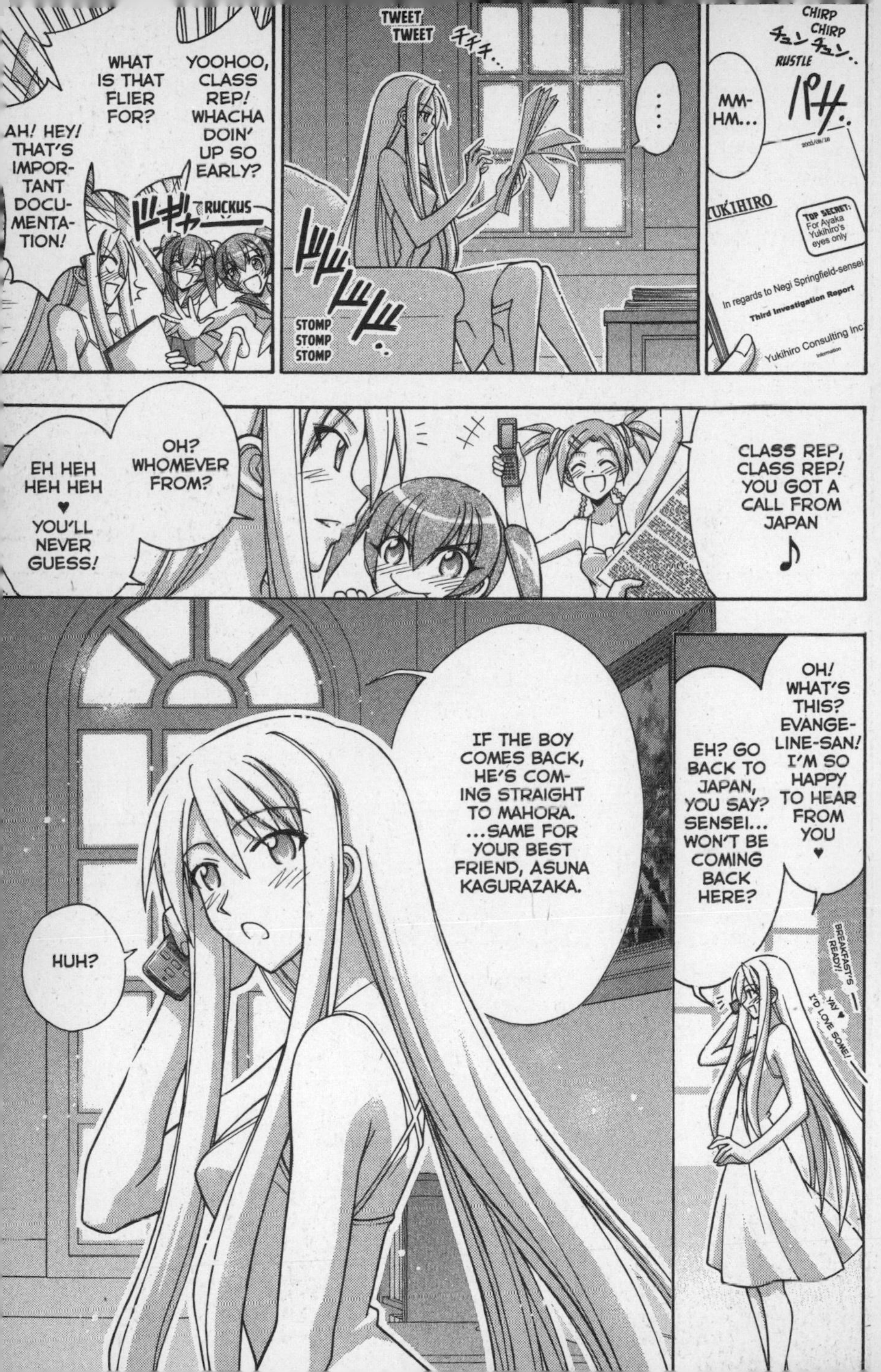
CHIRP CHIRP
チュンチュン..
RUSTLE
パサ..
MM-HM...
YUKIHIRO
TOP SECRET: For Ayaka Yukihiro's eyes only
In regards to Negi Springfield-sensei
Third Investigation Report
Yukihiro Consulting Inc.
Information
TWEET TWEET
チチチ...
....
ドドドドド
STOMP STOMP STOMP
YOOHOO, CLASS REP! WHACHA DOIN' UP SO EARLY?
WHAT IS THAT FLIER FOR?
ドギャー
RUCKUS
AH! HEY! THAT'S IMPORTANT DOCUMENTATION!
CLASS REP, CLASS REP! YOU GOT A CALL FROM JAPAN ♪
OH? WHOMEVER FROM?
EH HEH HEH HEH ♥ YOU'LL NEVER GUESS!
OH! WHAT'S THIS? EVANGELINE-SAN! I'M SO HAPPY TO HEAR FROM YOU ♥
EH? GO BACK TO JAPAN, YOU SAY? SENSEI... WON'T BE COMING BACK HERE?
BREAKFAST'S READY!
YAY ♥ I'D LOVE SOME!
IF THE BOY COMES BACK, HE'S COMING STRAIGHT TO MAHORA. ...SAME FOR YOUR BEST FRIEND, ASUNA KAGURAZAKA.
HUH?

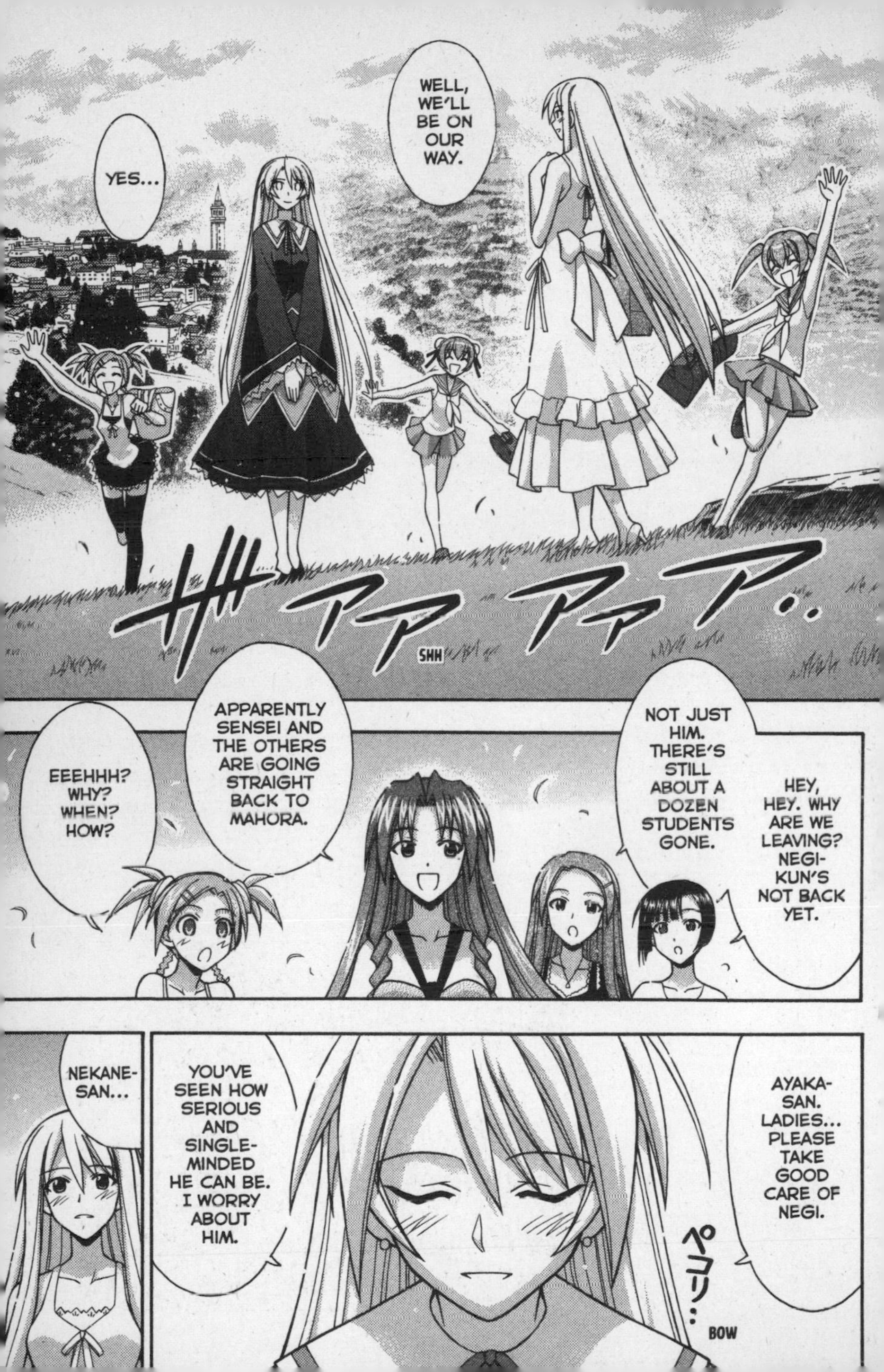

WELL, WE'LL BE ON OUR WAY.
YES...
SHH
HEY, HEY. WHY ARE WE LEAVING? NEGI-KUN'S NOT BACK YET.
NOT JUST HIM. THERE'S STILL ABOUT A DOZEN STUDENTS GONE.
APPARENTLY SENSEI AND THE OTHERS ARE GOING STRAIGHT BACK TO MAHORA.
EEEHHH? WHY? WHEN? HOW?
AYAKA-SAN. LADIES... PLEASE TAKE GOOD CARE OF NEGI.
ペコリ..
BOW
YOU'VE SEEN HOW SERIOUS AND SINGLE-MINDED HE CAN BE. I WORRY ABOUT HIM.
NEKANE-SAN...

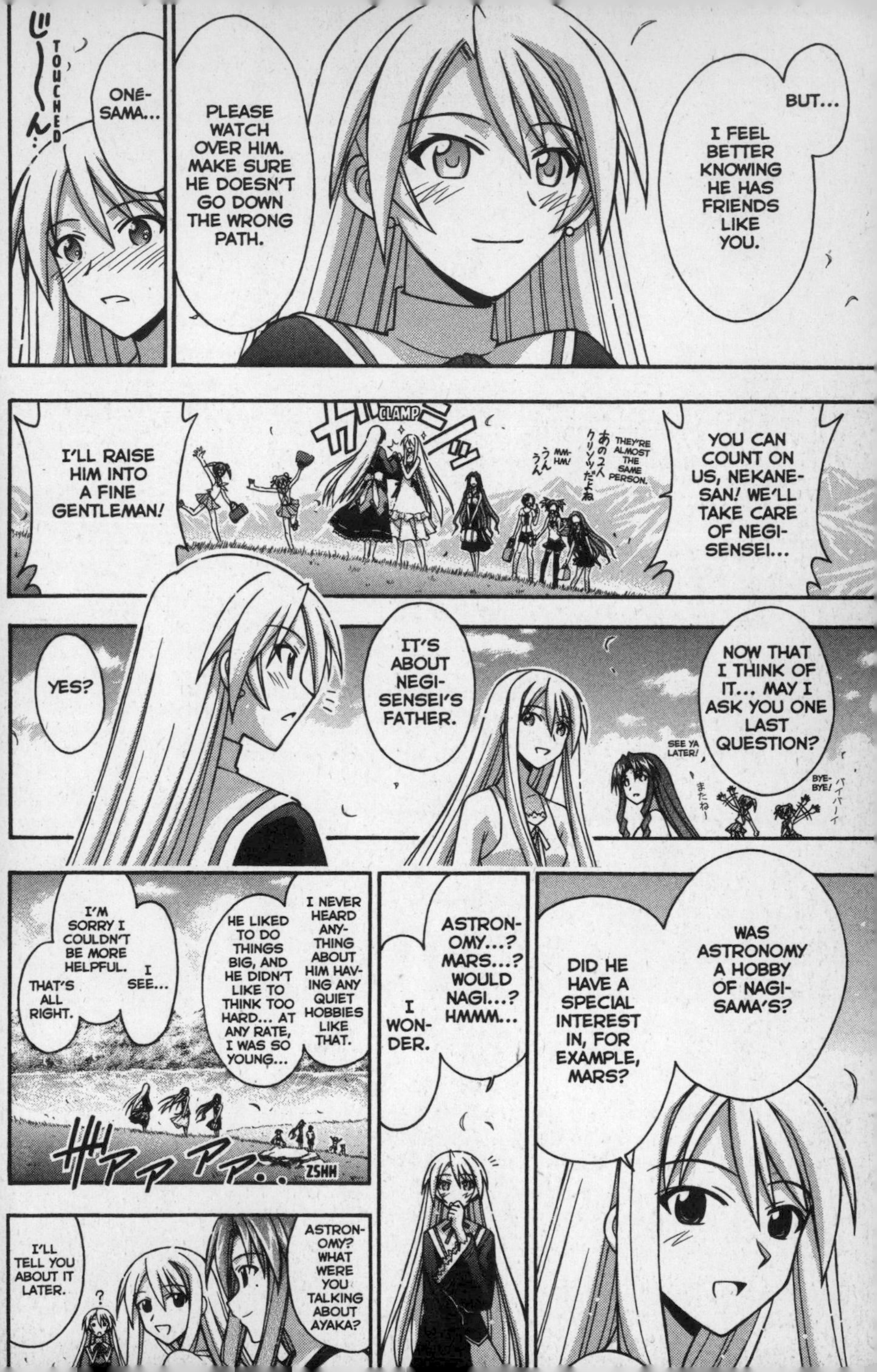
BUT...
I FEEL BETTER KNOWING HE HAS FRIENDS LIKE YOU.
PLEASE WATCH OVER HIM. MAKE SURE HE DOESN'T GO DOWN THE WRONG PATH.
ONE-SAMA...
じ～ん… TOUCHED
YOU CAN COUNT ON US, NEKANE-SAN! WE'LL TAKE CARE OF NEGI-SENSEI...
あの2人クリソツだよね
THEY'RE ALMOST THE SAME PERSON.
うんうん
MM-HM!
CLAMP
I'LL RAISE HIM INTO A FINE GENTLEMAN!
NOW THAT I THINK OF IT... MAY I ASK YOU ONE LAST QUESTION?
バイバーイ
BYE-BYE!
またねー
SEE YA LATER!
IT'S ABOUT NEGI-SENSEI'S FATHER.
YES?
WAS ASTRONOMY A HOBBY OF NAGI-SAMA'S?
DID HE HAVE A SPECIAL INTEREST IN, FOR EXAMPLE, MARS?
ASTRONOMY...? MARS...? WOULD NAGI...? HMMM...
I WONDER.
I NEVER HEARD ANYTHING ABOUT HIM HAVING ANY QUIET HOBBIES LIKE THAT.
HE LIKED TO DO THINGS BIG, AND HE DIDN'T LIKE TO THINK TOO HARD... AT ANY RATE, I WAS SO YOUNG...
I SEE...
I'M SORRY I COULDN'T BE MORE HELPFUL.
THAT'S ALL RIGHT.
ザァァァ… ZSHH
ASTRONOMY? WHAT WERE YOU TALKING ABOUT AYAKA?
I'LL TELL YOU ABOUT IT LATER.

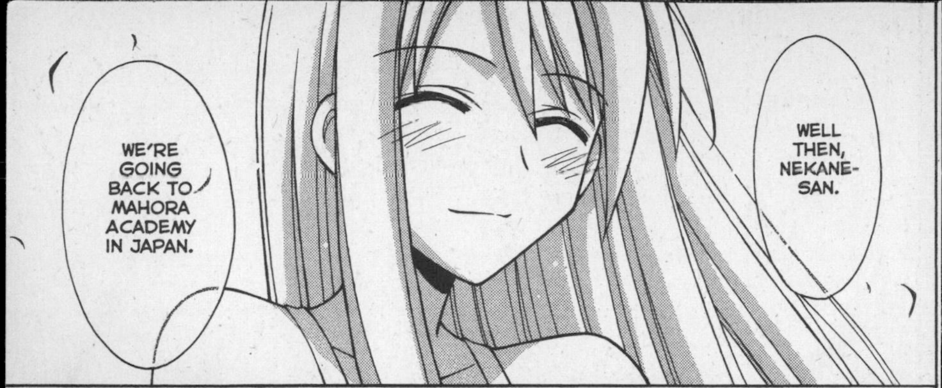
WELL THEN, NEKANE-SAN.
WE'RE GOING BACK TO MAHORA ACADEMY IN JAPAN.

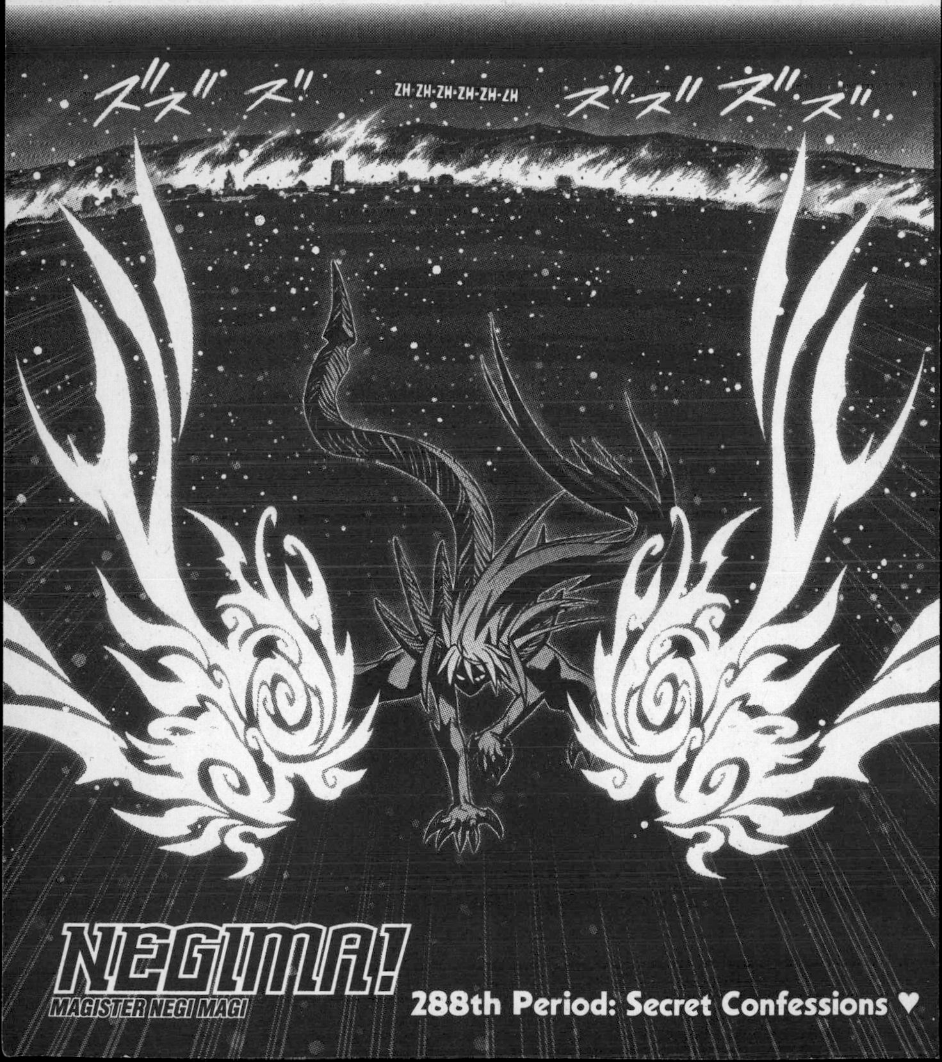
ズズズズ
ZH-ZH-ZH-ZH-ZH-ZH
ズズズ
NEGIMA!
MAGISTER NEGI MAGI
288th Period: Secret Confessions ♥

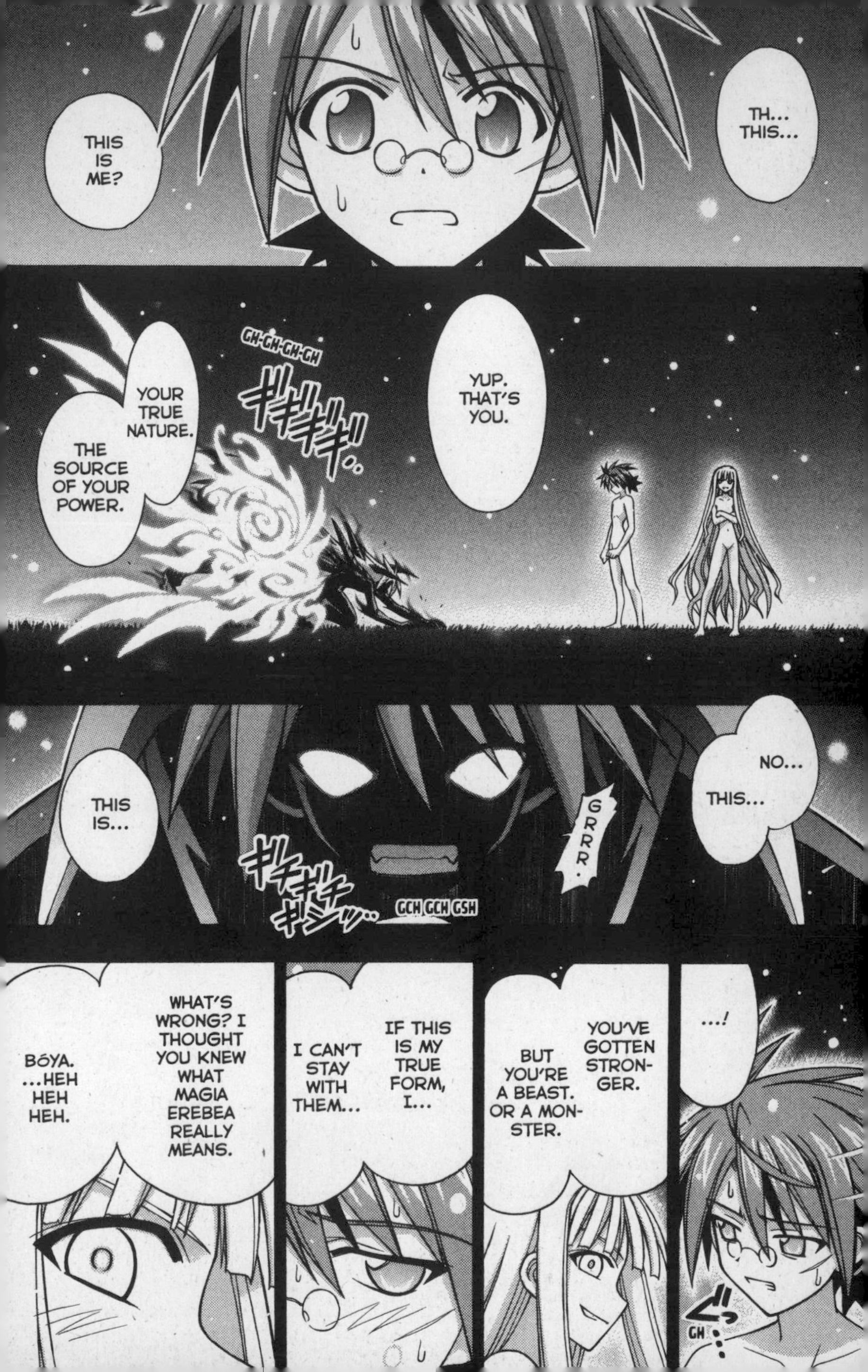
TH... THIS...
THIS IS ME?
YUP. THAT'S YOU.
GH-GH-GH-GH
YOUR TRUE NATURE.
THE SOURCE OF YOUR POWER.
NO... THIS...
GRRR.
GCH GCH GSH
THIS IS...
...!
GH...
YOU'VE GOTTEN STRONGER.
BUT YOU'RE A BEAST. OR A MONSTER.
IF THIS IS MY TRUE FORM, I...
I CAN'T STAY WITH THEM...
WHAT'S WRONG? I THOUGHT YOU KNEW WHAT MAGIA EREBEA REALLY MEANS.
BŌYA. ...HEH HEH HEH.

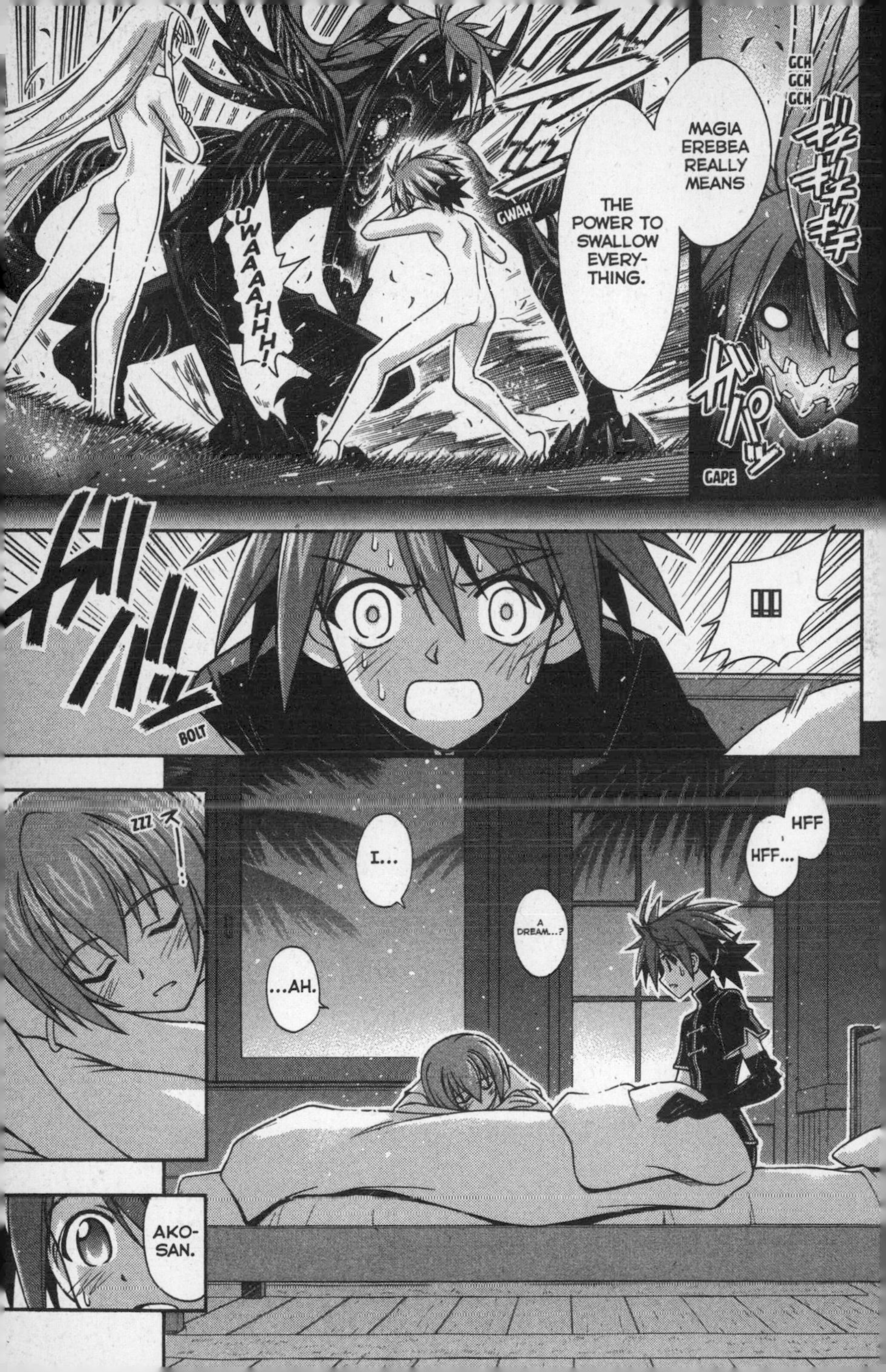
GCH GCH GCH
GAPE
MAGIA EREBEA REALLY MEANS
THE POWER TO SWALLOW EVERY-THING.
GWAH
UWAAAAHHH!
!!!
BOLT
HFF HFF...
A DREAM...?
I...
...AH.
ZZZ
AKO-SAN.

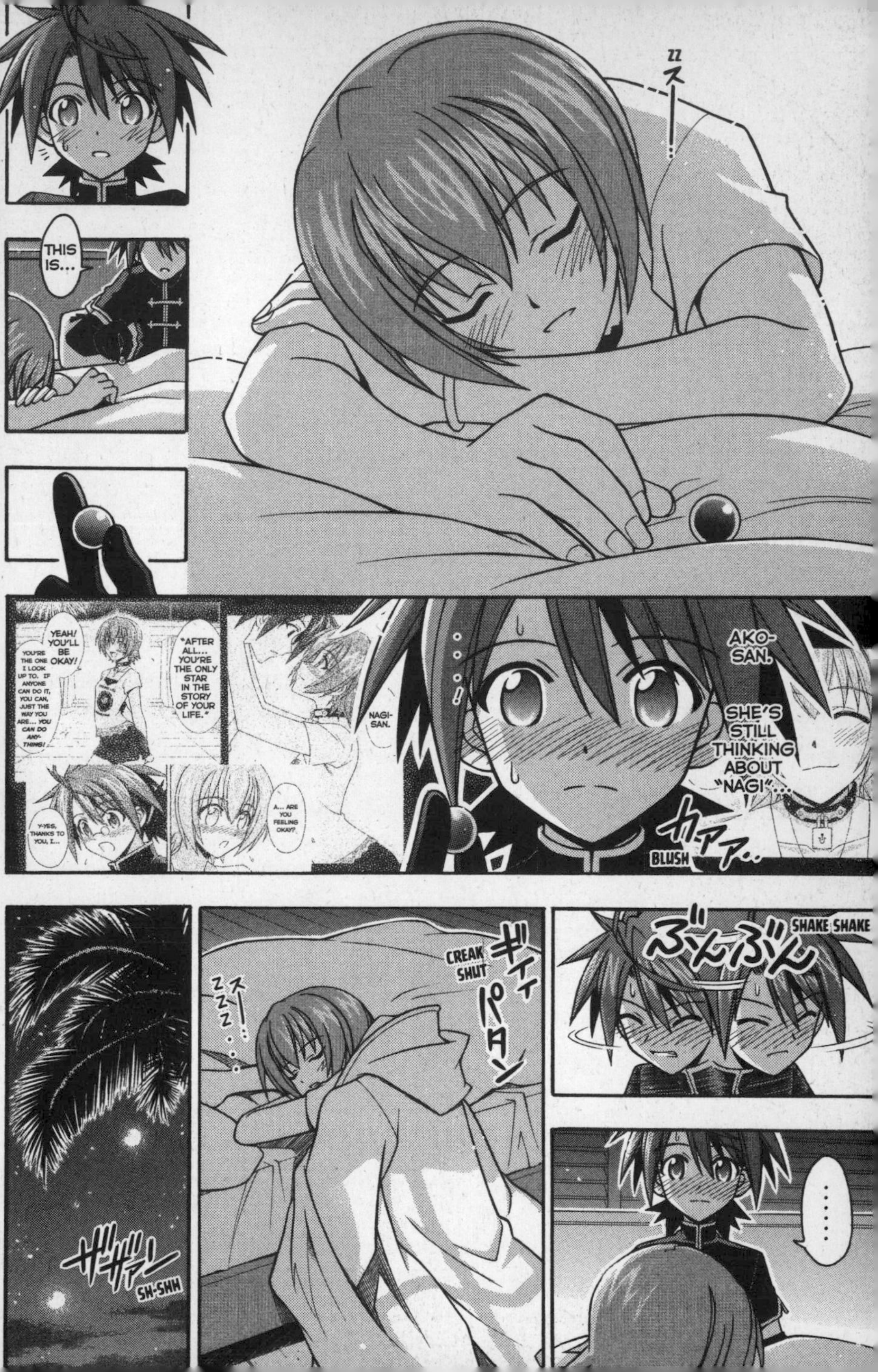
ZZ
スー…
THIS IS...
AKO-SAN.
SHE'S STILL THINKING ABOUT "NAGI"...
カァァ..
BLUSH
NAGI-SAN.
"AFTER ALL... YOU'RE THE ONLY STAR IN THE STORY OF YOUR LIFE."
YEAH! YOU'LL BE OKAY!
YOU'RE THE ONE I LOOK UP TO. IF ANYONE CAN DO IT, YOU CAN, JUST THE WAY YOU ARE... YOU CAN DO ANY-THING!
A... ARE YOU FEELING OKAY?
Y-YES, THANKS TO YOU, I...
ぶんぶん
SHAKE SHAKE
......
ギィィ パタン
CREAK SHUT
スー…
ZZZ...
ザザァー
SH-SHH

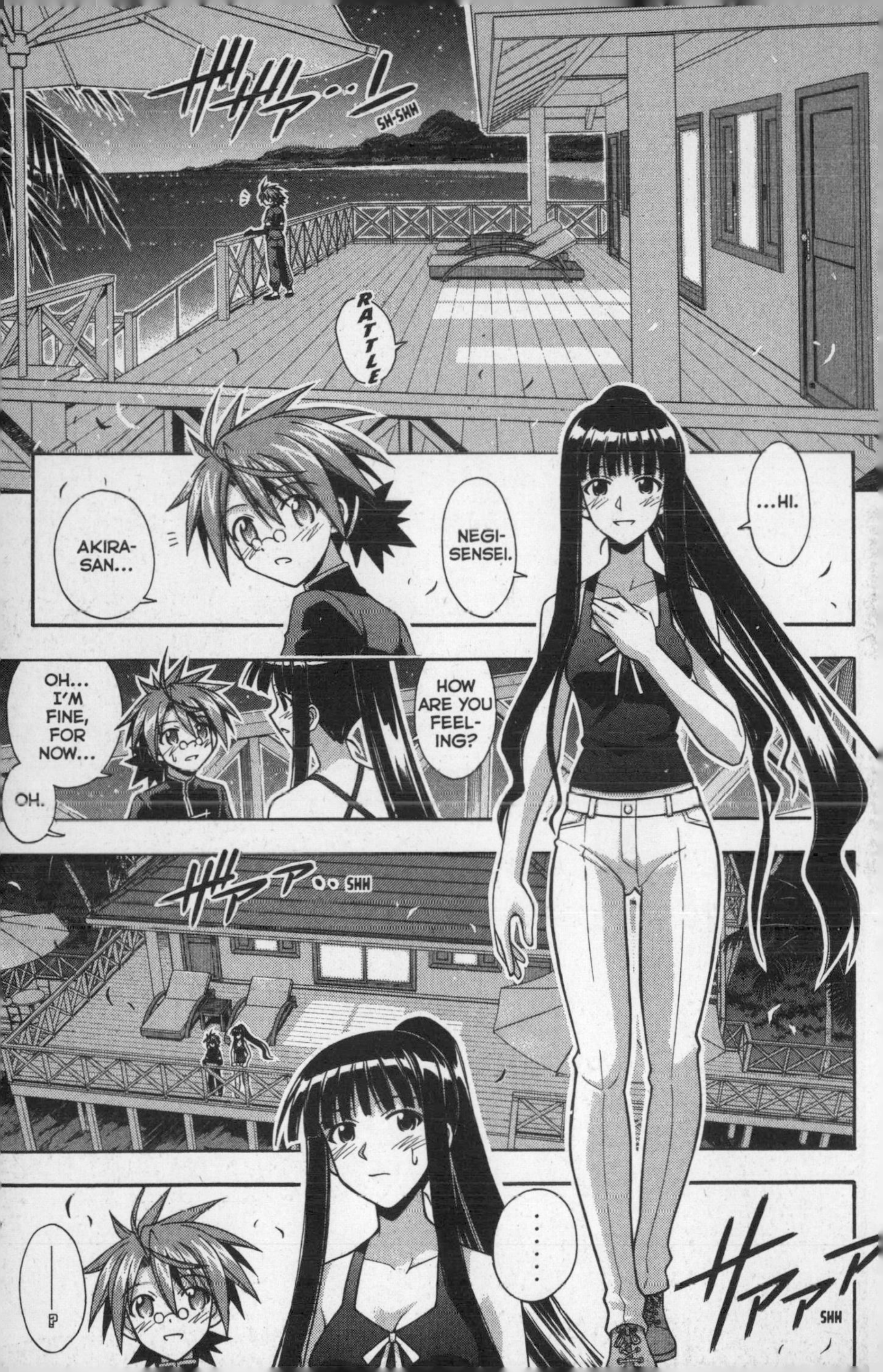
SH-SHH
RATTLE
...HI.
NEGI-SENSEI.
AKIRA-SAN...
HOW ARE YOU FEELING?
OH... I'M FINE, FOR NOW...
OH.
SHH
SHH
......
—!?

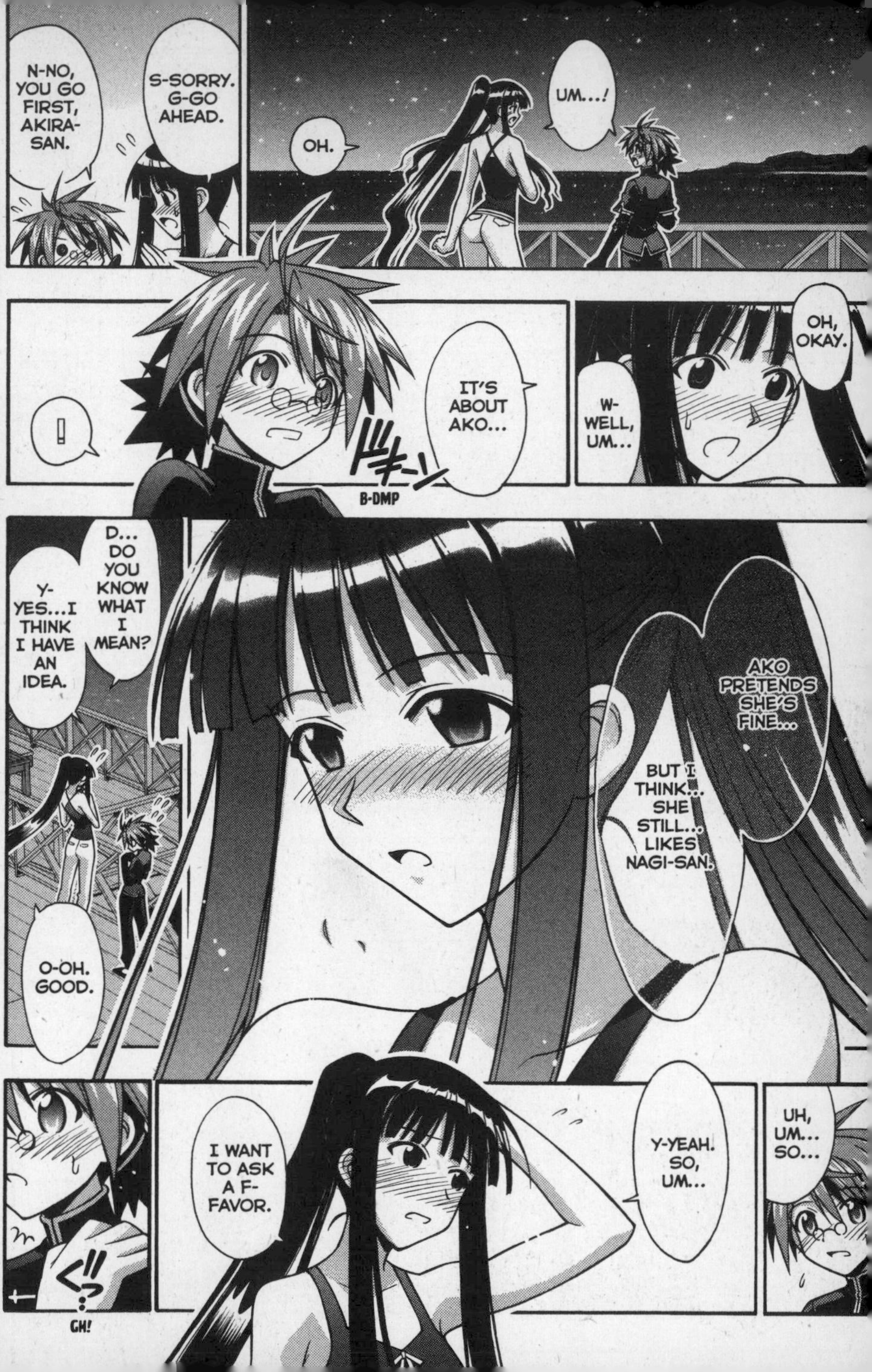
UM...!
OH.
S-SORRY. G-GO AHEAD.
N-NO, YOU GO FIRST, AKIRA-SAN.
OH, OKAY.
W-WELL, UM...
IT'S ABOUT AKO...
B-DMP
!
AKO PRETENDS SHE'S FINE...
BUT I THINK... SHE STILL... LIKES NAGI-SAN.
D... DO YOU KNOW WHAT I MEAN?
Y-YES...I THINK I HAVE AN IDEA.
O-OH. GOOD.
UH, UM... SO...
Y-YEAH. SO, UM...
I WANT TO ASK A F-FAVOR.
GH!

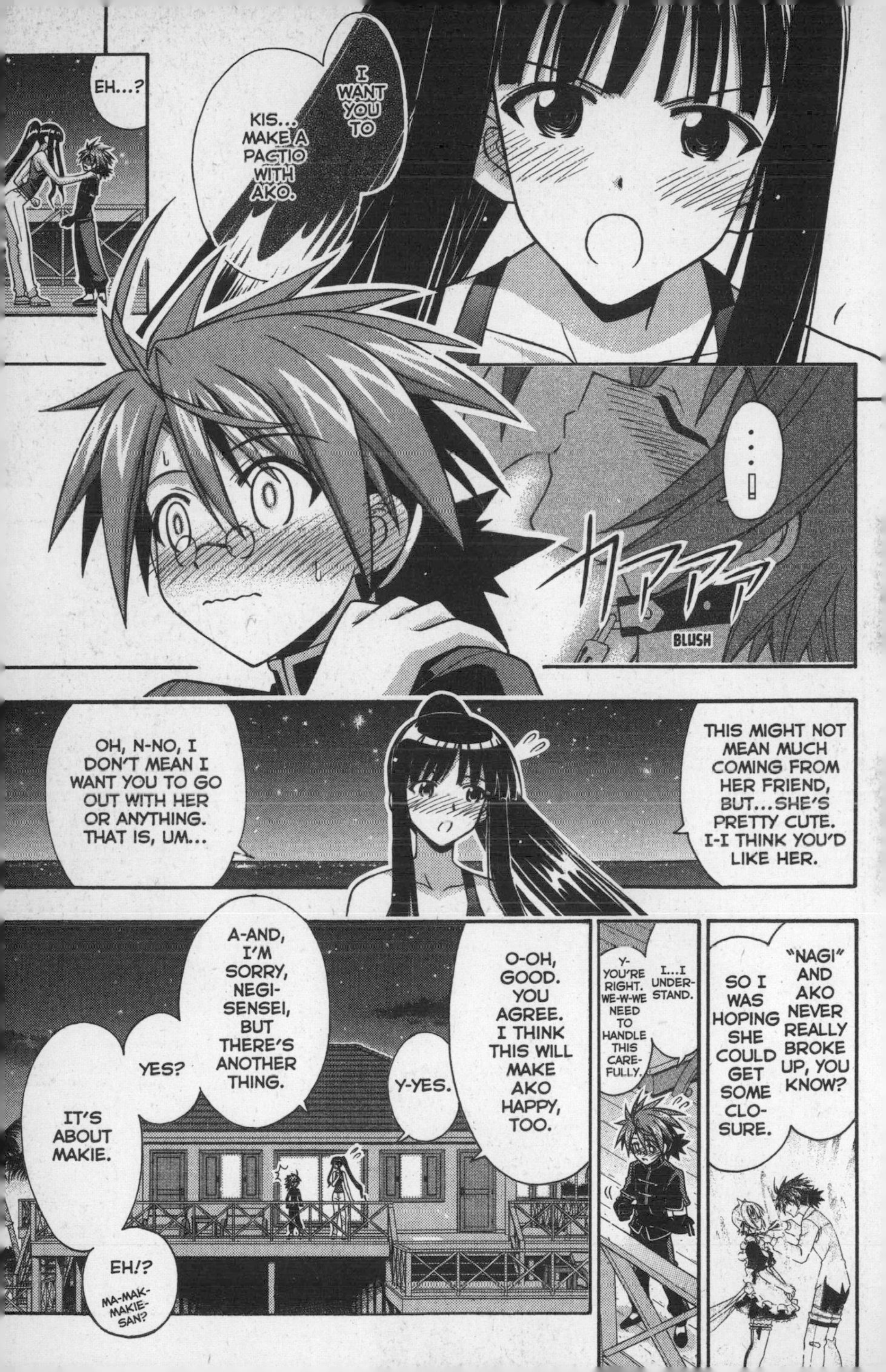
I WANT YOU TO KIS... MAKE A PACTIO WITH AKO.
EH...?
...!
カァァァ
BLUSH
THIS MIGHT NOT MEAN MUCH COMING FROM HER FRIEND, BUT...SHE'S PRETTY CUTE. I-I THINK YOU'D LIKE HER.
OH, N-NO, I DON'T MEAN I WANT YOU TO GO OUT WITH HER OR ANYTHING. THAT IS, UM...
"NAGI" AND AKO NEVER REALLY BROKE UP, YOU KNOW?
SO I WAS HOPING SHE COULD GET SOME CLO-SURE.
I...I UNDER-STAND.
Y-YOU'RE RIGHT. WE-W-WE NEED TO HANDLE THIS CARE-FULLY.
O-OH, GOOD. YOU AGREE. I THINK THIS WILL MAKE AKO HAPPY, TOO.
Y-YES.
A-AND, I'M SORRY, NEGI-SENSEI, BUT THERE'S ANOTHER THING.
YES?
IT'S ABOUT MAKIE.
EH!?
MA-MAK-MAKIE-SAN?

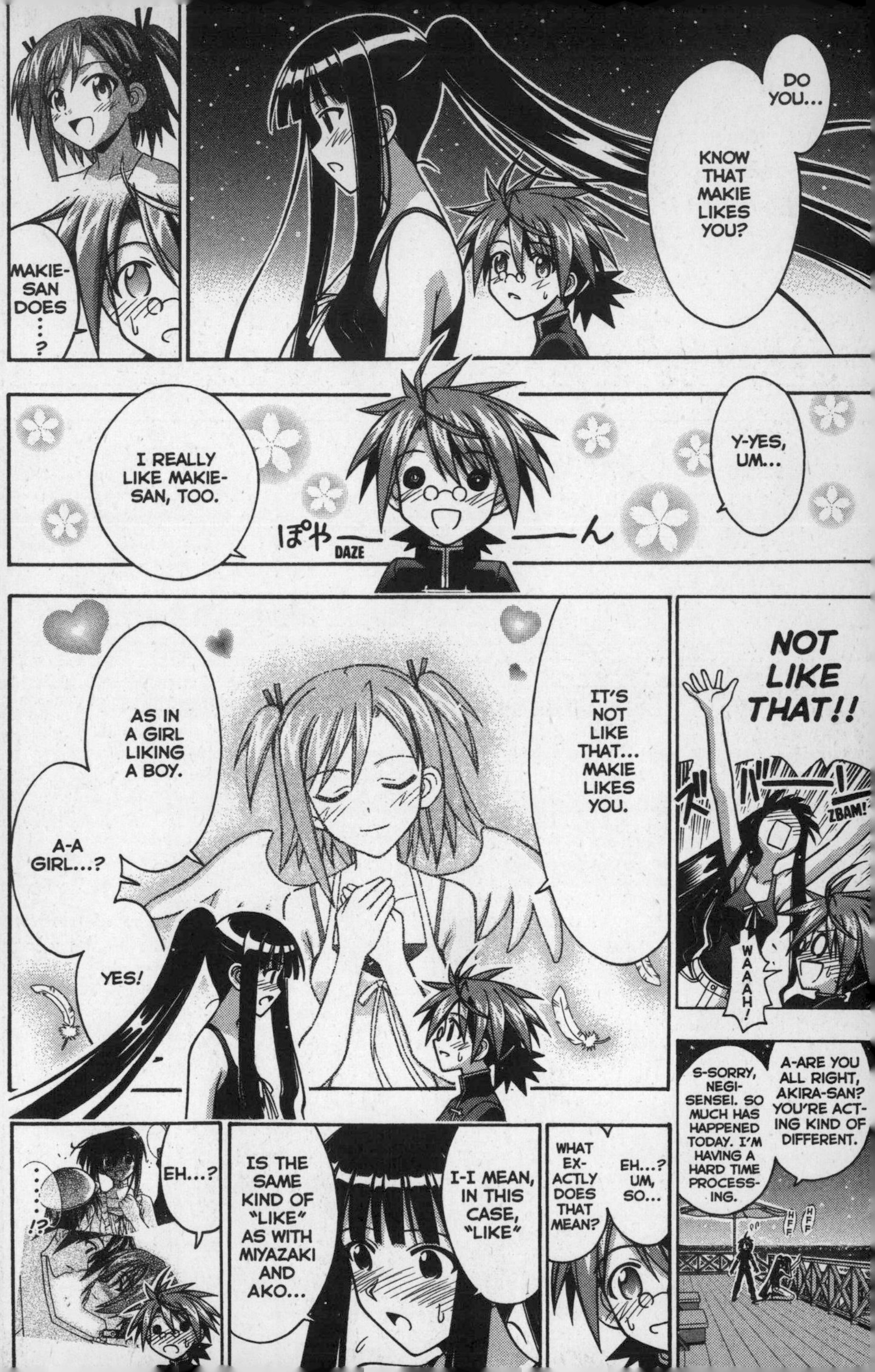
DO YOU... KNOW THAT MAKIE LIKES YOU?
MAKIE-SAN DOES...?
Y-YES, UM...
I REALLY LIKE MAKIE-SAN, TOO.
ぽや——ん
DAZE
NOT LIKE THAT!!
ZBAM!
WAAAAH!
A-ARE YOU ALL RIGHT, AKIRA-SAN? YOU'RE ACTING KIND OF DIFFERENT.
S-SORRY, NEGI-SENSEI. SO MUCH HAS HAPPENED TODAY. I'M HAVING A HARD TIME PROCESSING.
HFF
HFF
IT'S NOT LIKE THAT... MAKIE LIKES YOU.
AS IN A GIRL LIKING A BOY.
A-A GIRL...?
YES!
EH...? UM, SO...
WHAT EXACTLY DOES THAT MEAN?
I-I MEAN, IN THIS CASE, "LIKE"
IS THE SAME KIND OF "LIKE" AS WITH MIYAZAKI AND AKO...
EH...?
......!?

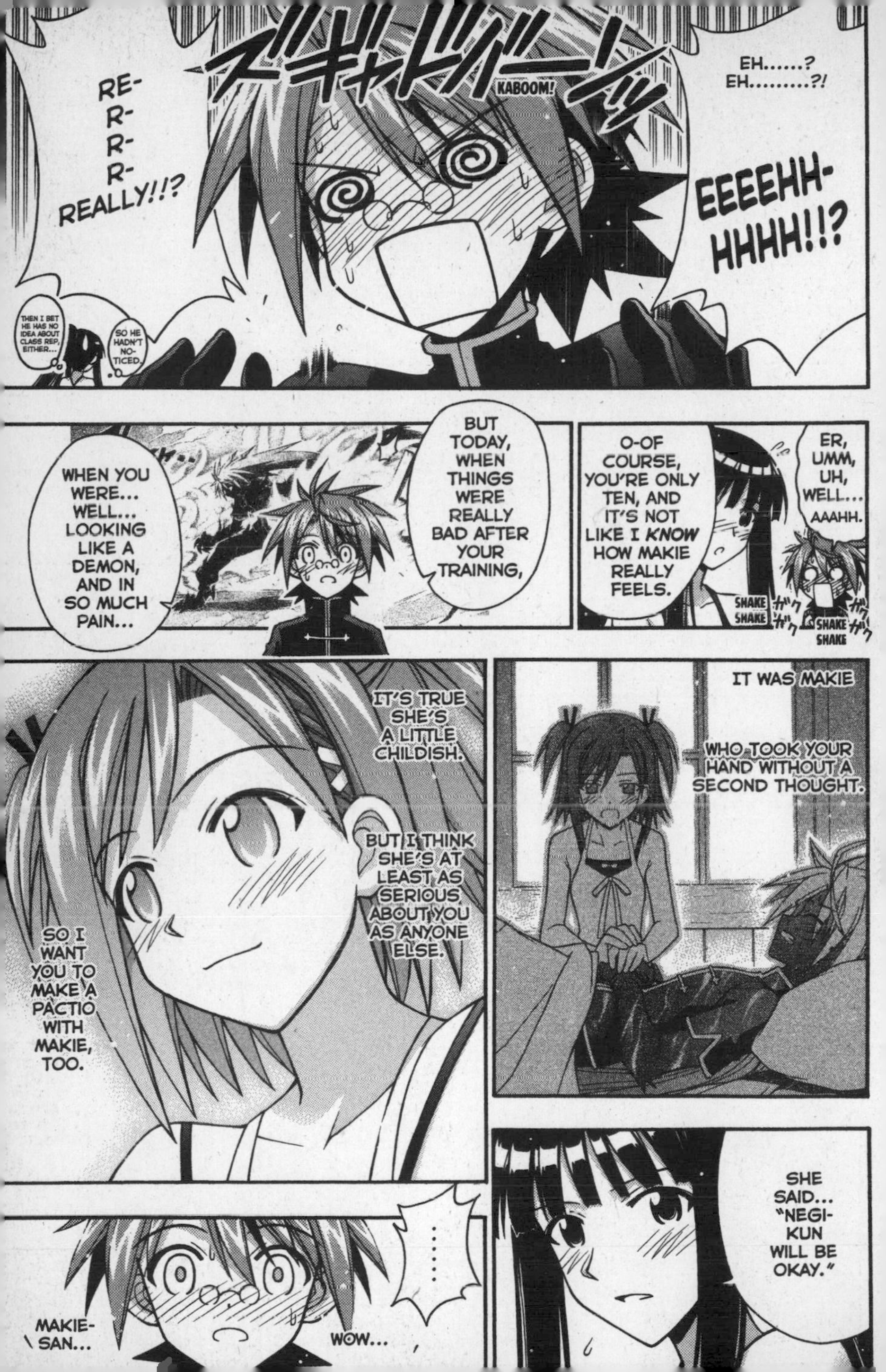
EH......?
EH.........?!
EEEEHH-HHHH!!?
KABOOM!
RE-R-R-R-REALLY!!?
SO HE HADN'T NOTICED.
THEN I BET HE HAS NO IDEA ABOUT CLASS REP, EITHER...
ER, UMM, UH, WELL...
AAAHH.
SHAKE SHAKE
SHAKE SHAKE
O-OF COURSE, YOU'RE ONLY TEN, AND IT'S NOT LIKE I KNOW HOW MAKIE REALLY FEELS.
BUT TODAY, WHEN THINGS WERE REALLY BAD AFTER YOUR TRAINING,
WHEN YOU WERE... WELL... LOOKING LIKE A DEMON, AND IN SO MUCH PAIN...
IT WAS MAKIE
WHO TOOK YOUR HAND WITHOUT A SECOND THOUGHT.
SHE SAID... "NEGI-KUN WILL BE OKAY."
IT'S TRUE SHE'S A LITTLE CHILDISH.
BUT I THINK SHE'S AT LEAST AS SERIOUS ABOUT YOU AS ANYONE ELSE.
SO I WANT YOU TO MAKE A PACTIO WITH MAKIE, TOO.
......
WOW...
MAKIE-SAN...

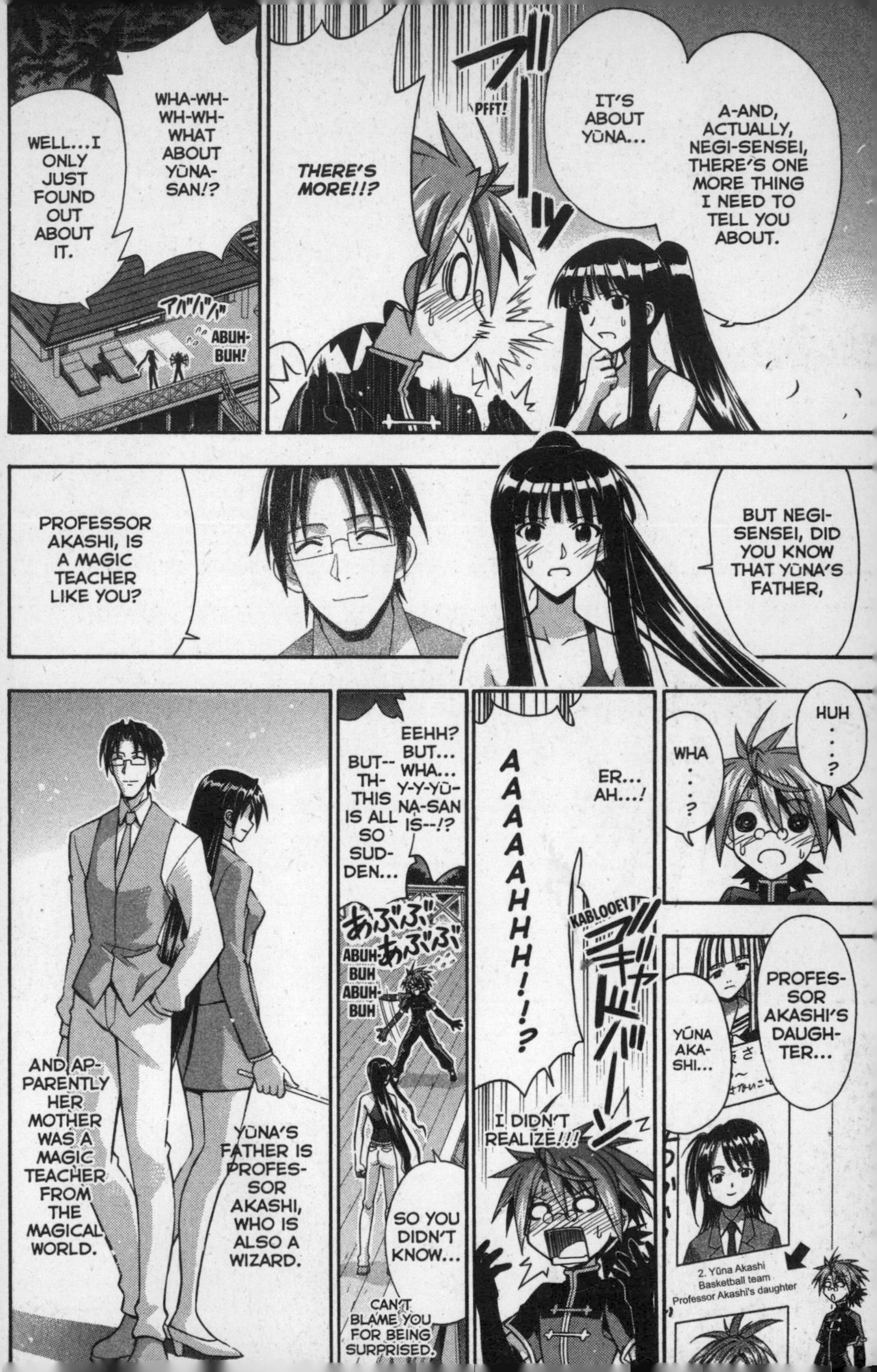
A-AND, ACTUALLY, NEGI-SENSEI, THERE'S ONE MORE THING I NEED TO TELL YOU ABOUT.
IT'S ABOUT YŪNA...
PFFT!
THERE'S MORE!!?
WHA-WH-WH-WH-WHAT ABOUT YŪNA-SAN!?
WELL...I ONLY JUST FOUND OUT ABOUT IT.
アババババ
ABUH-BUH!
BUT NEGI-SENSEI, DID YOU KNOW THAT YŪNA'S FATHER,
PROFESSOR AKASHI, IS A MAGIC TEACHER LIKE YOU?
HUH...?
WHA...?
PROFESSOR AKASHI'S DAUGHTER...
YŪNA AKASHI...
2. Yūna Akashi
Basketball team
Professor Akashi's daughter
ER... AH...!
AAAAAAHHH!!?
KABLOOEY
I DIDN'T REALIZE!!!
EEHH? BUT... WHA... Y-Y-YŪNA-SAN IS--!?
BUT--TH-THIS IS ALL SO SUDDEN...
あぶぶぶあぶぶ
ABUH-BUH ABUH-BUH
SO YOU DIDN'T KNOW...
CAN'T BLAME YOU FOR BEING SURPRISED.
YŪNA'S FATHER IS PROFESSOR AKASHI, WHO IS ALSO A WIZARD.
AND APPARENTLY HER MOTHER WAS A MAGIC TEACHER FROM THE MAGICAL WORLD.

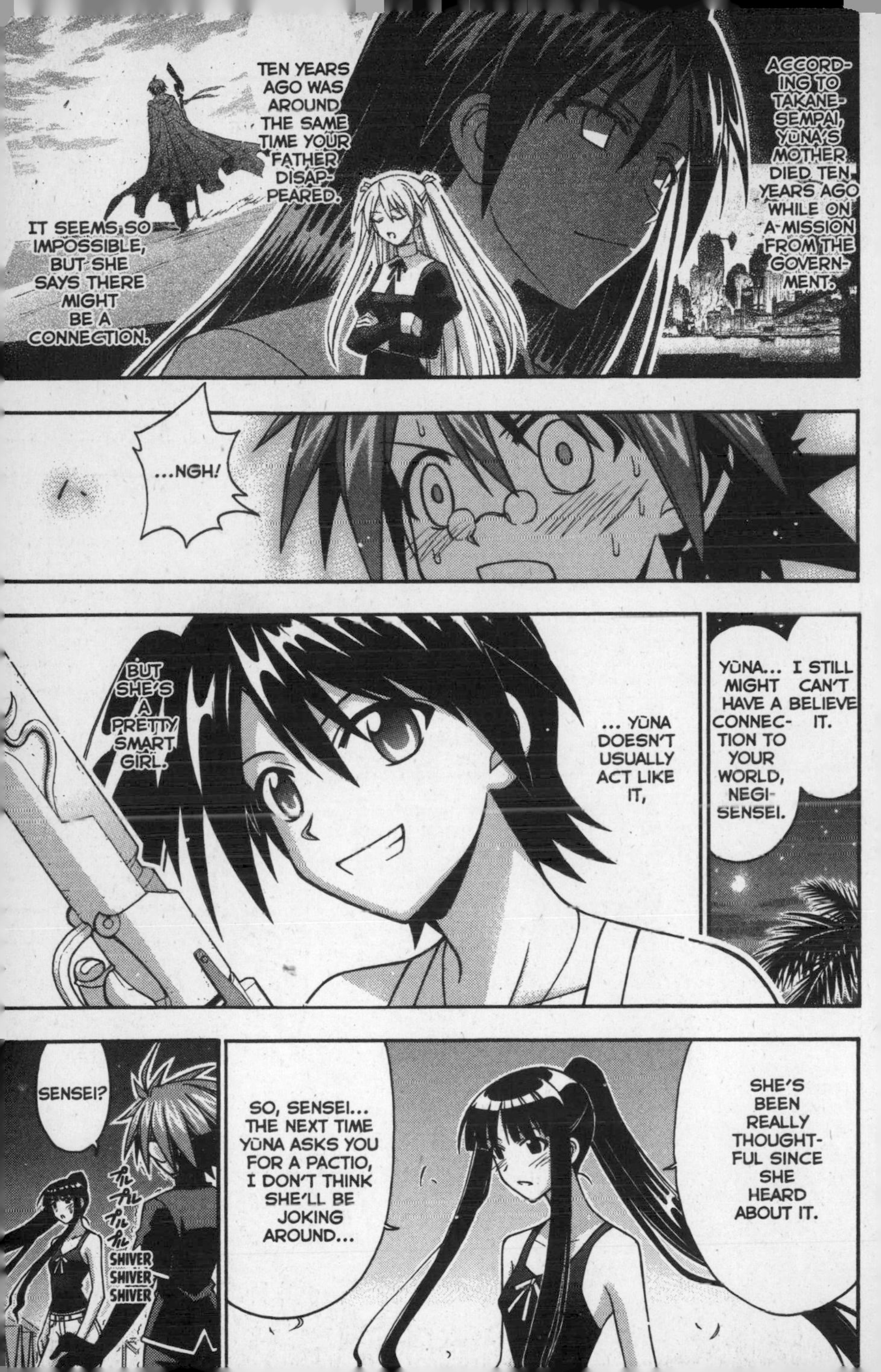
ACCORDING TO TAKANE-SEMPAI, YŪNA'S MOTHER DIED TEN YEARS AGO WHILE ON A MISSION FROM THE GOVERNMENT.
TEN YEARS AGO WAS AROUND THE SAME TIME YOUR FATHER DISAPPEARED.
IT SEEMS SO IMPOSSIBLE, BUT SHE SAYS THERE MIGHT BE A CONNECTION.
...NGH!
I STILL CAN'T BELIEVE IT.
YŪNA... MIGHT HAVE A CONNECTION TO YOUR WORLD, NEGI-SENSEI.
... YŪNA DOESN'T USUALLY ACT LIKE IT,
BUT SHE'S A PRETTY SMART GIRL.
SHE'S BEEN REALLY THOUGHTFUL SINCE SHE HEARD ABOUT IT.
SO, SENSEI... THE NEXT TIME YŪNA ASKS YOU FOR A PACTIO, I DON'T THINK SHE'LL BE JOKING AROUND...
SENSEI?
SHIVER SHIVER SHIVER

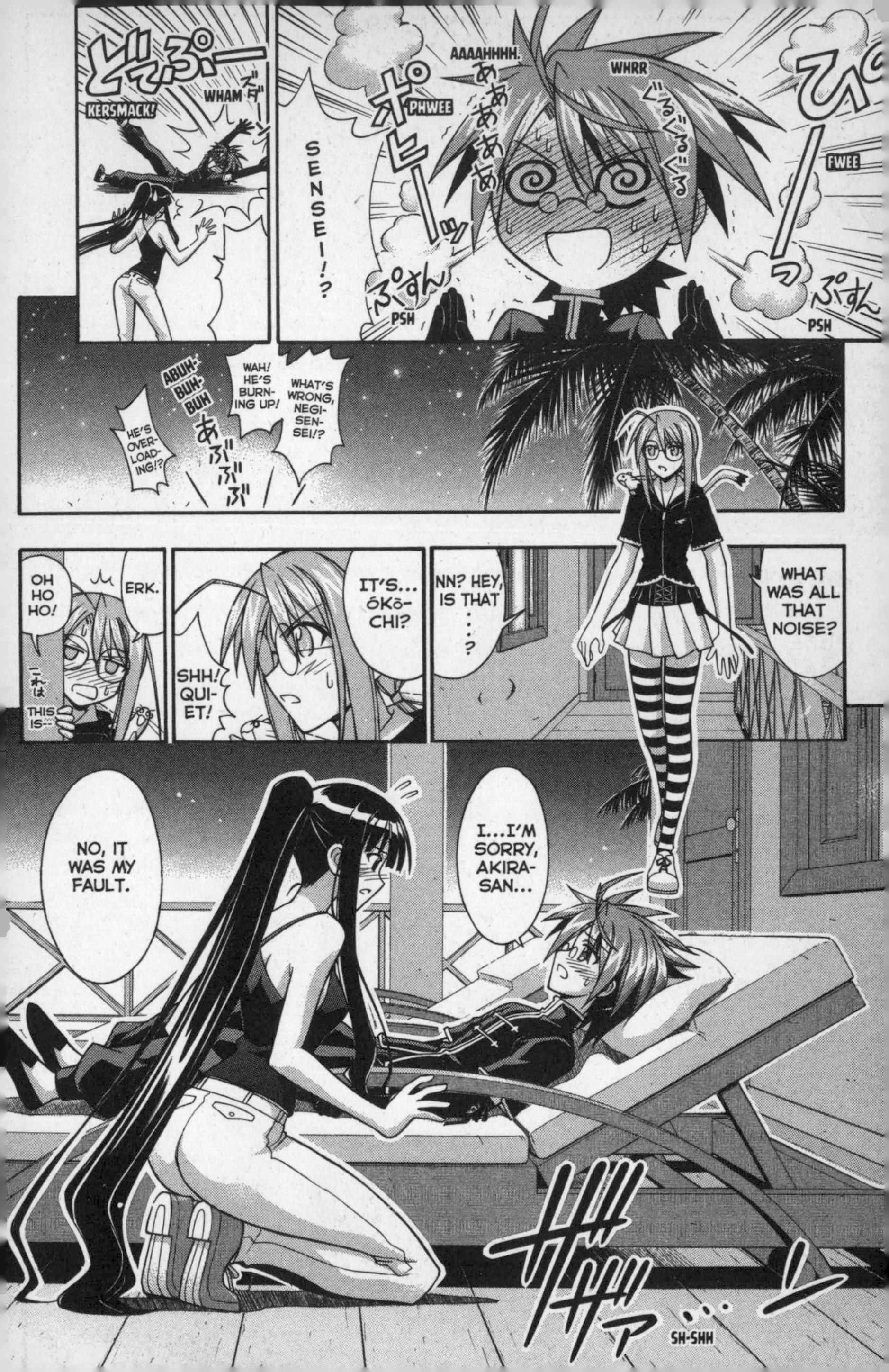
ぴ
FWEE
WHRR
ぐるぐるぐるぐる
AAAAHHHH.
あああああ
ポヒーッ
PHWEE
SENSEI!?
ぷすん
PSH
ぷすん
PSH
どてぷーー
KERSMACK!
ダーン
WHAM
WHAT'S WRONG, NEGI-SENSEI!?
WAH! HE'S BURNING UP!
ABUH-BUH-BUH
あぶぶぶ
HE'S OVER-LOADING!?
WHAT WAS ALL THAT NOISE?
NN? HEY, IS THAT ...?
IT'S... ŌKŌCHI?
SHH! QUIET!
ERK.
OH HO HO!
これは
THIS IS---
I...I'M SORRY, AKIRA-SAN...
NO, IT WAS MY FAULT.
ザザァ...
SH-SHH

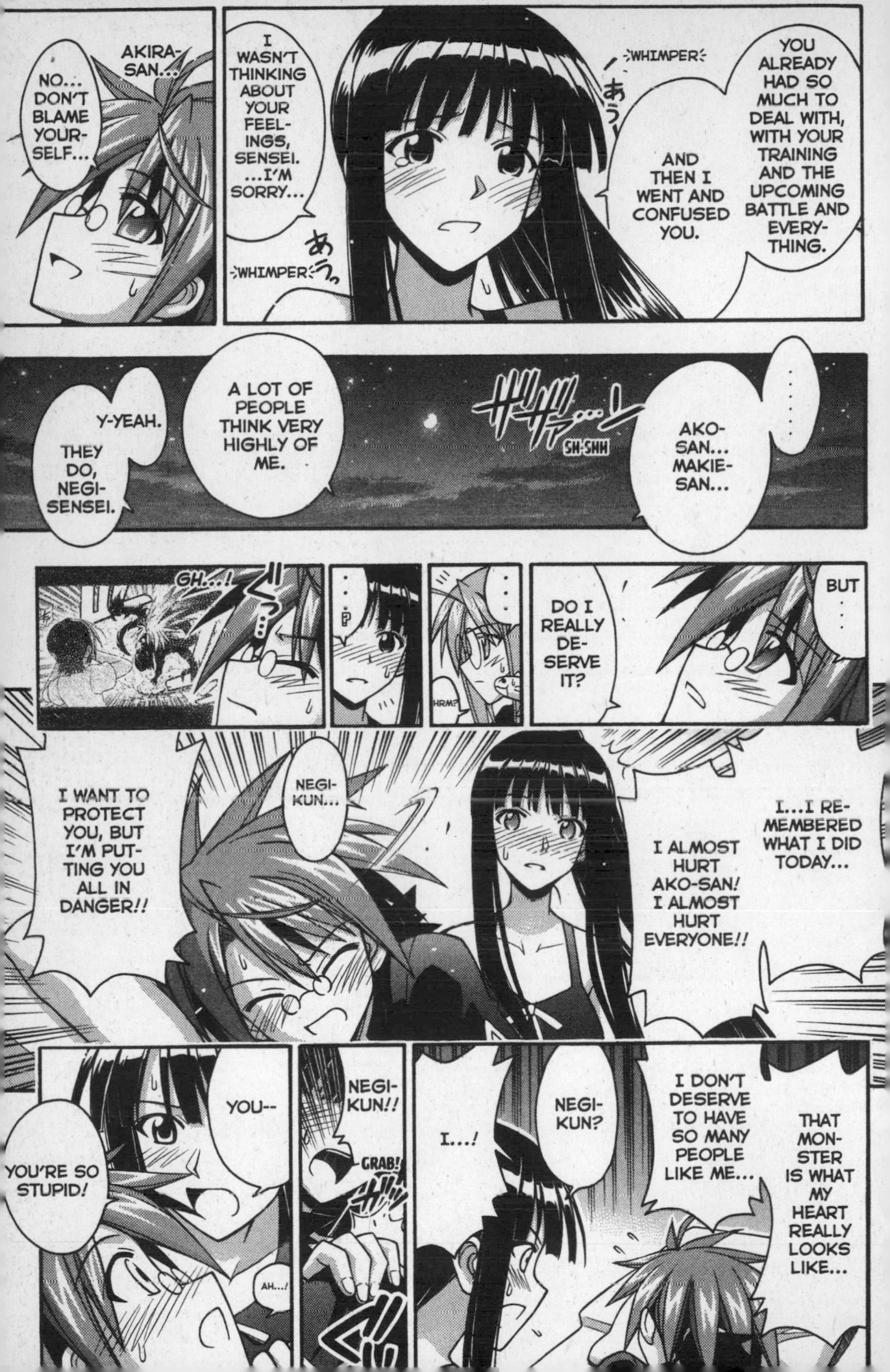
YOU ALREADY HAD SO MUCH TO DEAL WITH, WITH YOUR TRAINING AND THE UPCOMING BATTLE AND EVERYTHING.
WHIMPER
AND THEN I WENT AND CONFUSED YOU.
I WASN'T THINKING ABOUT YOUR FEELINGS, SENSEI. ...I'M SORRY...
WHIMPER
AKIRA-SAN...
NO... DON'T BLAME YOURSELF...
...
AKO-SAN... MAKIE-SAN...
SH-SHH
A LOT OF PEOPLE THINK VERY HIGHLY OF ME.
Y-YEAH.
THEY DO, NEGI-SENSEI.
BUT...
DO I REALLY DESERVE IT?
...
HRM?
...?
GH...!
I...I REMEMBERED WHAT I DID TODAY...
I ALMOST HURT AKO-SAN! I ALMOST HURT EVERYONE!!
NEGI-KUN...
I WANT TO PROTECT YOU, BUT I'M PUTTING YOU ALL IN DANGER!!
THAT MONSTER IS WHAT MY HEART REALLY LOOKS LIKE...
I DON'T DESERVE TO HAVE SO MANY PEOPLE LIKE ME...
NEGI-KUN?
I...!
NEGI-KUN!!
GRAB!
AH...!
YOU--
YOU'RE SO STUPID!

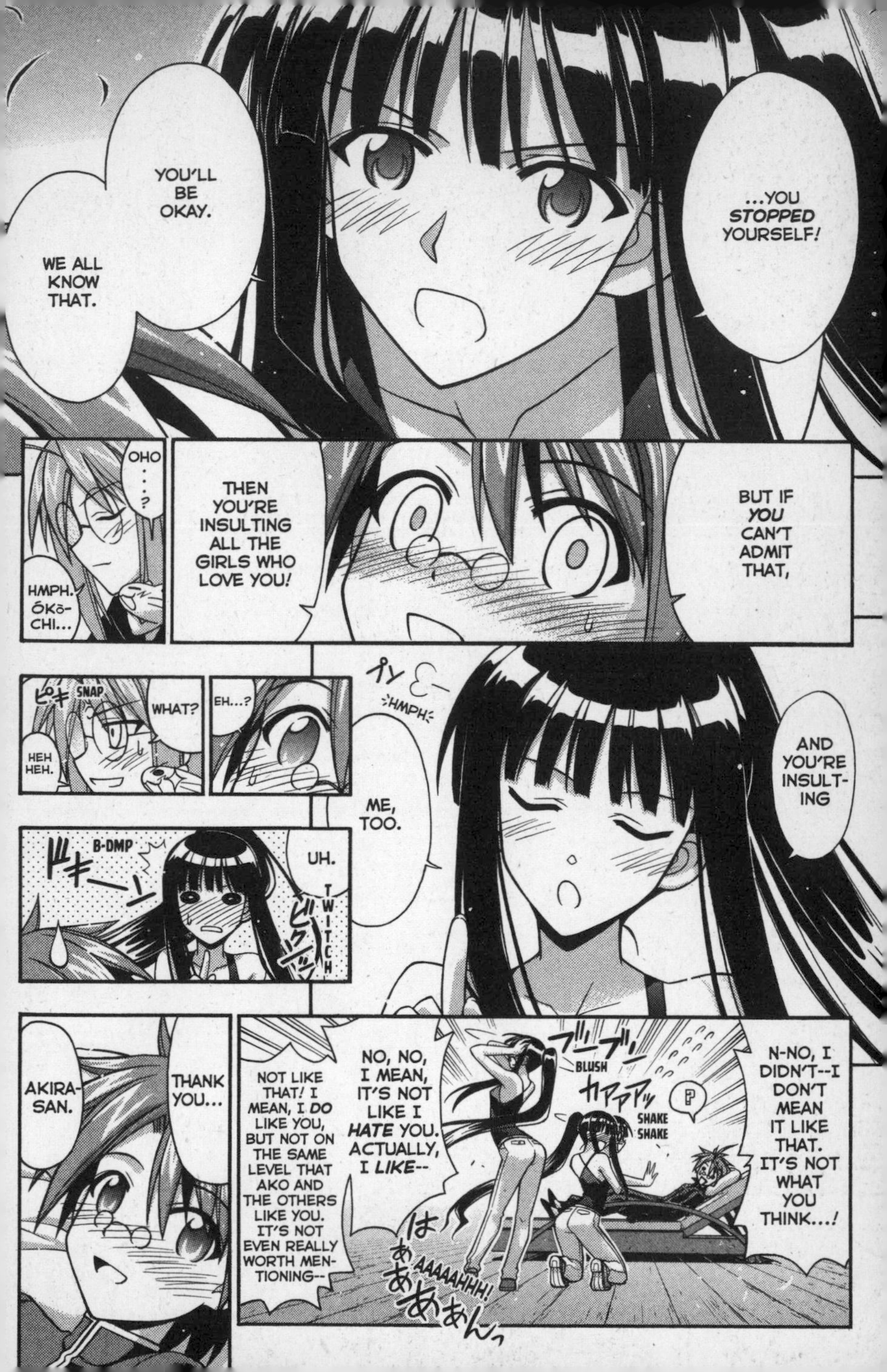
...YOU *STOPPED* YOURSELF!
YOU'LL BE OKAY.
WE ALL KNOW THAT.
BUT IF *YOU* CAN'T ADMIT THAT,
THEN YOU'RE INSULTING ALL THE GIRLS WHO LOVE YOU!
OHO...?
HMPH. ŌKŌCHI...
AND YOU'RE INSULTING
HMPH
ME, TOO.
EH...?
WHAT?
SNAP
HEH HEH.
UH.
B-DMP
TWITCH
N-NO, I DIDN'T--I DON'T MEAN IT LIKE THAT. IT'S NOT WHAT YOU THINK...!
BLUSH
SHAKE SHAKE
NO, NO, I MEAN, IT'S NOT LIKE I *HATE* YOU. ACTUALLY, I *LIKE*--
NOT LIKE THAT! I MEAN, I *DO* LIKE YOU, BUT NOT ON THE SAME LEVEL THAT AKO AND THE OTHERS LIKE YOU. IT'S NOT EVEN REALLY WORTH MENTIONING--
AAAAAHHH!
THANK YOU...
AKIRA-SAN.

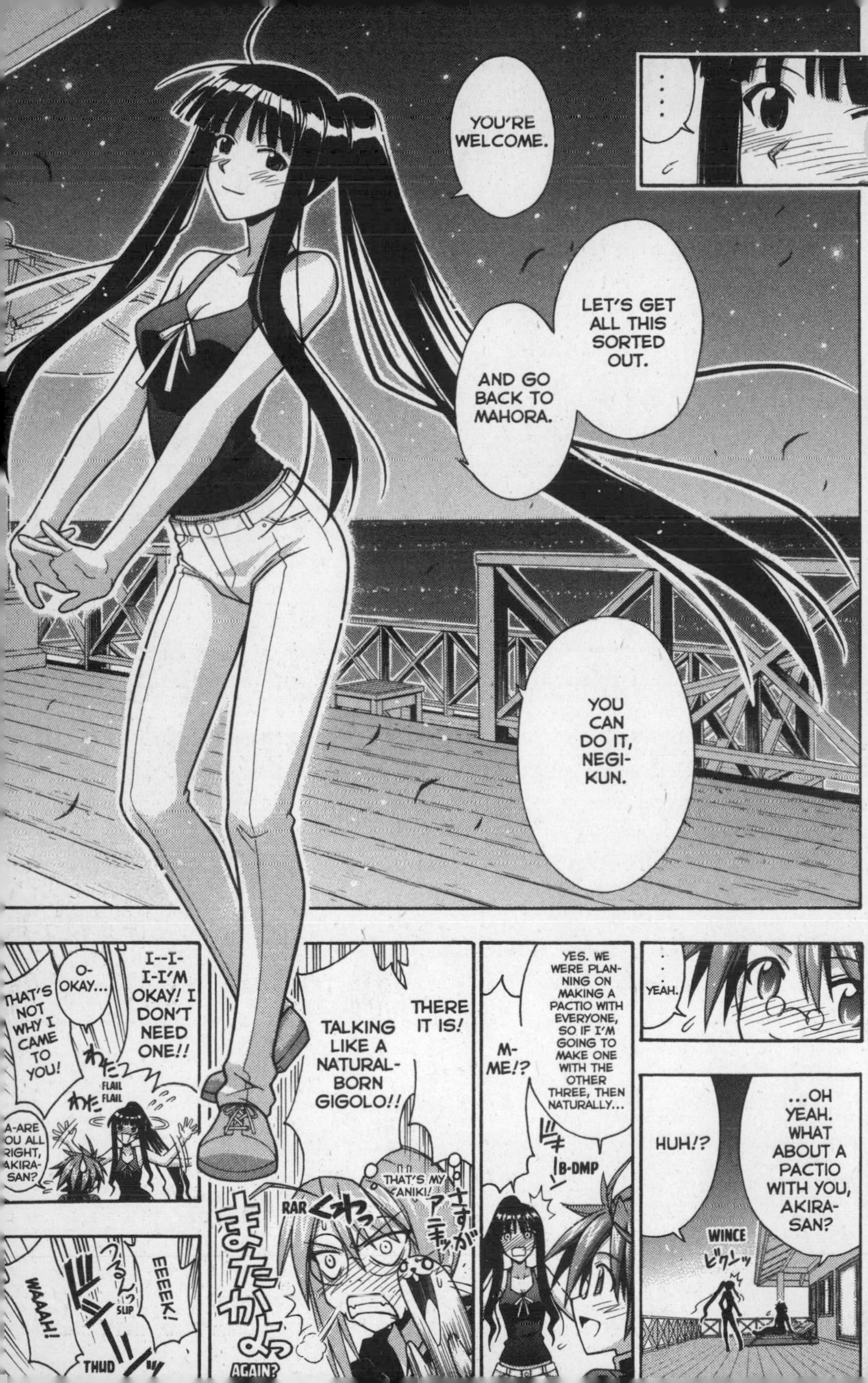
....
YOU'RE WELCOME.
LET'S GET ALL THIS SORTED OUT.
AND GO BACK TO MAHORA.
YOU CAN DO IT, NEGI-KUN.
... YEAH.
...OH YEAH. WHAT ABOUT A PACTIO WITH YOU, AKIRA-SAN?
HUH!?
ビクンッ
WINCE
YES. WE WERE PLANNING ON MAKING A PACTIO WITH EVERYONE, SO IF I'M GOING TO MAKE ONE WITH THE OTHER THREE, THEN NATURALLY...
M-ME!?
ドキ
B-DMP
THERE IT IS!
TALKING LIKE A NATURAL-BORN GIGOLO!!
さすがアニキッ
THAT'S MY ANIKI!
くわっ
RAR
またかよっ
AGAIN?
I--I-I-I'M OKAY! I DON'T NEED ONE!!
O-OKAY...
THAT'S NOT WHY I CAME TO YOU!
わたわた
FLAIL FLAIL
A-ARE OU ALL RIGHT, AKIRA-SAN?
EEEEK!
つるんっ
SLIP
WAAAH!
ドシーン
THUD

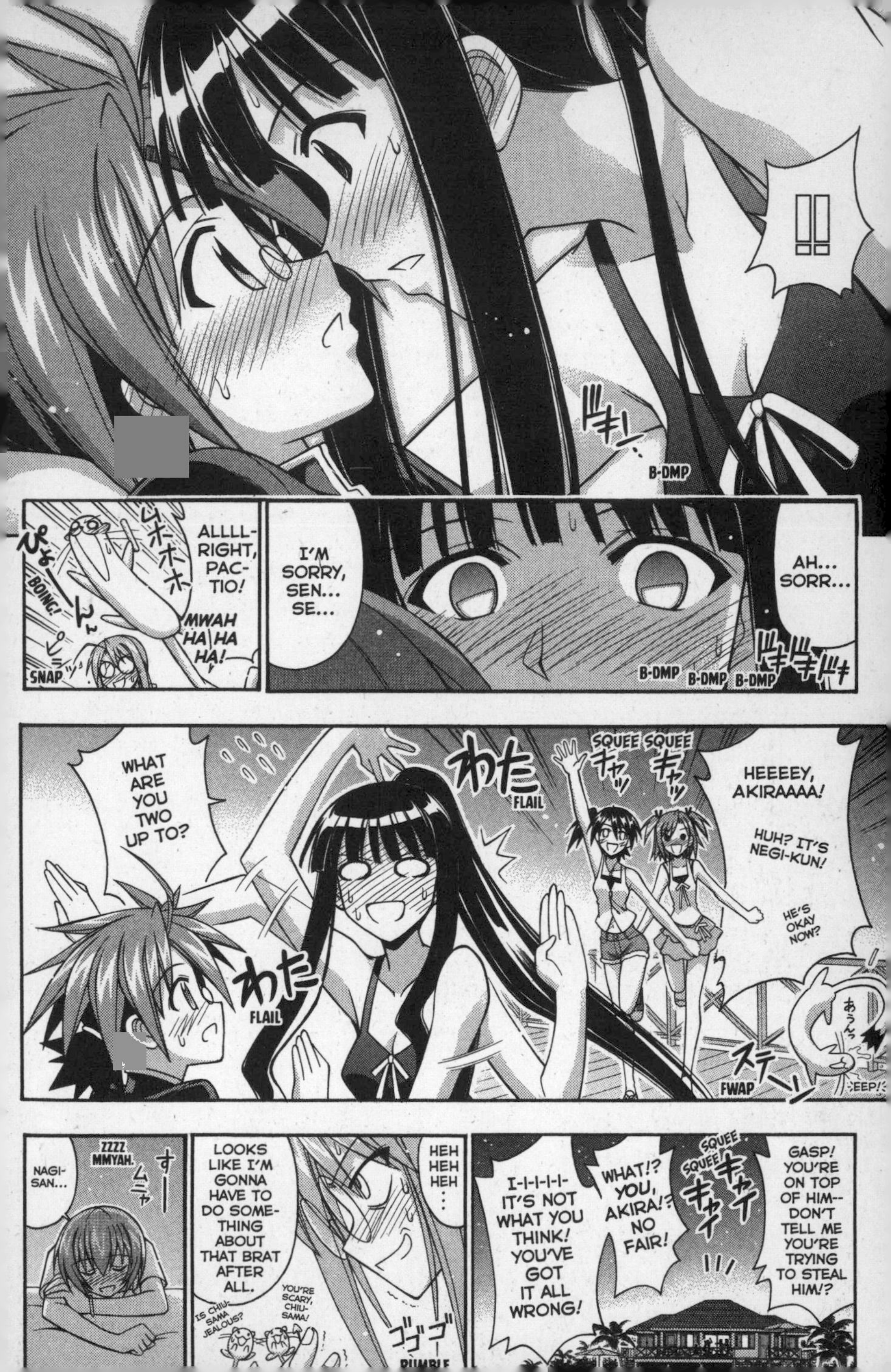
!!
B-DMP
AH... SORR...
B-DMP B-DMP B-DMP
I'M SORRY, SEN... SE...
ALLLL-RIGHT, PACTIO!
MWAH HA HA HA!
BOING!
SNAP
HEEEEY, AKIRAAAA!
SQUEE SQUEE
HUH? IT'S NEGI-KUN!
HE'S OKAY NOW?
EEP!
FWAP
FLAIL
WHAT ARE YOU TWO UP TO?
FLAIL
GASP! YOU'RE ON TOP OF HIM-- DON'T TELL ME YOU'RE TRYING TO STEAL HIM!?
SQUEE SQUEE
WHAT!? YOU, AKIRA!? NO FAIR!
I-I-I-I-I-IT'S NOT WHAT YOU THINK! YOU'VE GOT IT ALL WRONG!
HEH HEH HEH...
LOOKS LIKE I'M GONNA HAVE TO DO SOMETHING ABOUT THAT BRAT AFTER ALL.
YOU'RE SCARY, CHIU-SAMA!
IS CHIU-SAMA JEALOUS?
ZZZZ MMYAH.
NAGI-SAN...

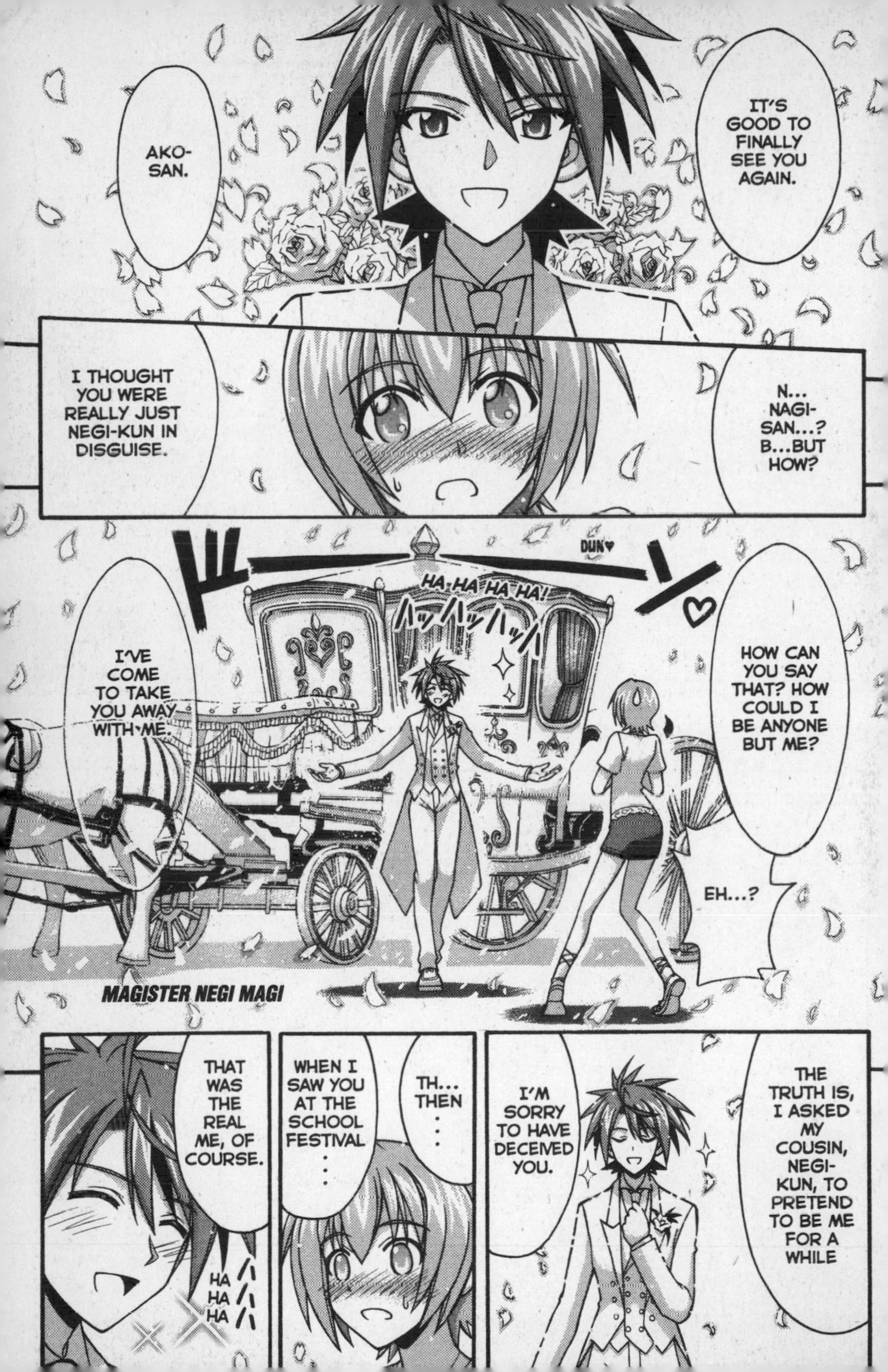
IT'S GOOD TO FINALLY SEE YOU AGAIN.
AKO-SAN.
N... NAGI-SAN...? B...BUT HOW?
I THOUGHT YOU WERE REALLY JUST NEGI-KUN IN DISGUISE.
DUN♥
HOW CAN YOU SAY THAT? HOW COULD I BE ANYONE BUT ME?
HA HA HA HA!
ハッハッハッハッ
I'VE COME TO TAKE YOU AWAY WITH ME.
EH...?
MAGISTER NEGI MAGI
THE TRUTH IS, I ASKED MY COUSIN, NEGI-KUN, TO PRETEND TO BE ME FOR A WHILE
I'M SORRY TO HAVE DECEIVED YOU.
TH... THEN...
WHEN I SAW YOU AT THE SCHOOL FESTIVAL...
THAT WAS THE REAL ME, OF COURSE.
HA HA HA

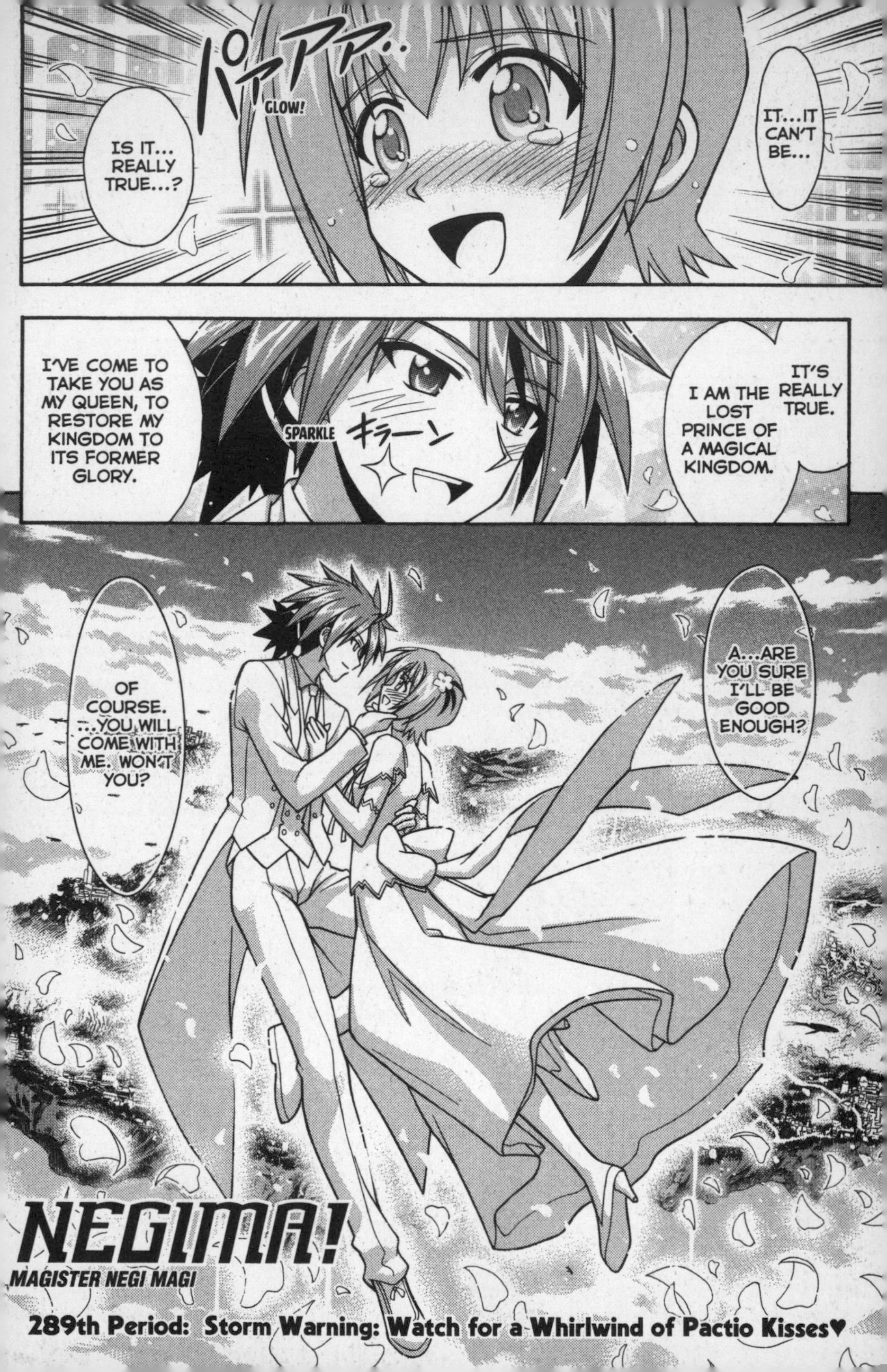
IT...IT CAN'T BE...
パァァァ..
GLOW!
IS IT... REALLY TRUE...?
IT'S REALLY TRUE. I AM THE LOST PRINCE OF A MAGICAL KINGDOM.
キラーン
SPARKLE
I'VE COME TO TAKE YOU AS MY QUEEN, TO RESTORE MY KINGDOM TO ITS FORMER GLORY.
A...ARE YOU SURE I'LL BE GOOD ENOUGH?
OF COURSE. ...YOU WILL COME WITH ME. WON'T YOU?
NEGIMA!
MAGISTER NEGI MAGI
289th Period: Storm Warning: Watch for a Whirlwind of Pactio Kisses♥

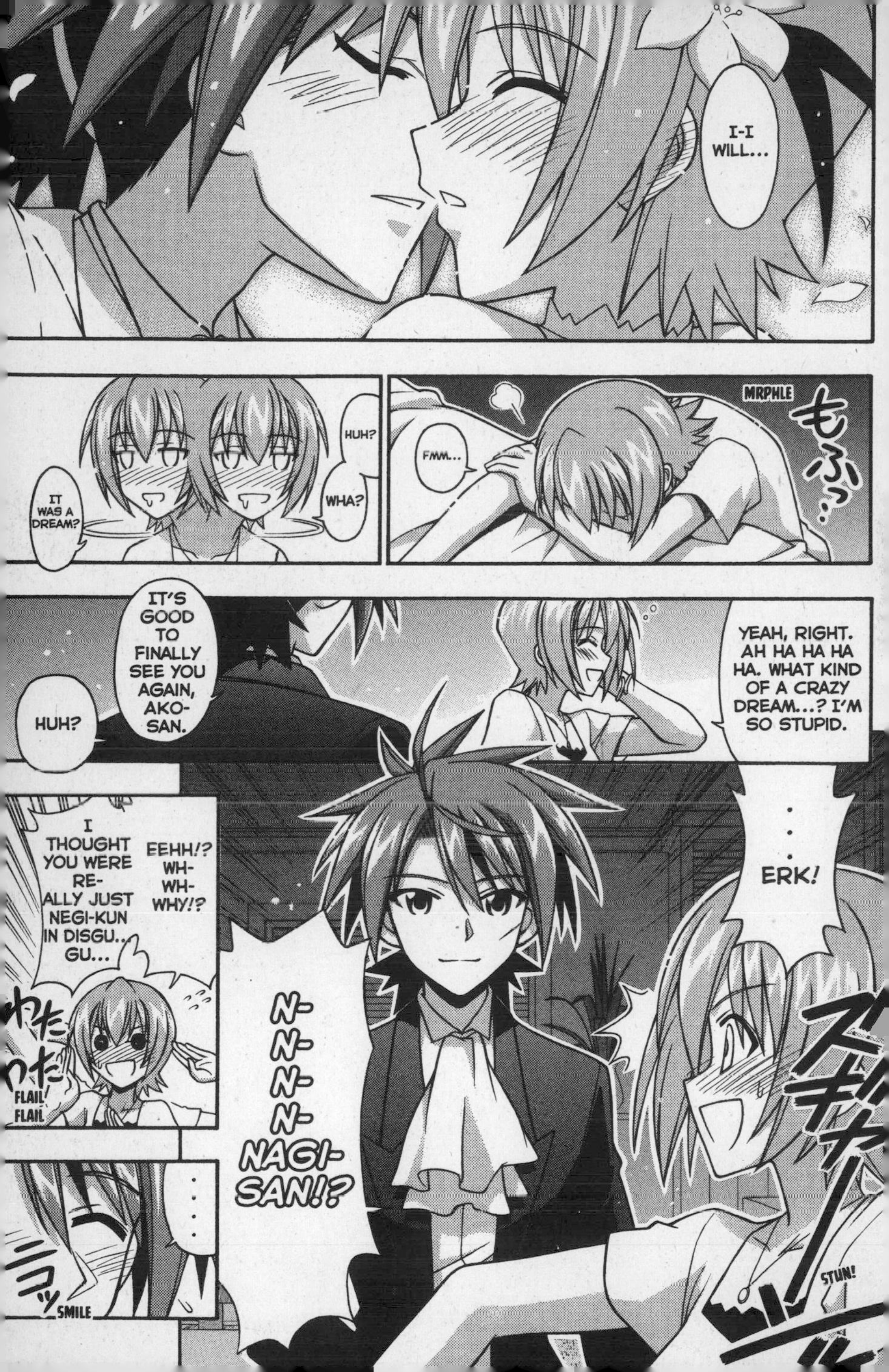

I-I WILL...
MRPHLE
もふっ...
FMM...
HUH?
WHA?
IT WAS A DREAM?
YEAH, RIGHT. AH HA HA HA HA. WHAT KIND OF A CRAZY DREAM...? I'M SO STUPID.
IT'S GOOD TO FINALLY SEE YOU AGAIN, AKO-SAN.
HUH?
...ERK!
N-N-N-N-NAGI-SAN!?
STUN!
EEHH!? WH-WH-WHY!?
I THOUGHT YOU WERE RE-ALLY JUST NEGI-KUN IN DISGU.. GU...
わたわた
FLAIL FLAIL
...
ニコッ
SMILE

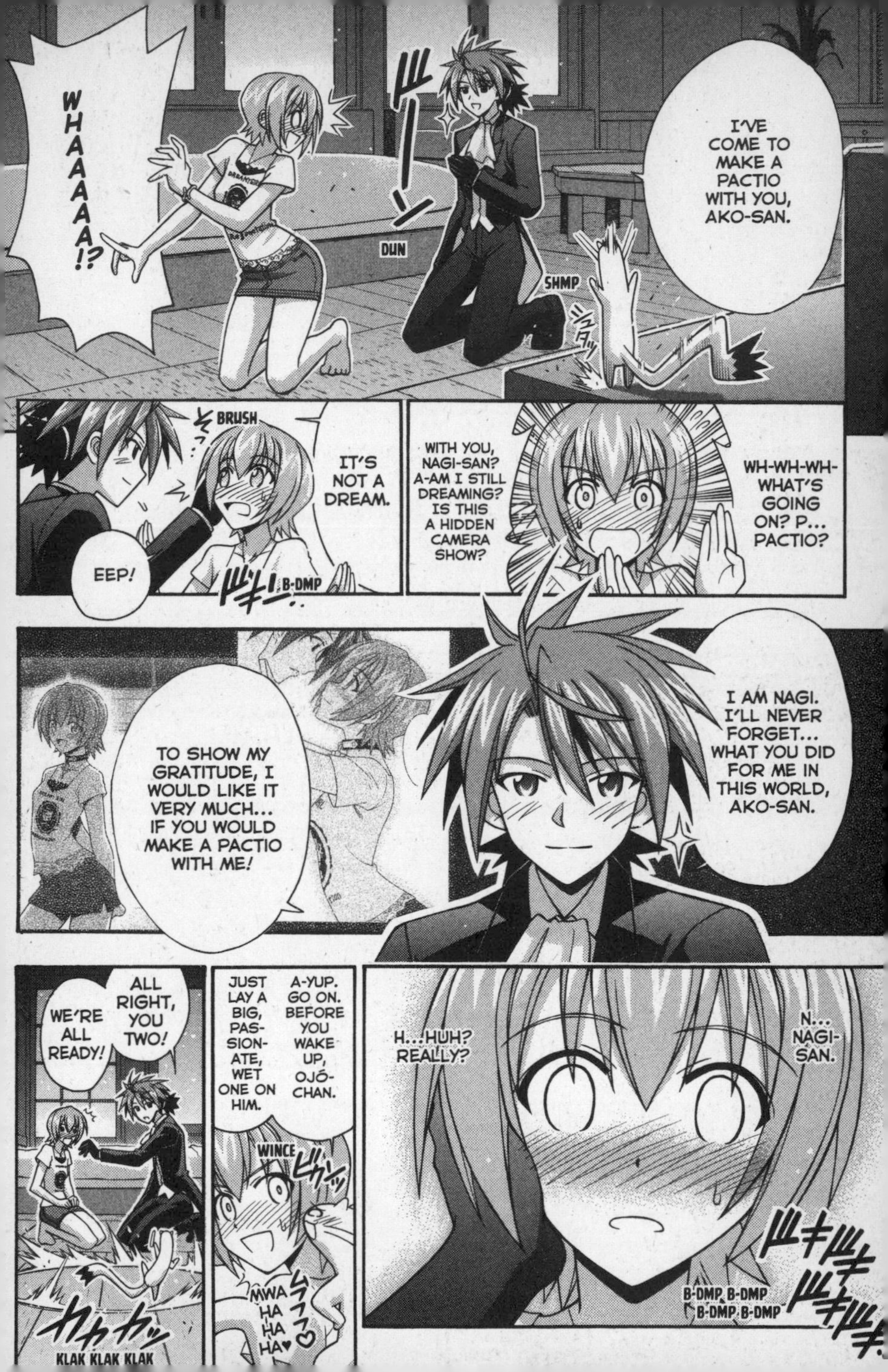
I'VE COME TO MAKE A PACTIO WITH YOU, AKO-SAN.
SHMP
DUN
WHAAAAAA!?
WH-WH-WH-WHAT'S GOING ON? P... PACTIO?
WITH YOU, NAGI-SAN? A-AM I STILL DREAMING? IS THIS A HIDDEN CAMERA SHOW?
IT'S NOT A DREAM.
BRUSH
EEP!
B-DMP
I AM NAGI. I'LL NEVER FORGET... WHAT YOU DID FOR ME IN THIS WORLD, AKO-SAN.
TO SHOW MY GRATITUDE, I WOULD LIKE IT VERY MUCH... IF YOU WOULD MAKE A PACTIO WITH ME!
N... NAGI-SAN.
H...HUH? REALLY?
B-DMP B-DMP
B-DMP B-DMP
A-YUP. GO ON. BEFORE YOU WAKE UP, OJŌ-CHAN.
JUST LAY A BIG, PAS-SION-ATE, WET ONE ON HIM.
WINCE
MWA HA HA HA♥
ALL RIGHT, YOU TWO!
WE'RE ALL READY!
KLAK KLAK KLAK

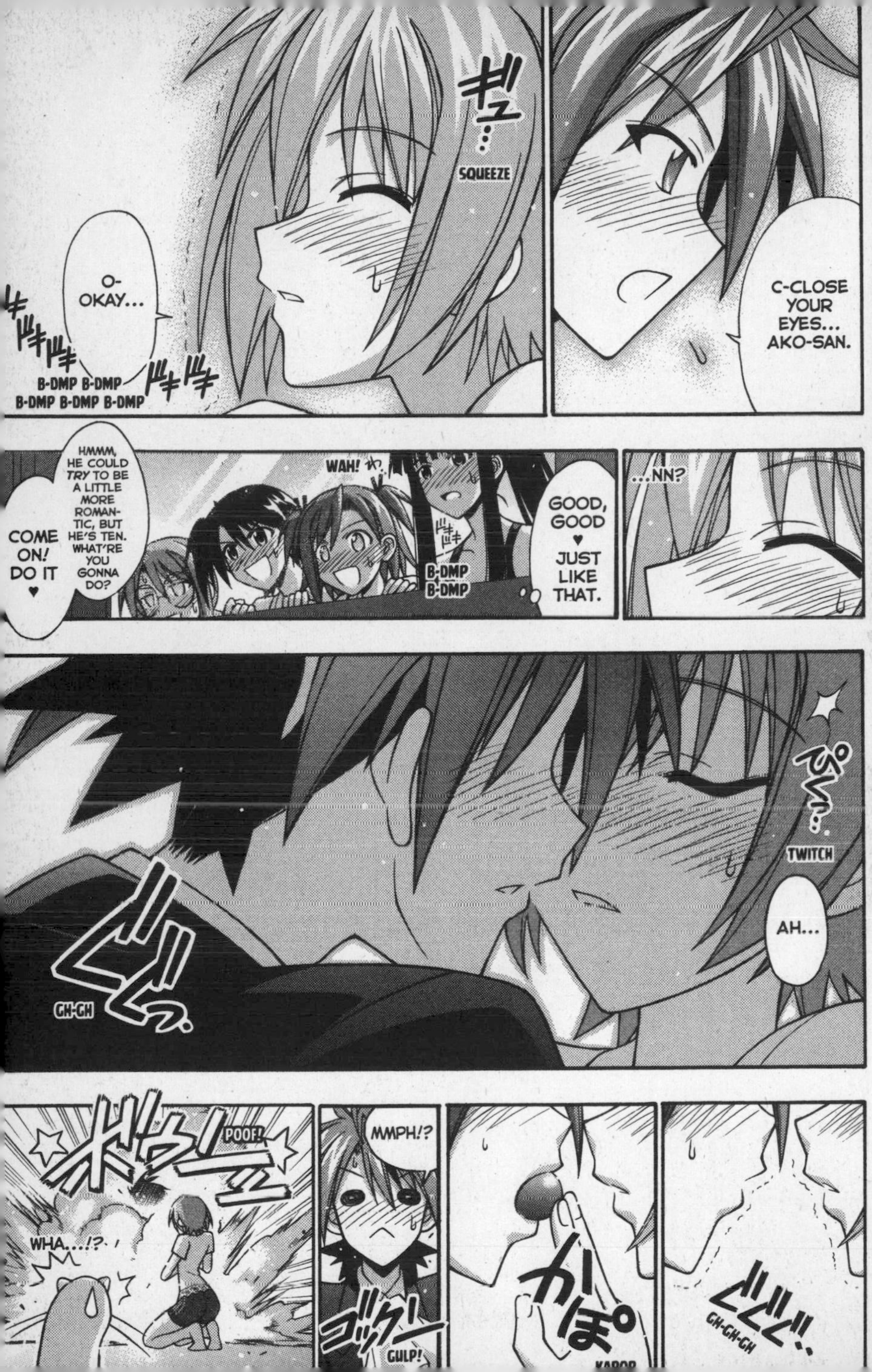
C-CLOSE YOUR EYES... AKO-SAN.
SQUEEZE
O-OKAY...
B-DMP B-DMP B-DMP B-DMP B-DMP
...NN?
GOOD, GOOD ♥ JUST LIKE THAT.
WAH!
B-DMP B-DMP
HMMM, HE COULD *TRY* TO BE A LITTLE MORE ROMANTIC, BUT HE'S TEN. WHAT'RE YOU GONNA DO?
COME ON! DO IT ♥
TWITCH
AH...
GH-GH
GH-GH-GH
MMPH!?
GULP!
POOF!
WHA...!?

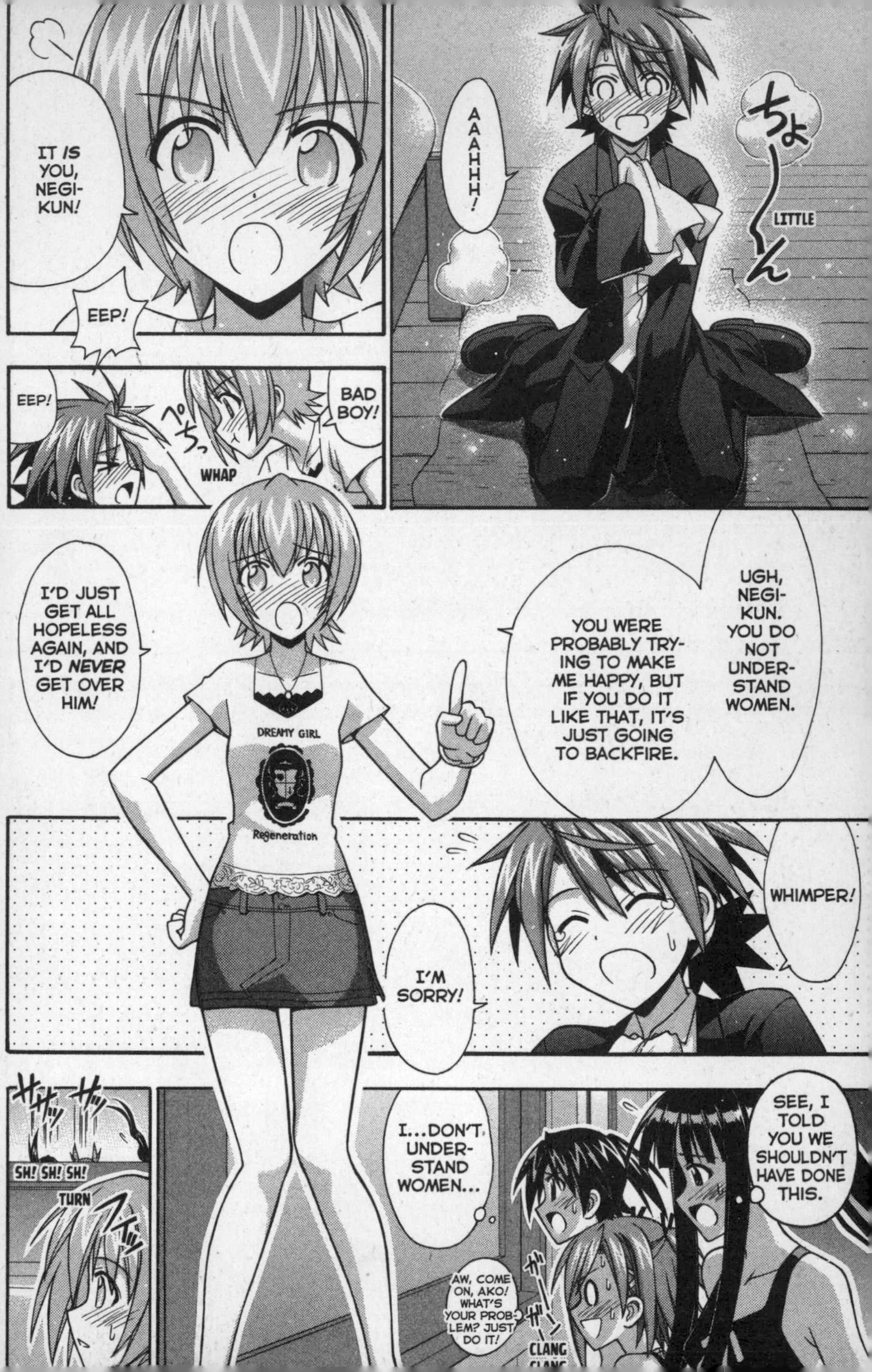
AAAHHH!
ちょーん
LITTLE
IT IS YOU, NEGI-KUN!
EEP!
BAD BOY!
EEP!
ぺちっ
WHAP
UGH, NEGI-KUN. YOU DO NOT UNDER-STAND WOMEN.
YOU WERE PROBABLY TRY-ING TO MAKE ME HAPPY, BUT IF YOU DO IT LIKE THAT, IT'S JUST GOING TO BACKFIRE.
I'D JUST GET ALL HOPELESS AGAIN, AND I'D NEVER GET OVER HIM!
DREAMY GIRL
Regeneration
WHIMPER!
I'M SORRY!
SEE, I TOLD YOU WE SHOULDN'T HAVE DONE THIS.
AW, COME ON, AKO! WHAT'S YOUR PROB-LEM? JUST DO IT!
CLANG
I...DON'T UNDER-STAND WOMEN...
SH! SH! SH!
TURN

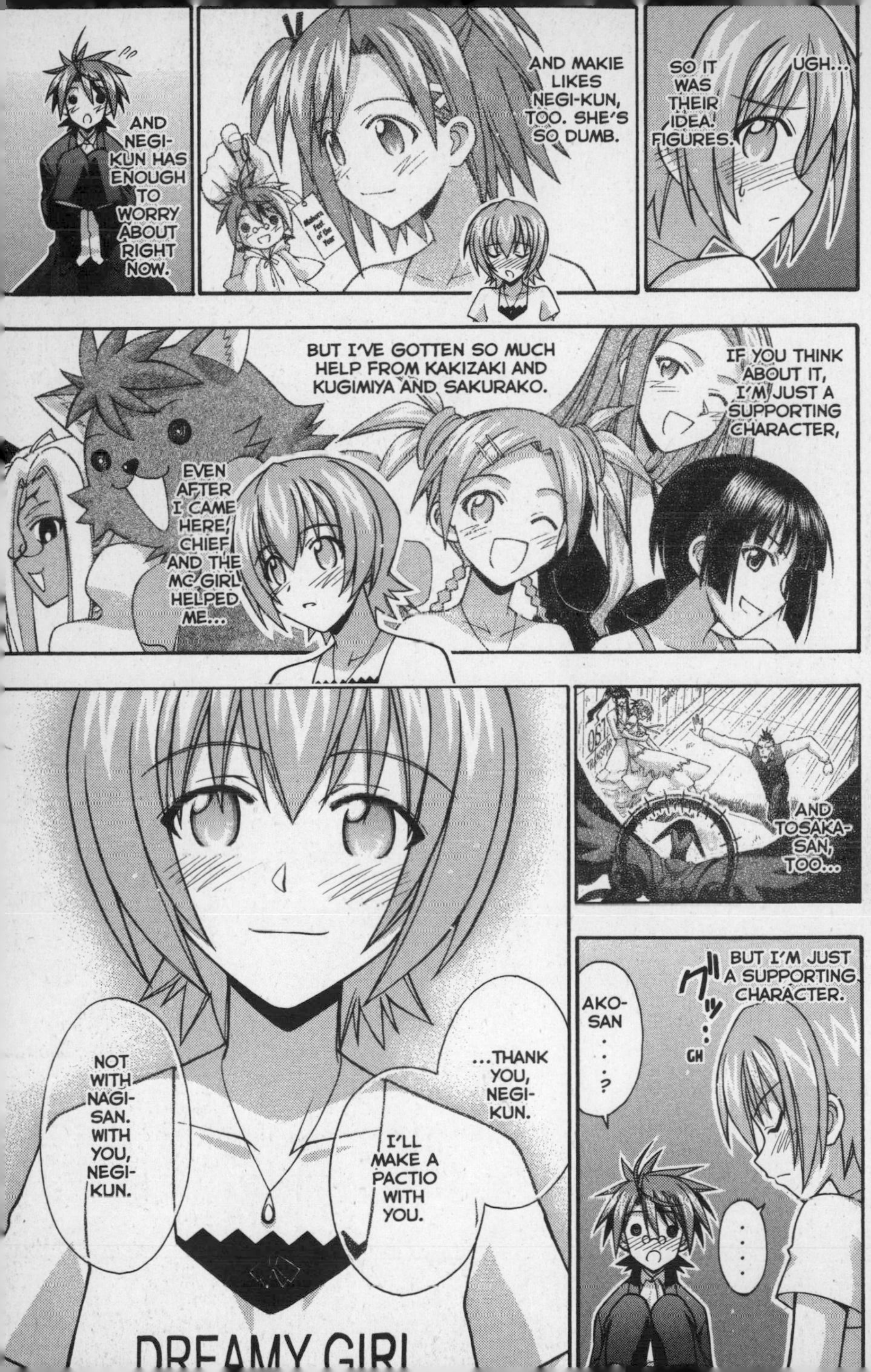
UGH...
SO IT WAS THEIR IDEA. FIGURES.
AND MAKIE LIKES NEGI-KUN, TOO. SHE'S SO DUMB.
AND NEGI-KUN HAS ENOUGH TO WORRY ABOUT RIGHT NOW.
IF YOU THINK ABOUT IT, I'M JUST A SUPPORTING CHARACTER,
BUT I'VE GOTTEN SO MUCH HELP FROM KAKIZAKI AND KUGIMIYA AND SAKURAKO.
EVEN AFTER I CAME HERE, CHIEF AND THE MC GIRL HELPED ME...
AND TOSAKA-SAN, TOO...
BUT I'M JUST A SUPPORTING CHARACTER.
グッ...
GH
AKO-SAN...?
....
...THANK YOU, NEGI-KUN.
I'LL MAKE A PACTIO WITH YOU.
NOT WITH NAGI-SAN. WITH YOU, NEGI-KUN.
DREAMY GIRL

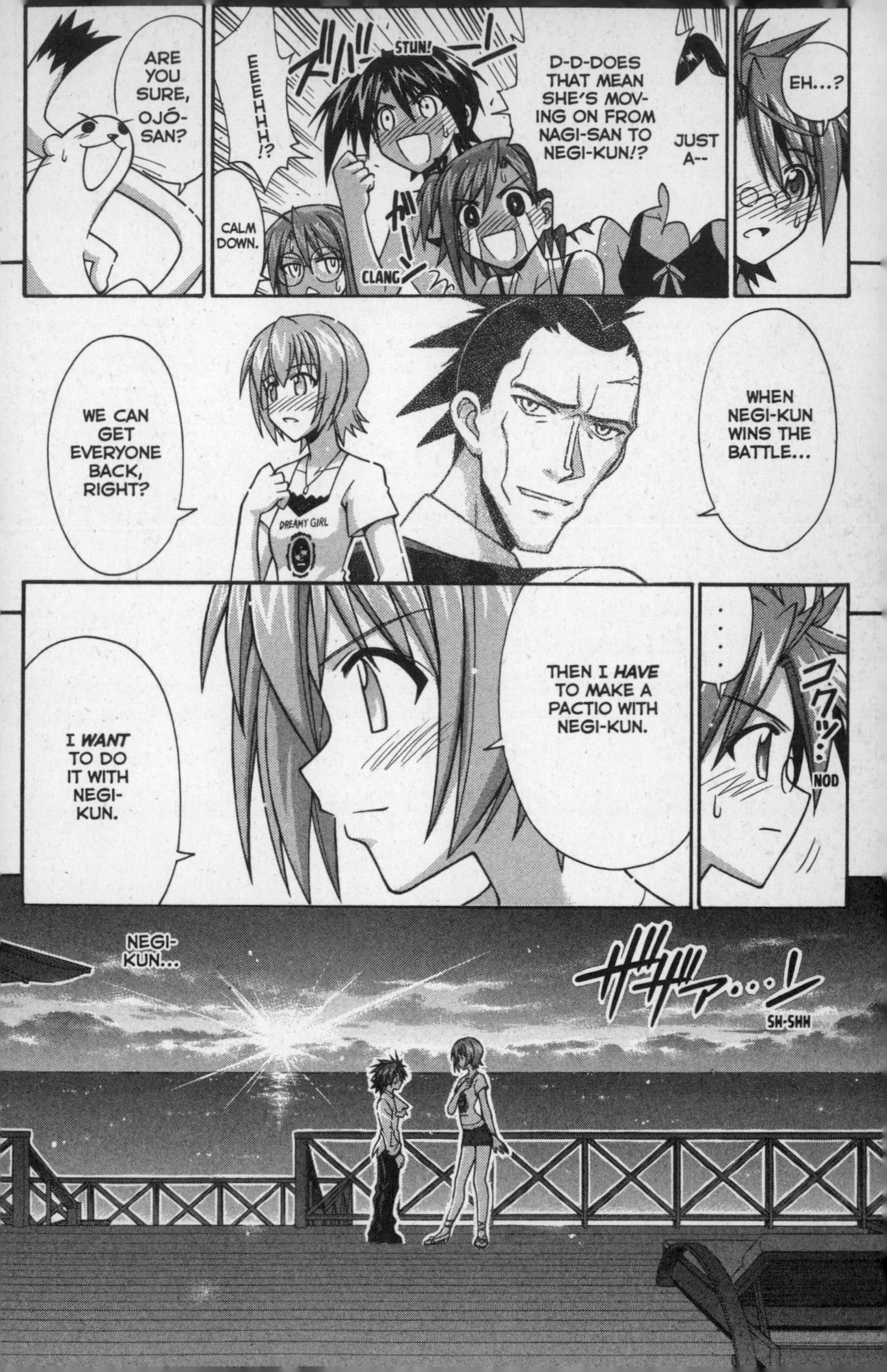
EH...?
JUST A--
D-D-DOES THAT MEAN SHE'S MOV-ING ON FROM NAGI-SAN TO NEGI-KUN!?
STUN!
EEEEHHH!?
CALM DOWN.
CLANG
ARE YOU SURE, OJÓ-SAN?
WHEN NEGI-KUN WINS THE BATTLE...
WE CAN GET EVERYONE BACK, RIGHT?
...
NOD
THEN I *HAVE* TO MAKE A PACTIO WITH NEGI-KUN.
I *WANT* TO DO IT WITH NEGI-KUN.
SH-SHH
NEGI-KUN...

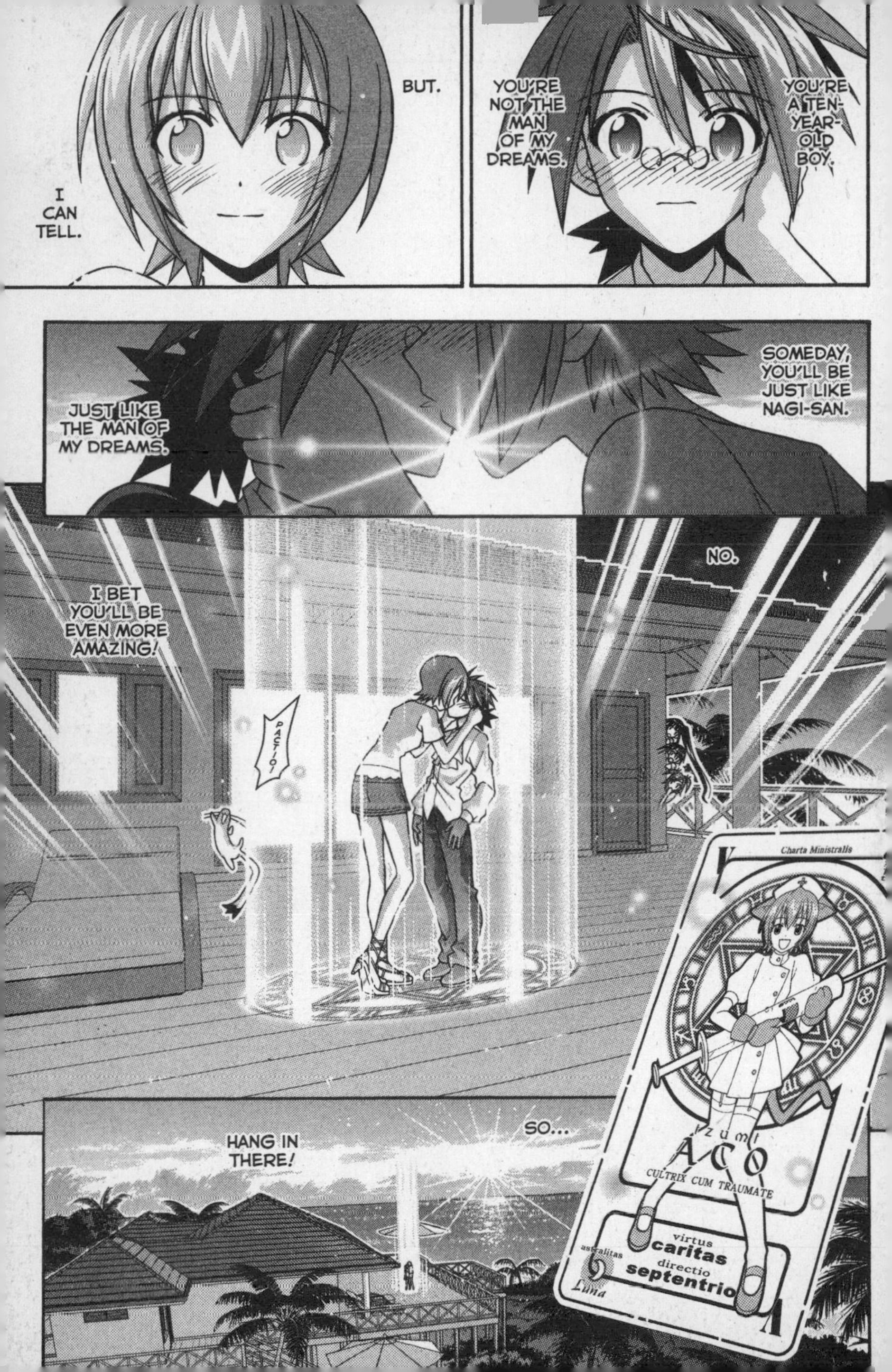
YOU'RE A TEN-YEAR-OLD BOY.
YOU'RE NOT THE MAN OF MY DREAMS.
BUT.
I CAN TELL.
SOMEDAY, YOU'LL BE JUST LIKE NAGI-SAN.
JUST LIKE THE MAN OF MY DREAMS.
NO.
I BET YOU'LL BE EVEN MORE AMAZING!
PACTIO!
Charta Ministralis
Izumi
ACO
CULTRIX CUM TRAUMATE
virtus
caritas
astralitas
Luna
directio
septentrio
SO...
HANG IN THERE!

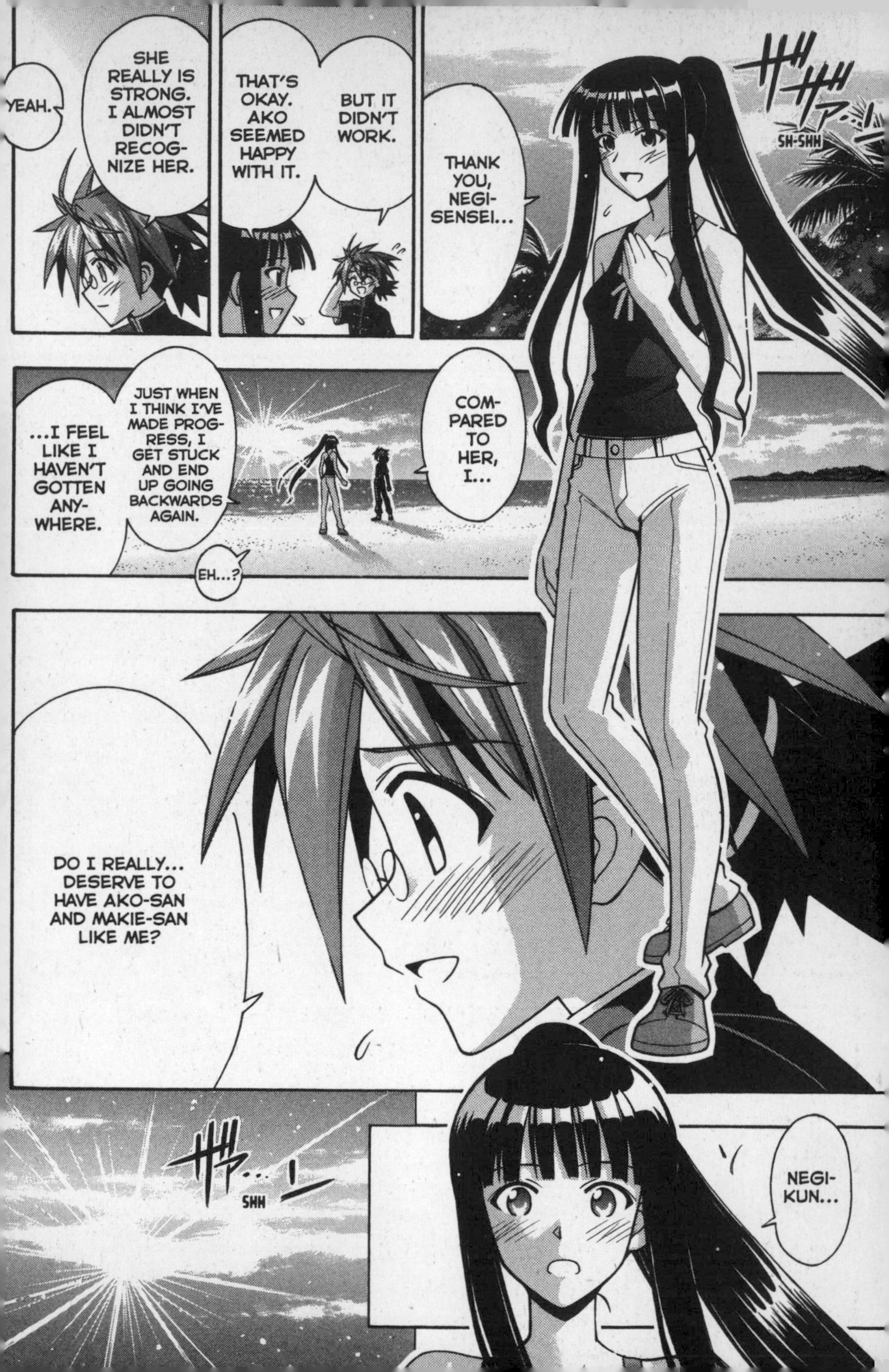
SH-SHH
THANK YOU, NEGI-SENSEI...
BUT IT DIDN'T WORK.
THAT'S OKAY. AKO SEEMED HAPPY WITH IT.
SHE REALLY IS STRONG. I ALMOST DIDN'T RECOGNIZE HER.
YEAH.
COMPARED TO HER, I...
JUST WHEN I THINK I'VE MADE PROGRESS, I GET STUCK AND END UP GOING BACKWARDS AGAIN.
...I FEEL LIKE I HAVEN'T GOTTEN ANYWHERE.
EH...?
DO I REALLY... DESERVE TO HAVE AKO-SAN AND MAKIE-SAN LIKE ME?
NEGI-KUN...
SHH

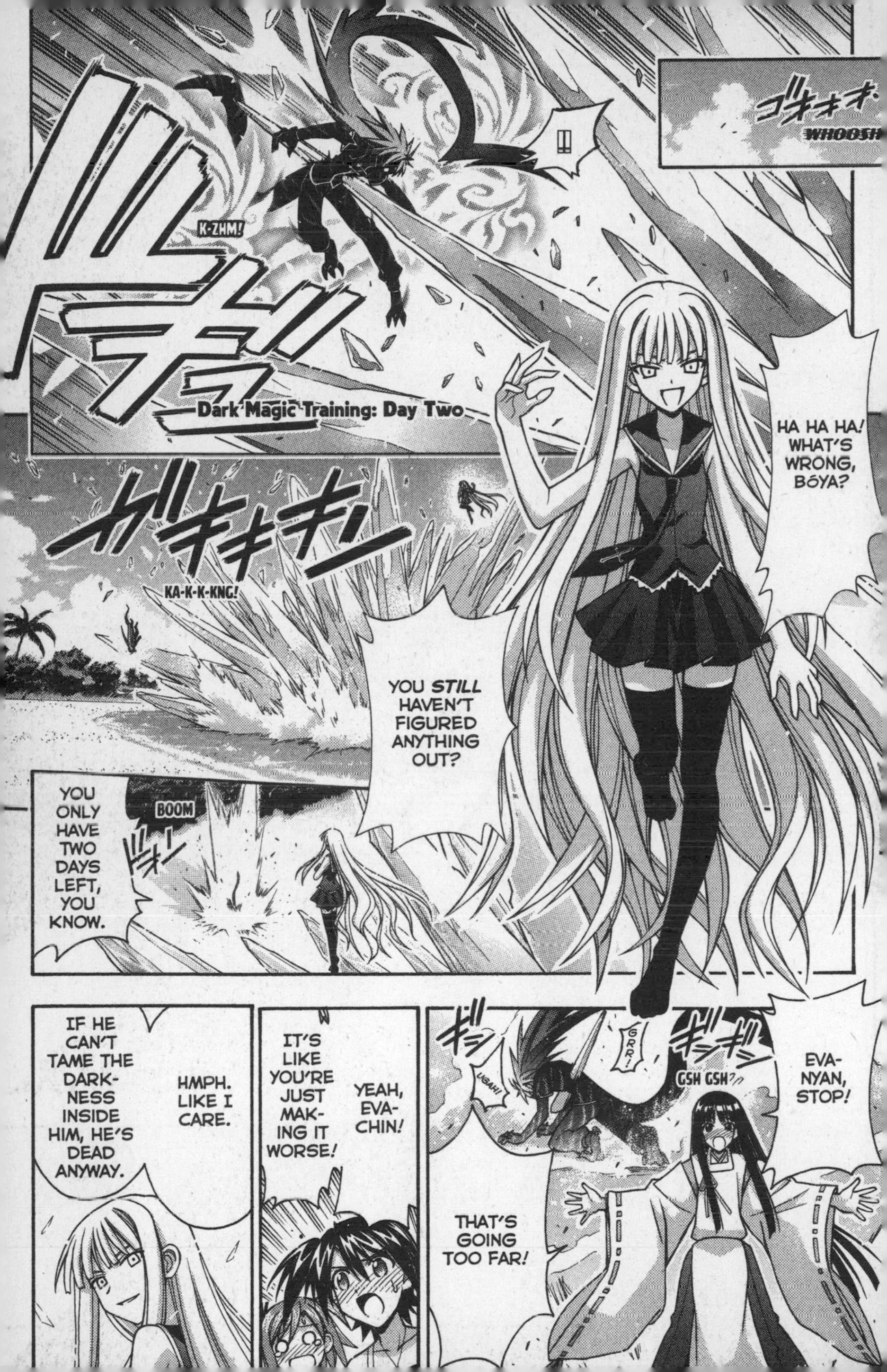

WHOOSH
!!
K-ZHM!
Dark Magic Training: Day Two
HA HA HA! WHAT'S WRONG, BŌYA?
YOU STILL HAVEN'T FIGURED ANYTHING OUT?
KA-K-K-KNG!
BOOM
YOU ONLY HAVE TWO DAYS LEFT, YOU KNOW.
EVA-NYAN, STOP!
GRR!
GSH GSH
UGAH!
THAT'S GOING TOO FAR!
IT'S LIKE YOU'RE JUST MAKING IT WORSE!
YEAH, EVA-CHIN!
IF HE CAN'T TAME THE DARKNESS INSIDE HIM, HE'S DEAD ANYWAY.
HMPH. LIKE I CARE.

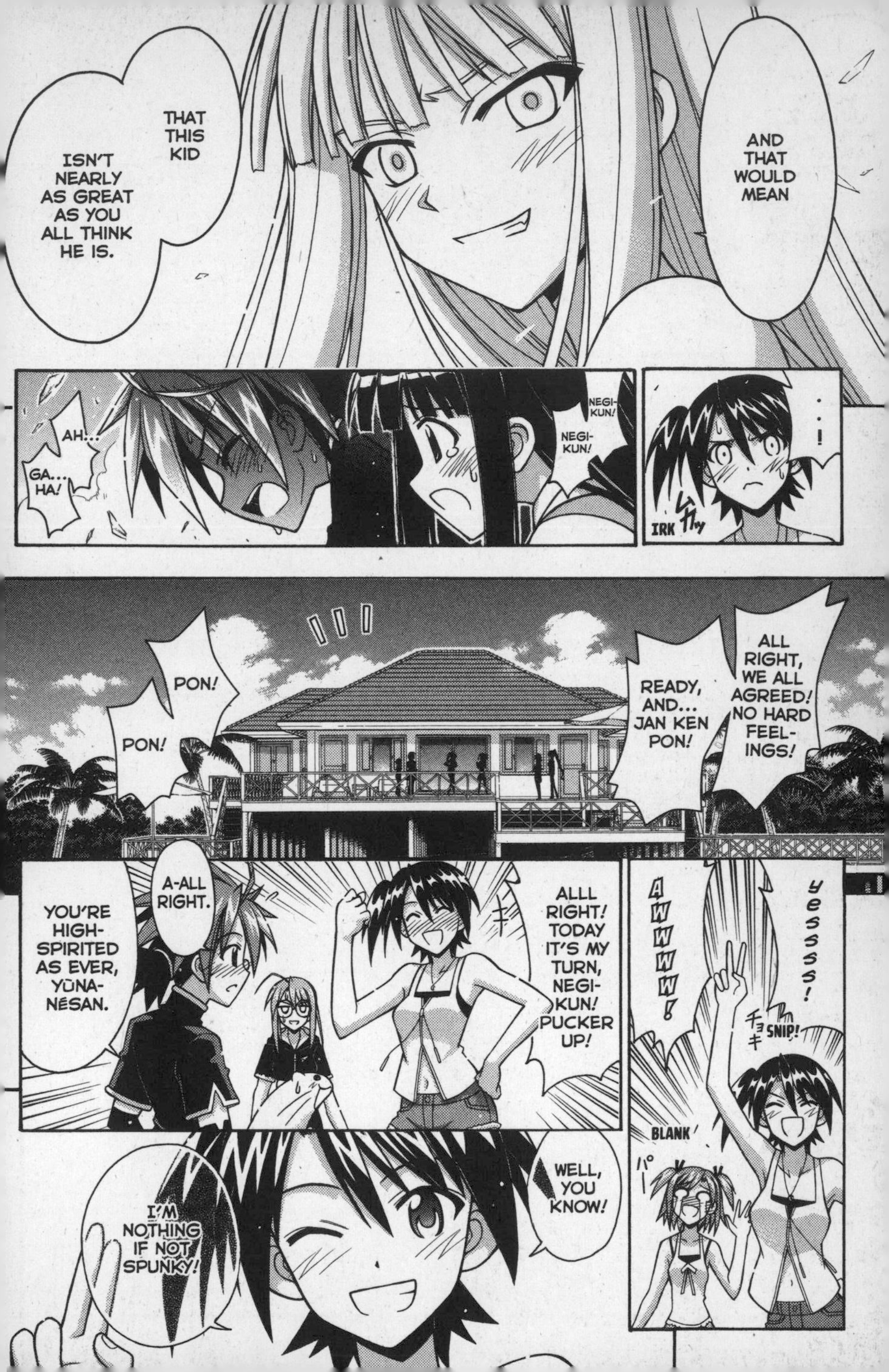
AND THAT WOULD MEAN
THAT THIS KID
ISN'T NEARLY AS GREAT AS YOU ALL THINK HE IS.
...!
IRK
NEGI-KUN!
NEGI-KUN!
AH...
GA... HA!
ALL RIGHT, WE ALL AGREED! NO HARD FEELINGS!
READY, AND... JAN KEN PON!
PON!
PON!
YESSSS!
AWWWWW!
SNIP!
BLANK
ALLL RIGHT! TODAY IT'S MY TURN, NEGI-KUN! PUCKER UP!
A-ALL RIGHT.
YOU'RE HIGH-SPIRITED AS EVER, YŪNA-NĒSAN.
WELL, YOU KNOW!
I'M NOTHING IF NOT SPUNKY!

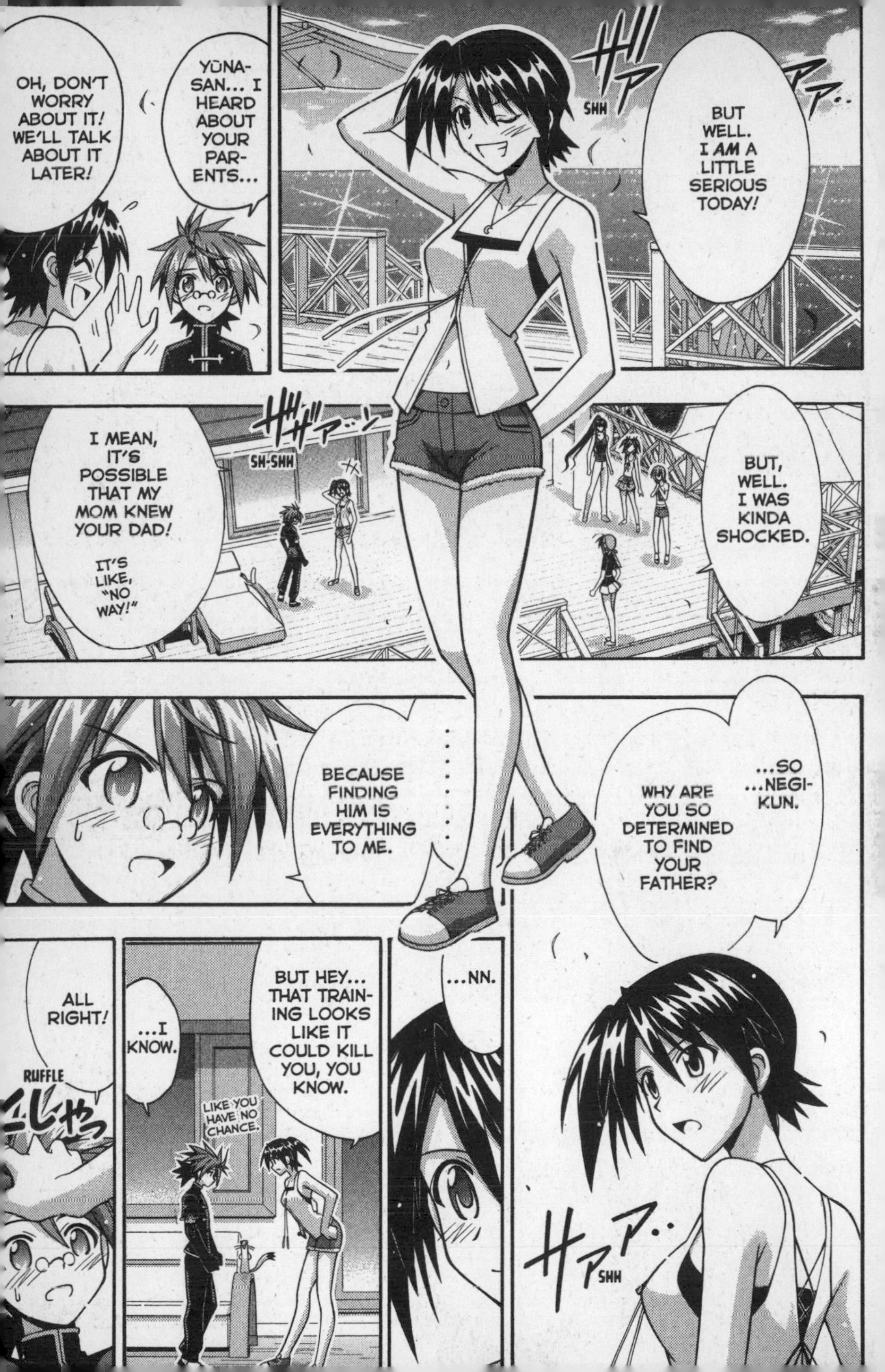
SHH
BUT WELL. I AM A LITTLE SERIOUS TODAY!
YŪNA-SAN... I HEARD ABOUT YOUR PARENTS...
OH, DON'T WORRY ABOUT IT! WE'LL TALK ABOUT IT LATER!
BUT, WELL. I WAS KINDA SHOCKED.
SH-SHH
I MEAN, IT'S POSSIBLE THAT MY MOM KNEW YOUR DAD!
IT'S LIKE, "NO WAY!"
...SO ...NEGI-KUN.
WHY ARE YOU SO DETERMINED TO FIND YOUR FATHER?
BECAUSE FINDING HIM IS EVERYTHING TO ME.
SHH
...NN.
BUT HEY... THAT TRAINING LOOKS LIKE IT COULD KILL YOU, YOU KNOW.
LIKE YOU HAVE NO CHANCE.
...I KNOW.
ALL RIGHT!
RUFFLE

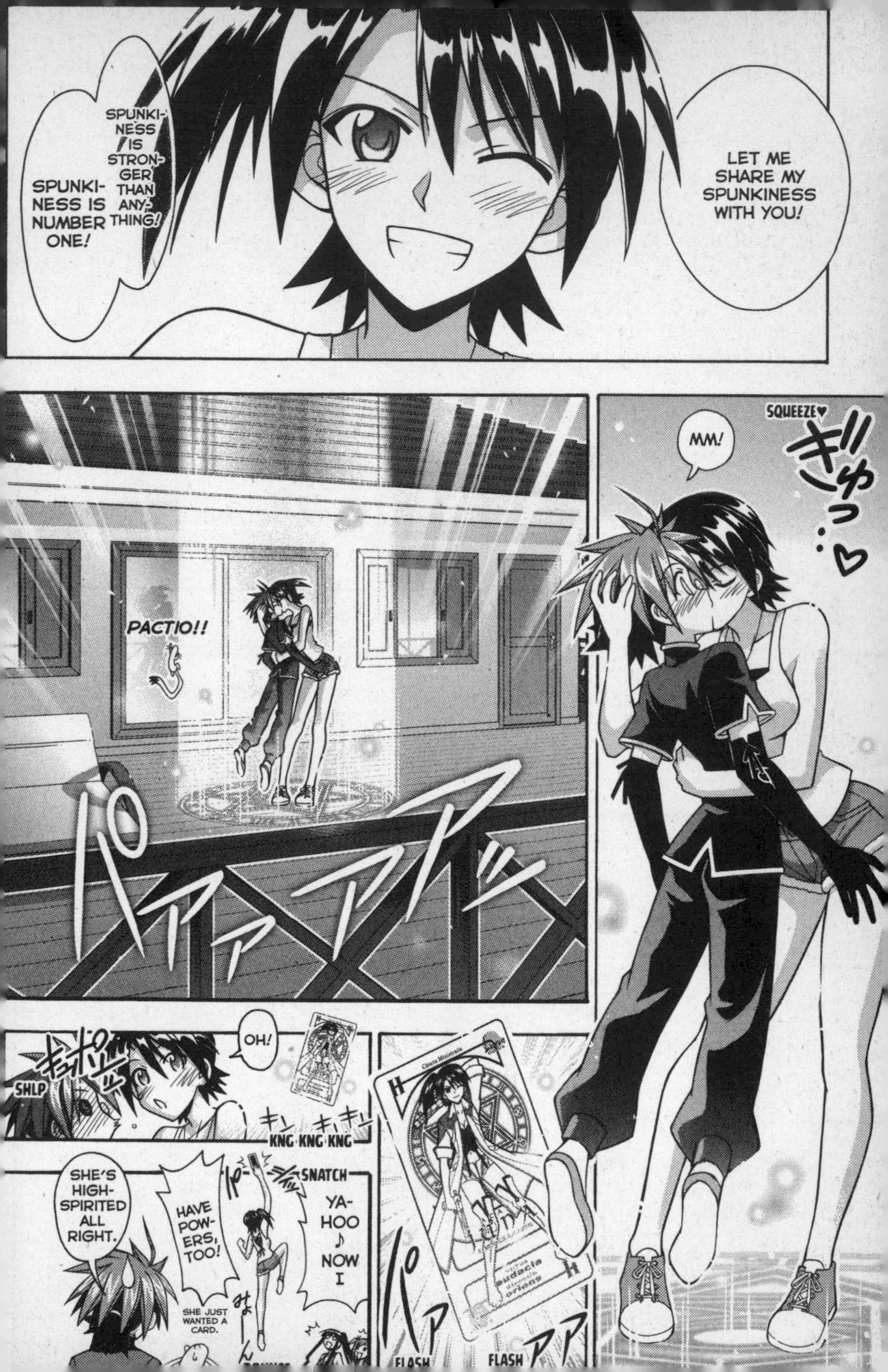

LET ME SHARE MY SPUNKINESS WITH YOU!
SPUNKINESS IS STRONGER THAN ANYTHING!
SPUNKINESS IS NUMBER ONE!
SQUEEZE♥
MM!
PACTIO!!
FLASH
FLASH
OH!
SHLP
KNG KNG KNG
YA-HOO♪ NOW I
HAVE POWERS, TOO!
SNATCH
SHE'S HIGH-SPIRITED ALL RIGHT.
SHE JUST WANTED A CARD.

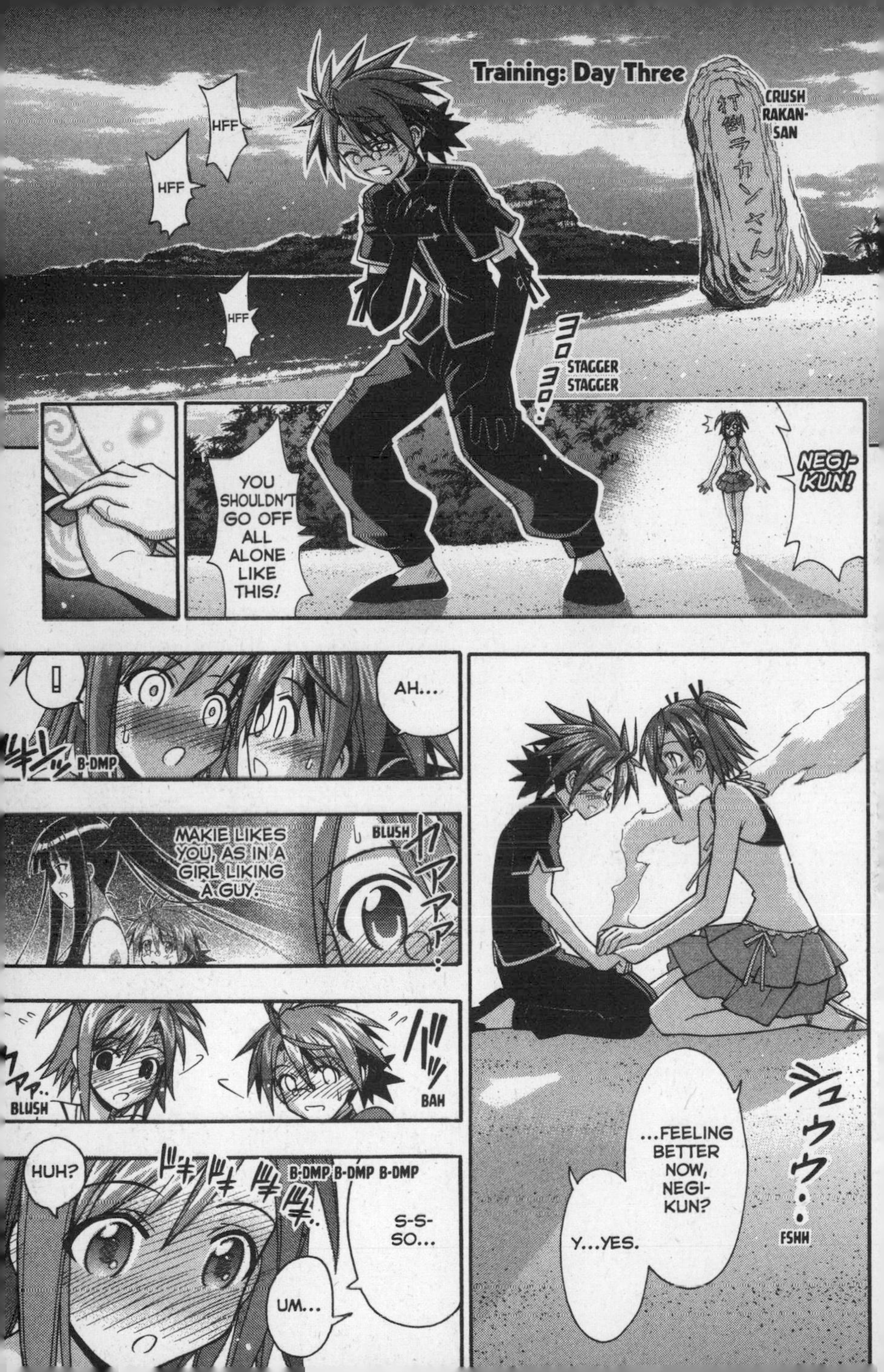
Training: Day Three
CRUSH RAKAN-SAN
HFF
HFF
HFF
STAGGER STAGGER
NEGI-KUN!
YOU SHOULDN'T GO OFF ALL ALONE LIKE THIS!
...FEELING BETTER NOW, NEGI-KUN?
Y...YES.
FSHH
AH...
!
B-DMP
BLUSH
MAKIE LIKES YOU, AS IN A GIRL LIKING A GUY.
BAH
BLUSH
B-DMP B-DMP B-DMP
HUH?
S-S-SO...
UM...

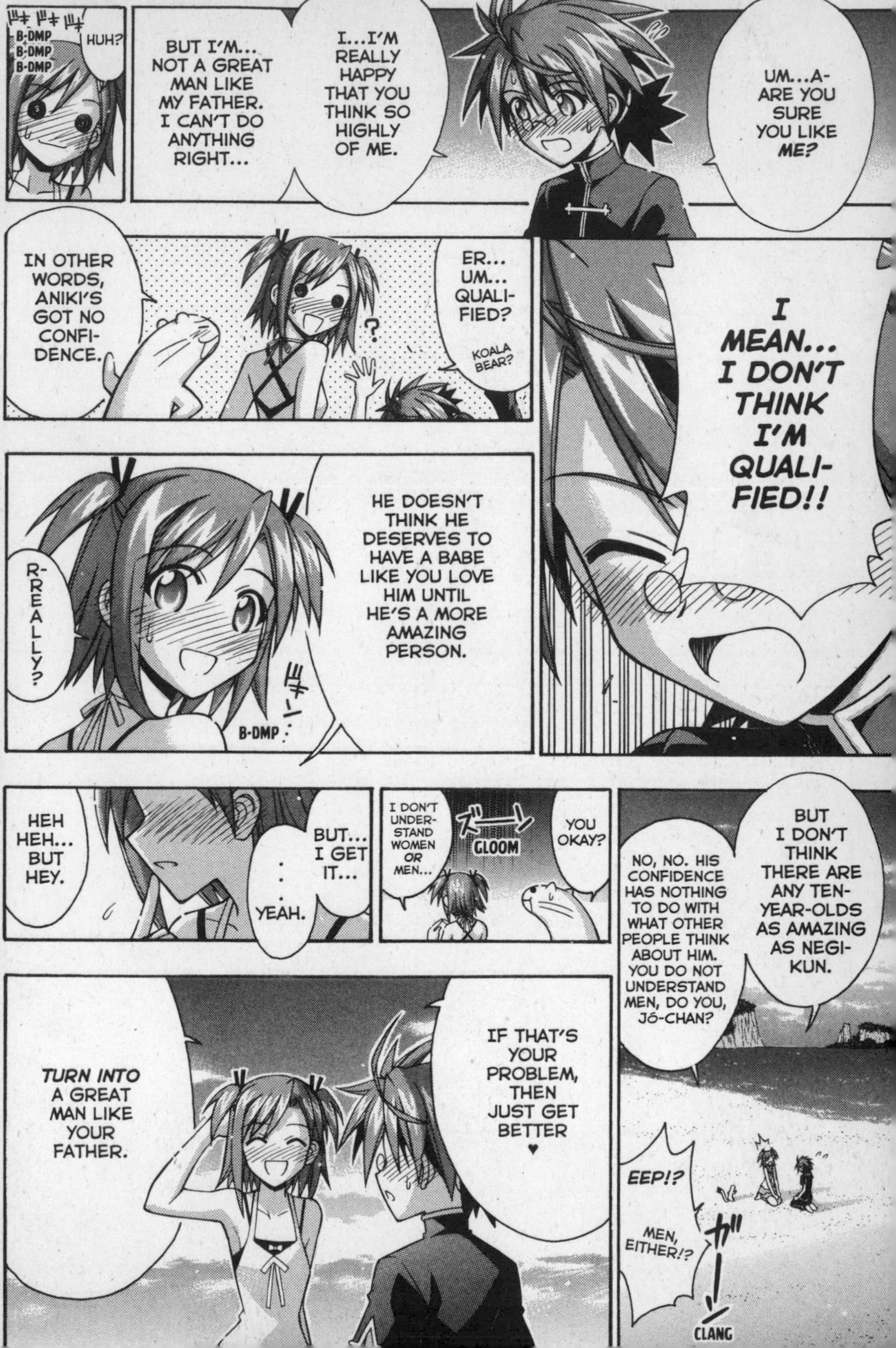
UM...A-ARE YOU SURE YOU LIKE *ME?*
I...I'M REALLY HAPPY THAT YOU THINK SO HIGHLY OF ME.
BUT I'M... NOT A GREAT MAN LIKE MY FATHER. I CAN'T DO ANYTHING RIGHT...
B-DMP B-DMP B-DMP
HUH?
I MEAN... I DON'T THINK I'M QUALIFIED!!
ER... UM... QUALIFIED?
KOALA BEAR?
IN OTHER WORDS, ANIKI'S GOT NO CONFIDENCE.
HE DOESN'T THINK HE DESERVES TO HAVE A BABE LIKE YOU LOVE HIM UNTIL HE'S A MORE AMAZING PERSON.
R-REALLY?
B-DMP
BUT I DON'T THINK THERE ARE ANY TEN-YEAR-OLDS AS AMAZING AS NEGI-KUN.
NO, NO. HIS CONFIDENCE HAS NOTHING TO DO WITH WHAT OTHER PEOPLE THINK ABOUT HIM. YOU DO NOT UNDERSTAND MEN, DO YOU, JŌ-CHAN?
YOU OKAY?
I DON'T UNDERSTAND WOMEN *OR* MEN...
GLOOM
BUT... I GET IT...
... YEAH.
HEH HEH... BUT HEY.
EEP!?
MEN, EITHER!?
CLANG
IF THAT'S YOUR PROBLEM, THEN JUST GET BETTER ♥
TURN INTO A GREAT MAN LIKE YOUR FATHER.

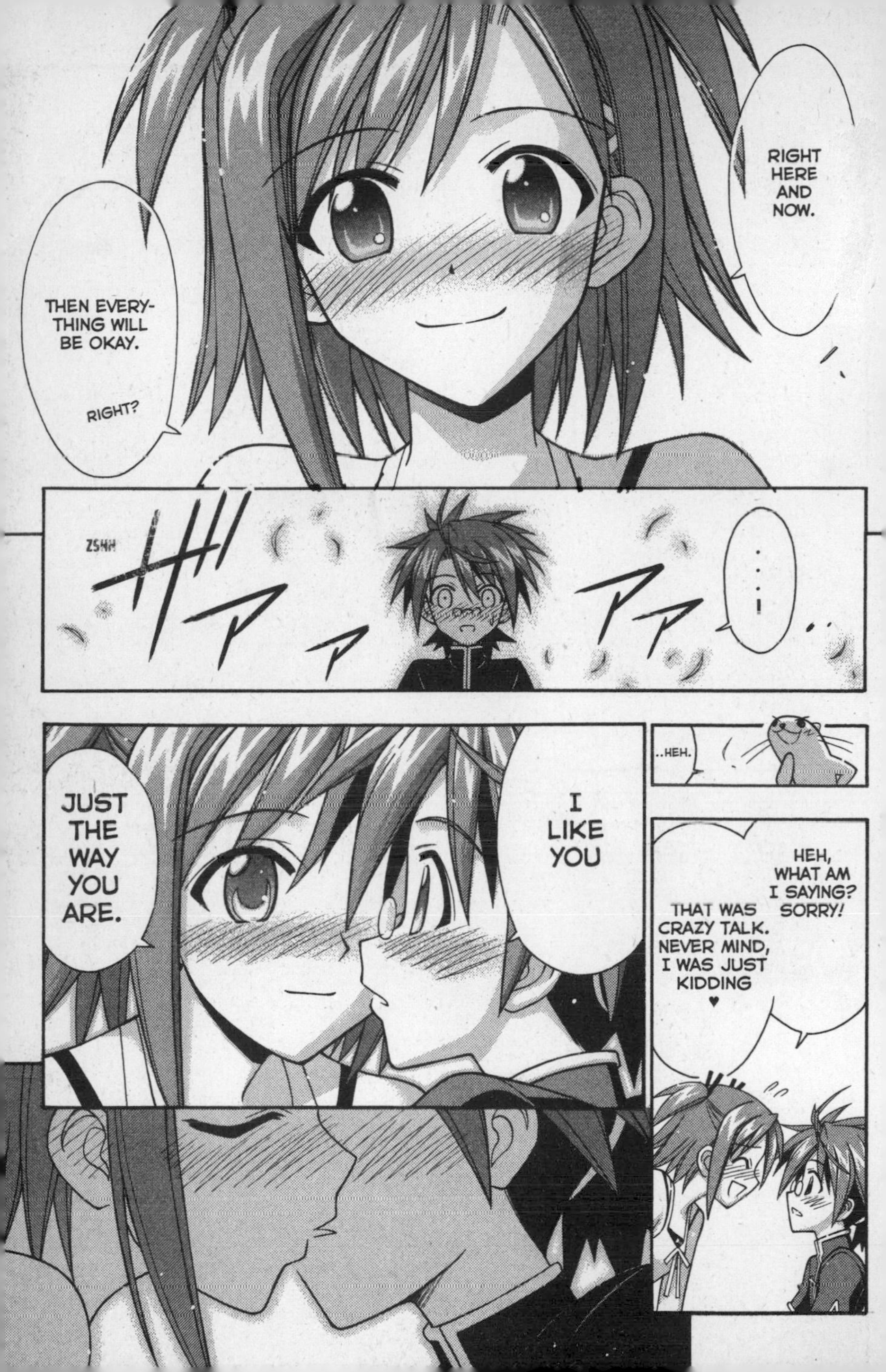
RIGHT HERE AND NOW.
THEN EVERY-THING WILL BE OKAY.
RIGHT?
...!
ZSHH
I LIKE YOU
JUST THE WAY YOU ARE.
..HEH.
HEH, WHAT AM I SAYING? SORRY!
THAT WAS CRAZY TALK. NEVER MIND, I WAS JUST KIDDING ♥

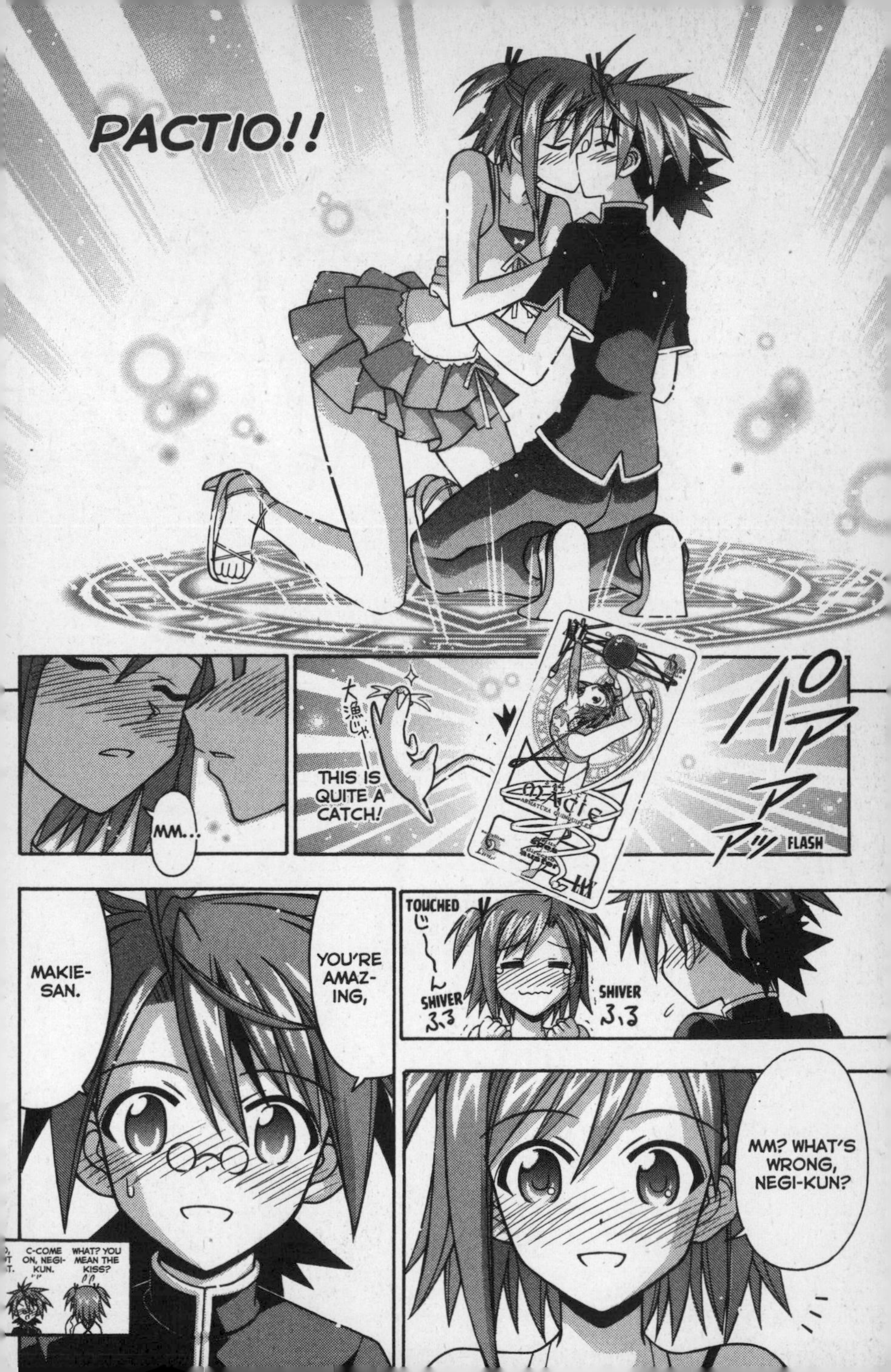

PACTIO!!
パァァァッ
FLASH
大漁じゃー
THIS IS QUITE A CATCH!
MM...
TOUCHED
じ～ん
SHIVER
ふる
SHIVER
ふる
MM? WHAT'S WRONG, NEGI-KUN?
YOU'RE AMAZING,
MAKIE-SAN.
WHAT? YOU MEAN THE KISS?
C-COME ON, NEGI-KUN.

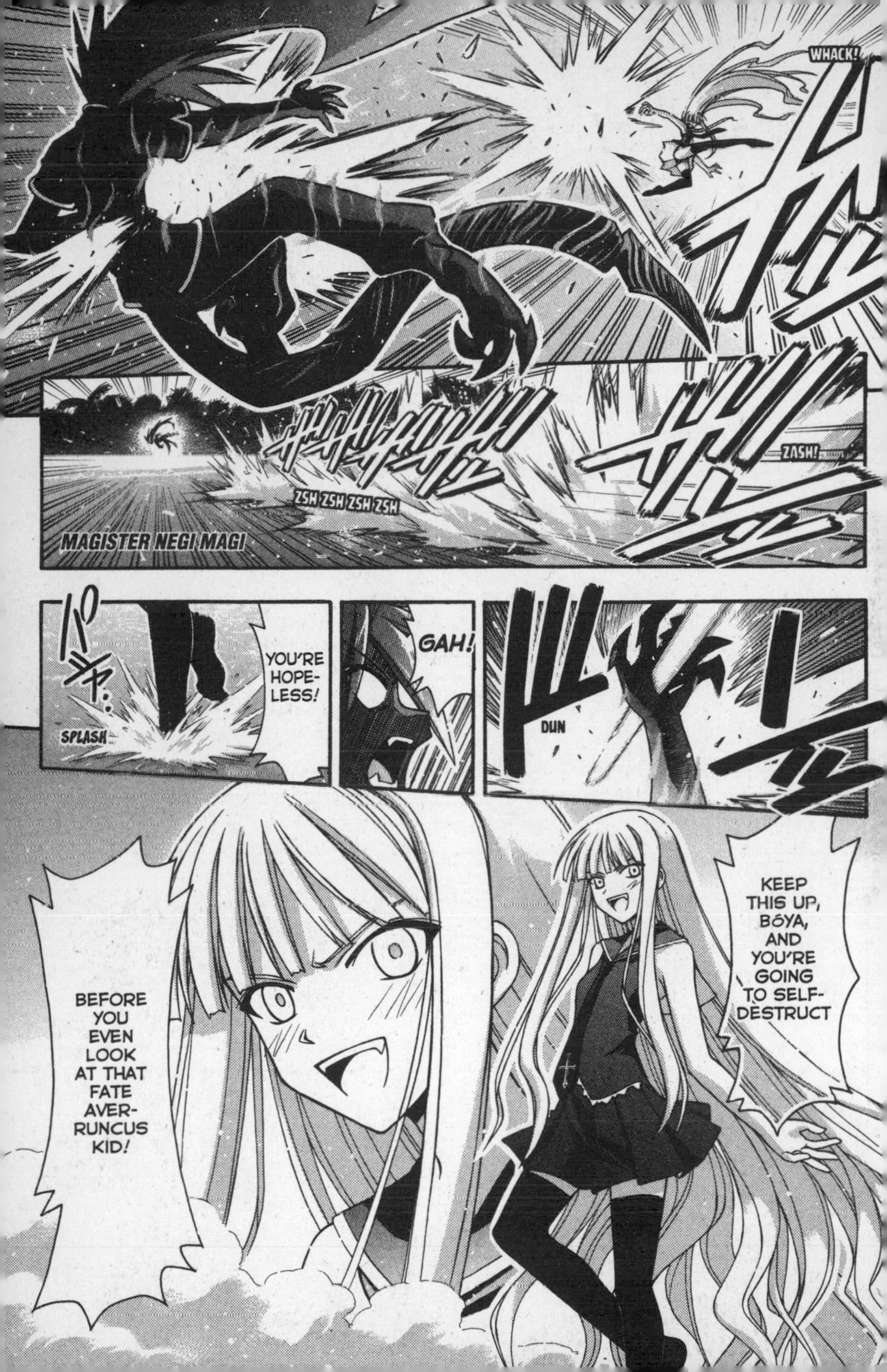
WHACK!
ZASH!
ZSH ZSH ZSH ZSH
MAGISTER NEGI MAGI
DUN
GAH!
YOU'RE HOPE-LESS!
SPLASH
KEEP THIS UP, BŌYA, AND YOU'RE GOING TO SELF-DESTRUCT
BEFORE YOU EVEN LOOK AT THAT FATE AVER-RUNCUS KID!

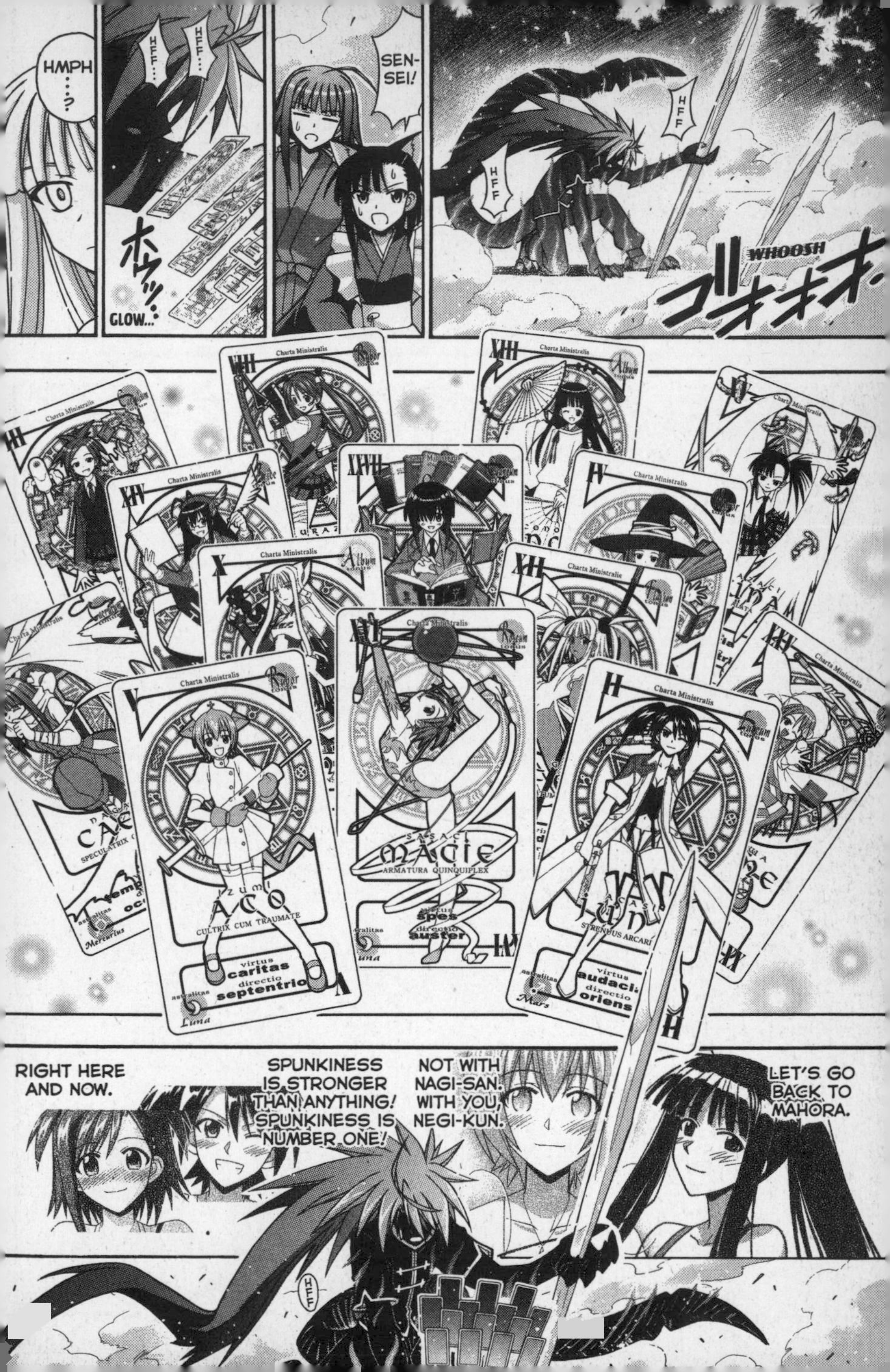
HFF
HFF
WHOOSH
ゴオオオ
SEN-SEI!
HFF...
HFF...
ホウッ
GLOW...
HMPH ...?
Charta Ministralis
IZUMI ACO
CULTRIX CUM TRAUMATE
virtus caritas directio septentrio
astralitas Luna
MAGIE
ARMATURA QUINQUIPLEX
virtus spes directio auster
virtus audacia directio oriens
Mars
SPECULATRIX
Mercurius
LET'S GO BACK TO MAHORA.
NOT WITH NAGI-SAN. WITH YOU, NEGI-KUN.
SPUNKINESS IS STRONGER THAN ANYTHING! SPUNKINESS IS NUMBER ONE!
RIGHT HERE AND NOW.
HFF

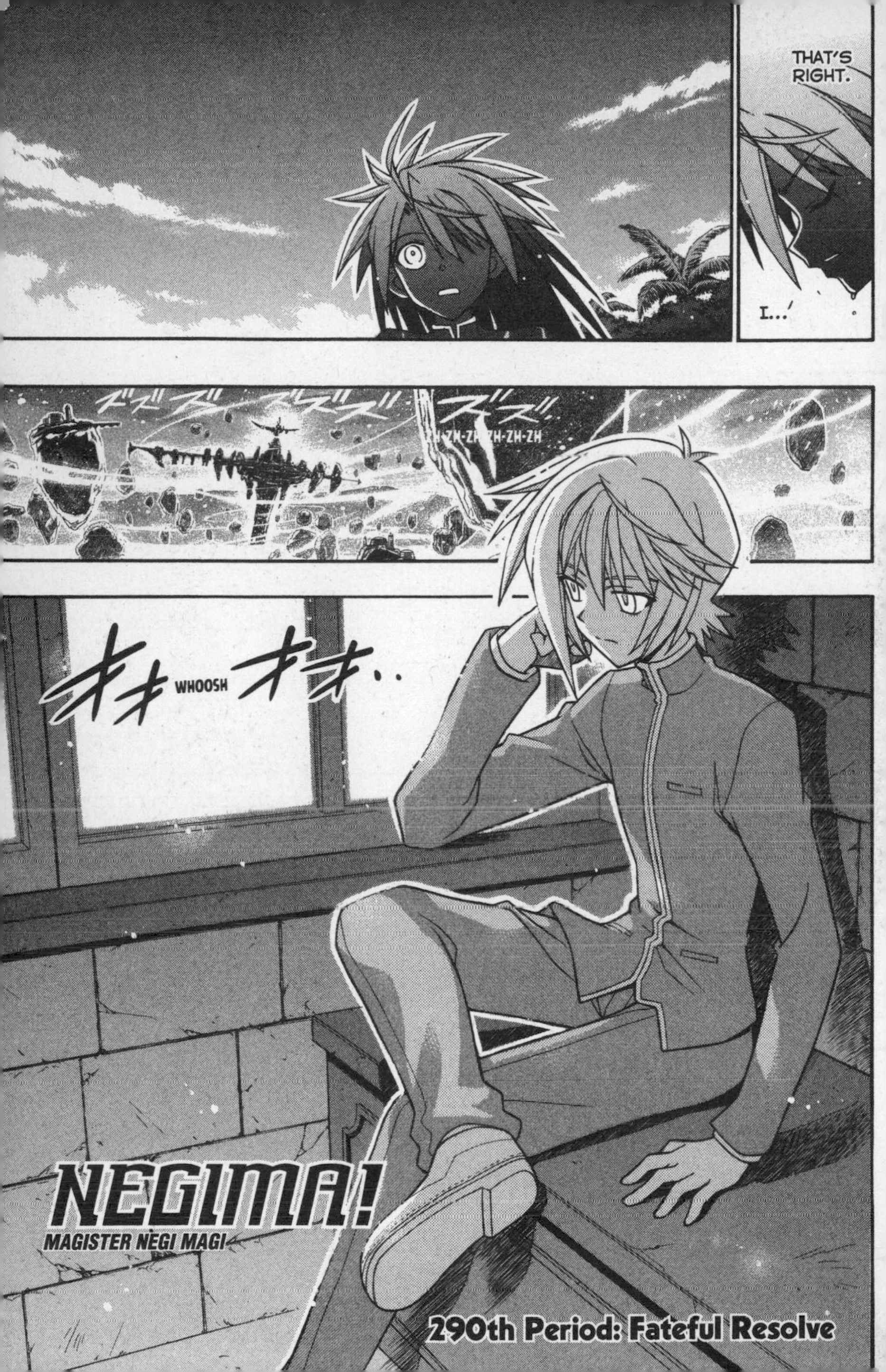
THAT'S RIGHT.
I...!
ZH-ZH-ZH-ZH-ZH-ZH
WHOOSH
NEGIMA!
MAGISTER NEGI MAGI
290th Period: Fateful Resolve

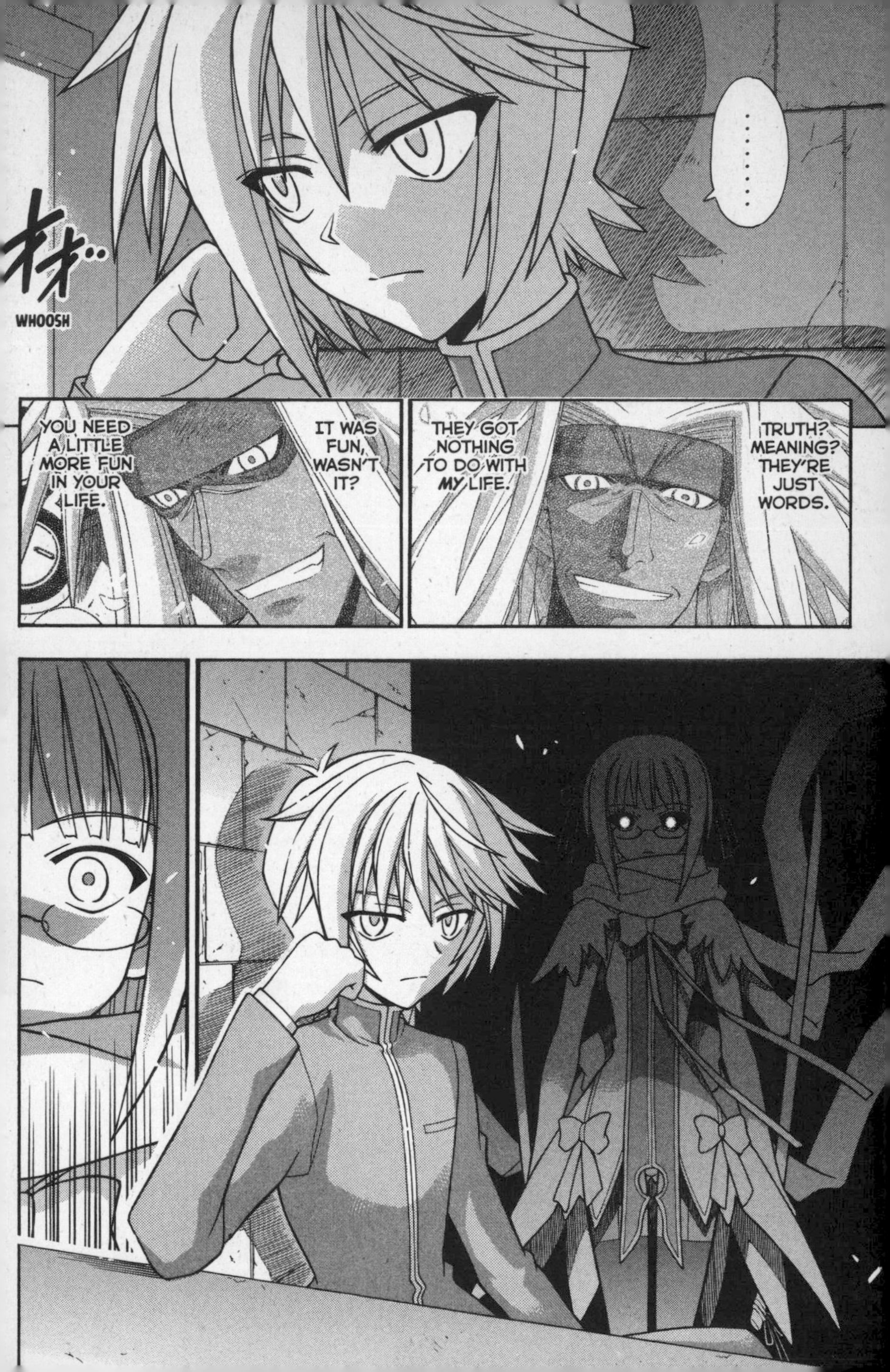
……
WHOOSH
TRUTH? MEANING? THEY'RE JUST WORDS.
THEY GOT NOTHING TO DO WITH *MY* LIFE.
IT WAS FUN, WASN'T IT?
YOU NEED A LITTLE MORE FUN IN YOUR LIFE.

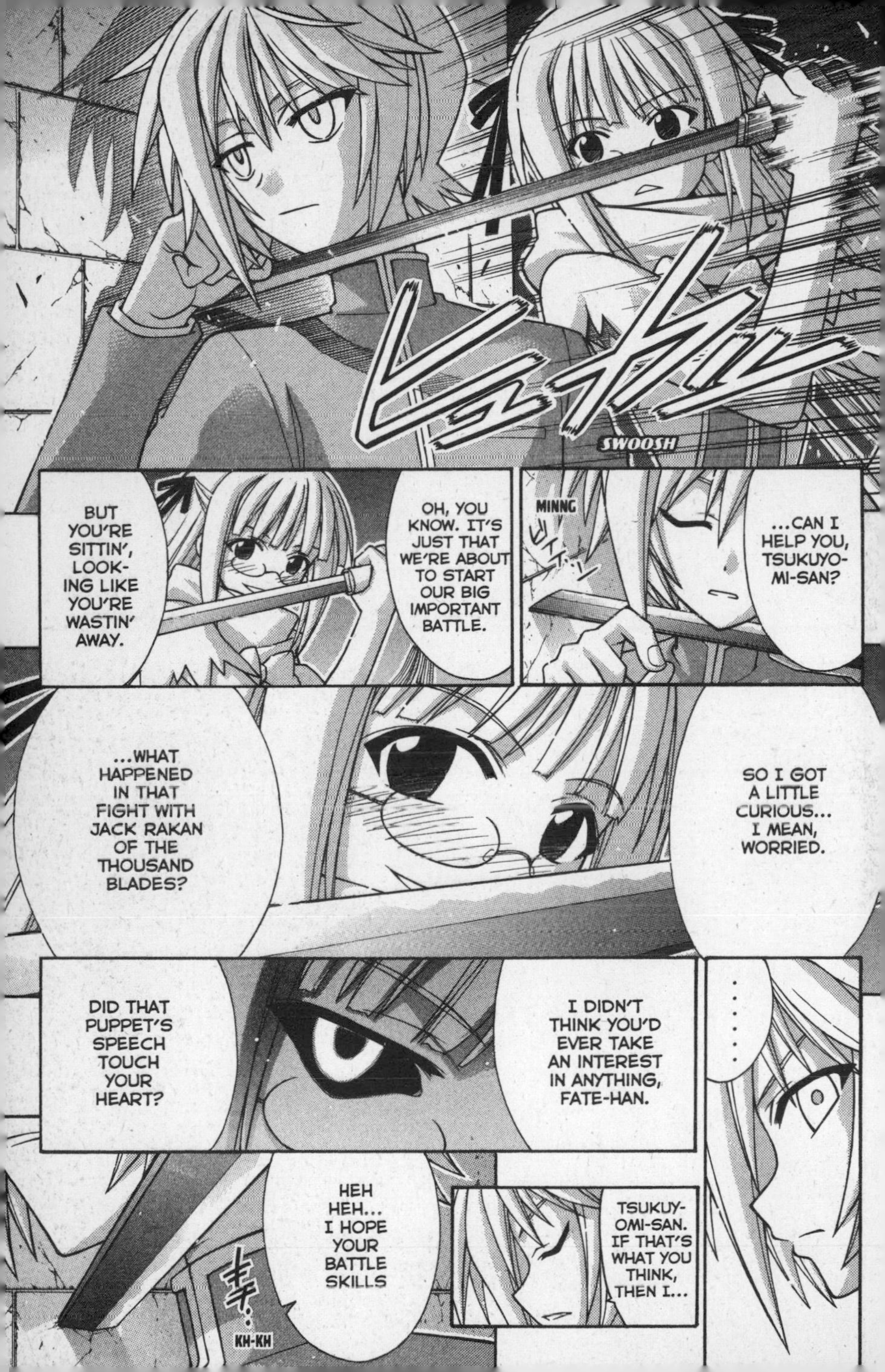
SWOOSH
MINNG
...CAN I HELP YOU, TSUKUYO-MI-SAN?
OH, YOU KNOW. IT'S JUST THAT WE'RE ABOUT TO START OUR BIG IMPORTANT BATTLE.
BUT YOU'RE SITTIN', LOOK-ING LIKE YOU'RE WASTIN' AWAY.
SO I GOT A LITTLE CURIOUS... I MEAN, WORRIED.
...WHAT HAPPENED IN THAT FIGHT WITH JACK RAKAN OF THE THOUSAND BLADES?
......
I DIDN'T THINK YOU'D EVER TAKE AN INTEREST IN ANYTHING, FATE-HAN.
DID THAT PUPPET'S SPEECH TOUCH YOUR HEART?
TSUKUY-OMI-SAN. IF THAT'S WHAT YOU THINK, THEN I...
HEH HEH... I HOPE YOUR BATTLE SKILLS
KH-KH

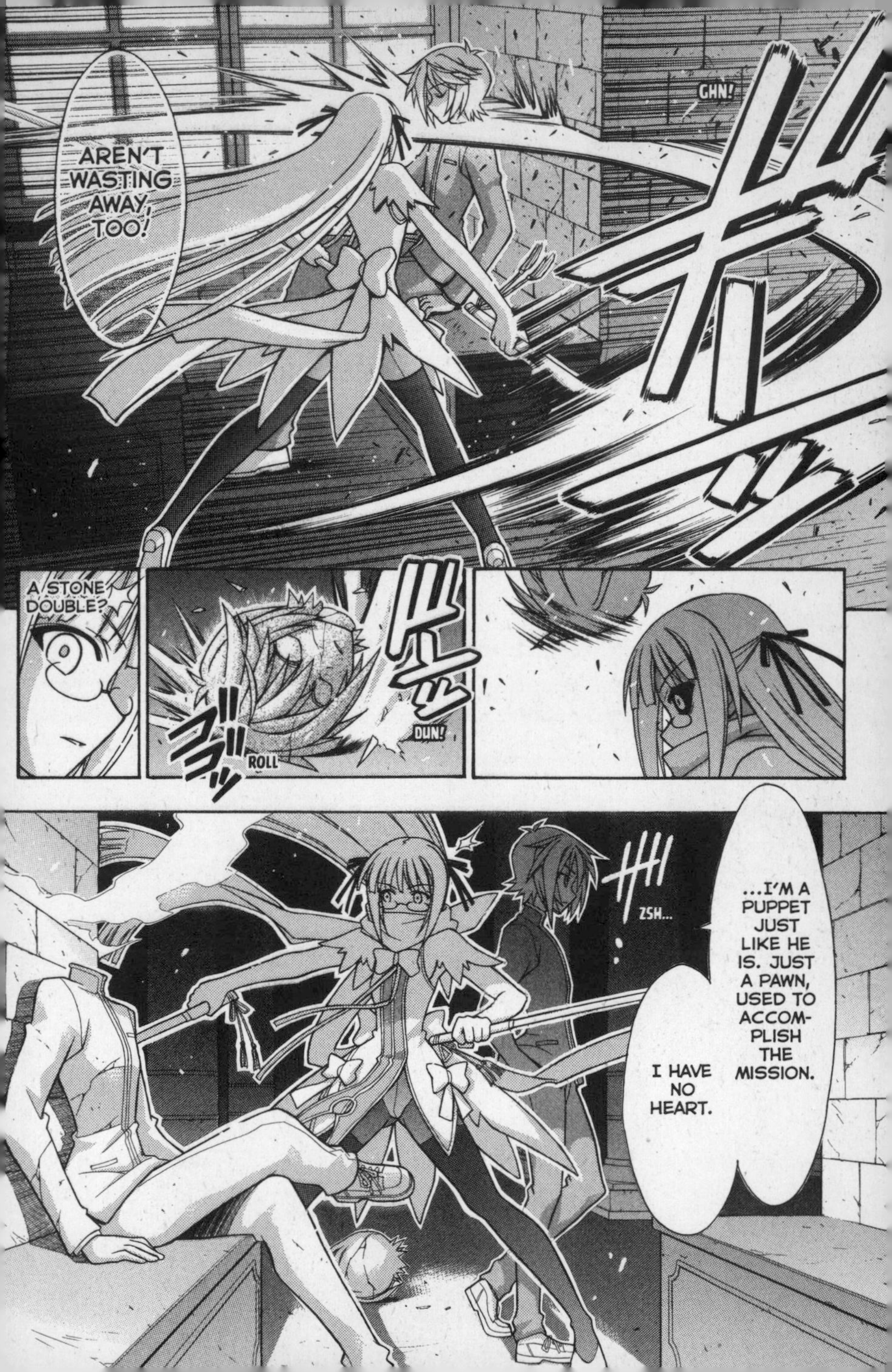
GHN!
AREN'T WASTING AWAY, TOO!
DUN!
ROLL
A STONE DOUBLE?
...I'M A PUPPET JUST LIKE HE IS. JUST A PAWN, USED TO ACCOMPLISH THE MISSION.
I HAVE NO HEART.
ZSH...

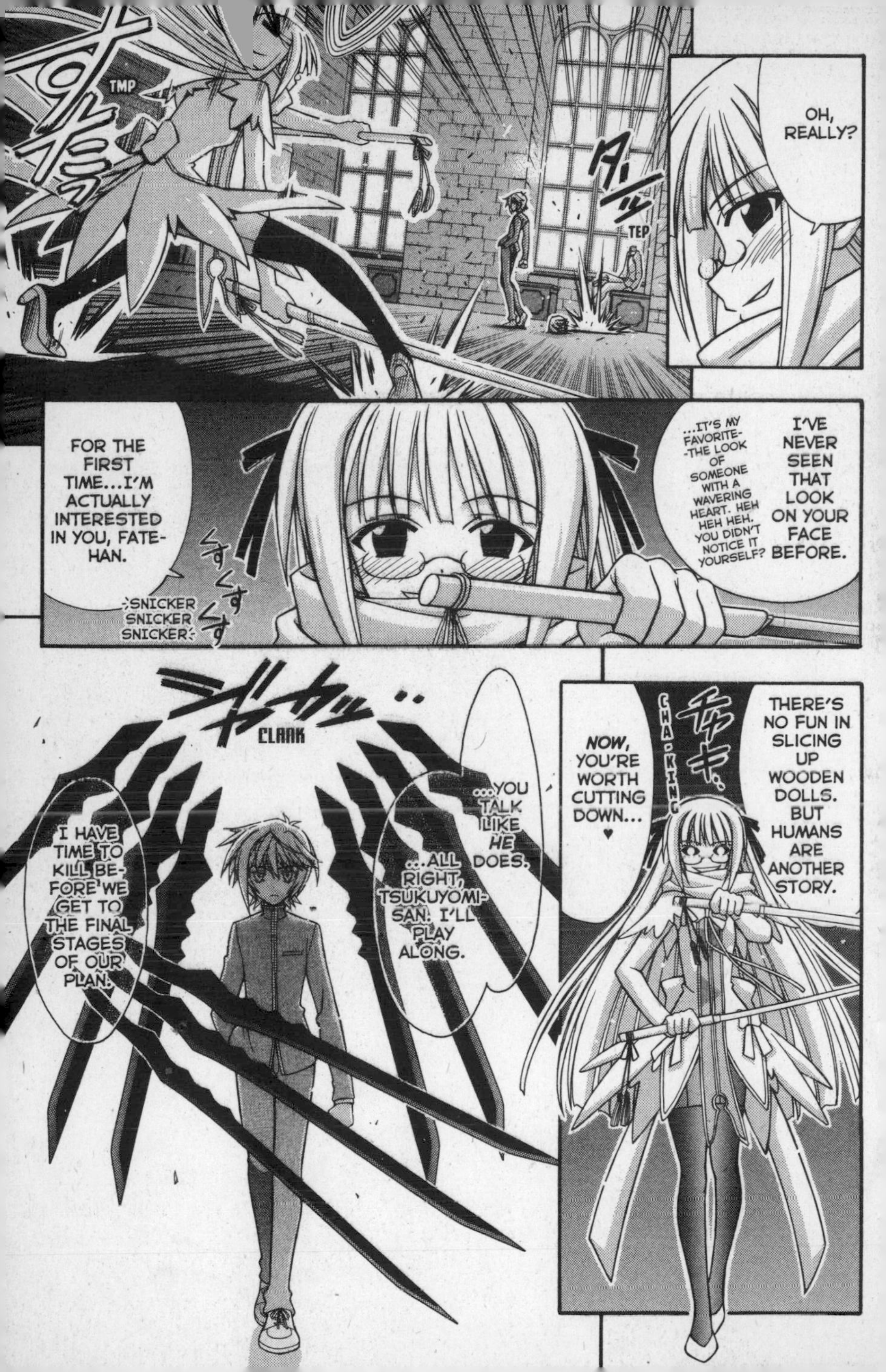
OH, REALLY?
TMP
TEP
I'VE NEVER SEEN THAT LOOK ON YOUR FACE BEFORE.
...IT'S MY FAVORITE--THE LOOK OF SOMEONE WITH A WAVERING HEART. HEH HEH HEH. YOU DIDN'T NOTICE IT YOURSELF?
FOR THE FIRST TIME...I'M ACTUALLY INTERESTED IN YOU, FATE-HAN.
くすくすくす
SNICKER SNICKER SNICKER
THERE'S NO FUN IN SLICING UP WOODEN DOLLS. BUT HUMANS ARE ANOTHER STORY.
チャキ
CHA-KING
NOW, YOU'RE WORTH CUTTING DOWN...♥
CLANK
...YOU TALK LIKE HE DOES.
...ALL RIGHT, TSUKUYOMI-SAN. I'LL PLAY ALONG.
I HAVE TIME TO KILL BEFORE WE GET TO THE FINAL STAGES OF OUR PLAN.

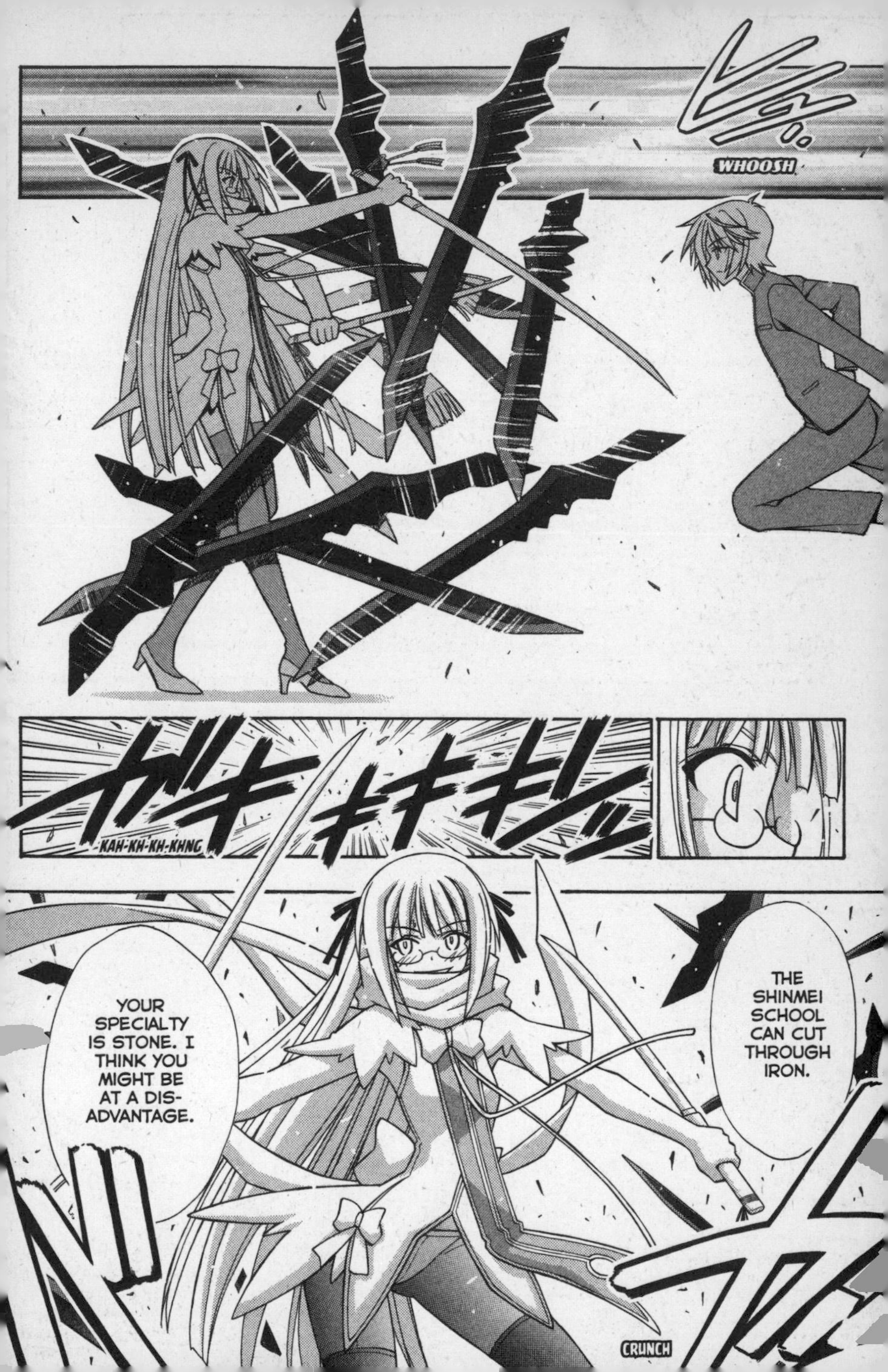
WHOOSH
KAH-KH-KH-KHNG
THE SHINMEI SCHOOL CAN CUT THROUGH IRON.
YOUR SPECIALTY IS STONE. I THINK YOU MIGHT BE AT A DIS-ADVANTAGE.
CRUNCH

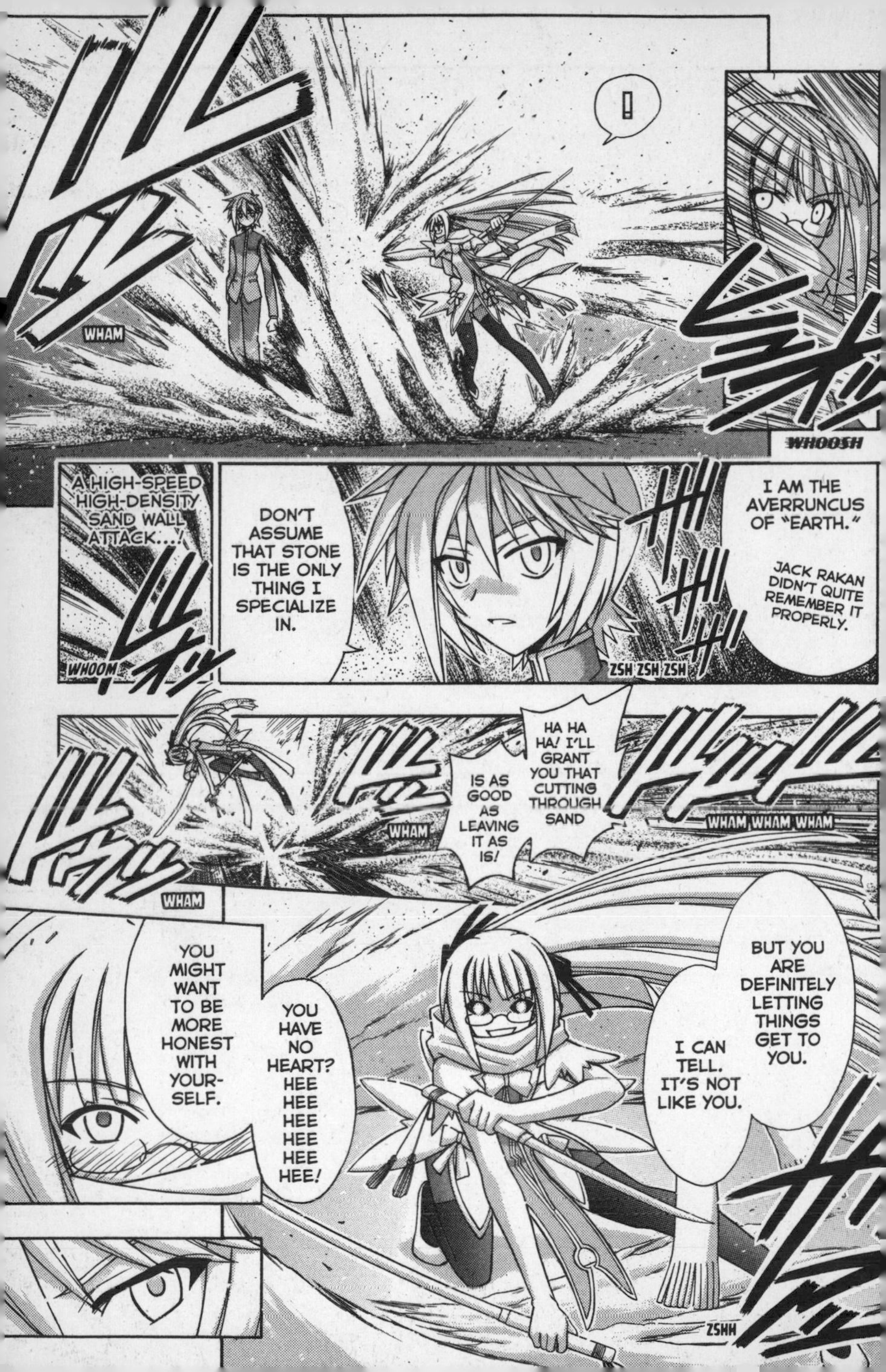
WHOOSH
!
WHAM
I AM THE AVERRUNCUS OF "EARTH."
JACK RAKAN DIDN'T QUITE REMEMBER IT PROPERLY.
ZSH ZSH ZSH
DON'T ASSUME THAT STONE IS THE ONLY THING I SPECIALIZE IN.
A HIGH-SPEED HIGH-DENSITY SAND WALL ATTACK...!
WHOOM
WHAM WHAM WHAM
HA HA HA! I'LL GRANT YOU THAT CUTTING THROUGH SAND
IS AS GOOD AS LEAVING IT AS IS!
WHAM
WHAM
BUT YOU ARE DEFINITELY LETTING THINGS GET TO YOU.
I CAN TELL. IT'S NOT LIKE YOU.
ZSHH
YOU HAVE NO HEART? HEE HEE HEE HEE HEE HEE!
YOU MIGHT WANT TO BE MORE HONEST WITH YOUR-SELF.

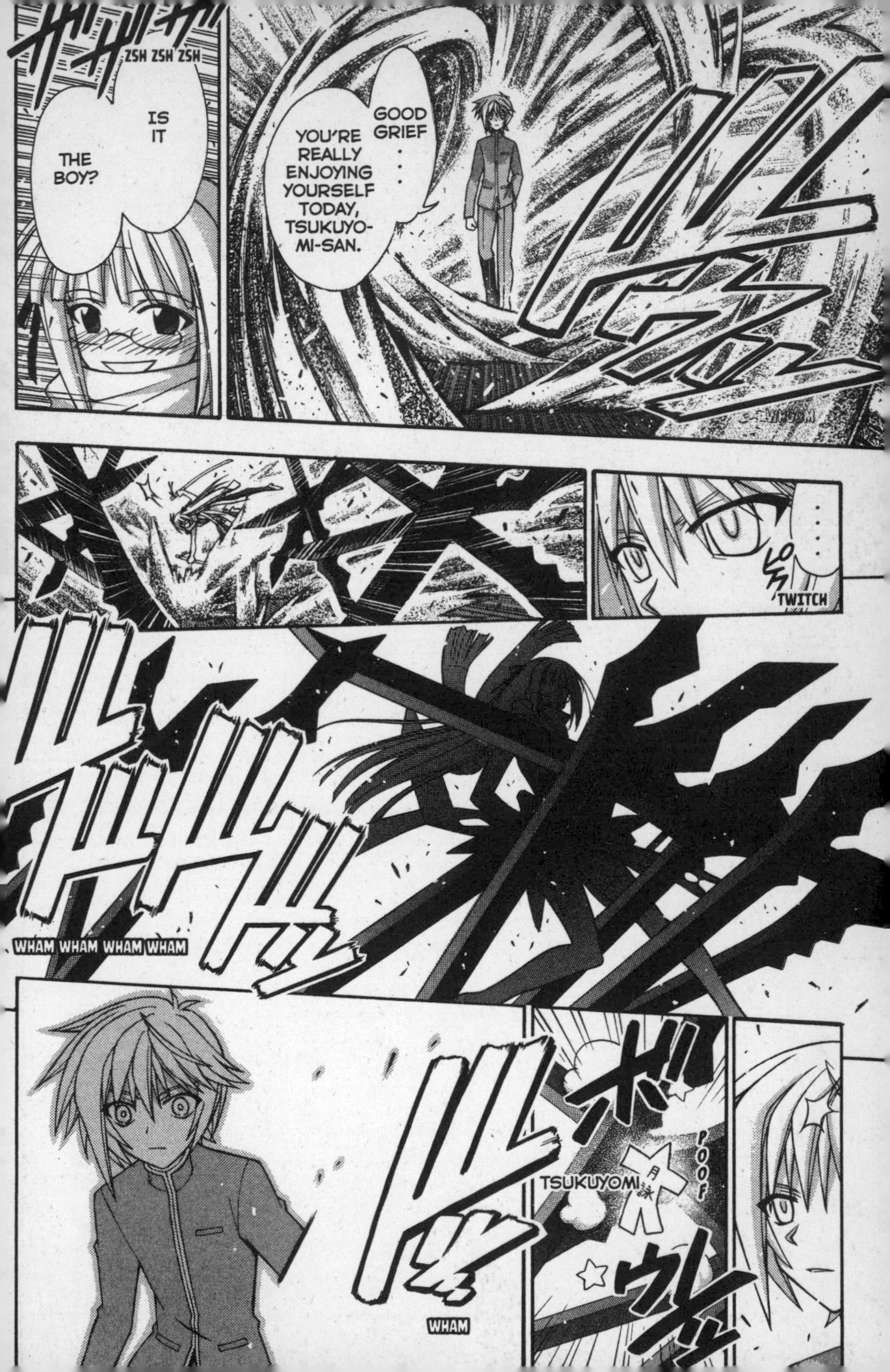

GOOD GRIEF . . . YOU'RE REALLY ENJOYING YOURSELF TODAY, TSUKUYOMI-SAN.
WHOOM
ZSH ZSH ZSH
IS IT THE BOY?
. . . .
TWITCH
WHAM WHAM WHAM WHAM
POOF
TSUKUYOMI
月詠
WHAM

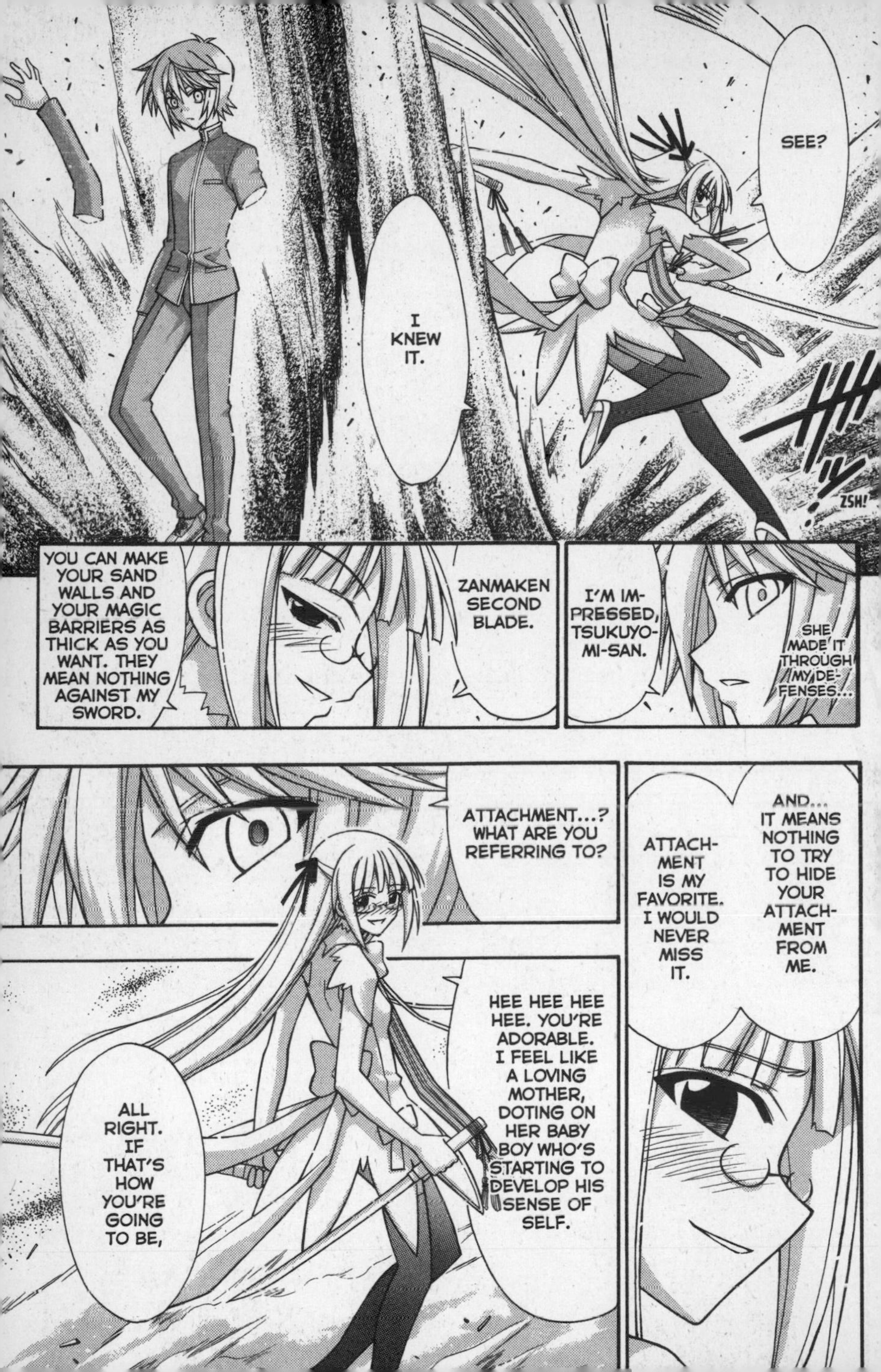
SEE?
ZSH!
I KNEW IT.
SHE MADE IT THROUGH MY DE-FENSES...
I'M IM-PRESSED, TSUKUYO-MI-SAN.
ZANMAKEN SECOND BLADE.
YOU CAN MAKE YOUR SAND WALLS AND YOUR MAGIC BARRIERS AS THICK AS YOU WANT. THEY MEAN NOTHING AGAINST MY SWORD.
AND... IT MEANS NOTHING TO TRY TO HIDE YOUR ATTACH-MENT FROM ME.
ATTACH-MENT IS MY FAVORITE. I WOULD NEVER MISS IT.
ATTACHMENT...? WHAT ARE YOU REFERRING TO?
HEE HEE HEE HEE. YOU'RE ADORABLE. I FEEL LIKE A LOVING MOTHER, DOTING ON HER BABY BOY WHO'S STARTING TO DEVELOP HIS SENSE OF SELF.
ALL RIGHT. IF THAT'S HOW YOU'RE GOING TO BE,

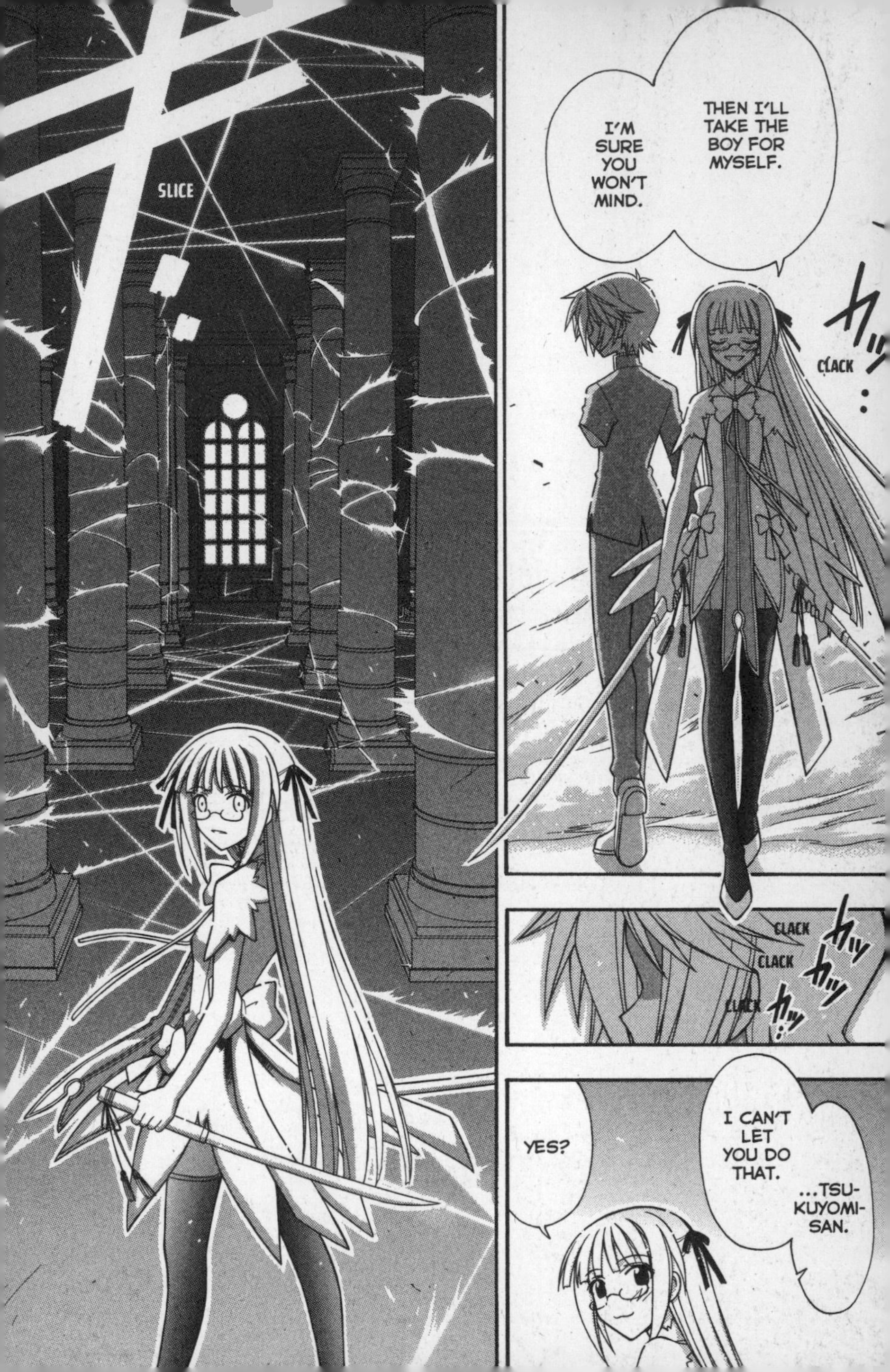
THEN I'LL TAKE THE BOY FOR MYSELF.
I'M SURE YOU WON'T MIND.
CLACK
CLACK
CLACK
CLACK
I CAN'T LET YOU DO THAT.
...TSU-KUYOMI-SAN.
YES?
SLICE

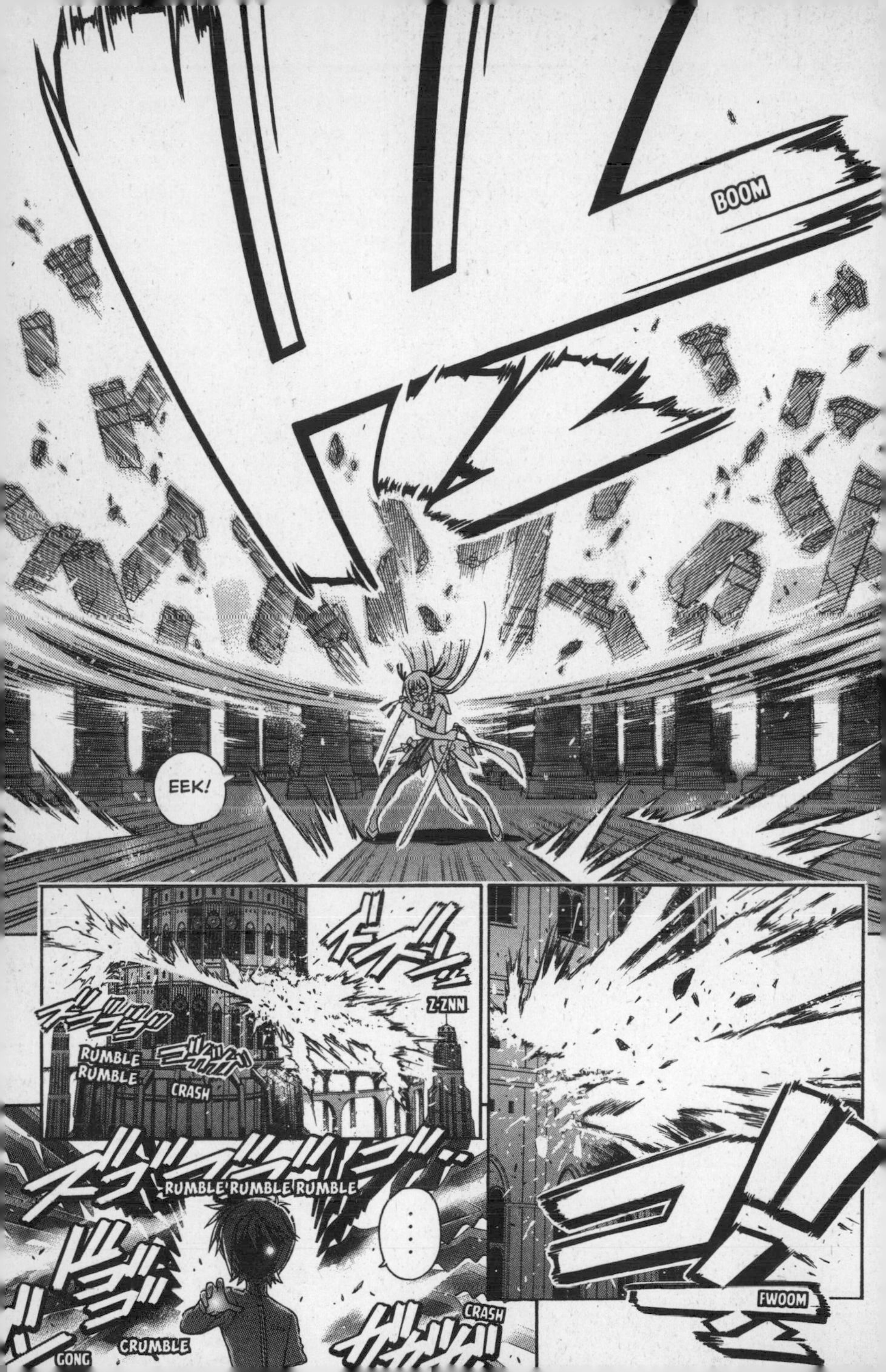
BOOM
EEK!
FWOOM
Z-ZNN
RUMBLE
RUMBLE
CRASH
RUMBLE RUMBLE RUMBLE
. . . .
CRASH
CRUMBLE
GONG

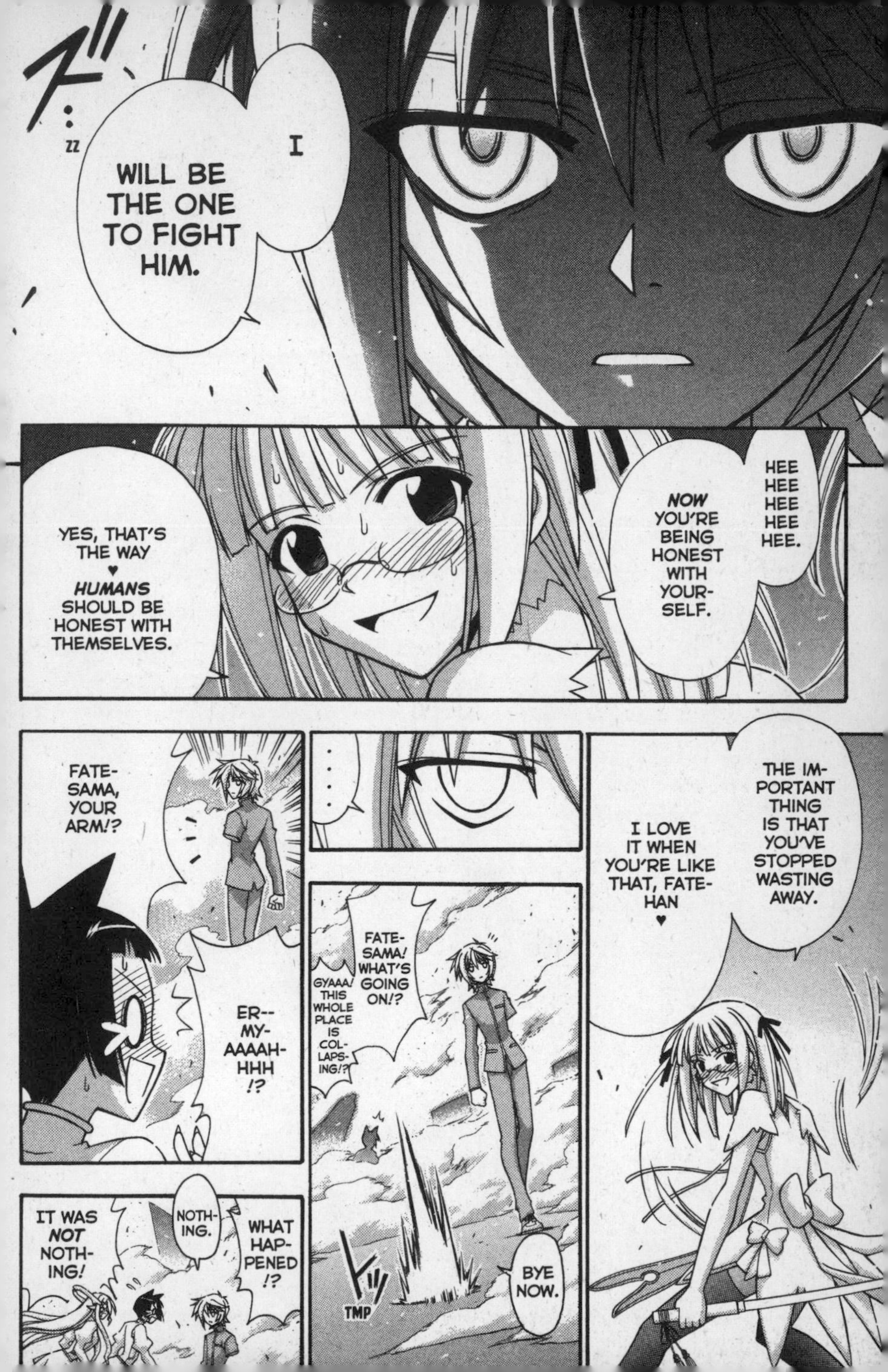
ZZ
I WILL BE THE ONE TO FIGHT HIM.
HEE HEE HEE HEE HEE.
NOW YOU'RE BEING HONEST WITH YOURSELF.
YES, THAT'S THE WAY ♥ *HUMANS* SHOULD BE HONEST WITH THEMSELVES.
THE IMPORTANT THING IS THAT YOU'VE STOPPED WASTING AWAY.
I LOVE IT WHEN YOU'RE LIKE THAT, FATE-HAN ♥
BYE NOW.
....
FATE-SAMA! WHAT'S GOING ON!?
GYAAA! THIS WHOLE PLACE IS COLLAPSING!?
TMP
FATE-SAMA, YOUR ARM!?
ER-- MY- AAAAHHHH !?
WHAT HAPPENED !?
NOTHING.
IT WAS *NOT* NOTHING!

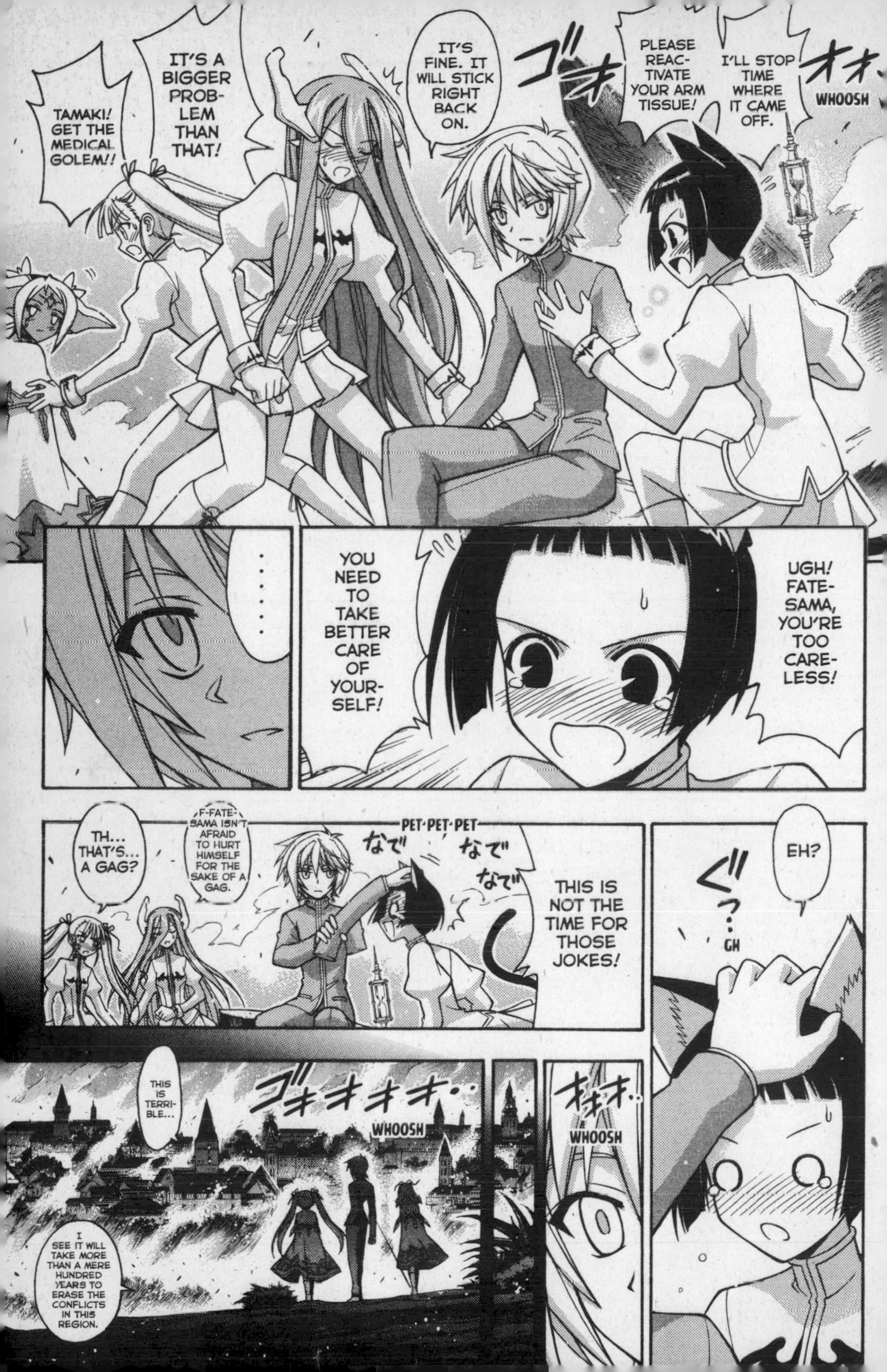オオ
WHOOSH
I'LL STOP TIME WHERE IT CAME OFF.
PLEASE REACTIVATE YOUR ARM TISSUE!
ゴォ
IT'S FINE. IT WILL STICK RIGHT BACK ON.
IT'S A BIGGER PROBLEM THAN THAT!
TAMAKI! GET THE MEDICAL GOLEM!!
UGH! FATE-SAMA, YOU'RE TOO CARELESS!
YOU NEED TO TAKE BETTER CARE OF YOURSELF!
......
EH?
ぐっ
GH
なで なで なで
PET PET PET
THIS IS NOT THE TIME FOR THOSE JOKES!
F-FATE-SAMA ISN'T AFRAID TO HURT HIMSELF FOR THE SAKE OF A GAG.
TH... THAT'S... A GAG?
オオオ..
WHOOSH
ゴオオオオ..
WHOOSH
THIS IS TERRIBLE...
I SEE IT WILL TAKE MORE THAN A MERE HUNDRED YEARS TO ERASE THE CONFLICTS IN THIS REGION.

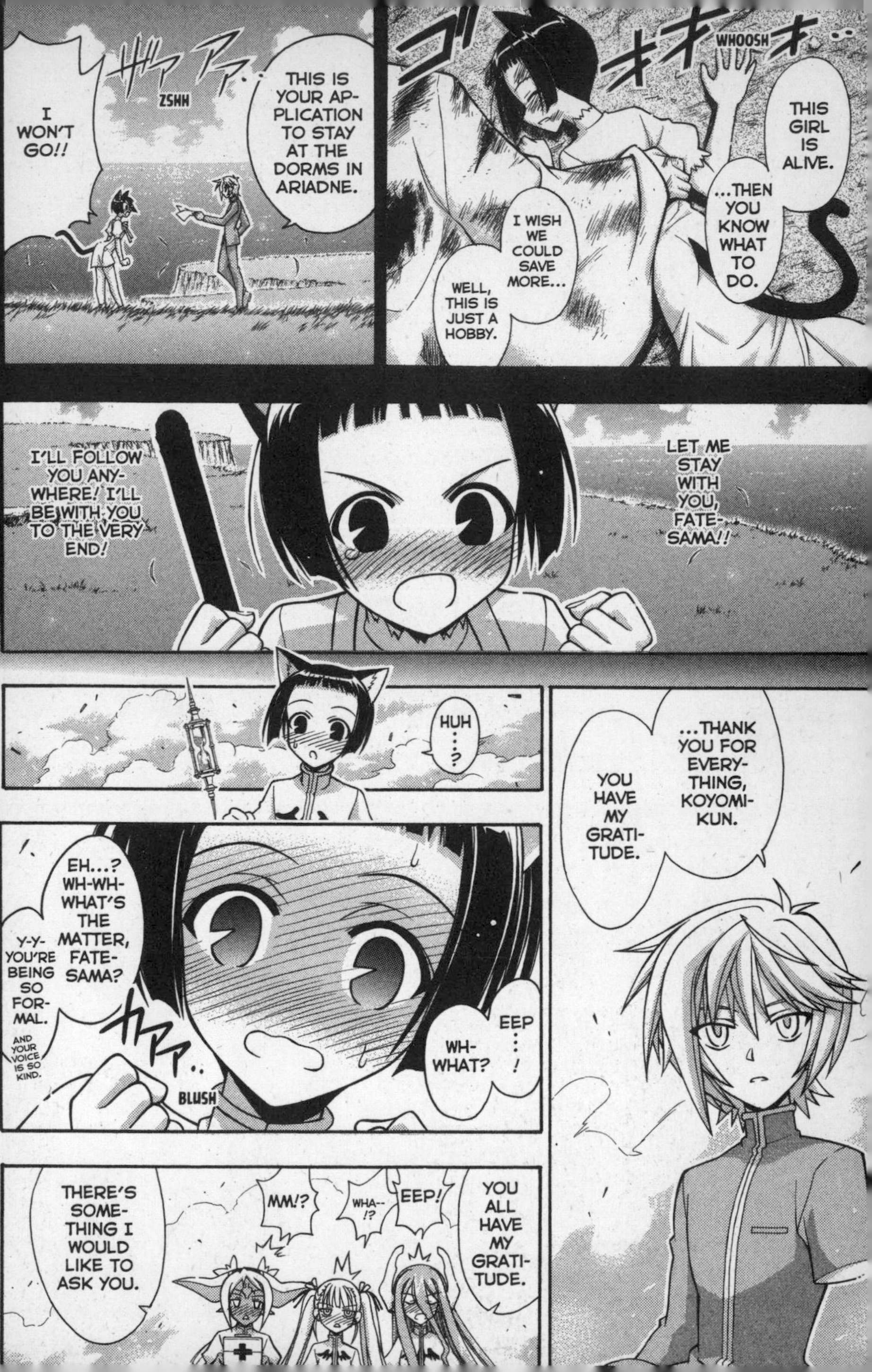
WHOOSH
THIS GIRL IS ALIVE.
...THEN YOU KNOW WHAT TO DO.
I WISH WE COULD SAVE MORE...
WELL, THIS IS JUST A HOBBY.
THIS IS YOUR APPLICATION TO STAY AT THE DORMS IN ARIADNE.
ZSHH
I WON'T GO!!
LET ME STAY WITH YOU, FATE-SAMA!!
I'LL FOLLOW YOU ANYWHERE! I'LL BE WITH YOU TO THE VERY END!
...THANK YOU FOR EVERYTHING, KOYOMI-KUN.
YOU HAVE MY GRATITUDE.
HUH...?
EEP...!
WH-WHAT?
EH...? WH-WH-WHAT'S THE MATTER, FATE-SAMA?
Y-Y-YOU'RE BEING SO FORMAL.
AND YOUR VOICE IS SO KIND.
BLUSH
YOU ALL HAVE MY GRATITUDE.
EEP!
WHA--!?
MM!?
THERE'S SOMETHING I WOULD LIKE TO ASK YOU.

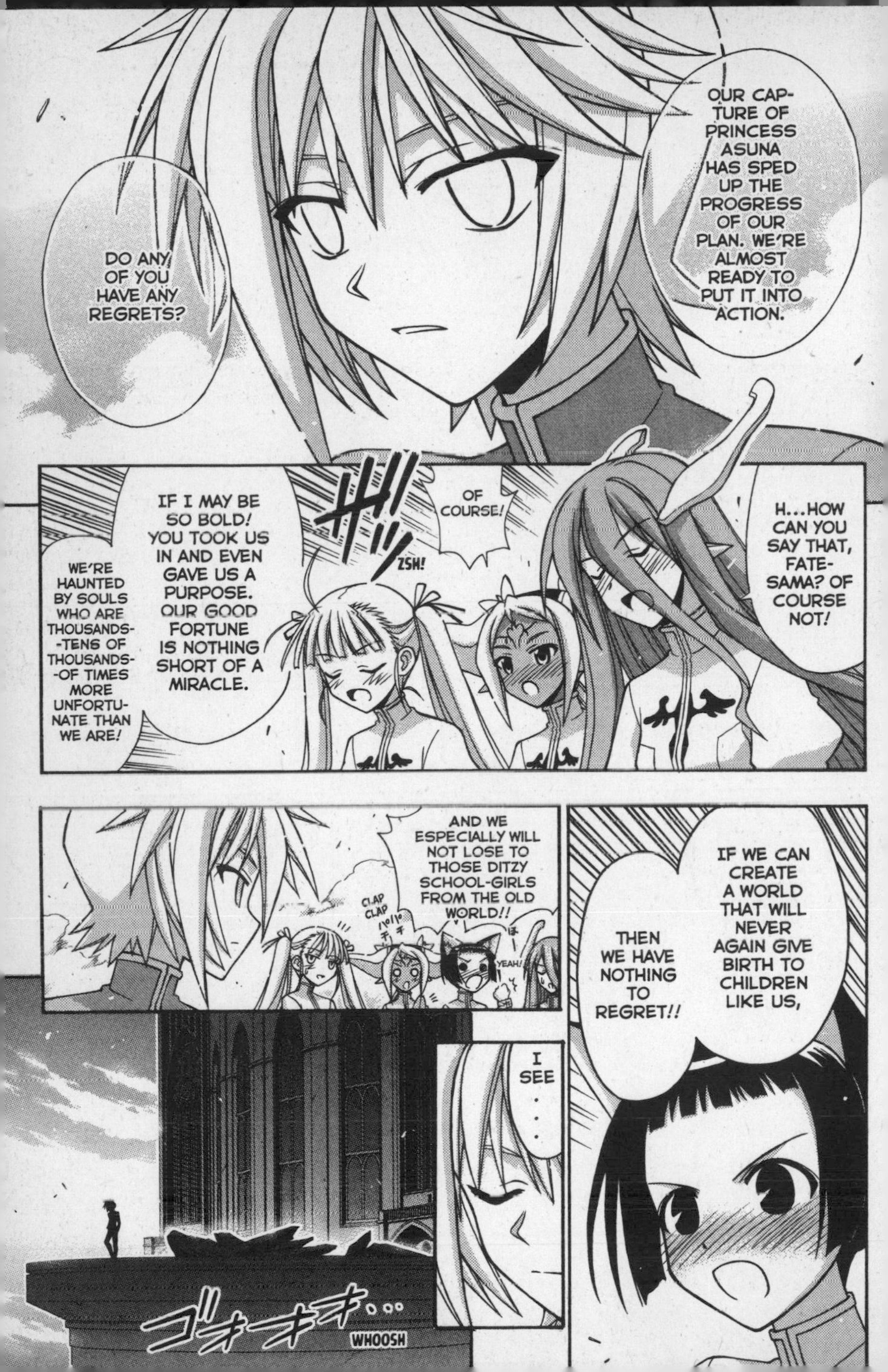
OUR CAPTURE OF PRINCESS ASUNA HAS SPED UP THE PROGRESS OF OUR PLAN. WE'RE ALMOST READY TO PUT IT INTO ACTION.
DO ANY OF YOU HAVE ANY REGRETS?
H...HOW CAN YOU SAY THAT, FATE-SAMA? OF COURSE NOT!
OF COURSE!
ZSH!
IF I MAY BE SO BOLD! YOU TOOK US IN AND EVEN GAVE US A PURPOSE. OUR GOOD FORTUNE IS NOTHING SHORT OF A MIRACLE.
WE'RE HAUNTED BY SOULS WHO ARE THOUSANDS-TENS OF THOUSANDS-OF TIMES MORE UNFORTUNATE THAN WE ARE!
IF WE CAN CREATE A WORLD THAT WILL NEVER AGAIN GIVE BIRTH TO CHILDREN LIKE US,
THEN WE HAVE NOTHING TO REGRET!!
AND WE ESPECIALLY WILL NOT LOSE TO THOSE DITZY SCHOOL-GIRLS FROM THE OLD WORLD!!
CLAP CLAP
YEAH!
I SEE...
WHOOSH

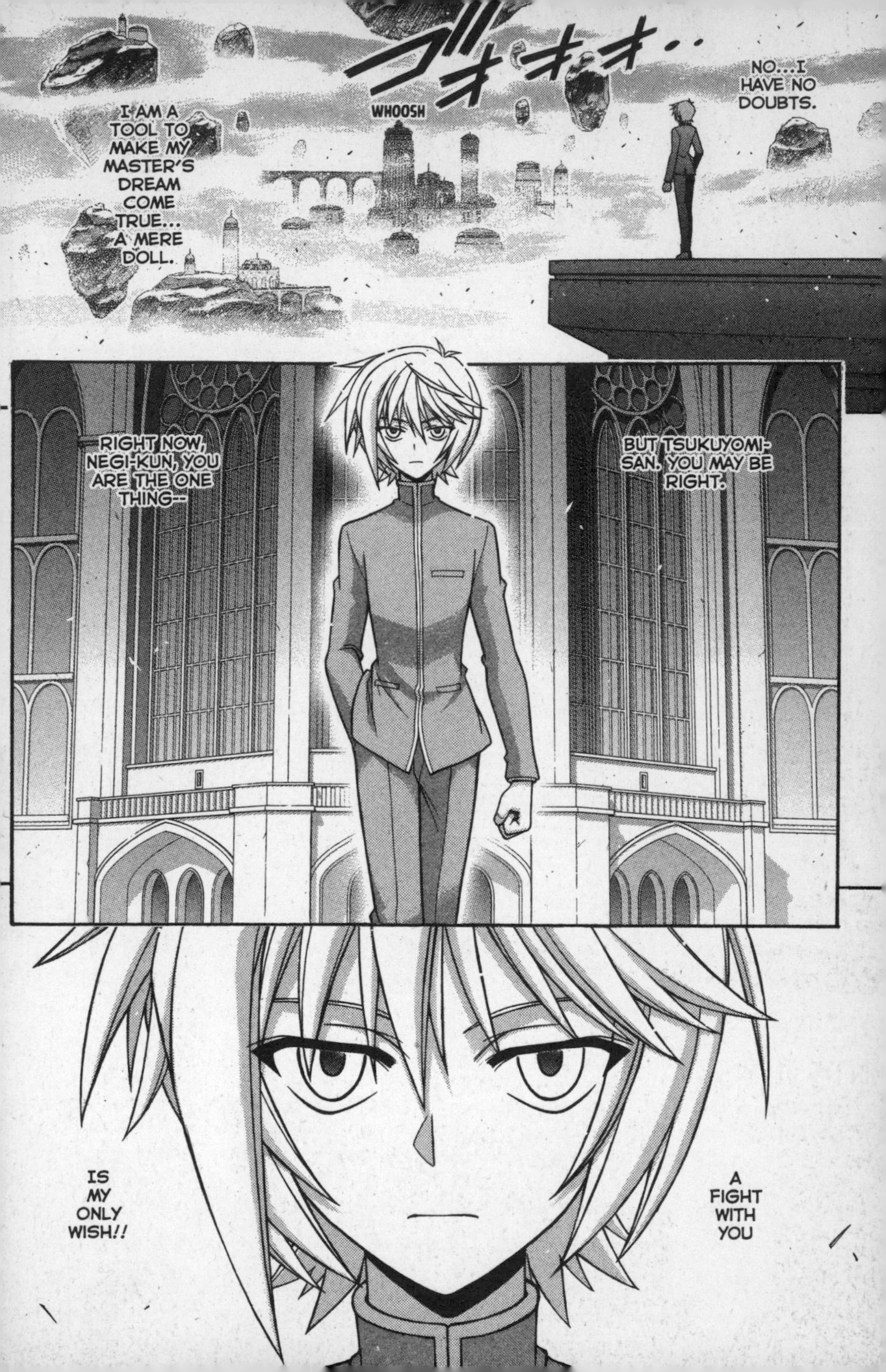
NO...I HAVE NO DOUBTS.
ゴォォォ…
WHOOSH
I AM A TOOL TO MAKE MY MASTER'S DREAM COME TRUE... A MERE DOLL.
BUT TSUKUYOMI-SAN. YOU MAY BE RIGHT.
RIGHT NOW, NEGI-KUN, YOU ARE THE ONE THING--
A FIGHT WITH YOU
IS MY ONLY WISH!!

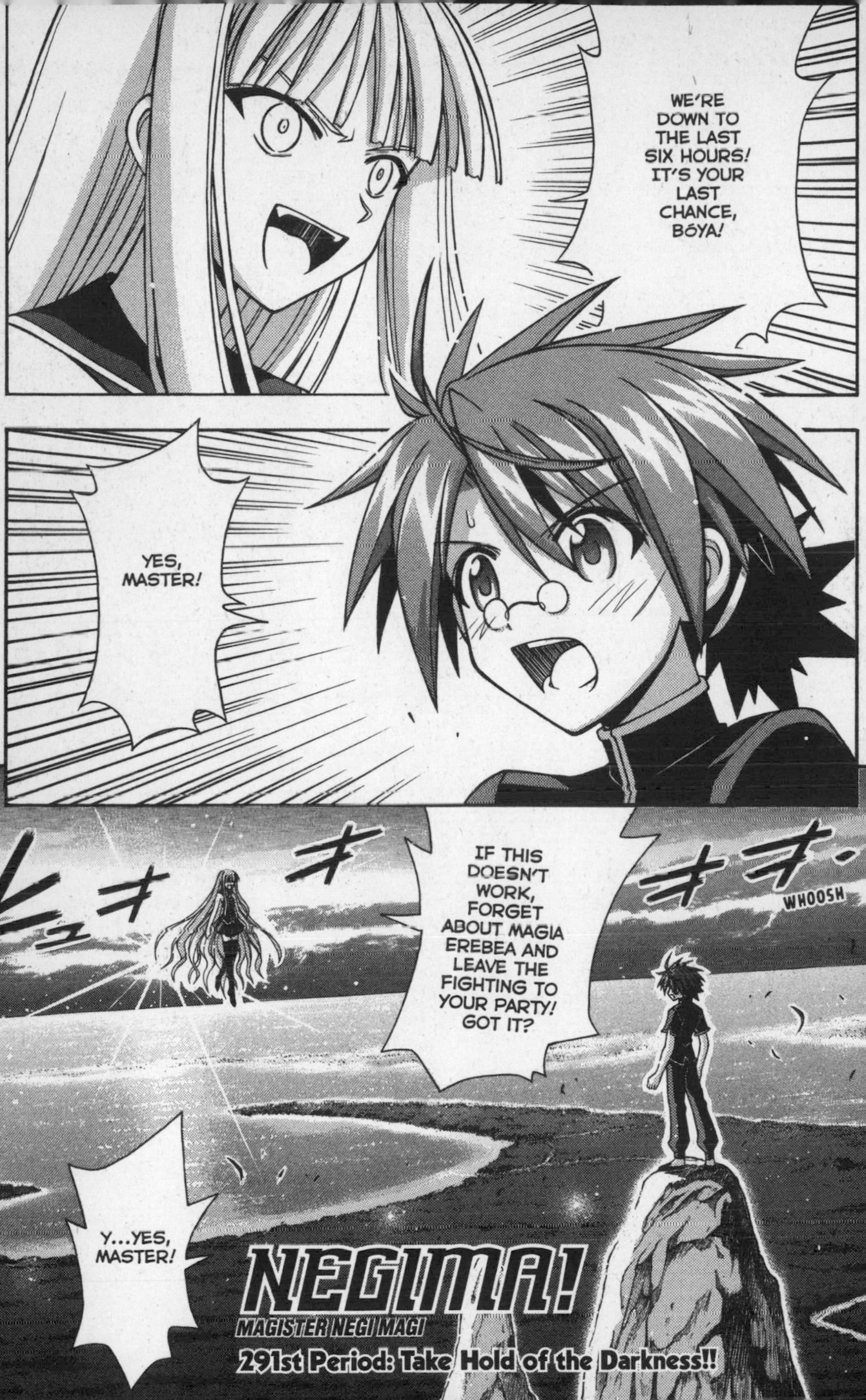
WE'RE DOWN TO THE LAST SIX HOURS! IT'S YOUR LAST CHANCE, BŌYA!
YES, MASTER!
ヒュオオオオ・
WHOOSH
IF THIS DOESN'T WORK, FORGET ABOUT MAGIA EREBEA AND LEAVE THE FIGHTING TO YOUR PARTY! GOT IT?
Y...YES, MASTER!
NEGIMA!
MAGISTER NEGI MAGI
291st Period: Take Hold of the Darkness!!

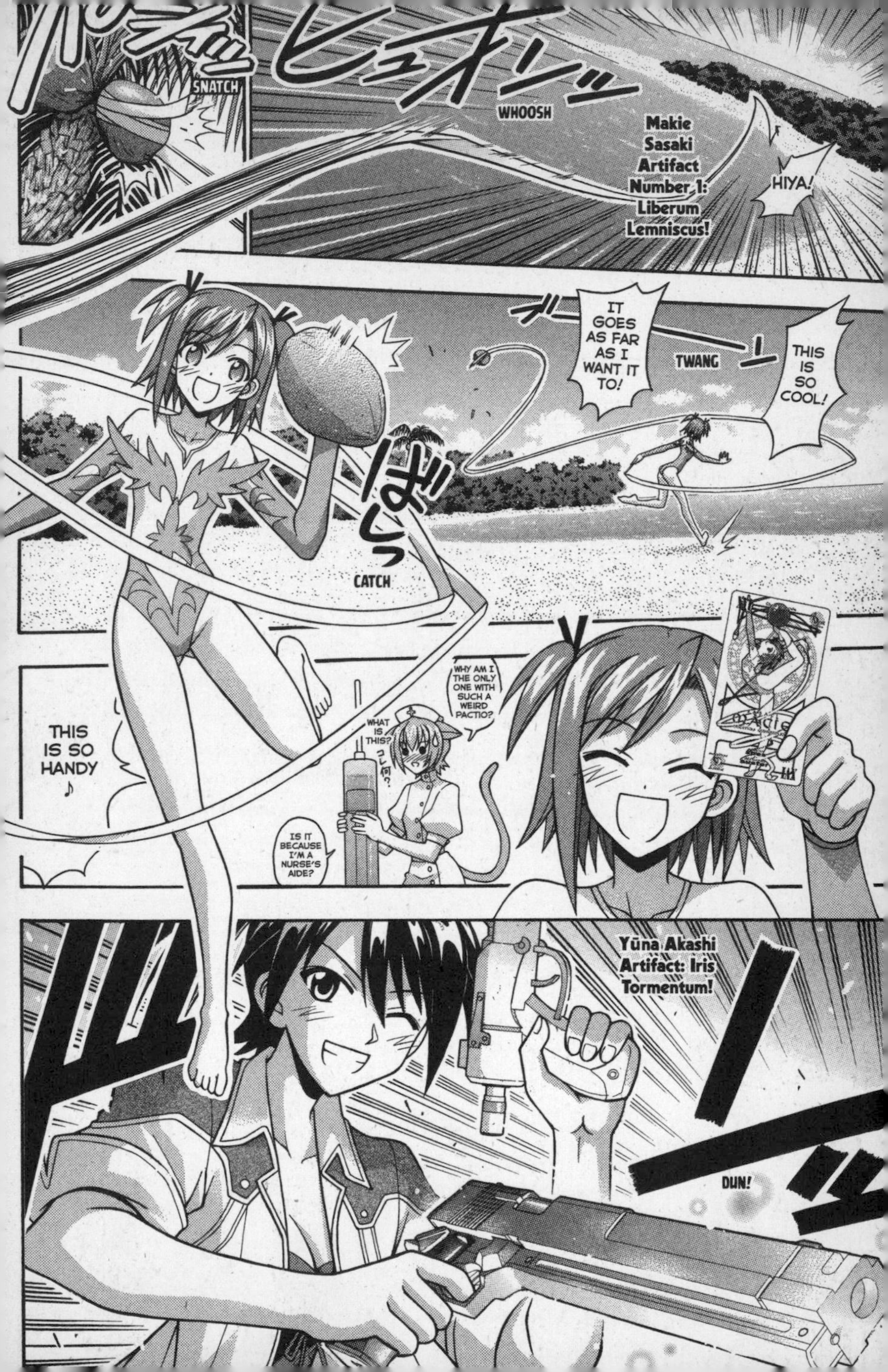
Makie Sasaki Artifact Number 1: Liberum Lemniscus!
HIYA!
ヒュオンッ
WHOOSH
SNATCH
THIS IS SO COOL!
TWANG
IT GOES AS FAR AS I WANT IT TO!
ばくっ
CATCH
WHY AM I THE ONLY ONE WITH SUCH A WEIRD PACTIO?
WHAT IS THIS?
コレ何?
IS IT BECAUSE I'M A NURSE'S AIDE?
THIS IS SO HANDY ♪
Yūna Akashi Artifact: Iris Tormentum!
DUN!

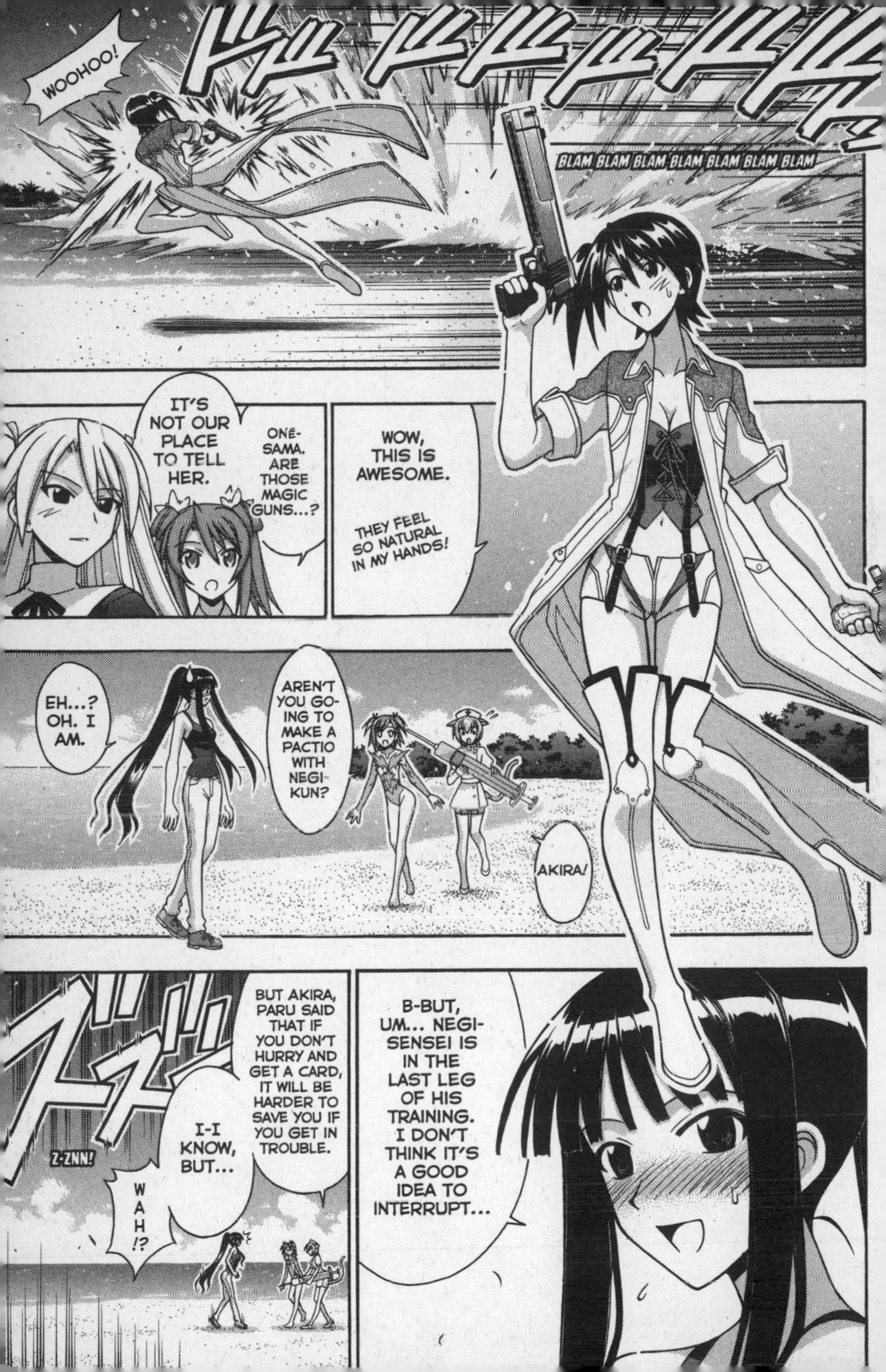
BLAM BLAM BLAM BLAM BLAM BLAM BLAM
WOOHOO!
WOW, THIS IS AWESOME.
THEY FEEL SO NATURAL IN MY HANDS!
ONE-SAMA. ARE THOSE MAGIC GUNS...?
IT'S NOT OUR PLACE TO TELL HER.
AKIRA!
AREN'T YOU GOING TO MAKE A PACTIO WITH NEGI-KUN?
EH...? OH. I AM.
B-BUT, UM... NEGI-SENSEI IS IN THE LAST LEG OF HIS TRAINING. I DON'T THINK IT'S A GOOD IDEA TO INTERRUPT...
BUT AKIRA, PARU SAID THAT IF YOU DON'T HURRY AND GET A CARD, IT WILL BE HARDER TO SAVE YOU IF YOU GET IN TROUBLE.
I-I KNOW, BUT...
Z-ZNN!
WAH!?

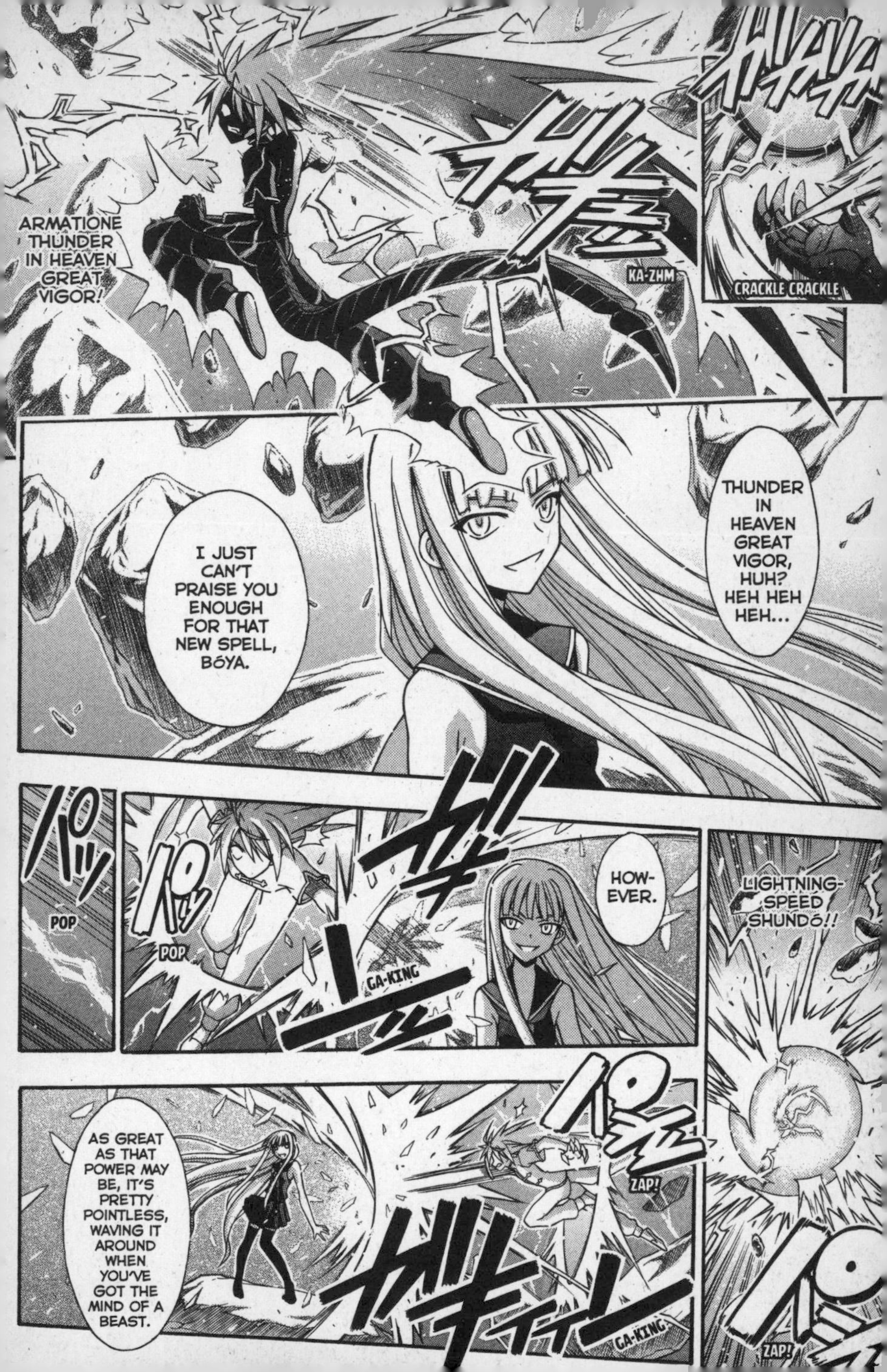
CRACKLE CRACKLE
KA-ZHM
ARMATIONE THUNDER IN HEAVEN GREAT VIGOR!
THUNDER IN HEAVEN GREAT VIGOR, HUH? HEH HEH HEH...
I JUST CAN'T PRAISE YOU ENOUGH FOR THAT NEW SPELL, BÔYA.
LIGHTNING-SPEED SHUNDÔ!!
HOW-EVER.
GA-KING
POP
POP
ZAP!
ZAP!
GA-KING
AS GREAT AS THAT POWER MAY BE, IT'S PRETTY POINTLESS, WAVING IT AROUND WHEN YOU'VE GOT THE MIND OF A BEAST.

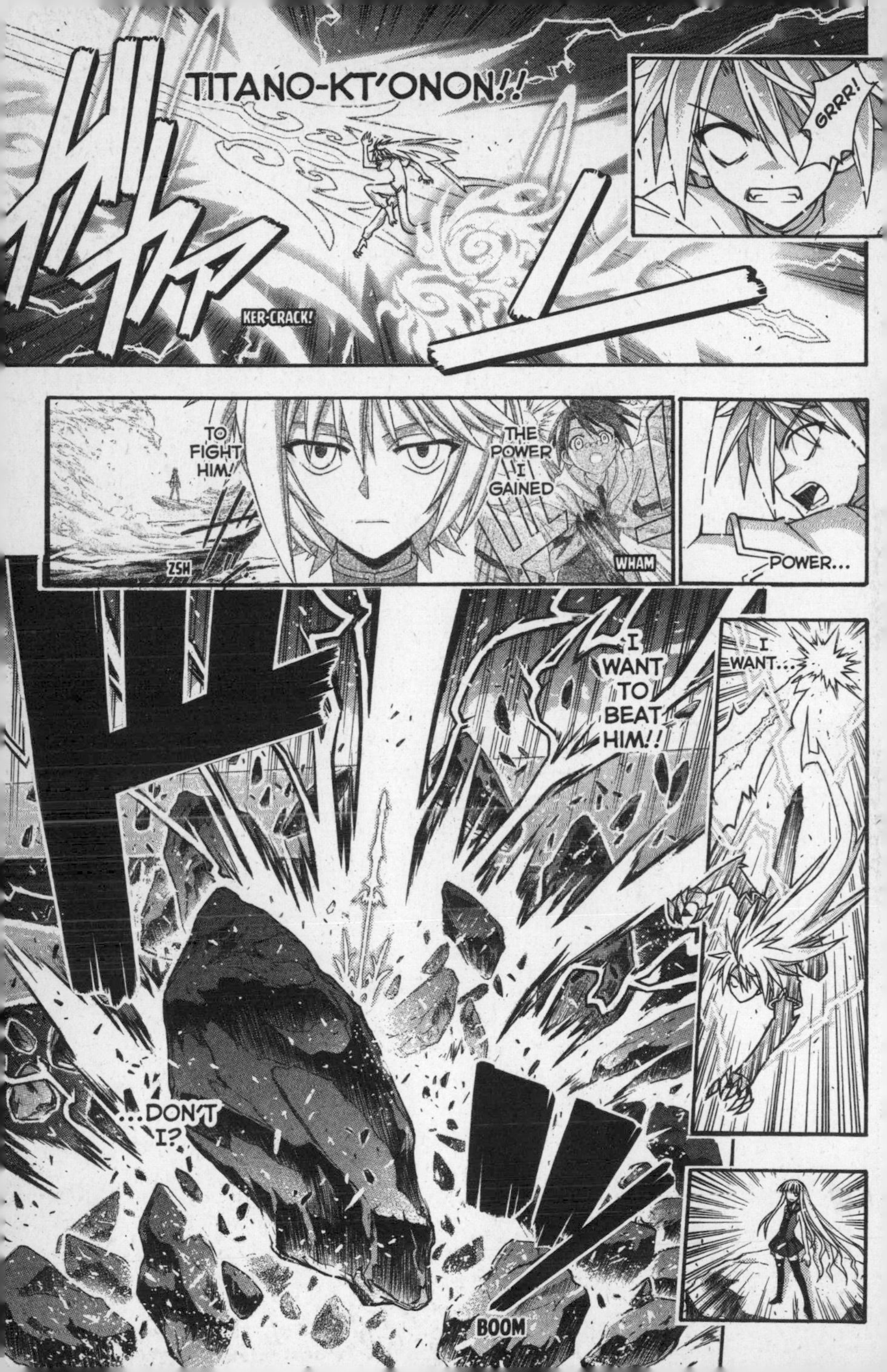
GRRR!
TITANO-KT'ONON!!
KER-CRACK!
POWER...
THE POWER I GAINED
WHAM
TO FIGHT HIM!
ZSH
I WANT...
I WANT TO BEAT HIM!!
...DON'T I?
BOOM

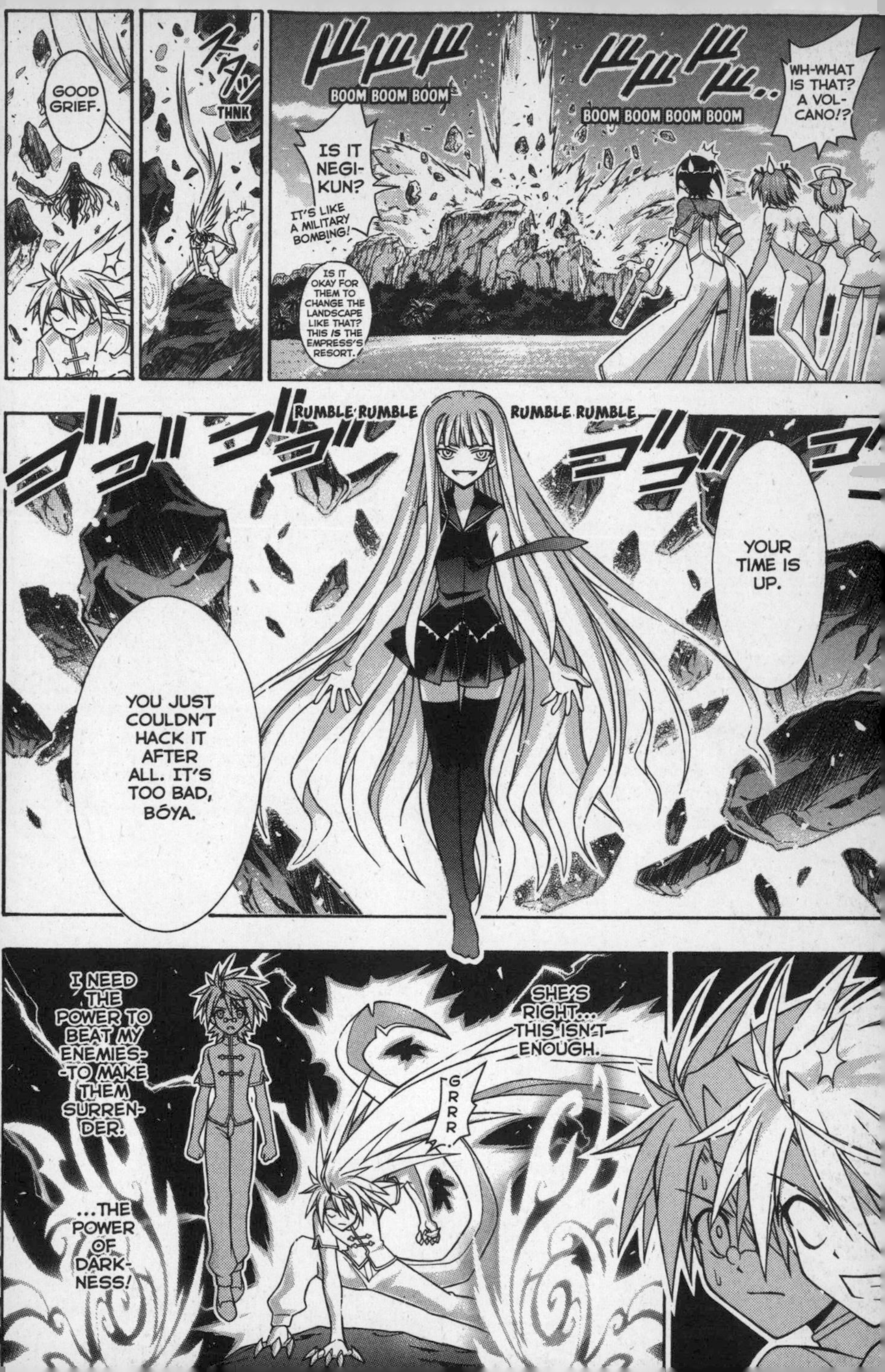
WH-WHAT IS THAT? A VOL-CANO!?
BOOM BOOM BOOM BOOM
BOOM BOOM BOOM
IS IT NEGI-KUN?
IT'S LIKE A MILITARY BOMBING!
IS IT OKAY FOR THEM TO CHANGE THE LANDSCAPE LIKE THAT? THIS *IS* THE EMPRESS'S RESORT.
THNK
GOOD GRIEF.
RUMBLE RUMBLE
RUMBLE RUMBLE
YOUR TIME IS UP.
YOU JUST COULDN'T HACK IT AFTER ALL. IT'S TOO BAD, BÓYA.
SHE'S RIGHT... THIS ISN'T ENOUGH.
GRRR...
I NEED THE POWER TO BEAT MY ENEMIES--TO MAKE THEM SURREN-DER.
...THE POWER OF DARK-NESS!

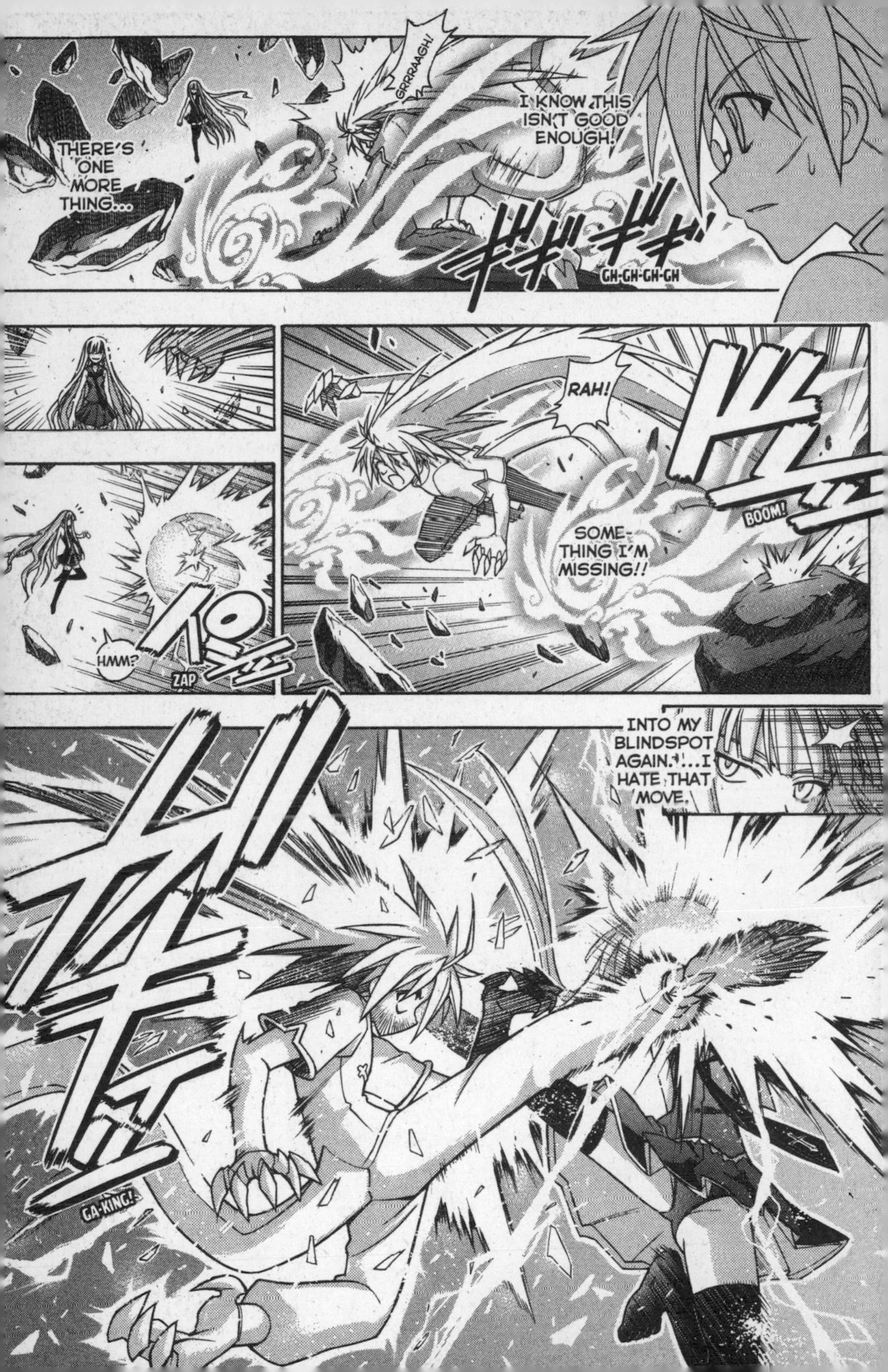

GRRRAAGH!
I KNOW THIS ISN'T GOOD ENOUGH!
GH-GH-GH-GH
THERE'S ONE MORE THING...
RAH!
BOOM!
SOME-THING I'M MISSING!!
HMM?
ZAP
INTO MY BLINDSPOT AGAIN. ...I HATE THAT MOVE.
GA-KING!

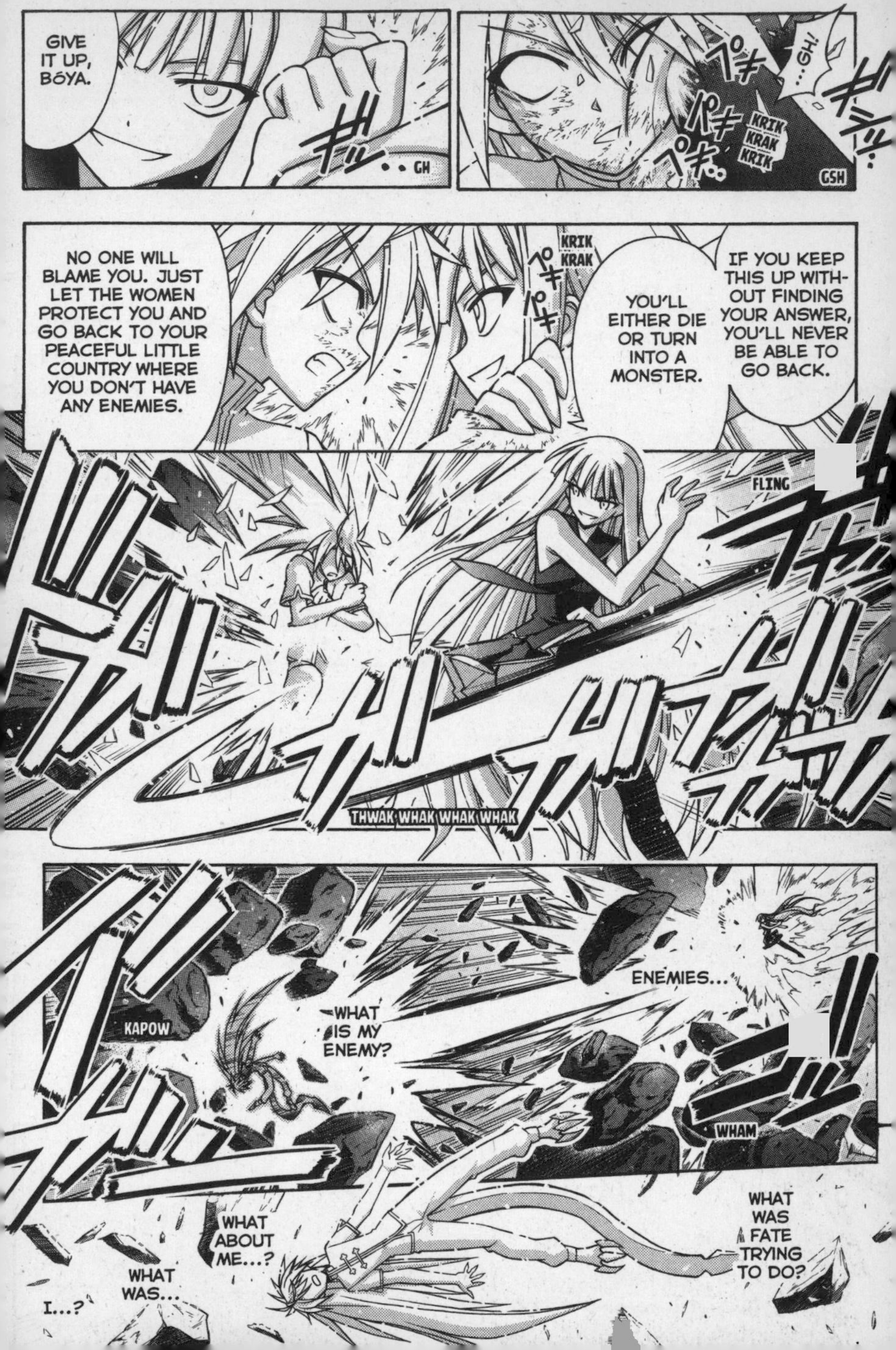
...GH!
KRIK KRAK KRIK
GSH
GIVE IT UP, BŌYA.
...GH
IF YOU KEEP THIS UP WITHOUT FINDING YOUR ANSWER, YOU'LL NEVER BE ABLE TO GO BACK.
YOU'LL EITHER DIE OR TURN INTO A MONSTER.
KRIK KRAK
NO ONE WILL BLAME YOU. JUST LET THE WOMEN PROTECT YOU AND GO BACK TO YOUR PEACEFUL LITTLE COUNTRY WHERE YOU DON'T HAVE ANY ENEMIES.
FLING
THWAK WHAK WHAK WHAK
ENEMIES...
WHAM
WHAT IS MY ENEMY?
KAPOW
WHAT WAS FATE TRYING TO DO?
WHAT ABOUT ME...?
WHAT WAS...
I...?

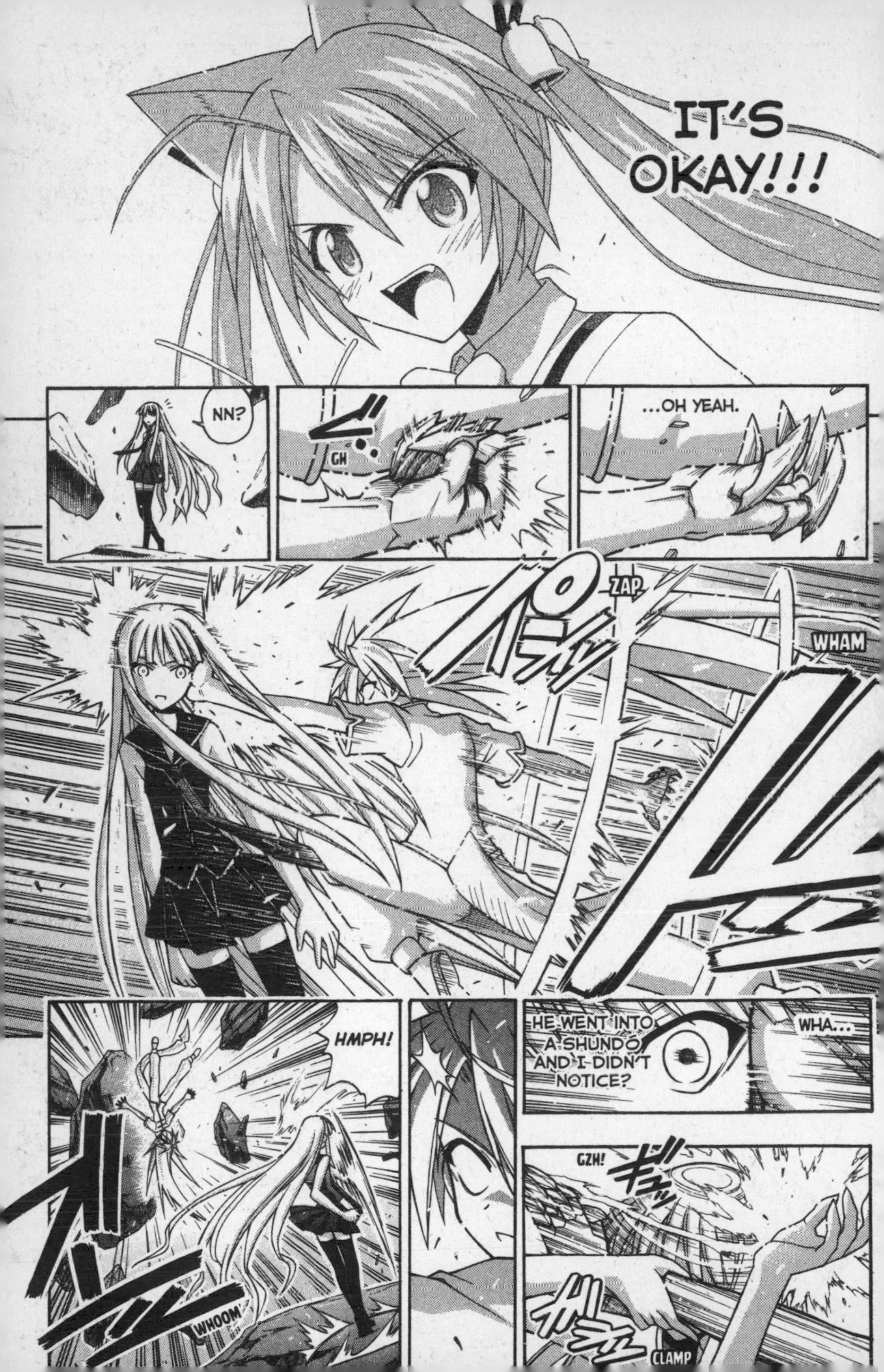
IT'S OKAY!!!
...OH YEAH.
GH
NN?
ZAP
WHAM
WHA...
HE WENT INTO A SHUNDO AND I DIDN'T NOTICE?
GZH!
CLAMP
HMPH!
WHOOM

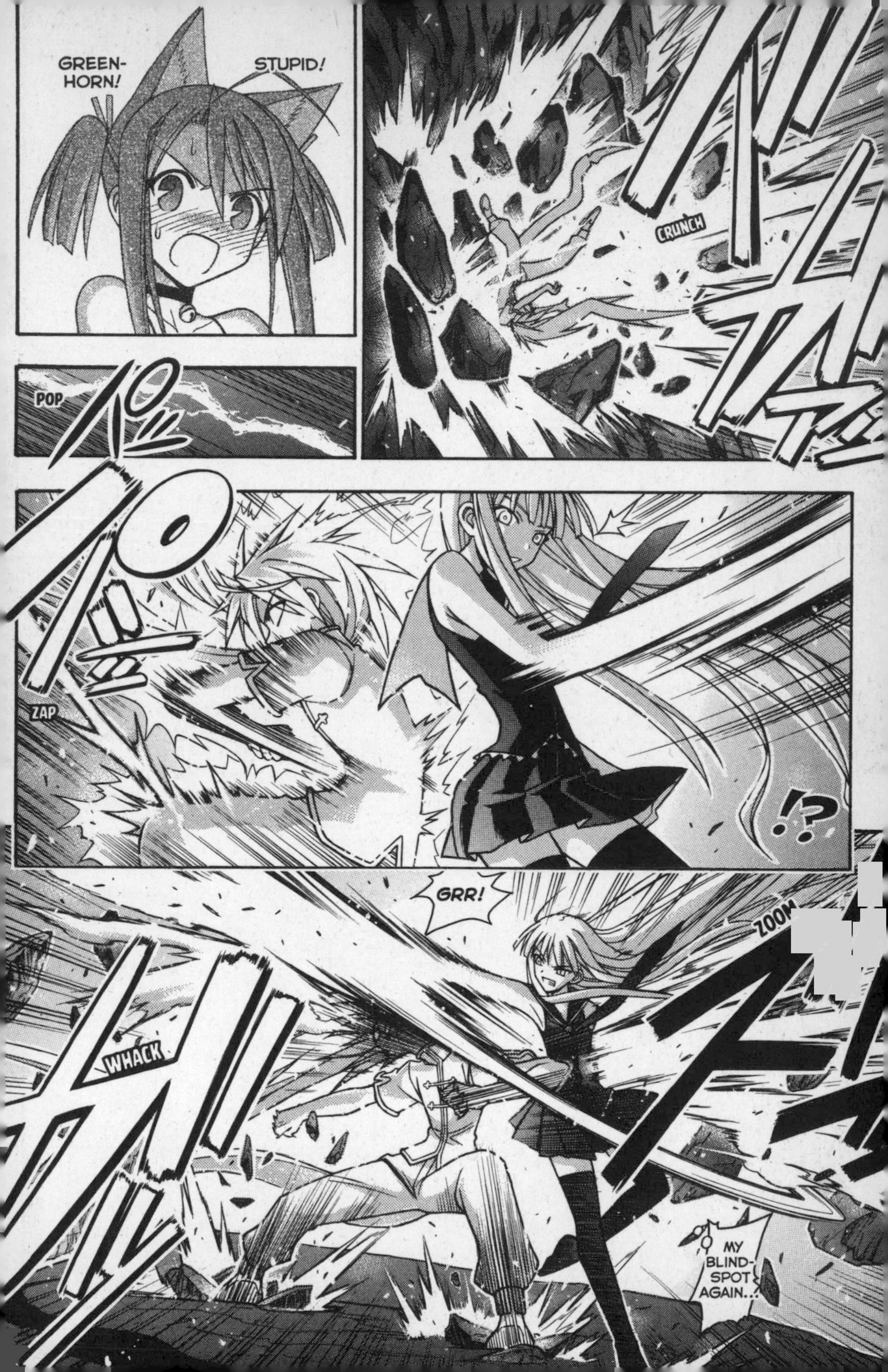

CRUNCH
STUPID!
GREEN-HORN!
POP
!?
ZAP
GRR!
ZOOM
WHACK
MY BLIND-SPOT AGAIN...

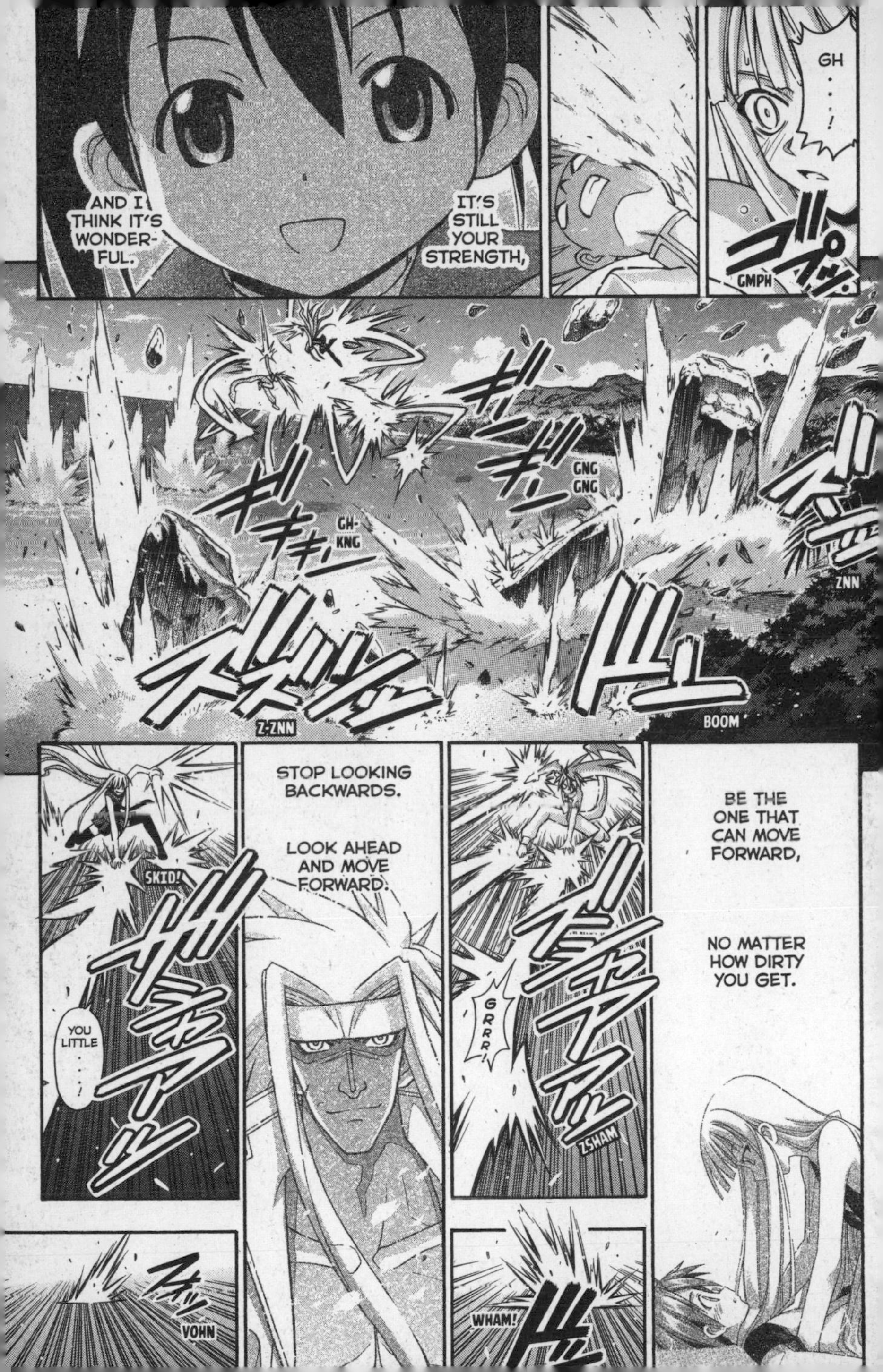
GH...!
GMPH
IT'S STILL YOUR STRENGTH,
AND I THINK IT'S WONDERFUL.
ZNN
GNG GNG
GH-KNG
BOOM
Z-ZNN
BE THE ONE THAT CAN MOVE FORWARD,
NO MATTER HOW DIRTY YOU GET.
GRRR!
ZSHAM
STOP LOOKING BACKWARDS.
LOOK AHEAD AND MOVE FORWARD.
SKID!
YOU LITTLE...!
WHAM!
VOHN

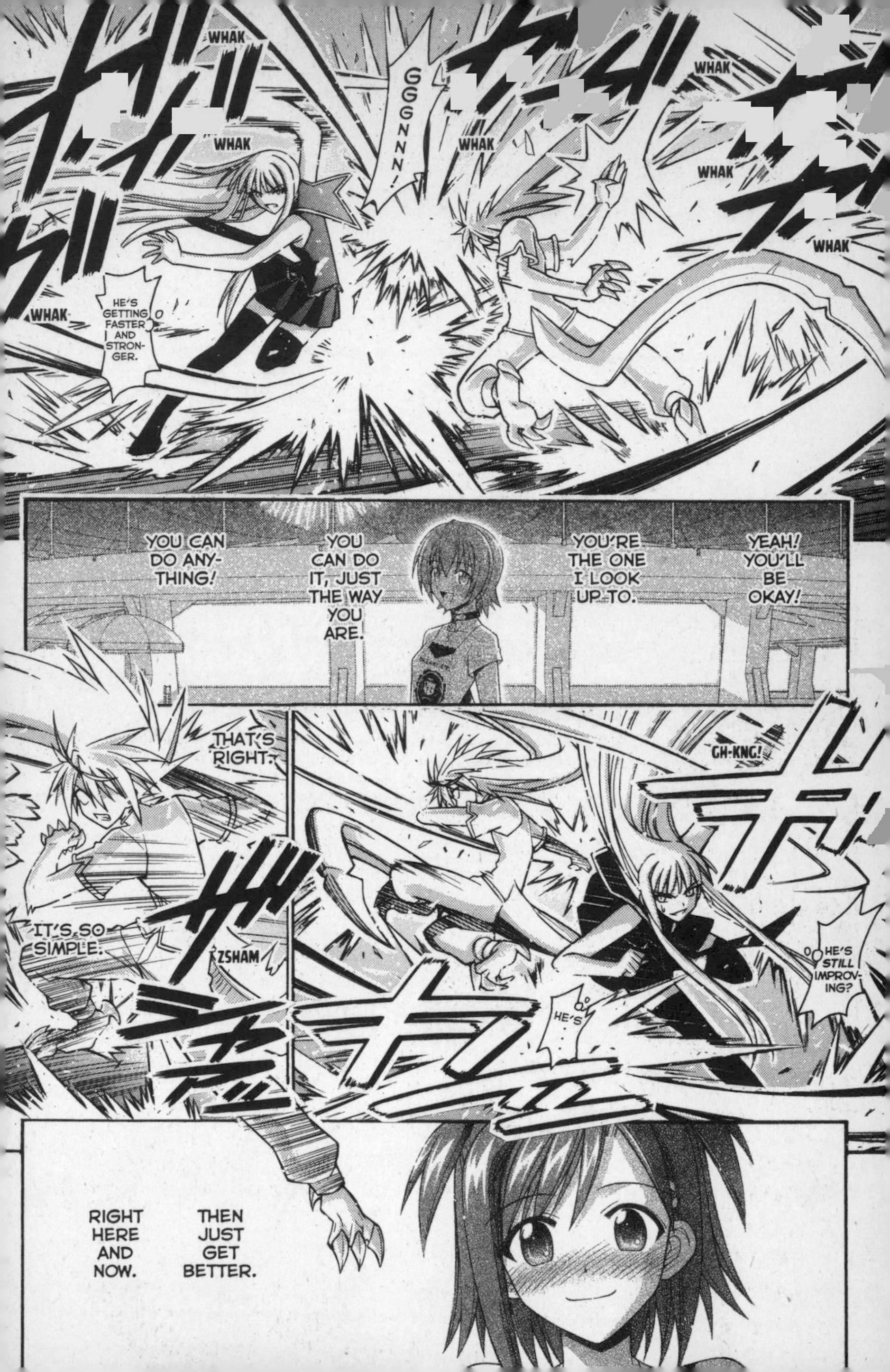
WHAK
WHAK
WHAK
GGGNNN!
WHAK
WHAK
WHAK
HE'S GETTING FASTER AND STRONGER.
WHAK
YEAH! YOU'LL BE OKAY!
YOU'RE THE ONE I LOOK UP TO.
YOU CAN DO IT, JUST THE WAY YOU ARE.
YOU CAN DO ANYTHING!
GH-KNG!
HE'S STILL IMPROVING?
HE'S
THAT'S RIGHT.
ZSHAM
IT'S SO SIMPLE.
THEN JUST GET BETTER.
RIGHT HERE AND NOW.

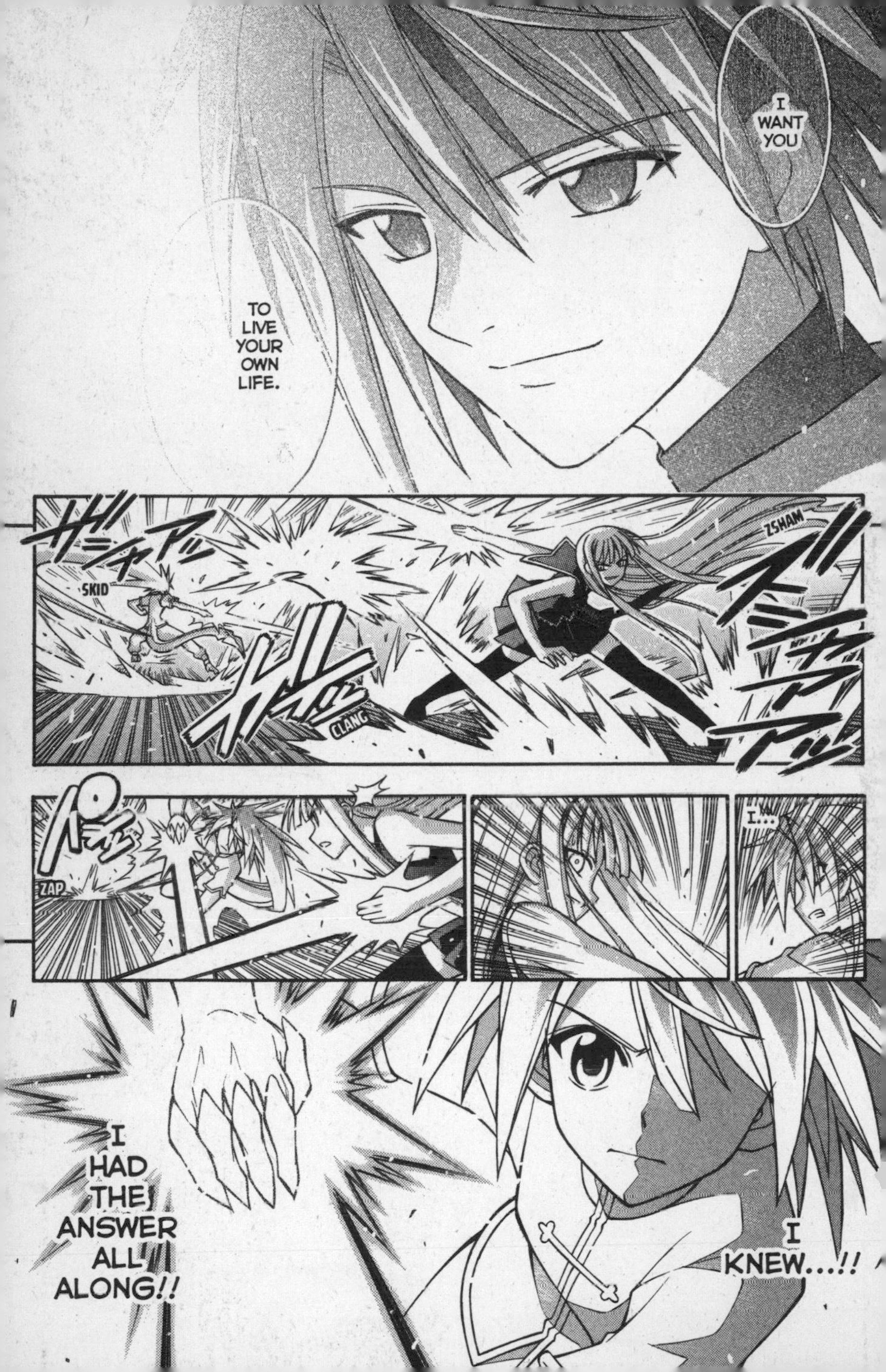
I WANT YOU
TO LIVE YOUR OWN LIFE.
ZSHAM
SKID
CLANG
I...
ZAP
I KNEW...!!
I HAD THE ANSWER ALL ALONG!!

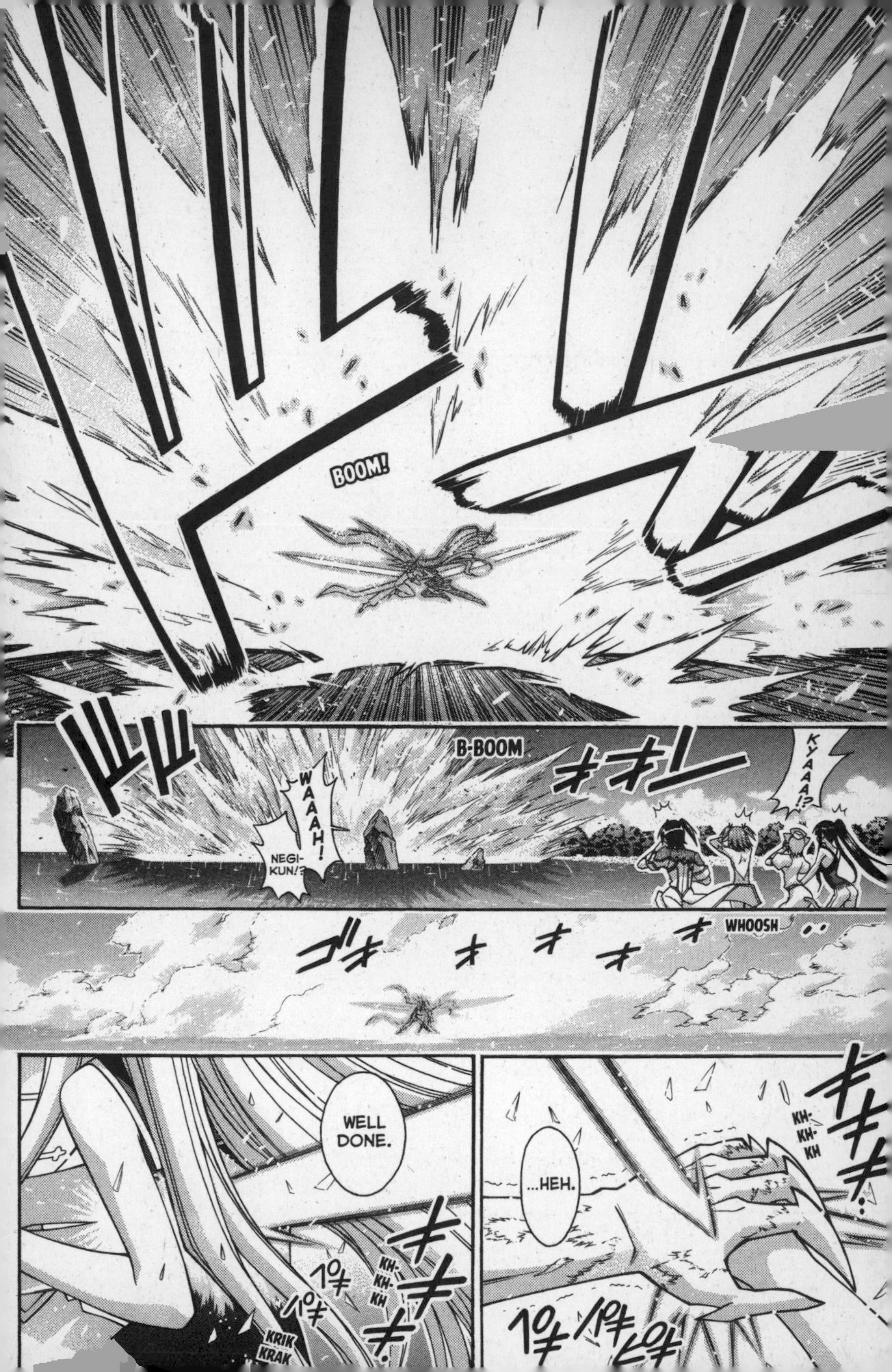
BOOM!
KYAAAA!?
B-BOOM
WAAAAH!
NEGI-KUN!?
WHOOSH
KH-KH-KH
...HEH.
WELL DONE.
KH-KH-KH
KRIK KRAK

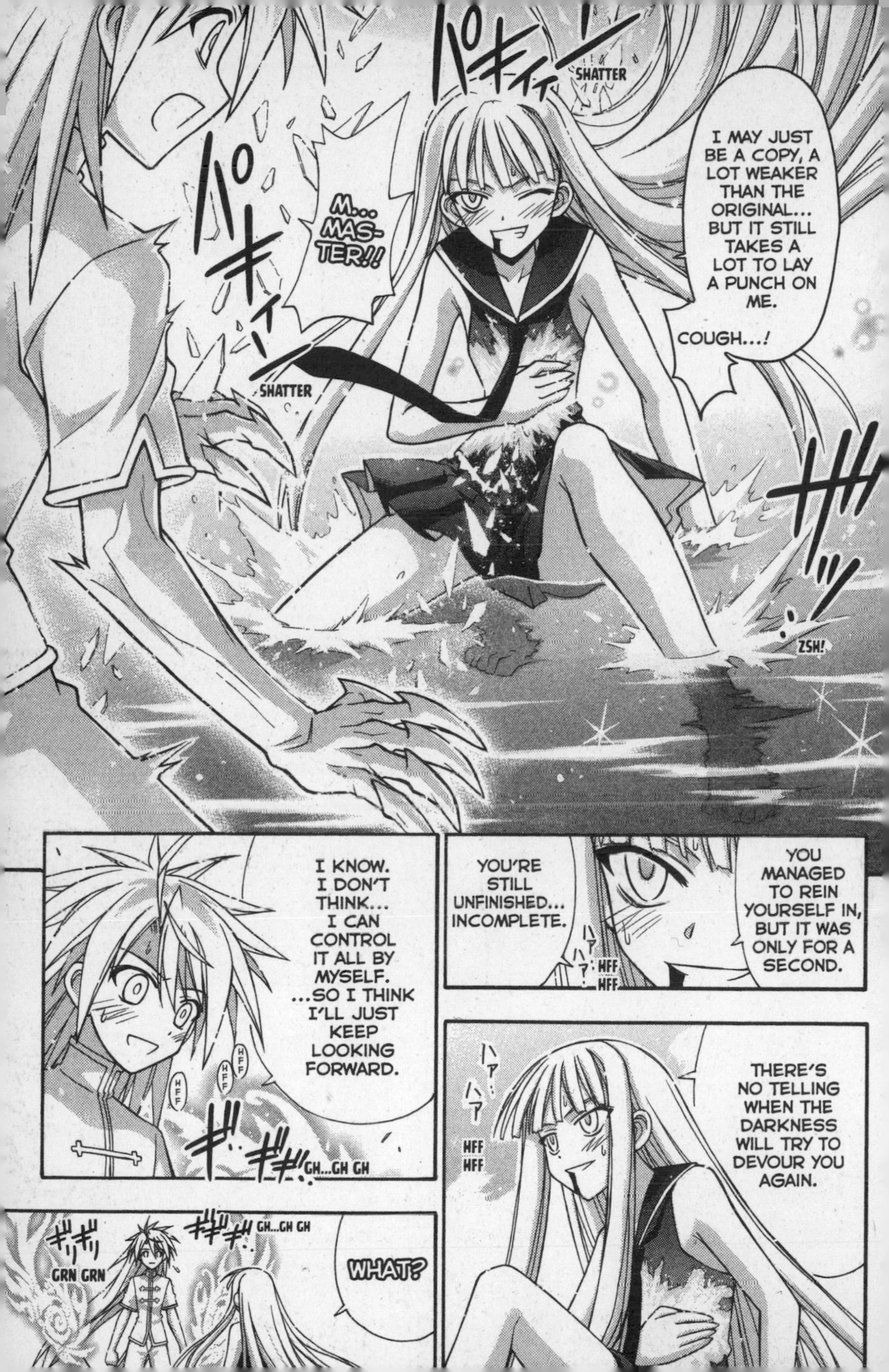
SHATTER
I MAY JUST BE A COPY, A LOT WEAKER THAN THE ORIGINAL... BUT IT STILL TAKES A LOT TO LAY A PUNCH ON ME.
COUGH...!
M... MASTER!!
SHATTER
ZSH!
YOU MANAGED TO REIN YOURSELF IN, BUT IT WAS ONLY FOR A SECOND.
YOU'RE STILL UNFINISHED... INCOMPLETE.
HFF HFF
I KNOW. I DON'T THINK... I CAN CONTROL IT ALL BY MYSELF. ...SO I THINK I'LL JUST KEEP LOOKING FORWARD.
HFF HFF HFF
GH...GH GH
THERE'S NO TELLING WHEN THE DARKNESS WILL TRY TO DEVOUR YOU AGAIN.
HFF HFF
WHAT?
GH...GH GH
GRN GRN

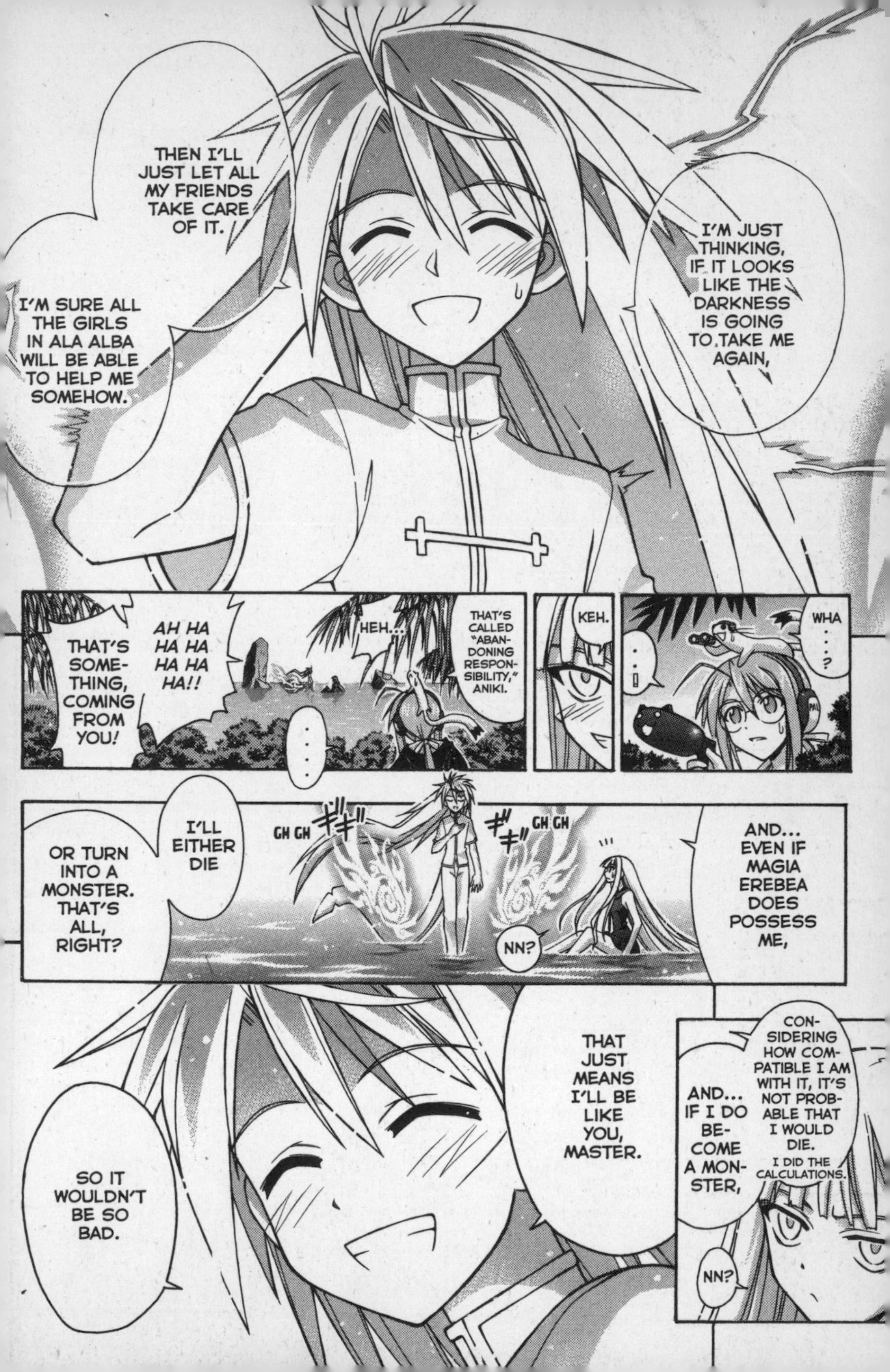
I'M JUST THINKING, IF IT LOOKS LIKE THE DARKNESS IS GOING TO TAKE ME AGAIN,
THEN I'LL JUST LET ALL MY FRIENDS TAKE CARE OF IT.
I'M SURE ALL THE GIRLS IN ALA ALBA WILL BE ABLE TO HELP ME SOMEHOW.
WHA . . . ?
KEH.
. . !
THAT'S CALLED "ABANDONING RESPONSIBILITY," ANIKI.
HEH...
AH HA HA HA HA HA HA!!
THAT'S SOMETHING, COMING FROM YOU!
. . . . .
AND... EVEN IF MAGIA EREBEA DOES POSSESS ME,
NN?
GH GH
GH GH
I'LL EITHER DIE
OR TURN INTO A MONSTER. THAT'S ALL, RIGHT?
CONSIDERING HOW COMPATIBLE I AM WITH IT, IT'S NOT PROBABLE THAT I WOULD DIE.
I DID THE CALCULATIONS.
AND... IF I DO BECOME A MONSTER,
NN?
THAT JUST MEANS I'LL BE LIKE YOU, MASTER.
SO IT WOULDN'T BE SO BAD.

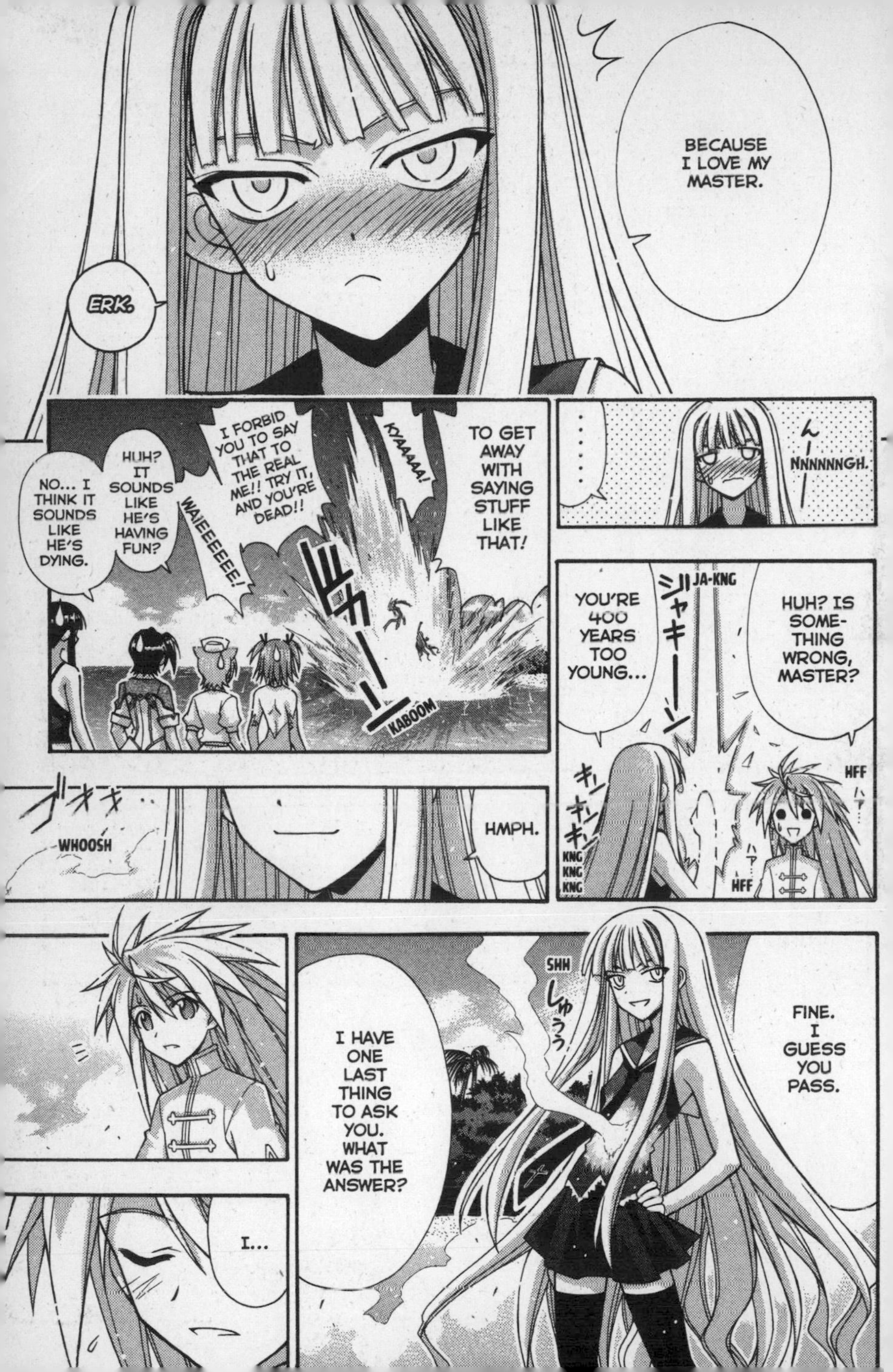
BECAUSE I LOVE MY MASTER.
ERK.
. . . .
NNNNNNGH.
TO GET AWAY WITH SAYING STUFF LIKE THAT!
KYAAAAA!
I FORBID YOU TO SAY THAT TO THE REAL ME!! TRY IT, AND YOU'RE DEAD!!
WAIEEEEEEE!
HUH? IT SOUNDS LIKE HE'S HAVING FUN?
NO... I THINK IT SOUNDS LIKE HE'S DYING.
KABOOM
HUH? IS SOME-THING WRONG, MASTER?
JA-KNG
YOU'RE 400 YEARS TOO YOUNG...
HFF
KNG KNG KNG
HFF
HMPH.
WHOOSH
FINE. I GUESS YOU PASS.
SHH
I HAVE ONE LAST THING TO ASK YOU. WHAT WAS THE ANSWER?
I...

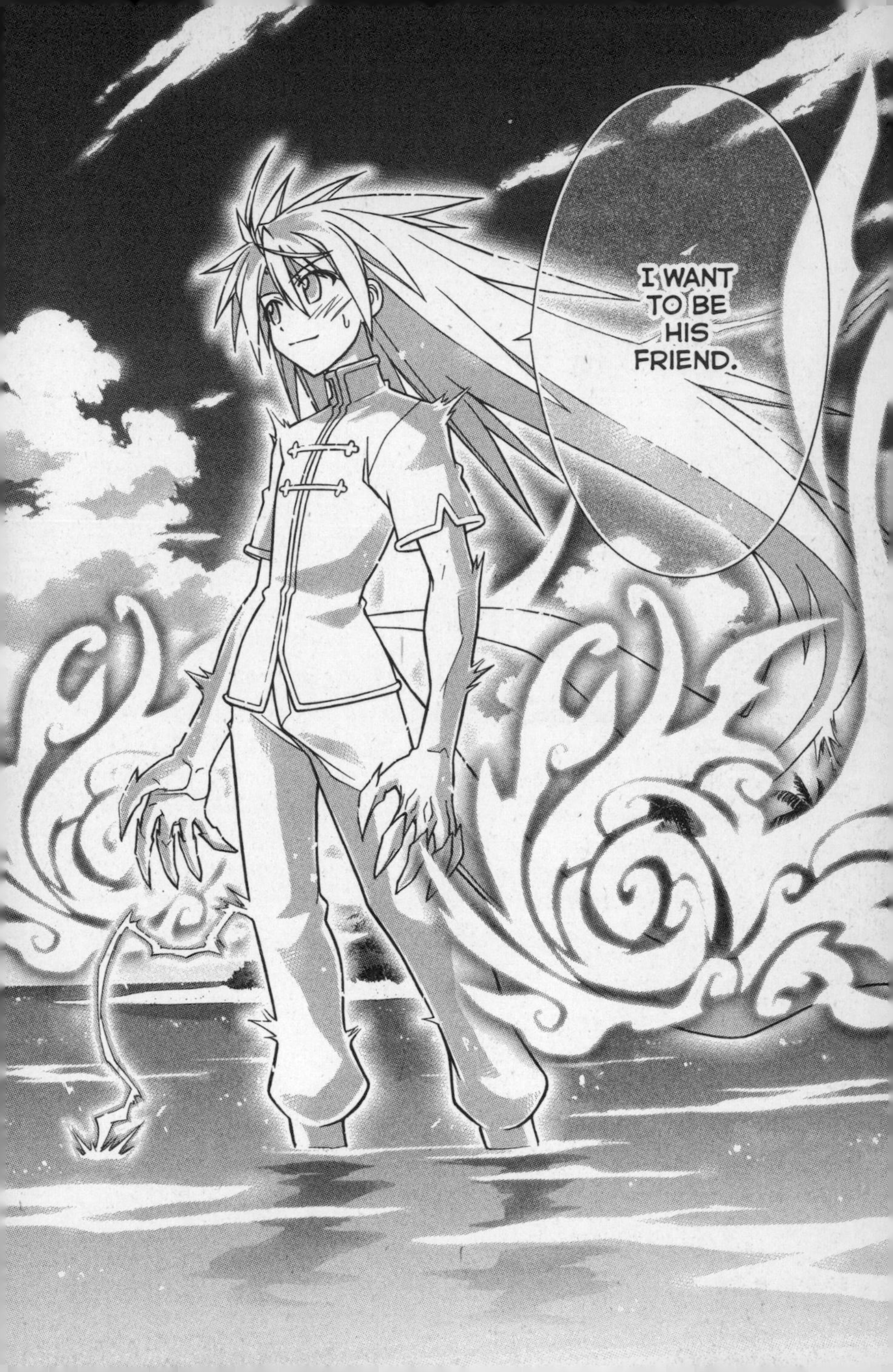
I WANT TO BE HIS FRIEND.

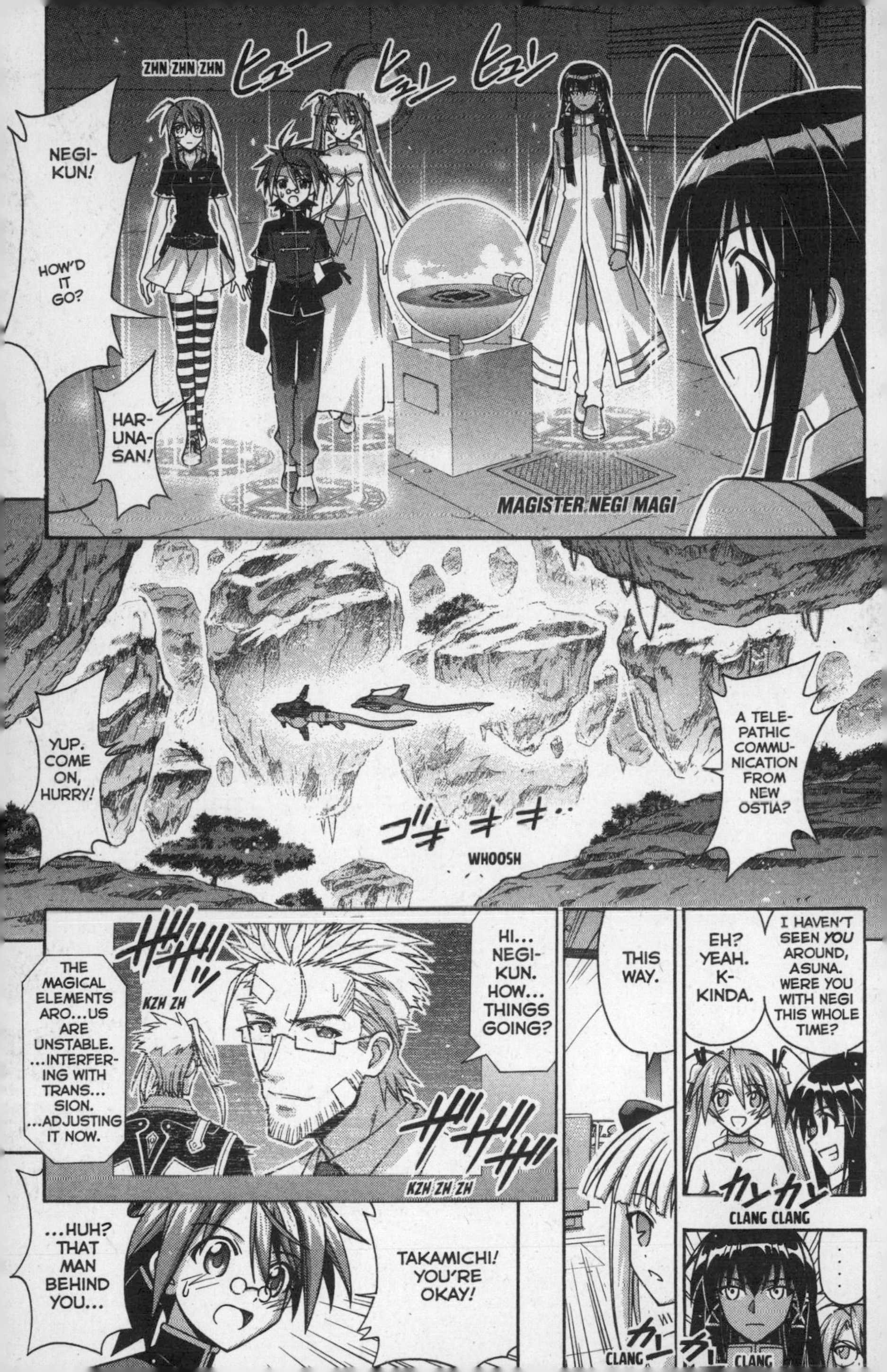
ZHN ZHN ZHN
NEGI-KUN!
HOW'D IT GO?
HARUNA-SAN!
MAGISTER NEGI MAGI
A TELEPATHIC COMMUNICATION FROM NEW OSTIA?
YUP. COME ON, HURRY!
WHOOSH
I HAVEN'T SEEN *YOU* AROUND, ASUNA. WERE YOU WITH NEGI THIS WHOLE TIME?
EH? YEAH. K-KINDA.
CLANG CLANG
...
CLANG
CLANG
THIS WAY.
HI... NEGI-KUN. HOW... THINGS GOING?
KZH ZH
THE MAGICAL ELEMENTS ARO...US ARE UNSTABLE. ...INTERFERING WITH TRANS...SION. ...ADJUSTING IT NOW.
KZH ZH ZH
TAKAMICHI! YOU'RE OKAY!
...HUH? THAT MAN BEHIND YOU...

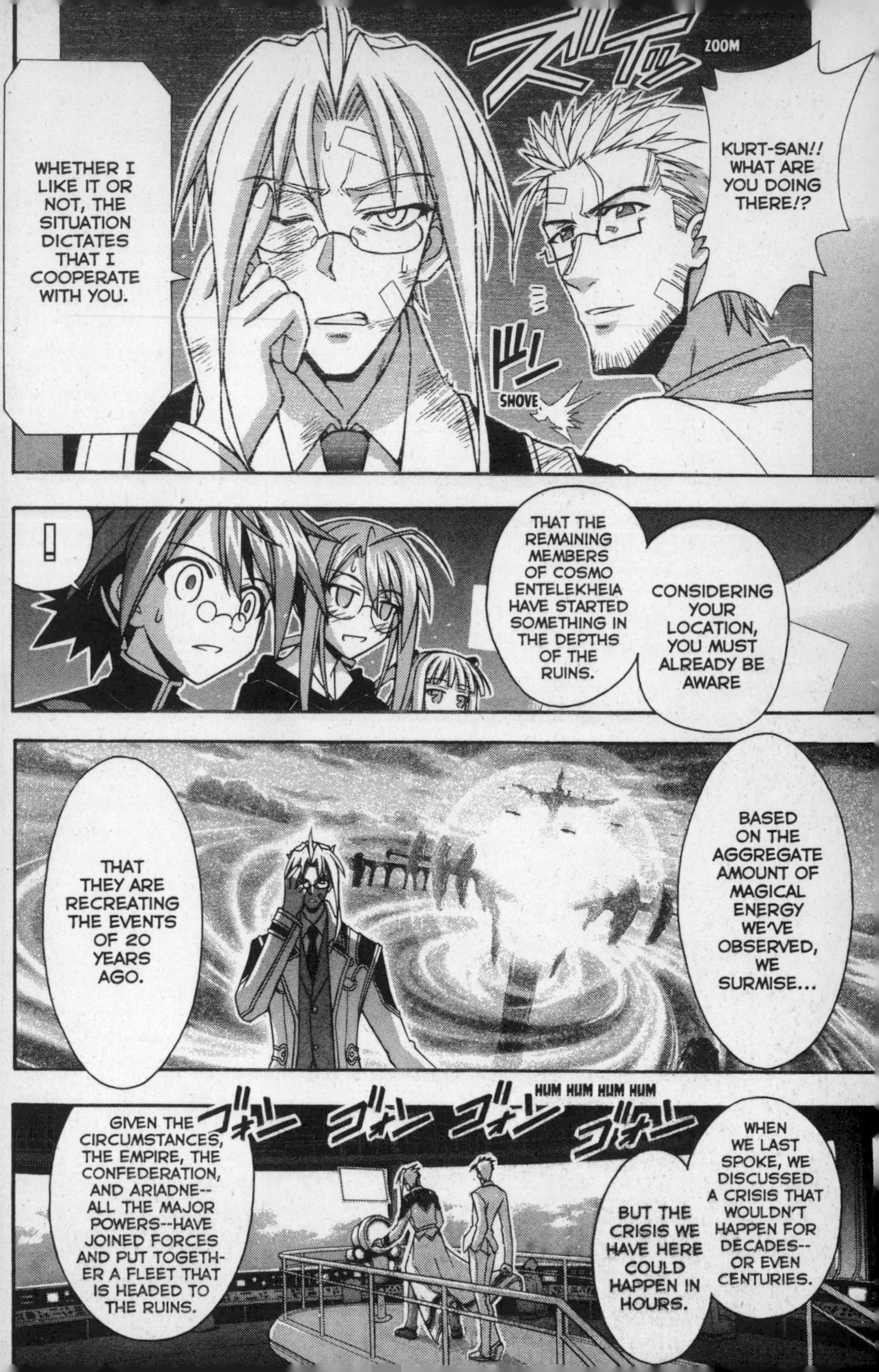
ZOOM
KURT-SAN!! WHAT ARE YOU DOING THERE!?
SHOVE
WHETHER I LIKE IT OR NOT, THE SITUATION DICTATES THAT I COOPERATE WITH YOU.
CONSIDERING YOUR LOCATION, YOU MUST ALREADY BE AWARE
THAT THE REMAINING MEMBERS OF COSMO ENTELEKHEIA HAVE STARTED SOMETHING IN THE DEPTHS OF THE RUINS.
!
BASED ON THE AGGREGATE AMOUNT OF MAGICAL ENERGY WE'VE OBSERVED, WE SURMISE...
THAT THEY ARE RECREATING THE EVENTS OF 20 YEARS AGO.
HUM HUM HUM HUM
WHEN WE LAST SPOKE, WE DISCUSSED A CRISIS THAT WOULDN'T HAPPEN FOR DECADES--OR EVEN CENTURIES.
BUT THE CRISIS WE HAVE HERE COULD HAPPEN IN HOURS.
GIVEN THE CIRCUMSTANCES, THE EMPIRE, THE CONFEDERATION, AND ARIADNE--ALL THE MAJOR POWERS--HAVE JOINED FORCES AND PUT TOGETHER A FLEET THAT IS HEADED TO THE RUINS.

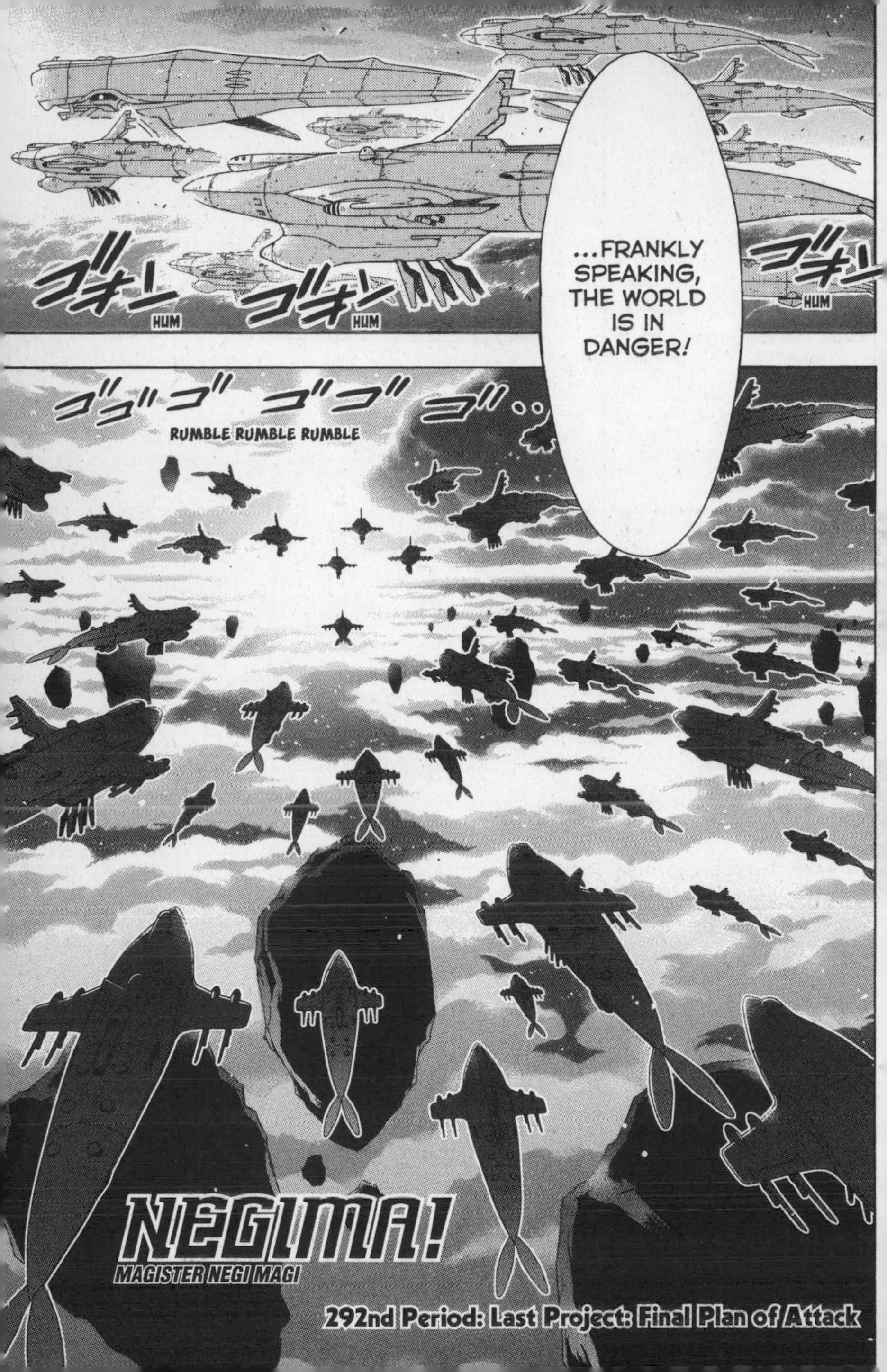
ゴォン
HUM
...FRANKLY SPEAKING, THE WORLD IS IN DANGER!
ゴォン
HUM
ゴォン
HUM
ゴゴゴ ゴゴ ゴ..
RUMBLE RUMBLE RUMBLE
NEGIMA!
MAGISTER NEGI MAGI
292nd Period: Last Project: Final Plan of Attack

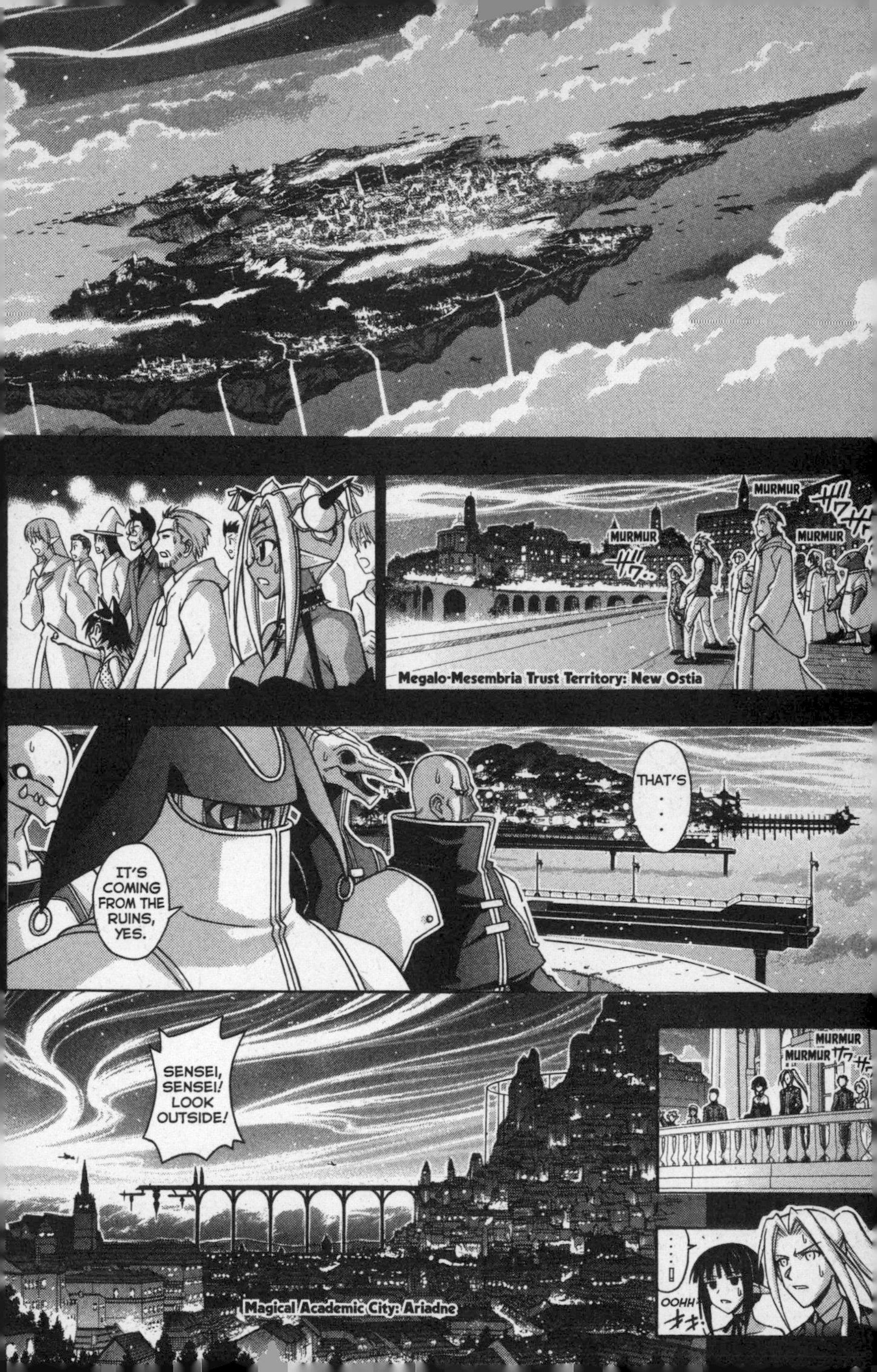
MURMUR
MURMUR
MURMUR
Megalo-Mesembria Trust Territory: New Ostia
THAT'S . . .
IT'S COMING FROM THE RUINS, YES.
MURMUR
MURMUR
. . . !
OOHH
SENSEI, SENSEI! LOOK OUTSIDE!
Magical Academic City: Ariadne

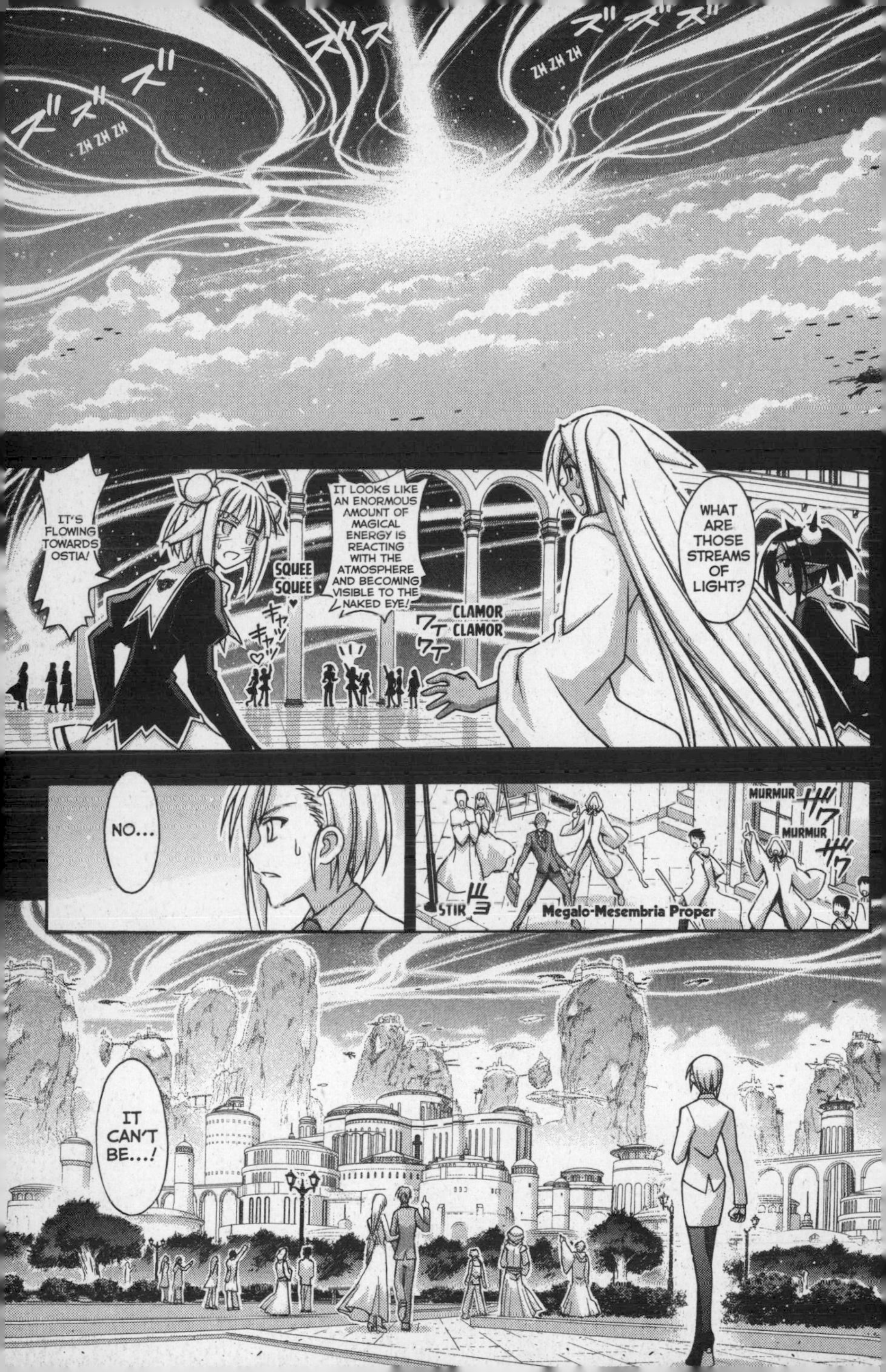
ズズズ
ZH ZH ZH
ズズ
ズズズ
ZH ZH ZH
WHAT ARE THOSE STREAMS OF LIGHT?
CLAMOR CLAMOR
ワイワイ
IT LOOKS LIKE AN ENORMOUS AMOUNT OF MAGICAL ENERGY IS REACTING WITH THE ATMOSPHERE AND BECOMING VISIBLE TO THE NAKED EYE!
SQUEE SQUEE
キャッキャッ
IT'S FLOWING TOWARDS OSTIA!
MURMUR ザワ
MURMUR ザワ
STIR ドヨ
Megalo-Mesembria Proper
NO...
IT CAN'T BE...!

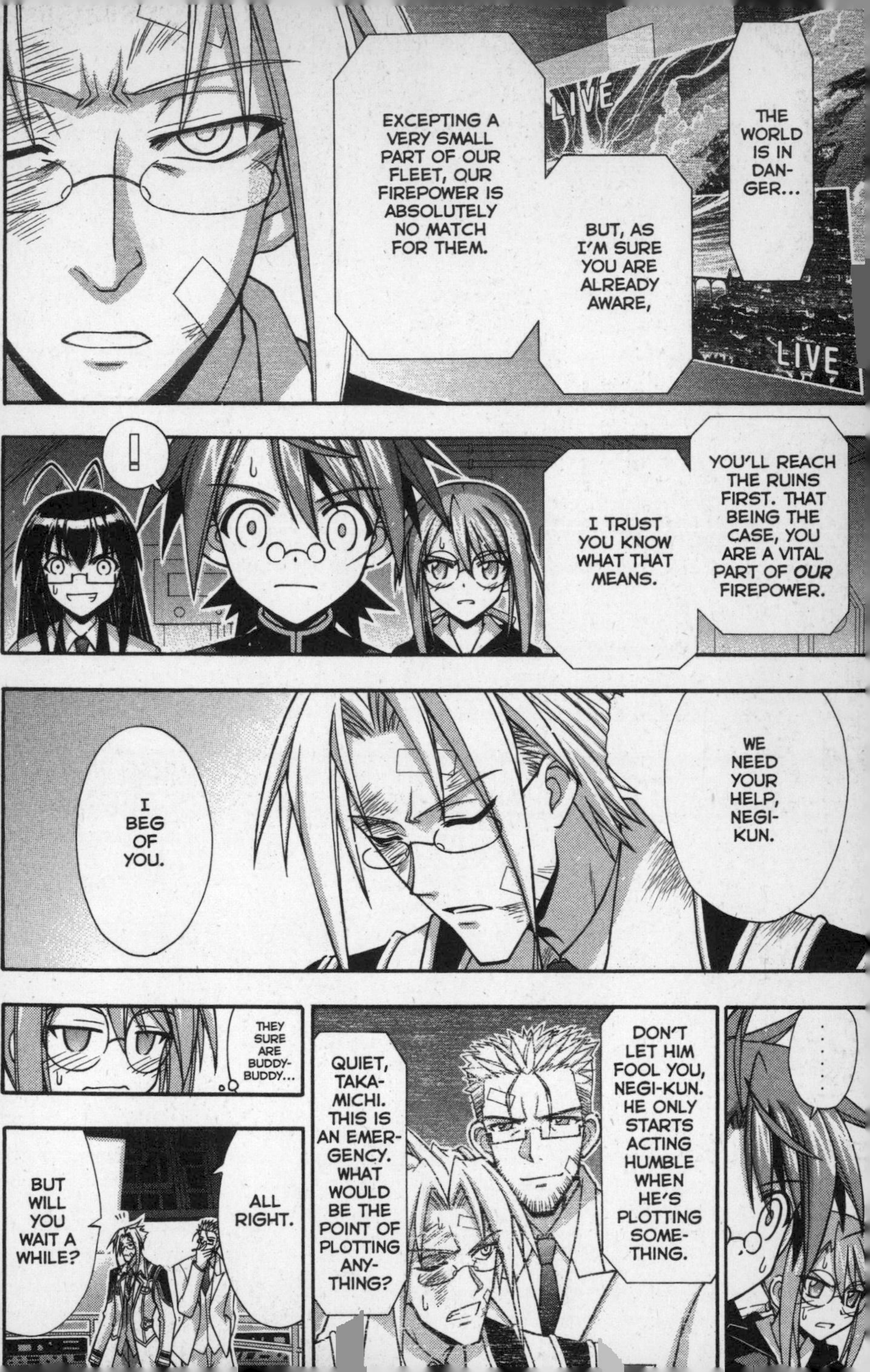
LIVE
LIVE
THE WORLD IS IN DANGER...
BUT, AS I'M SURE YOU ARE ALREADY AWARE,
EXCEPTING A VERY SMALL PART OF OUR FLEET, OUR FIREPOWER IS ABSOLUTELY NO MATCH FOR THEM.
YOU'LL REACH THE RUINS FIRST. THAT BEING THE CASE, YOU ARE A VITAL PART OF *OUR* FIREPOWER.
I TRUST YOU KNOW WHAT THAT MEANS.
!
WE NEED YOUR HELP, NEGI-KUN.
I BEG OF YOU.
.....
DON'T LET HIM FOOL YOU, NEGI-KUN. HE ONLY STARTS ACTING HUMBLE WHEN HE'S PLOTTING SOMETHING.
QUIET, TAKAMICHI. THIS IS AN EMERGENCY. WHAT WOULD BE THE POINT OF PLOTTING ANYTHING?
THEY SURE ARE BUDDY-BUDDY...
ALL RIGHT.
BUT WILL YOU WAIT A WHILE?

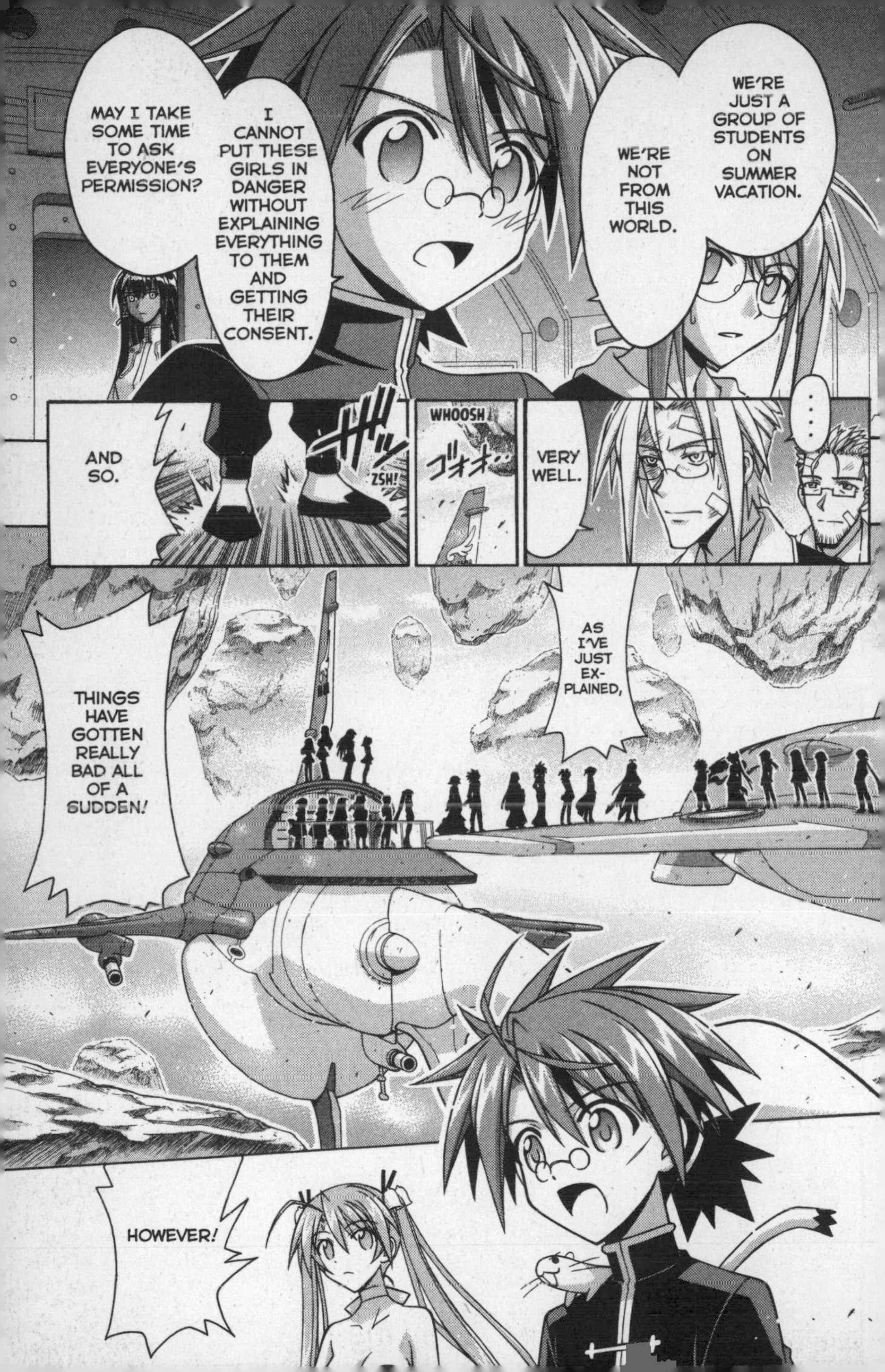
WE'RE JUST A GROUP OF STUDENTS ON SUMMER VACATION.
WE'RE NOT FROM THIS WORLD.
I CANNOT PUT THESE GIRLS IN DANGER WITHOUT EXPLAINING EVERYTHING TO THEM AND GETTING THEIR CONSENT.
MAY I TAKE SOME TIME TO ASK EVERYONE'S PERMISSION?
...
VERY WELL.
WHOOSH
ゴォオ…
ZSH!
ザッ
AND SO.
AS I'VE JUST EX-PLAINED,
THINGS HAVE GOTTEN REALLY BAD ALL OF A SUDDEN!
HOWEVER!

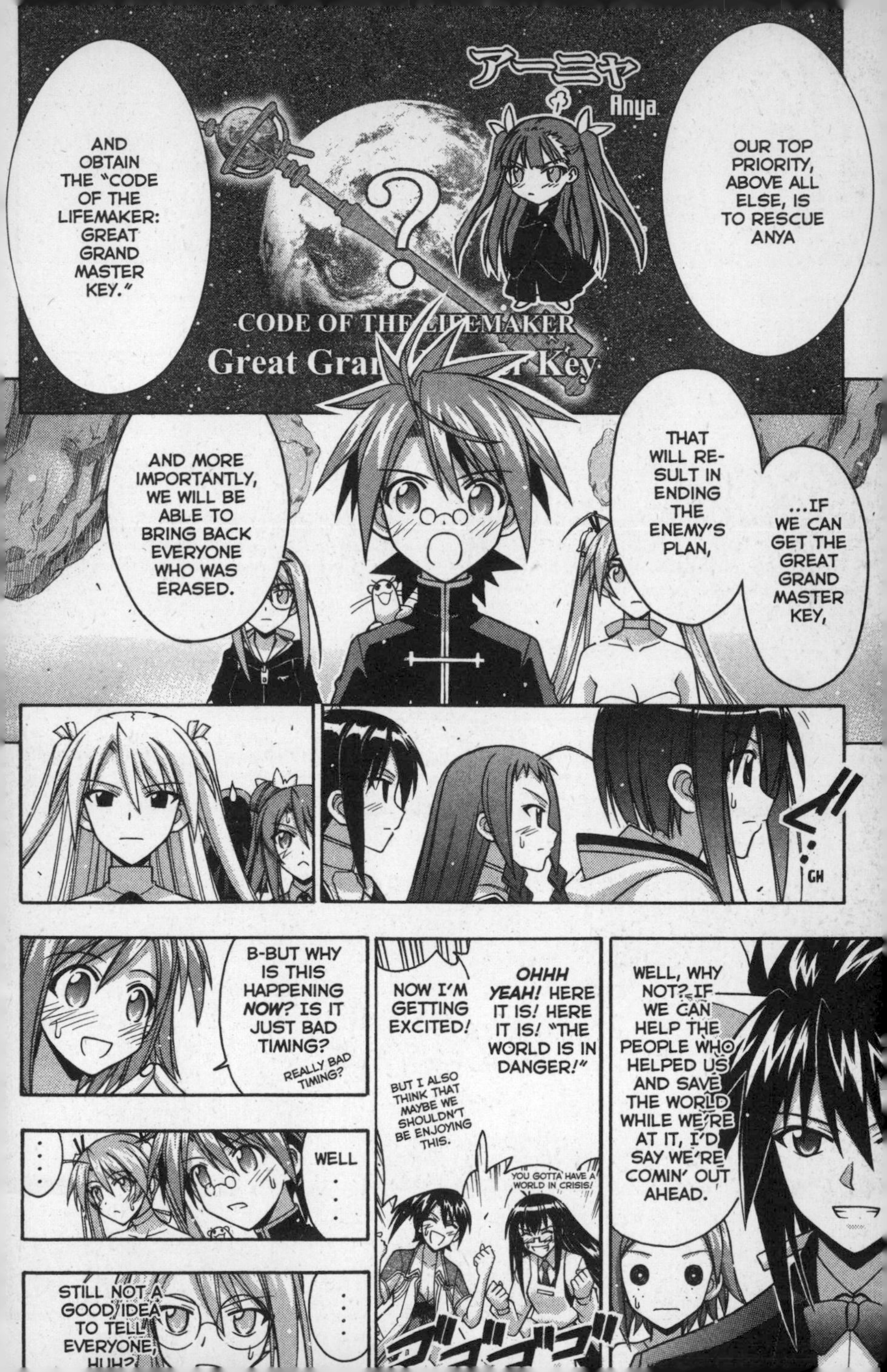

アーニャ
Anya
OUR TOP PRIORITY, ABOVE ALL ELSE, IS TO RESCUE ANYA
AND OBTAIN THE "CODE OF THE LIFEMAKER: GREAT GRAND MASTER KEY."
...IF WE CAN GET THE GREAT GRAND MASTER KEY,
THAT WILL RESULT IN ENDING THE ENEMY'S PLAN,
AND MORE IMPORTANTLY, WE WILL BE ABLE TO BRING BACK EVERYONE WHO WAS ERASED.
GH
WELL, WHY NOT? IF WE CAN HELP THE PEOPLE WHO HELPED US AND SAVE THE WORLD WHILE WE'RE AT IT, I'D SAY WE'RE COMIN' OUT AHEAD.
OHHH YEAH! HERE IT IS! HERE IT IS! "THE WORLD IS IN DANGER!"
NOW I'M GETTING EXCITED!
BUT I ALSO THINK THAT MAYBE WE SHOULDN'T BE ENJOYING THIS.
YOU GOTTA HAVE A WORLD IN CRISIS!
B-BUT WHY IS THIS HAPPENING NOW? IS IT JUST BAD TIMING?
REALLY BAD TIMING?
WELL
......
......
STILL NOT A GOOD IDEA TO TELL EVERYONE, HUH?
......

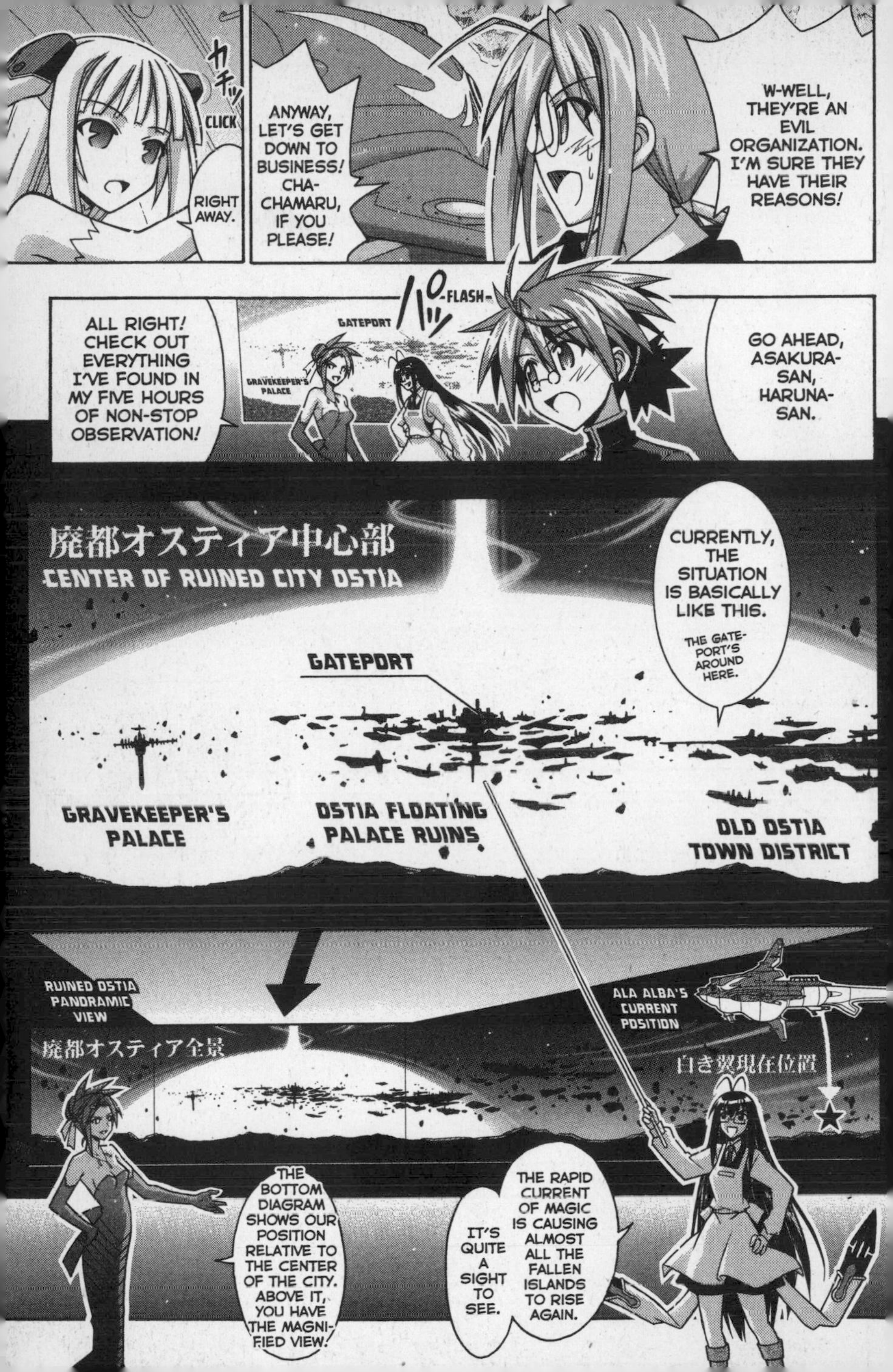
W-WELL, THEY'RE AN EVIL ORGANIZATION. I'M SURE THEY HAVE THEIR REASONS!
ANYWAY, LET'S GET DOWN TO BUSINESS! CHA-CHAMARU, IF YOU PLEASE!
カチッ
CLICK
RIGHT AWAY.
GO AHEAD, ASAKURA-SAN, HARUNA-SAN.
パッ
-FLASH-
GATEPORT
GRAVEKEEPER'S PALACE
ALL RIGHT! CHECK OUT EVERYTHING I'VE FOUND IN MY FIVE HOURS OF NON-STOP OBSERVATION!
CURRENTLY, THE SITUATION IS BASICALLY LIKE THIS.
THE GATE-PORT'S AROUND HERE.
廃都オスティア中心部
CENTER OF RUINED CITY OSTIA
GATEPORT
OLD OSTIA TOWN DISTRICT
OSTIA FLOATING PALACE RUINS
GRAVEKEEPER'S PALACE
ALA ALBA'S CURRENT POSITION
白き翼現在位置
RUINED OSTIA PANORAMIC VIEW
廃都オスティア全景
THE RAPID CURRENT OF MAGIC IS CAUSING ALMOST ALL THE FALLEN ISLANDS TO RISE AGAIN.
IT'S QUITE A SIGHT TO SEE.
THE BOTTOM DIAGRAM SHOWS OUR POSITION RELATIVE TO THE CENTER OF THE CITY. ABOVE IT, YOU HAVE THE MAGNIFIED VIEW.

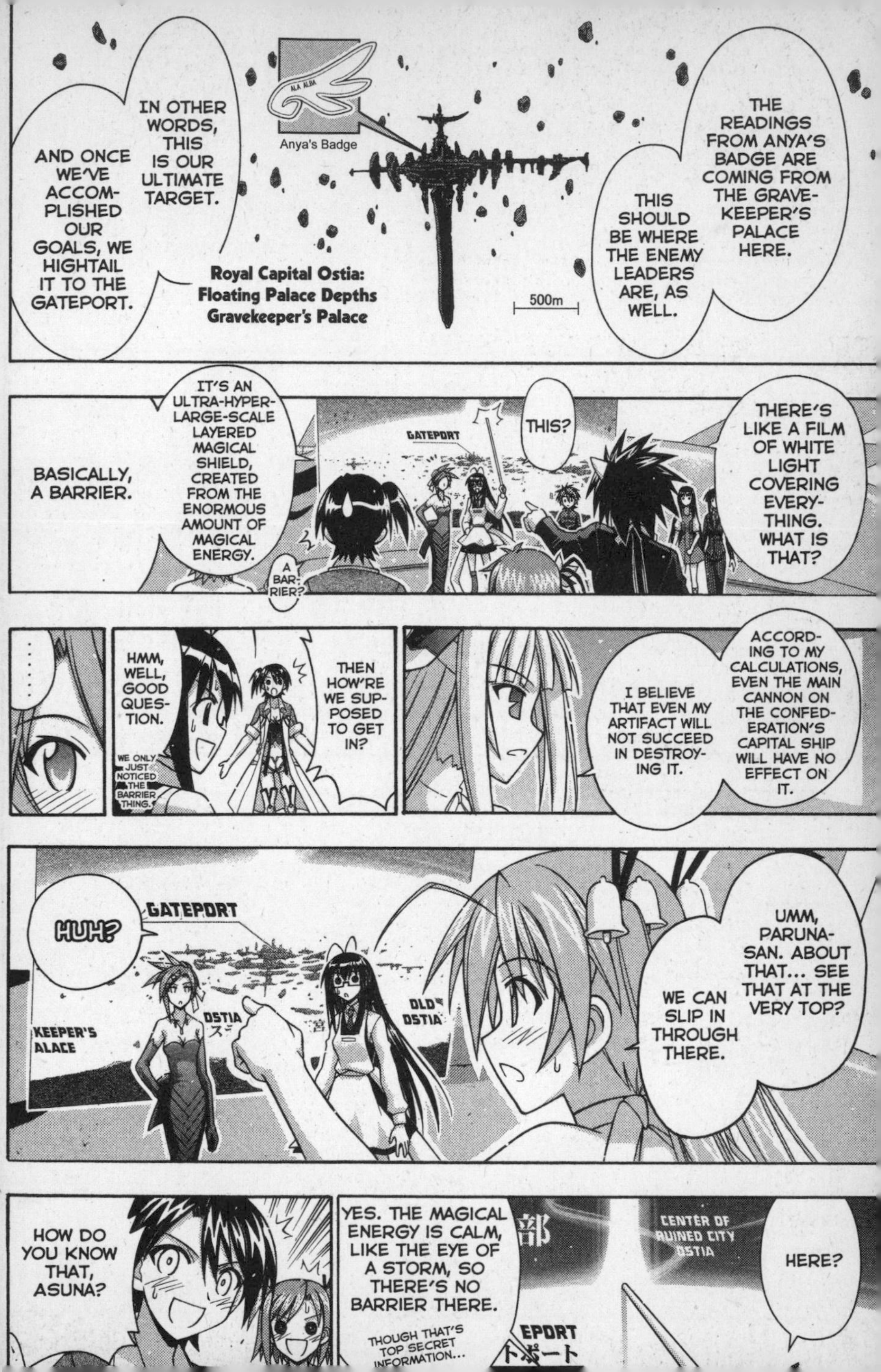
THE READINGS FROM ANYA'S BADGE ARE COMING FROM THE GRAVE-KEEPER'S PALACE HERE.
THIS SHOULD BE WHERE THE ENEMY LEADERS ARE, AS WELL.
500m
ALA ALBA
Anya's Badge
Royal Capital Ostia: Floating Palace Depths Gravekeeper's Palace
IN OTHER WORDS, THIS IS OUR ULTIMATE TARGET.
AND ONCE WE'VE ACCOM-PLISHED OUR GOALS, WE HIGHTAIL IT TO THE GATEPORT.
THERE'S LIKE A FILM OF WHITE LIGHT COVERING EVERY-THING. WHAT IS THAT?
THIS?
GATEPORT
IT'S AN ULTRA-HYPER-LARGE-SCALE LAYERED MAGICAL SHIELD, CREATED FROM THE ENORMOUS AMOUNT OF MAGICAL ENERGY.
BASICALLY, A BARRIER.
A BAR-RIER?
ACCORD-ING TO MY CALCULATIONS, EVEN THE MAIN CANNON ON THE CONFED-ERATION'S CAPITAL SHIP WILL HAVE NO EFFECT ON IT.
I BELIEVE THAT EVEN MY ARTIFACT WILL NOT SUCCEED IN DESTROY-ING IT.
THEN HOW'RE WE SUP-POSED TO GET IN?
HMM, WELL, GOOD QUES-TION.
WE ONLY JUST NOTICED THE BARRIER THING.
......
UMM, PARUNA-SAN. ABOUT THAT... SEE THAT AT THE VERY TOP?
WE CAN SLIP IN THROUGH THERE.
OLD OSTIA
GATEPORT
HUH?
OSTIA
KEEPER'S ALACE
HERE?
CENTER OF RUINED CITY OSTIA
部
EPORT
トポート
YES. THE MAGICAL ENERGY IS CALM, LIKE THE EYE OF A STORM, SO THERE'S NO BARRIER THERE.
THOUGH THAT'S TOP SECRET INFORMATION...
HOW DO YOU KNOW THAT, ASUNA?

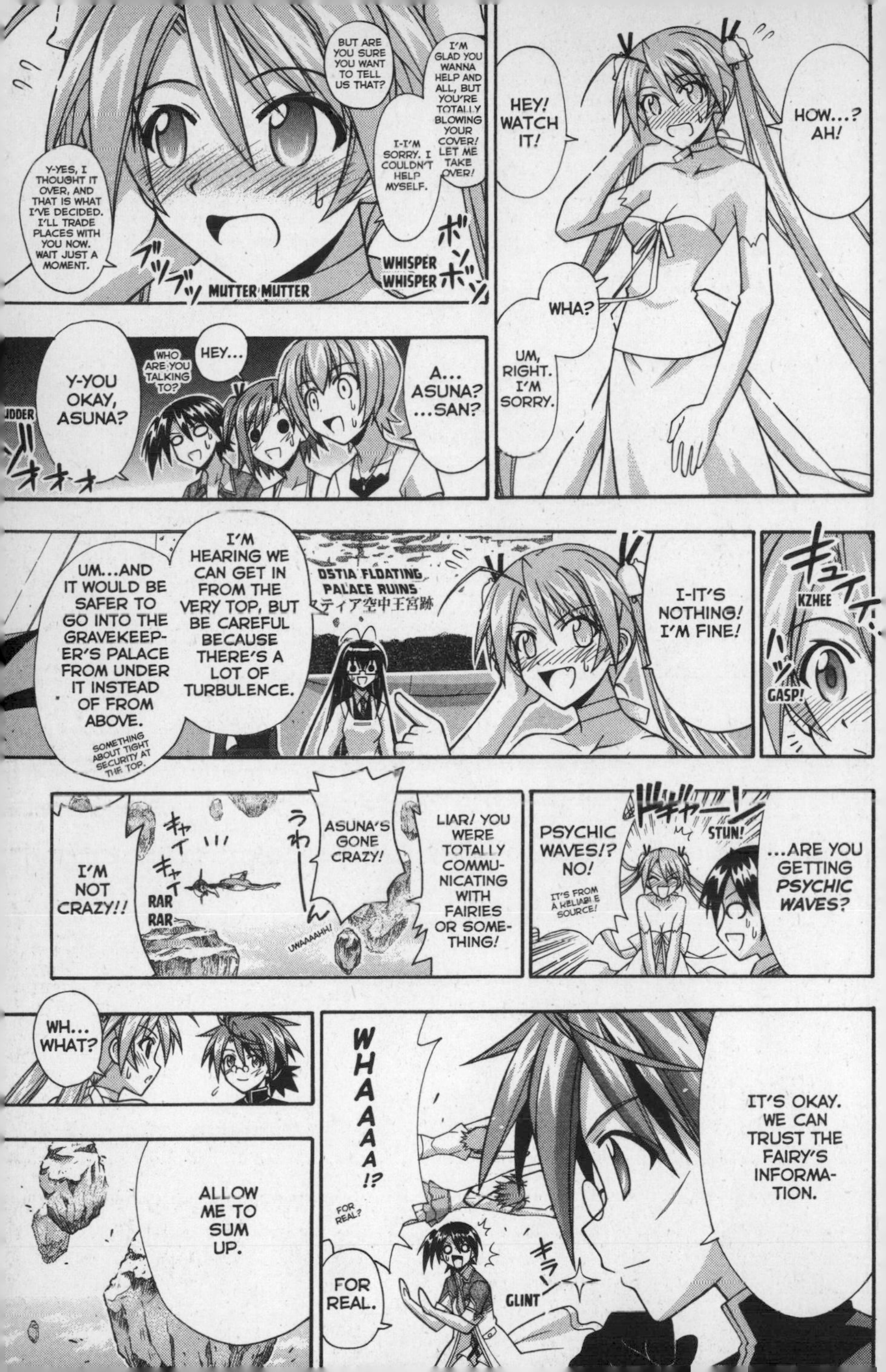
HOW...? AH!
HEY! WATCH IT!
WHA?
UM, RIGHT. I'M SORRY.
I'M GLAD YOU WANNA HELP AND ALL, BUT YOU'RE TOTALLY BLOWING YOUR COVER! LET ME TAKE OVER!
BUT ARE YOU SURE YOU WANT TO TELL US THAT?
I-I'M SORRY. I COULDN'T HELP MYSELF.
WHISPER WHISPER
Y-YES, I THOUGHT IT OVER, AND THAT IS WHAT I'VE DECIDED. I'LL TRADE PLACES WITH YOU NOW. WAIT JUST A MOMENT.
MUTTER MUTTER
A... ASUNA? ...SAN?
HEY...
WHO ARE YOU TALKING TO?
Y-YOU OKAY, ASUNA?
KZHEE
GASP!
I-IT'S NOTHING! I'M FINE!
OSTIA FLOATING PALACE RUINS
I'M HEARING WE CAN GET IN FROM THE VERY TOP, BUT BE CAREFUL BECAUSE THERE'S A LOT OF TURBULENCE.
UM...AND IT WOULD BE SAFER TO GO INTO THE GRAVEKEEPER'S PALACE FROM UNDER IT INSTEAD OF FROM ABOVE.
SOMETHING ABOUT TIGHT SECURITY AT THE TOP.
...ARE YOU GETTING PSYCHIC WAVES?
STUN!
PSYCHIC WAVES!? NO!
IT'S FROM A RELIABLE SOURCE!
LIAR! YOU WERE TOTALLY COMMUNICATING WITH FAIRIES OR SOMETHING!
ASUNA'S GONE CRAZY!
UWAAAAHH!
RAR RAR
I'M NOT CRAZY!!
IT'S OKAY. WE CAN TRUST THE FAIRY'S INFORMATION.
GLINT
WHAAAAA!?
FOR REAL?
FOR REAL.
WH... WHAT?
ALLOW ME TO SUM UP.

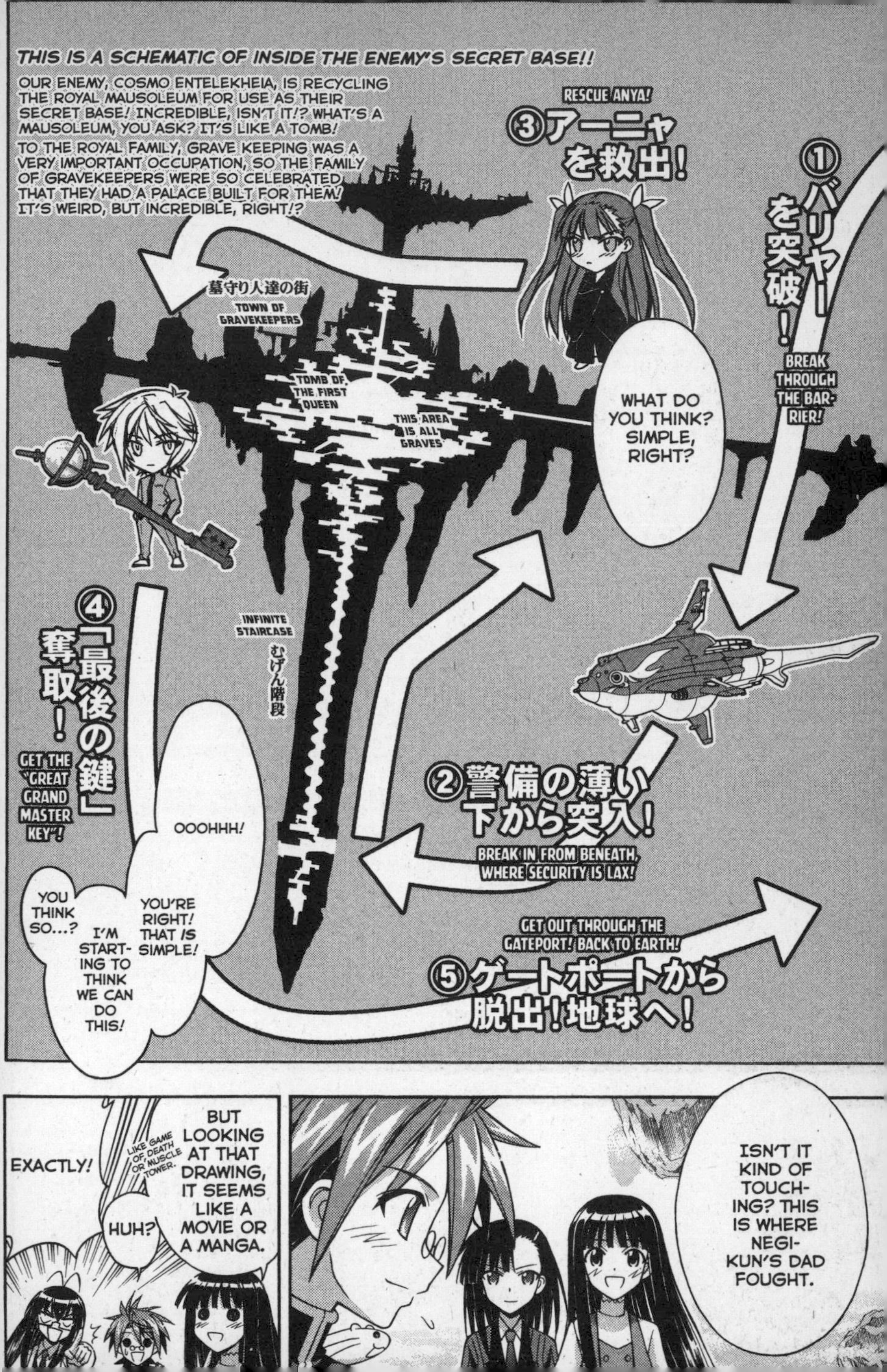
THIS IS A SCHEMATIC OF INSIDE THE ENEMY'S SECRET BASE!!
OUR ENEMY, COSMO ENTELEKHEIA, IS RECYCLING THE ROYAL MAUSOLEUM FOR USE AS THEIR SECRET BASE! INCREDIBLE, ISN'T IT!? WHAT'S A MAUSOLEUM, YOU ASK? IT'S LIKE A TOMB!
TO THE ROYAL FAMILY, GRAVE KEEPING WAS A VERY IMPORTANT OCCUPATION, SO THE FAMILY OF GRAVEKEEPERS WERE SO CELEBRATED THAT THEY HAD A PALACE BUILT FOR THEM! IT'S WEIRD, BUT INCREDIBLE, RIGHT!?
①バリヤーを突破!
BREAK THROUGH THE BAR-RIER!
②警備の薄い下から突入!
BREAK IN FROM BENEATH, WHERE SECURITY IS LAX!
③アーニャを救出!
RESCUE ANYA!
④「最後の鍵」奪取!
GET THE "GREAT GRAND MASTER KEY"!
⑤ゲートポートから脱出!地球へ!
GET OUT THROUGH THE GATEPORT! BACK TO EARTH!
墓守り人達の街
TOWN OF GRAVEKEEPERS
TOMB OF THE FIRST QUEEN
THIS AREA IS ALL GRAVES
INFINITE STAIRCASE
むげん階段
WHAT DO YOU THINK? SIMPLE, RIGHT?
OOOHHH!
YOU'RE RIGHT! THAT IS SIMPLE!
YOU THINK SO...?
I'M STARTING TO THINK WE CAN DO THIS!
ISN'T IT KIND OF TOUCHING? THIS IS WHERE NEGI-KUN'S DAD FOUGHT.
BUT LOOKING AT THAT DRAWING, IT SEEMS LIKE A MOVIE OR A MANGA.
LIKE GAME OF DEATH OR MUSCLE TOWER.
HUH?
EXACTLY!

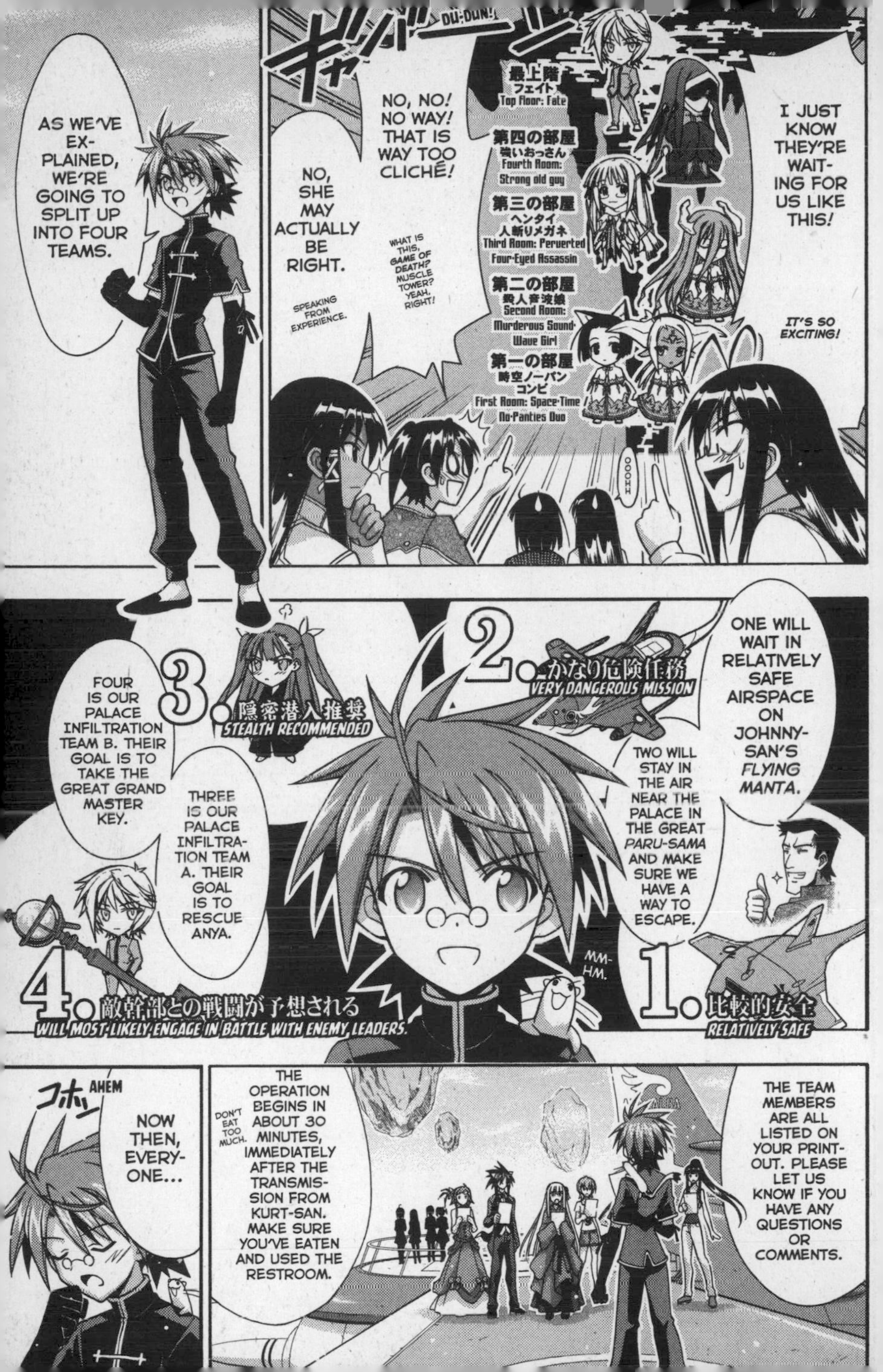

DU-DUN!
I JUST KNOW THEY'RE WAITING FOR US LIKE THIS!
IT'S SO EXCITING!
最上階 フェイト Top Floor: Fate
第四の部屋 強いおっさん Fourth Room: Strong old guy
第三の部屋 ヘンタイ人斬りメガネ Third Room: Perverted Four-Eyed Assassin
第二の部屋 殺人音波娘 Second Room: Murderous Sound-Wave Girl
第一の部屋 時空ノーパンコンビ First Room: Space-Time No-Panties Duo
NO, NO! NO WAY! THAT IS WAY TOO CLICHÉ!
WHAT IS THIS, GAME OF DEATH? MUSCLE TOWER? YEAH, RIGHT!
NO, SHE MAY ACTUALLY BE RIGHT.
SPEAKING FROM EXPERIENCE.
OOOKH
AS WE'VE EXPLAINED, WE'RE GOING TO SPLIT UP INTO FOUR TEAMS.
ONE WILL WAIT IN RELATIVELY SAFE AIRSPACE ON JOHNNY-SAN'S FLYING MANTA.
1. 比較的安全 RELATIVELY SAFE
2. かなり危険任務 VERY DANGEROUS MISSION
TWO WILL STAY IN THE AIR NEAR THE PALACE IN THE GREAT PARU-SAMA AND MAKE SURE WE HAVE A WAY TO ESCAPE.
MM-HM.
THREE IS OUR PALACE INFILTRATION TEAM A. THEIR GOAL IS TO RESCUE ANYA.
3. 隠密潜入推奨 STEALTH RECOMMENDED
FOUR IS OUR PALACE INFILTRATION TEAM B. THEIR GOAL IS TO TAKE THE GREAT GRAND MASTER KEY.
4. 敵幹部との戦闘が予想される WILL MOST LIKELY ENGAGE IN BATTLE WITH ENEMY LEADERS.
THE TEAM MEMBERS ARE ALL LISTED ON YOUR PRINTOUT. PLEASE LET US KNOW IF YOU HAVE ANY QUESTIONS OR COMMENTS.
THE OPERATION BEGINS IN ABOUT 30 MINUTES, IMMEDIATELY AFTER THE TRANSMISSION FROM KURT-SAN. MAKE SURE YOU'VE EATEN AND USED THE RESTROOM.
DON'T EAT TOO MUCH.
コホン AHEM
NOW THEN, EVERYONE...

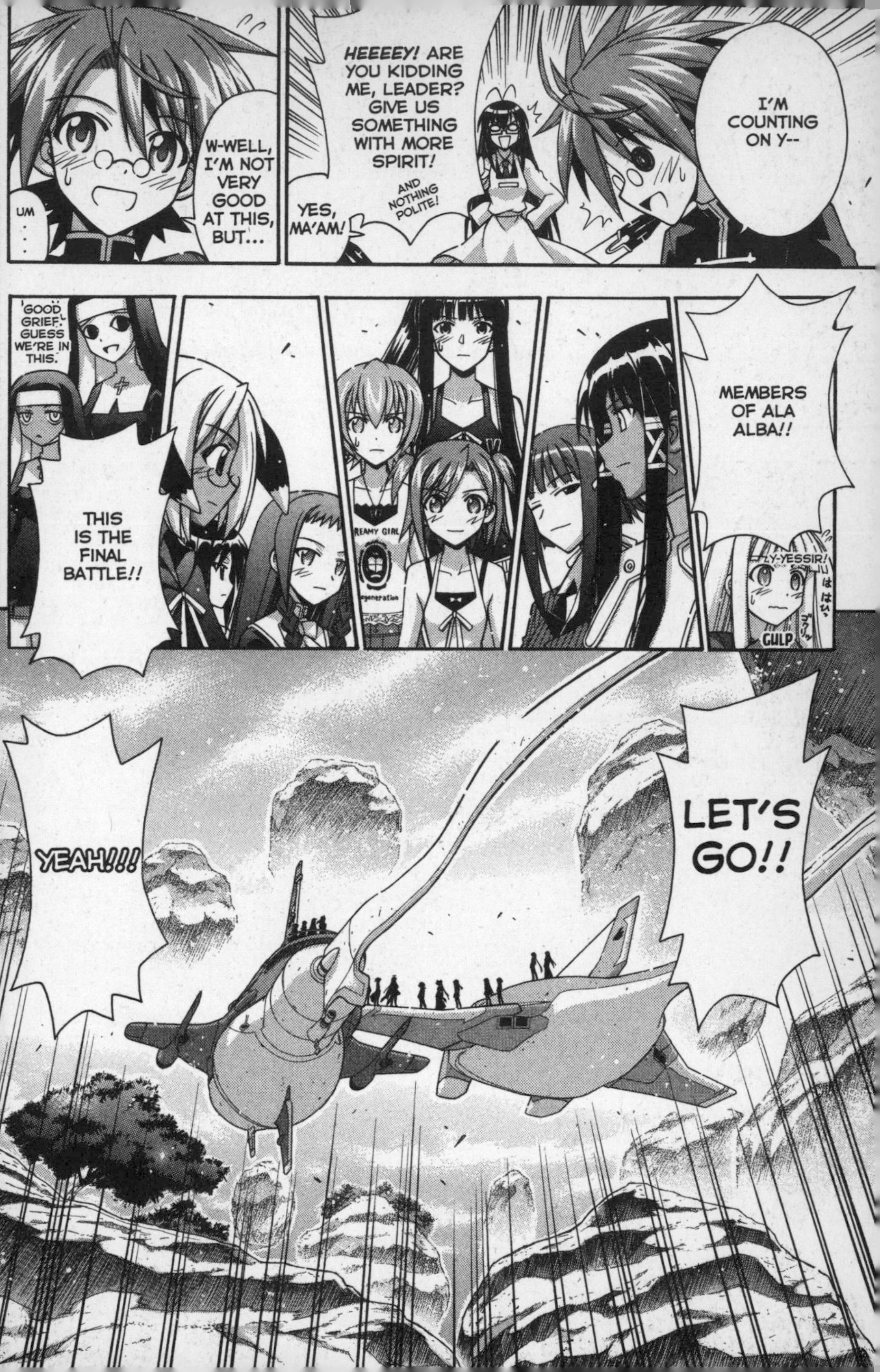
I'M COUNTING ON Y--
HEEEEY! ARE YOU KIDDING ME, LEADER? GIVE US SOMETHING WITH MORE SPIRIT!
AND NOTHING POLITE!
YES, MA'AM!
W-WELL, I'M NOT VERY GOOD AT THIS, BUT...
UM...
MEMBERS OF ALA ALBA!!
LY-YESSIR!
GULP
THIS IS THE FINAL BATTLE!!
GOOD GRIEF. GUESS WE'RE IN THIS.
LET'S GO!!
YEAH!!!

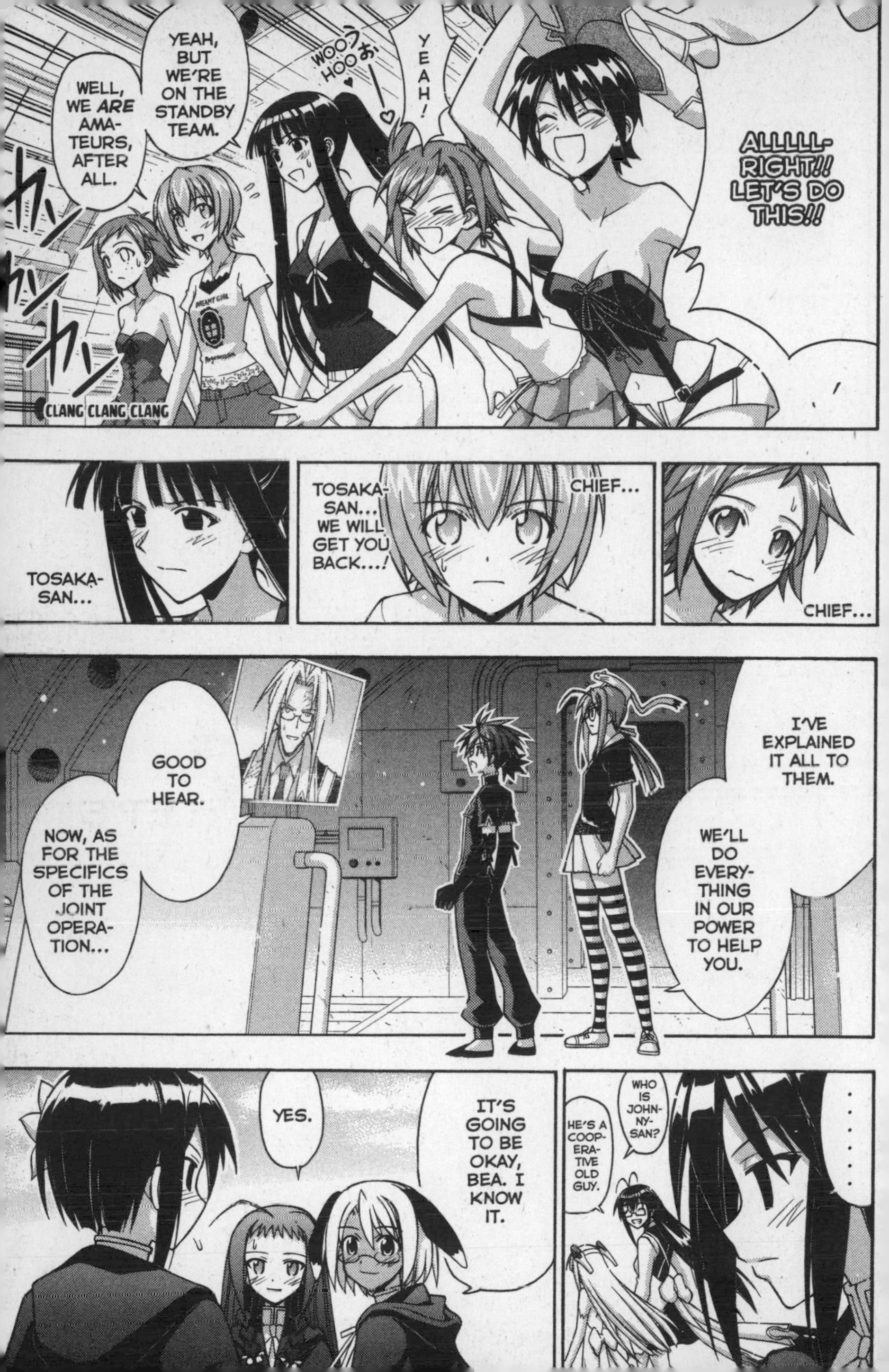
ALLLLL-RIGHT!! LET'S DO THIS!!
YEAH!
WOO HOO ♥
YEAH, BUT WE'RE ON THE STANDBY TEAM.
WELL, WE *ARE* AMATEURS, AFTER ALL.
CLANG CLANG CLANG
CHIEF...
CHIEF...
TOSAKA-SAN... WE WILL GET YOU BACK...!
TOSAKA-SAN...
I'VE EXPLAINED IT ALL TO THEM.
WE'LL DO EVERYTHING IN OUR POWER TO HELP YOU.
GOOD TO HEAR.
NOW, AS FOR THE SPECIFICS OF THE JOINT OPERATION...
......
WHO IS JOHNNY-SAN?
HE'S A COOPERATIVE OLD GUY.
IT'S GOING TO BE OKAY, BEA. I KNOW IT.
YES.

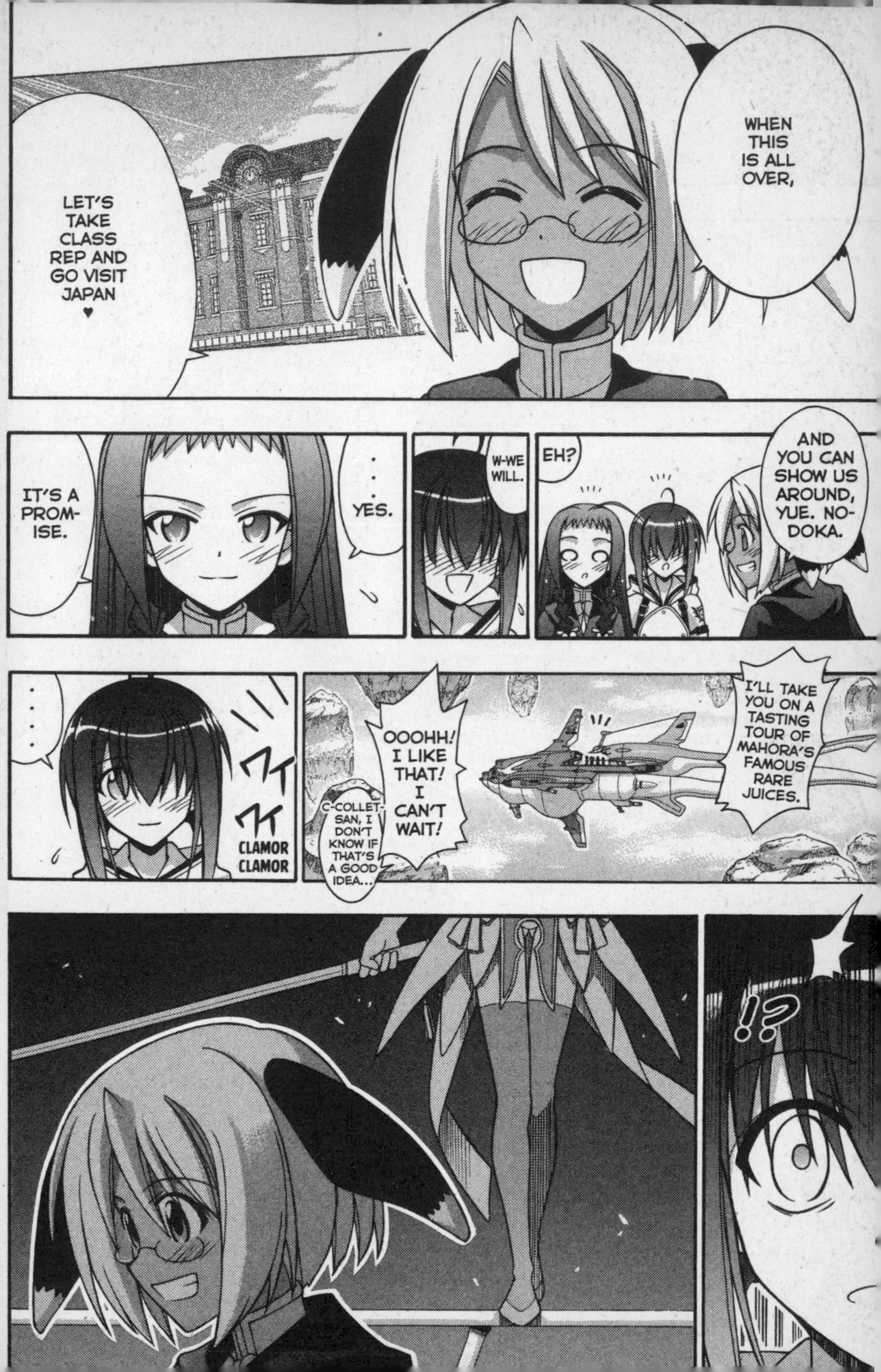
WHEN THIS IS ALL OVER,
LET'S TAKE CLASS REP AND GO VISIT JAPAN ♥
AND YOU CAN SHOW US AROUND, YUE. NO-DOKA.
EH?
W-WE WILL.
...YES.
IT'S A PROM-ISE.
I'LL TAKE YOU ON A TASTING TOUR OF MAHORA'S FAMOUS RARE JUICES.
OOOHH! I LIKE THAT! I CAN'T WAIT!
C-COLLET-SAN, I DON'T KNOW IF THAT'S A GOOD IDEA...
....
CLAMOR CLAMOR
!?

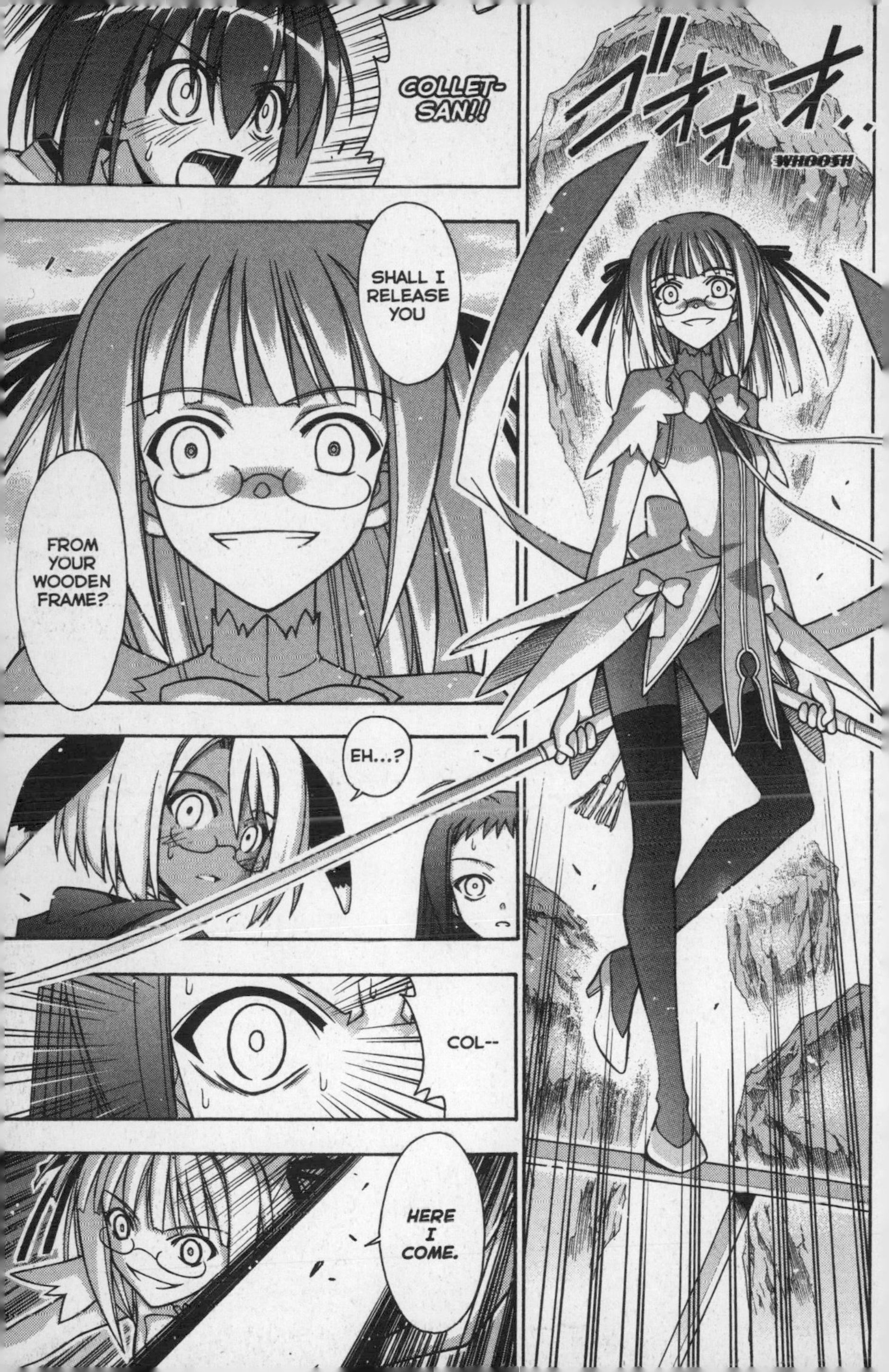
ゴォォオ..
WHOOSH
COLLET-SAN!!
SHALL I RELEASE YOU
FROM YOUR WOODEN FRAME?
EH...?
COL--
HERE I COME.

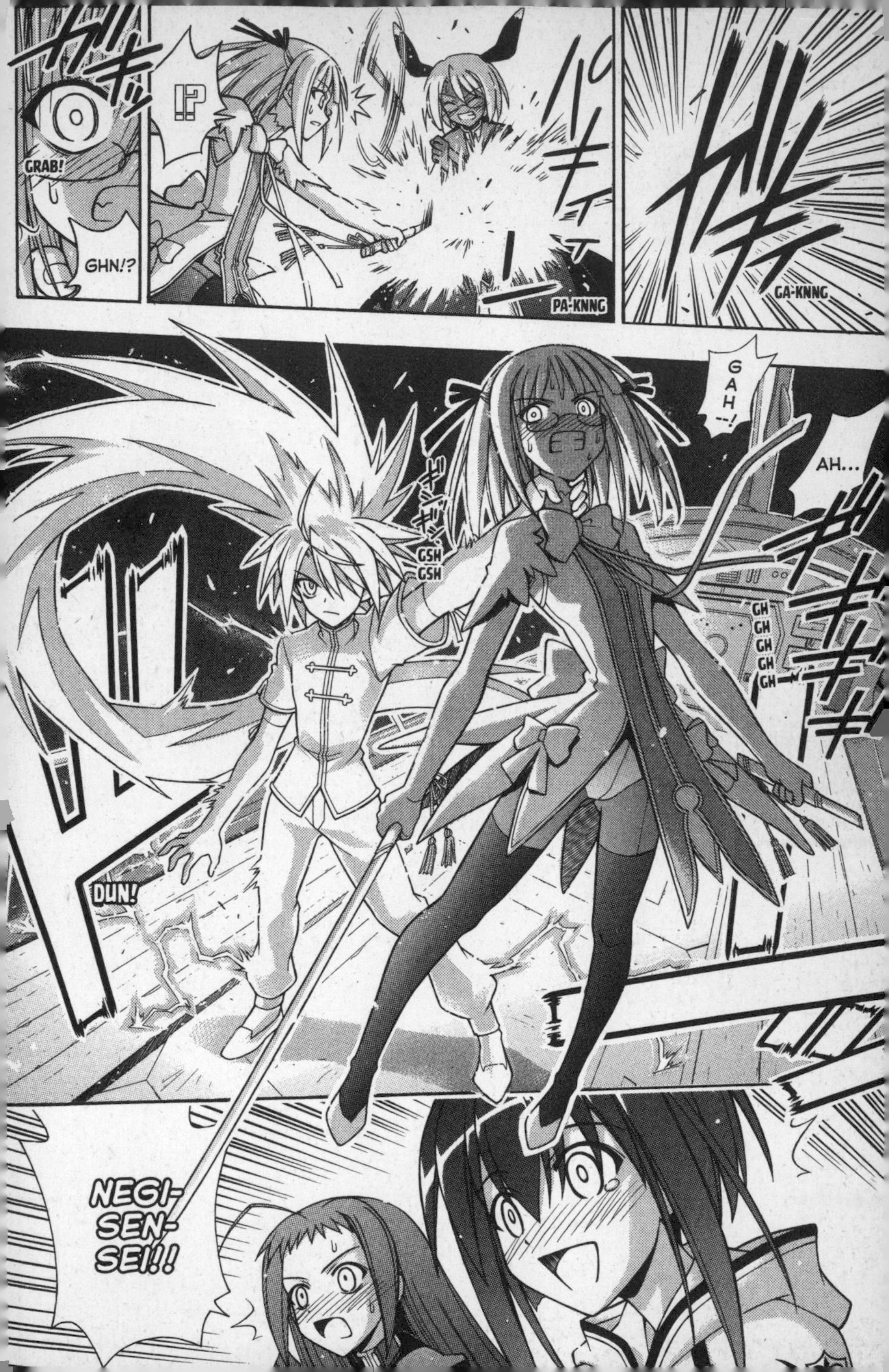
GA-KNNG
PA-KNNG
!?
GRAB!
GHN!?
GAH --!
AH...
GH
GH
GH
GH
GH
GSH
GSH
DUN!
NEGI-SEN-SEI!!

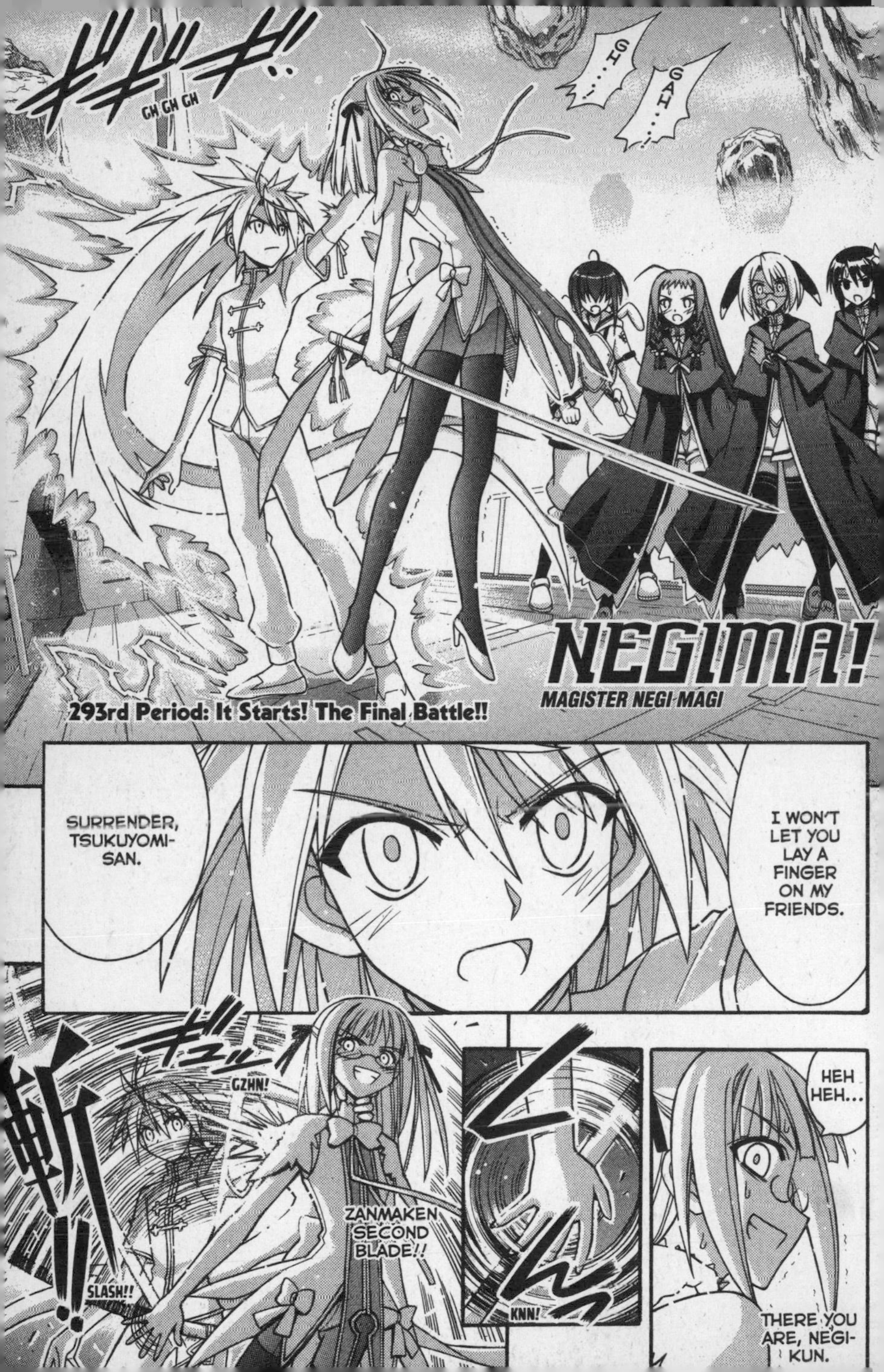
GAH...!
GH...!
GH GH GH
NEGIMA!
MAGISTER NEGI MAGI
293rd Period: It Starts! The Final Battle!!
I WON'T LET YOU LAY A FINGER ON MY FRIENDS.
SURRENDER, TSUKUYOMI-SAN.
HEH HEH...
THERE YOU ARE, NEGI-KUN.
KNN!
GZHN!
ZANMAKEN SECOND BLADE!!
SLASH!!

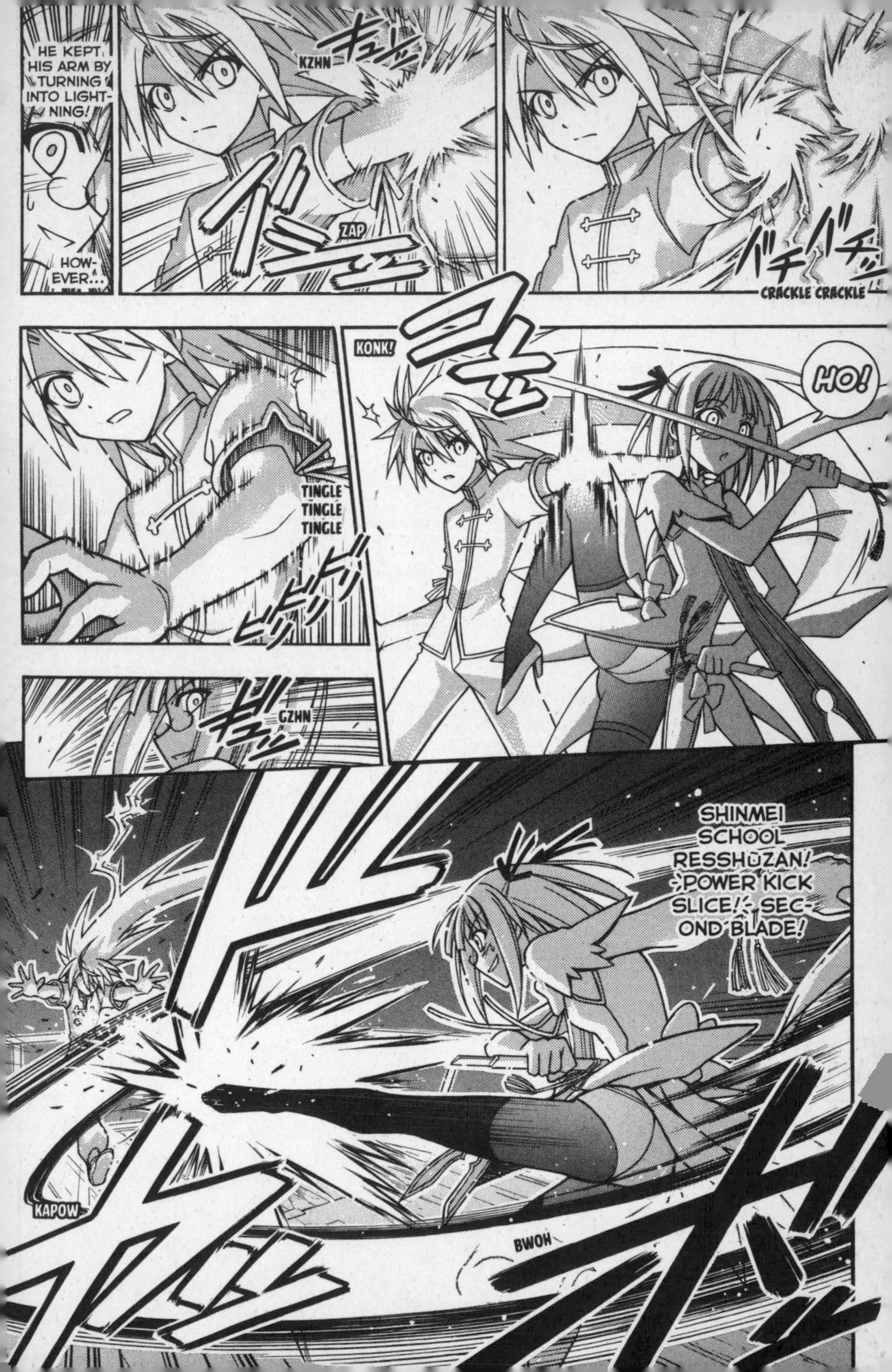
CRACKLE CRACKLE
KZHN
ZAP
HE KEPT HIS ARM BY TURNING INTO LIGHT-NING!
HOW-EVER...
HO!
KONK!
TINGLE TINGLE TINGLE
GZHN
SHINMEI SCHOOL RESSHŪZAN! POWER KICK SLICE! SEC-OND BLADE!
KAPOW
BWOH

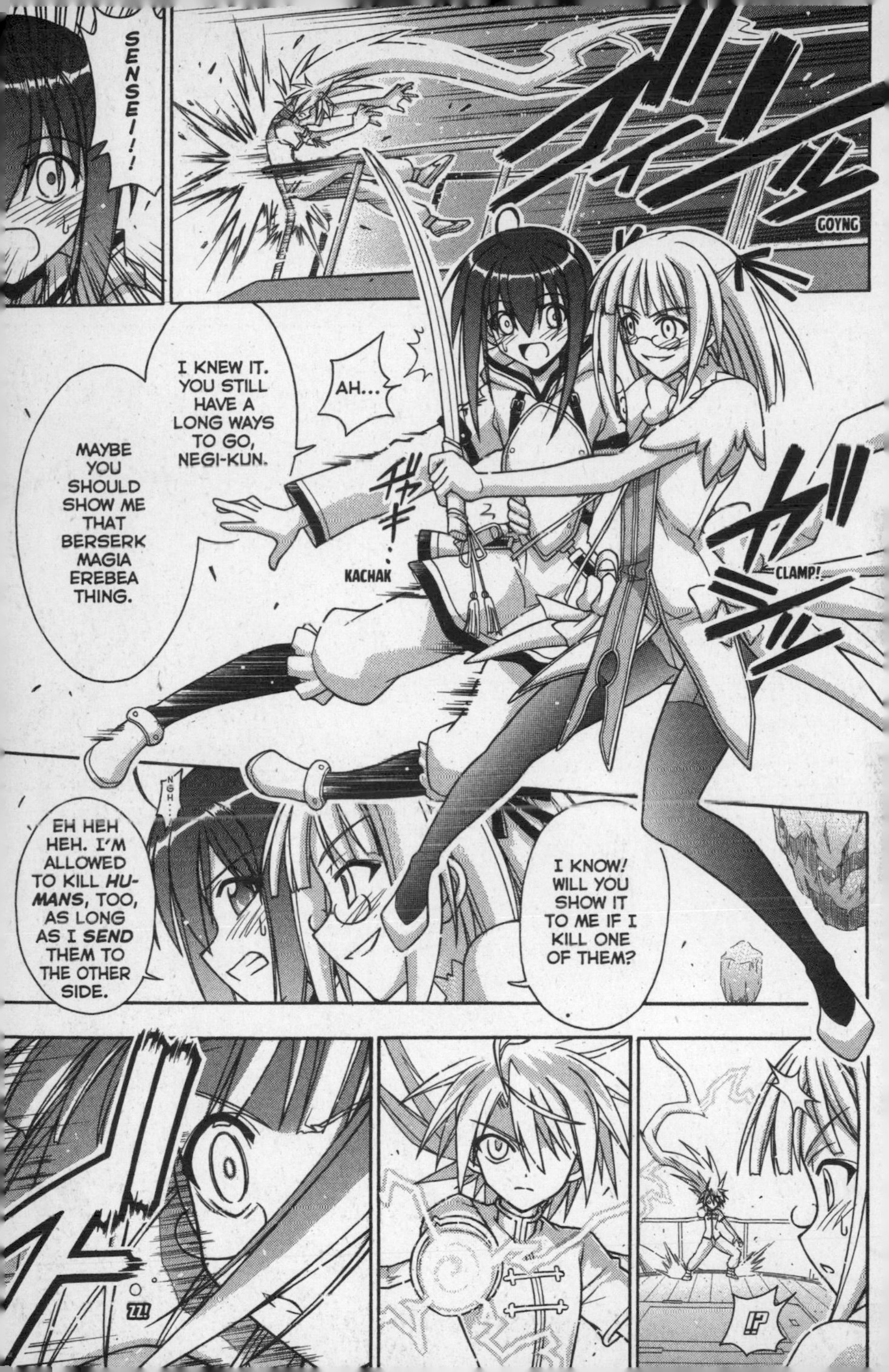
GOYNG
SENSEI!!
CLAMP!
KACHAK
AH...
I KNEW IT. YOU STILL HAVE A LONG WAYS TO GO, NEGI-KUN.
MAYBE YOU SHOULD SHOW ME THAT BERSERK MAGIA EREBEA THING.
I KNOW! WILL YOU SHOW IT TO ME IF I KILL ONE OF THEM?
NGH...
EH HEH HEH. I'M ALLOWED TO KILL *HUMANS*, TOO, AS LONG AS I *SEND* THEM TO THE OTHER SIDE.
!?

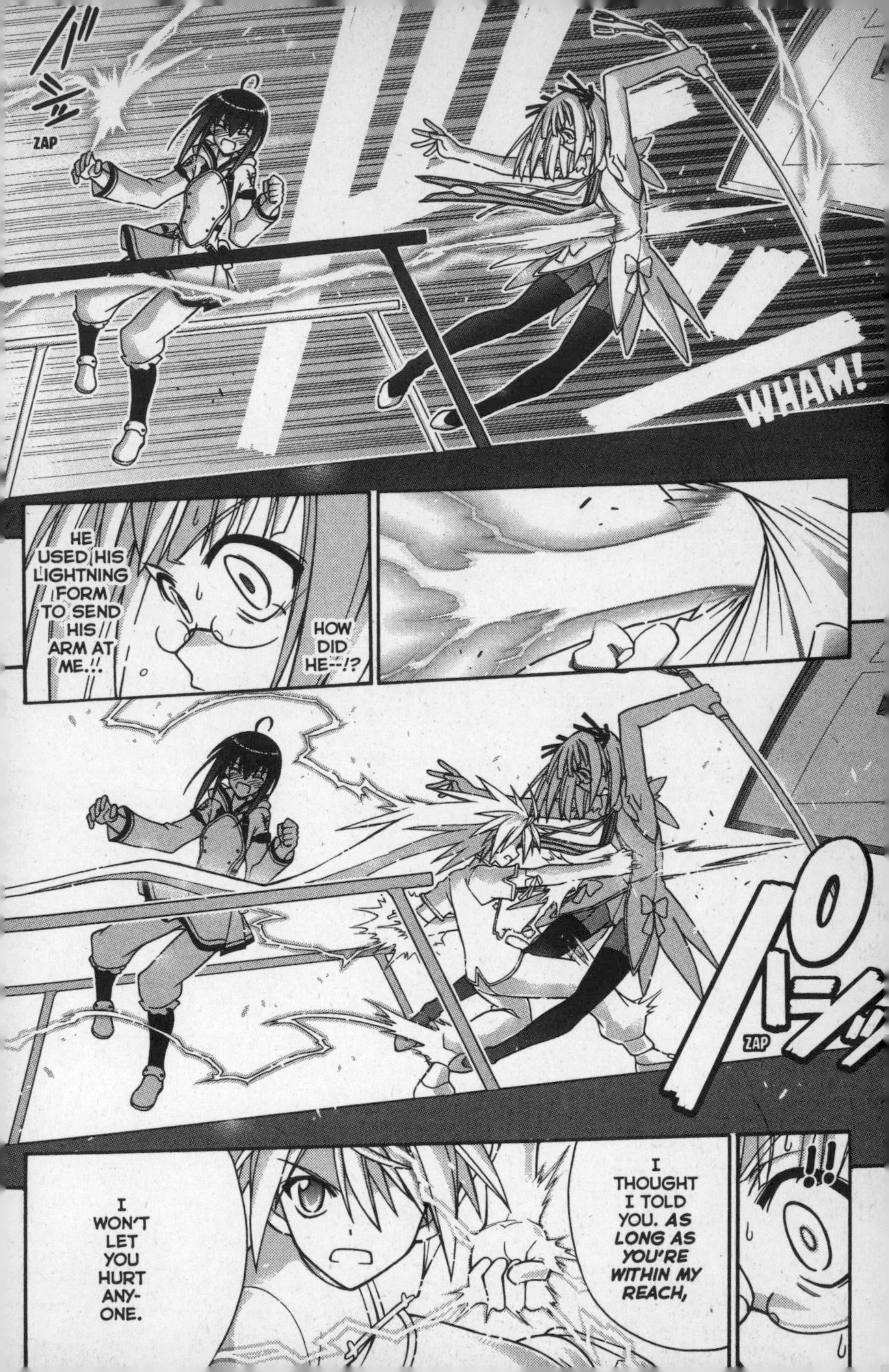
ZAP
WHAM!
HOW DID HE--!?
HE USED HIS LIGHTNING FORM TO SEND HIS ARM AT ME..!!
ZAP
!!
I THOUGHT I TOLD YOU. AS LONG AS YOU'RE WITHIN MY REACH,
I WON'T LET YOU HURT ANYONE.

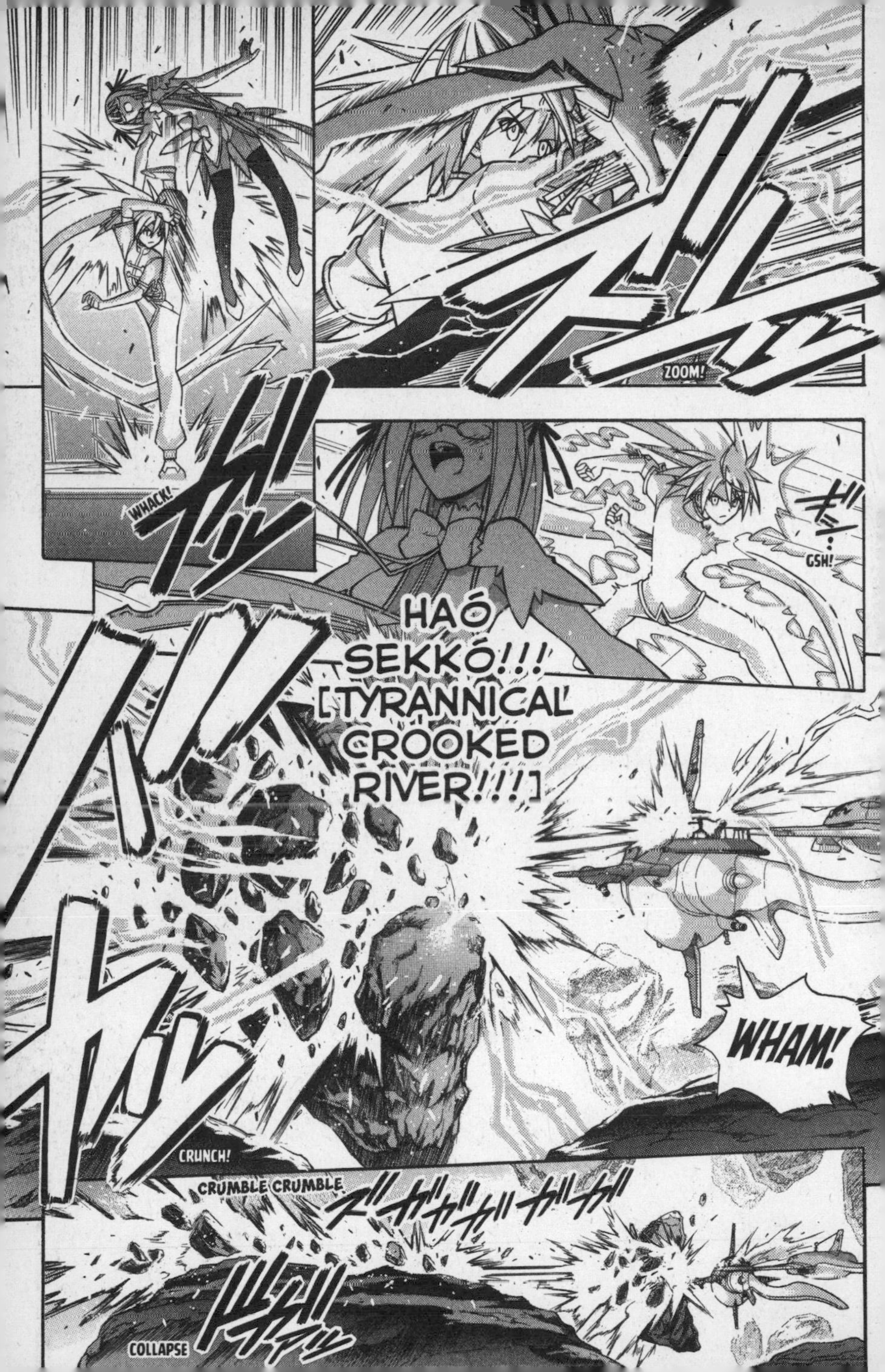
ZOOM!
GSH!
WHACK!
HAÓ SEKKÓ!!! [TYRANNICAL CROOKED RIVER!!!]
WHAM!
CRUNCH!
CRUMBLE CRUMBLE
COLLAPSE

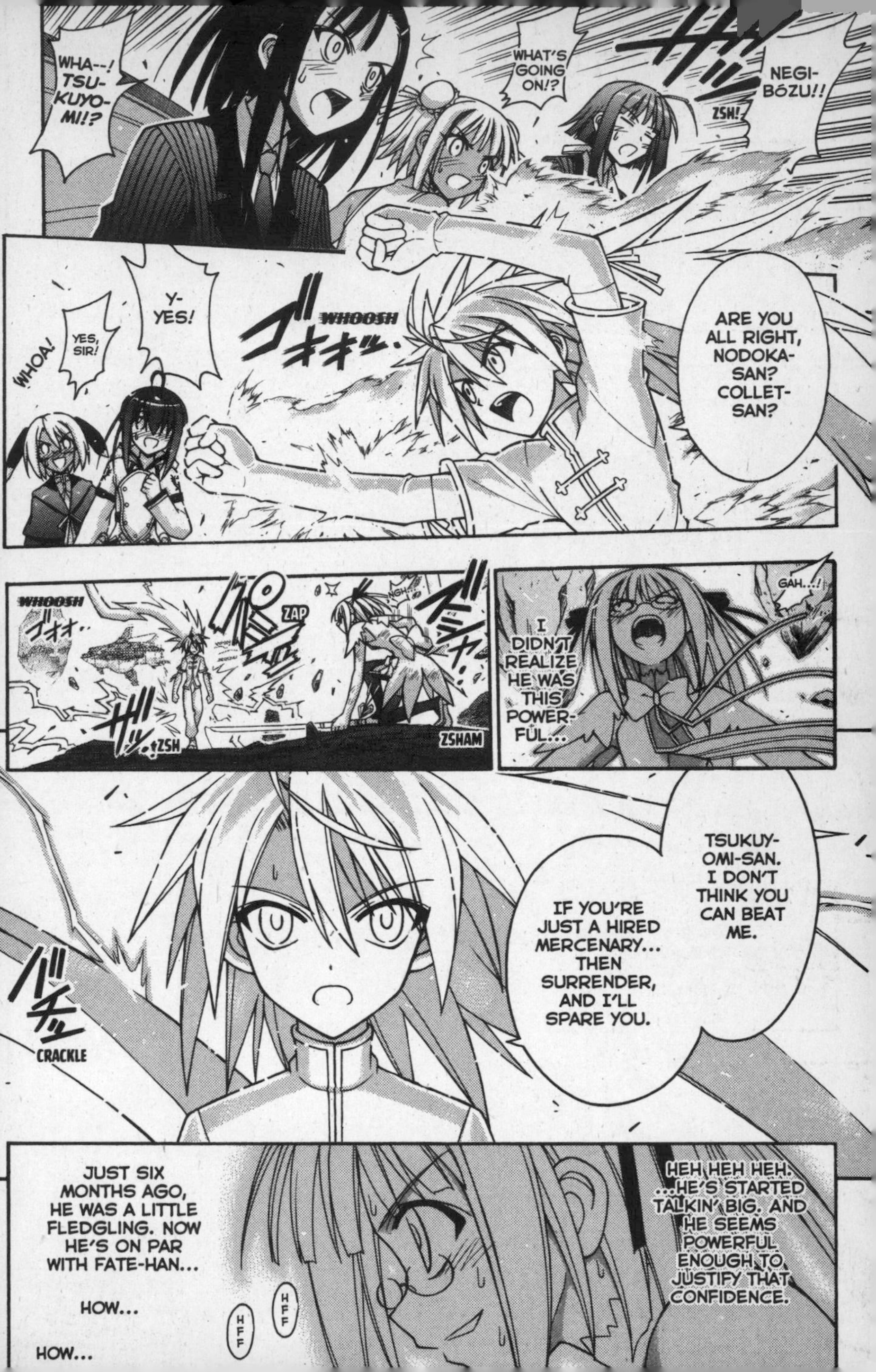
NEGI-BŌZU!!
ZSH!
WHAT'S GOING ON!?
WHA--! TSUKUYOMI!?
ARE YOU ALL RIGHT, NODOKA-SAN? COLLET-SAN?
WHOOSH
Y-YES!
YES, SIR!
WHOA!
GAH...!
I DIDN'T REALIZE HE WAS THIS POWERFUL...
NGH...
ZSHAM
ZAP
WHOOSH
ZSH
TSUKUYOMI-SAN. I DON'T THINK YOU CAN BEAT ME.
IF YOU'RE JUST A HIRED MERCENARY... THEN SURRENDER, AND I'LL SPARE YOU.
CRACKLE
HEH HEH HEH. ...HE'S STARTED TALKIN' BIG. AND HE SEEMS POWERFUL ENOUGH TO JUSTIFY THAT CONFIDENCE.
HFF
HFF
JUST SIX MONTHS AGO, HE WAS A LITTLE FLEDGLING. NOW HE'S ON PAR WITH FATE-HAN...
HOW...
HOW...

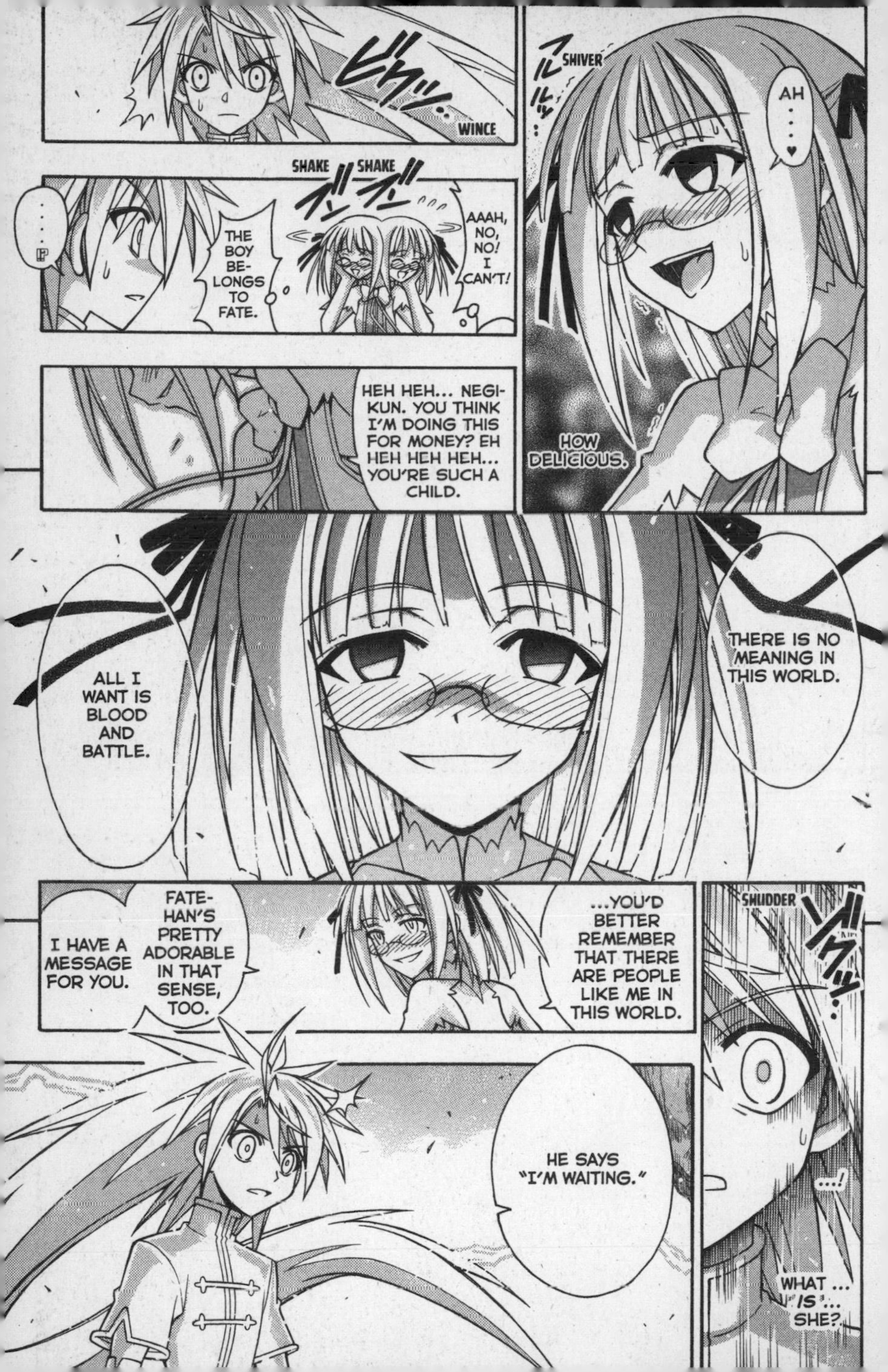
SHIVER
AH . . . . ♥
HOW DELICIOUS.
WINCE
SHAKE SHAKE
AAAH, NO, NO! I CAN'T!
THE BOY BE-LONGS TO FATE.
. . . . !?
HEH HEH... NEGI-KUN. YOU THINK I'M DOING THIS FOR MONEY? EH HEH HEH HEH... YOU'RE SUCH A CHILD.
THERE IS NO MEANING IN THIS WORLD.
ALL I WANT IS BLOOD AND BATTLE.
SHUDDER
...!
WHAT ... IS ... SHE?
...YOU'D BETTER REMEMBER THAT THERE ARE PEOPLE LIKE ME IN THIS WORLD.
FATE-HAN'S PRETTY ADORABLE IN THAT SENSE, TOO.
I HAVE A MESSAGE FOR YOU.
HE SAYS "I'M WAITING."

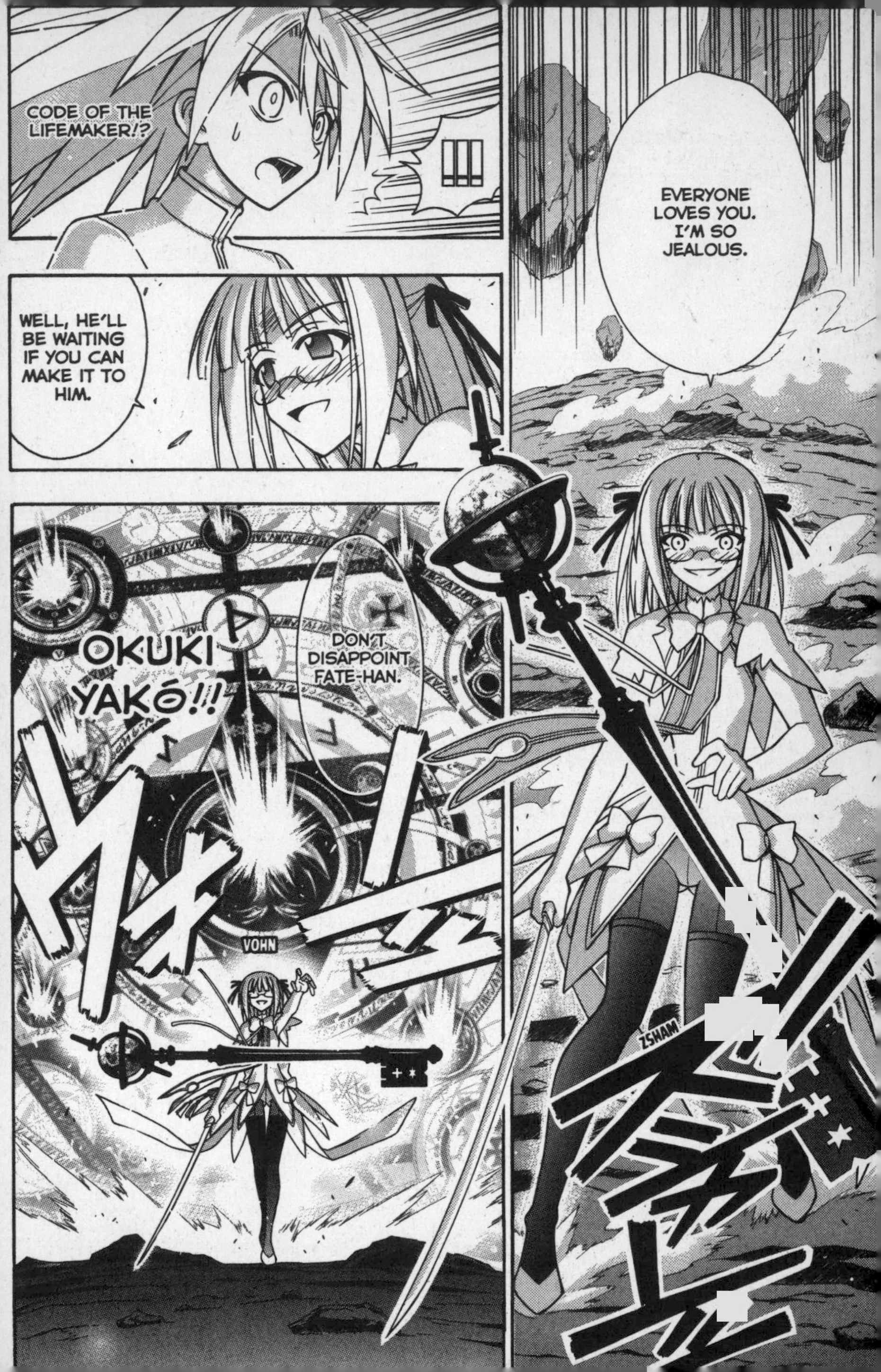
EVERYONE LOVES YOU. I'M SO JEALOUS.
ZSHAM
CODE OF THE LIFEMAKER!?
WELL, HE'LL BE WAITING IF YOU CAN MAKE IT TO HIM.
DON'T DISAPPOINT FATE-HAN.
OKUKI YAKŌ!!!
VOHN

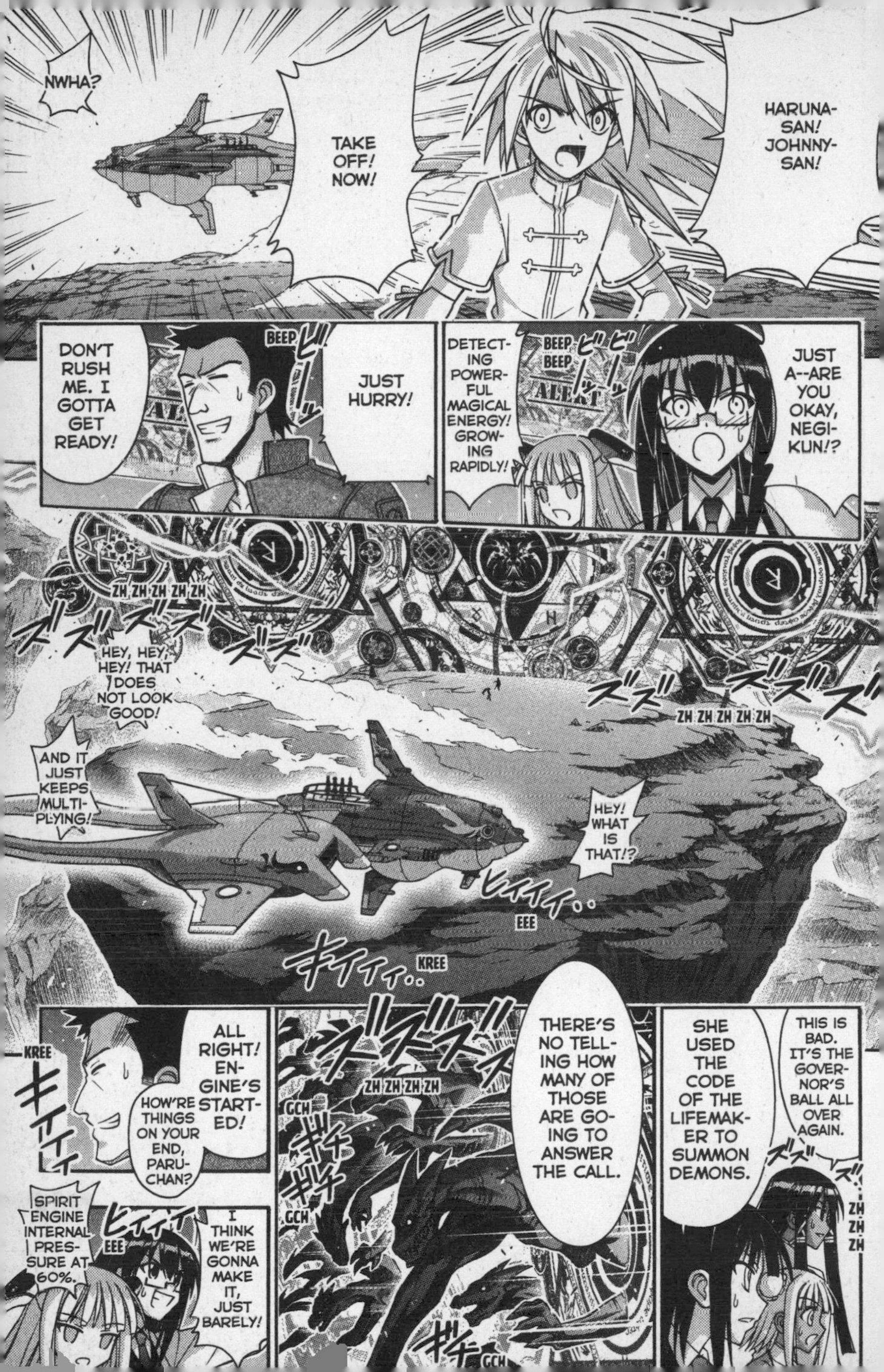
HARUNA-SAN! JOHNNY-SAN!
TAKE OFF! NOW!
NWHA?
JUST A--ARE YOU OKAY, NEGI-KUN!?
BEEP BEEP
ALERT
DETECTING POWERFUL MAGICAL ENERGY! GROWING RAPIDLY!
JUST HURRY!
BEEP
DON'T RUSH ME. I GOTTA GET READY!
ZH ZH ZH ZH ZH
ZH ZH ZH ZH ZH
HEY! WHAT IS THAT!?
HEY, HEY, HEY! THAT DOES NOT LOOK GOOD!
AND IT JUST KEEPS MULTI-PLYING!
EEE
KREE
THIS IS BAD. IT'S THE GOVERNOR'S BALL ALL OVER AGAIN.
ZH ZH ZH
SHE USED THE CODE OF THE LIFEMAKER TO SUMMON DEMONS.
THERE'S NO TELLING HOW MANY OF THOSE ARE GOING TO ANSWER THE CALL.
ZH ZH ZH ZH
GCH
GCH
GCH
KREE
ALL RIGHT! ENGINE'S STARTED!
HOW'RE THINGS ON YOUR END, PARU-CHAN?
I THINK WE'RE GONNA MAKE IT, JUST BARELY!
EEE
SPIRIT ENGINE INTERNAL PRESSURE AT 60%.

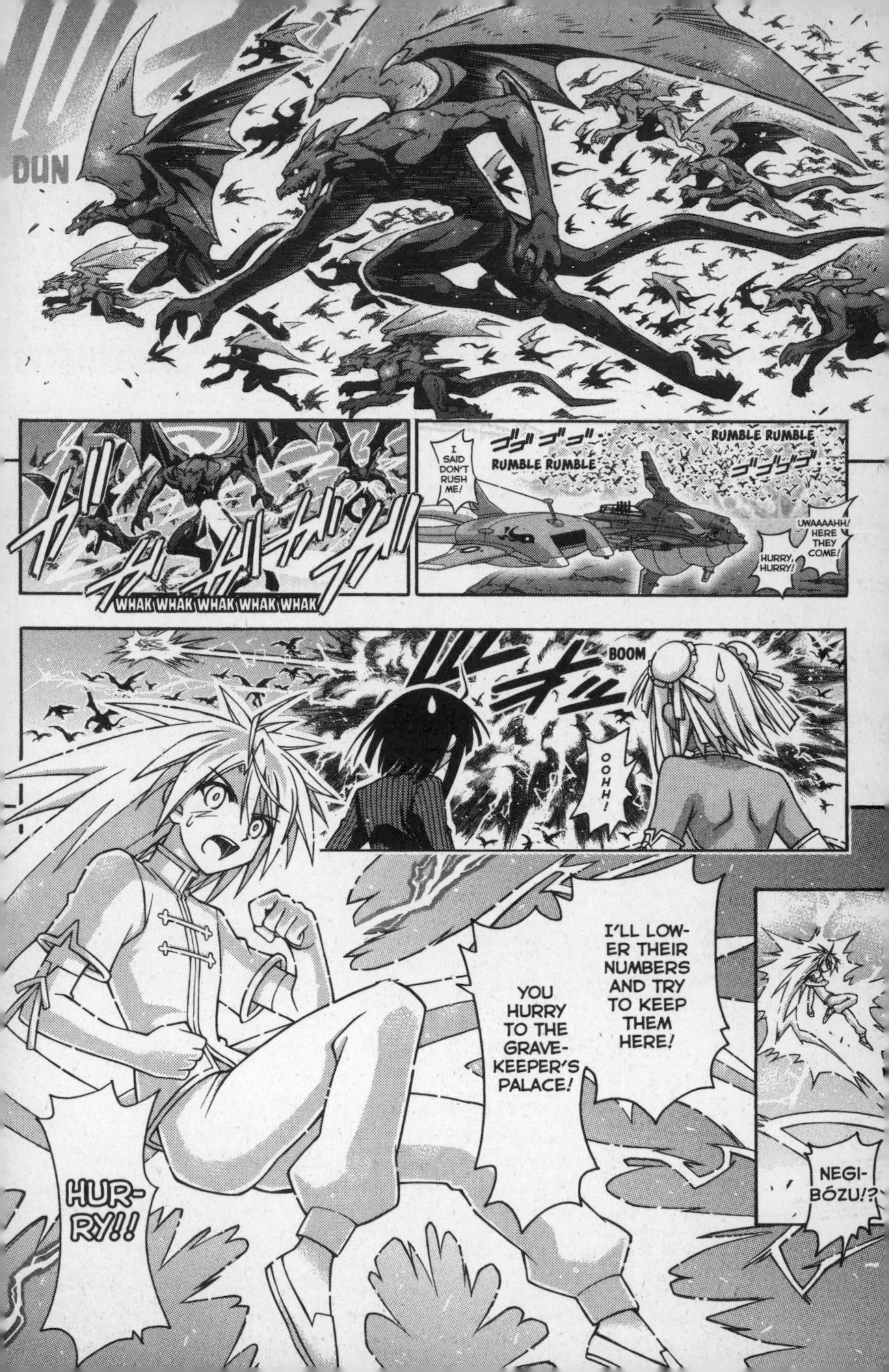
DUN
RUMBLE RUMBLE
I SAID DON'T RUSH ME!
RUMBLE RUMBLE
UWAAAAHH! HERE THEY COME!
HURRY, HURRY!
WHAK WHAK WHAK WHAK WHAK
BOOM
OOHH!
NEGI-BÓZU!?
I'LL LOWER THEIR NUMBERS AND TRY TO KEEP THEM HERE!
YOU HURRY TO THE GRAVEKEEPER'S PALACE!
HURRY!!

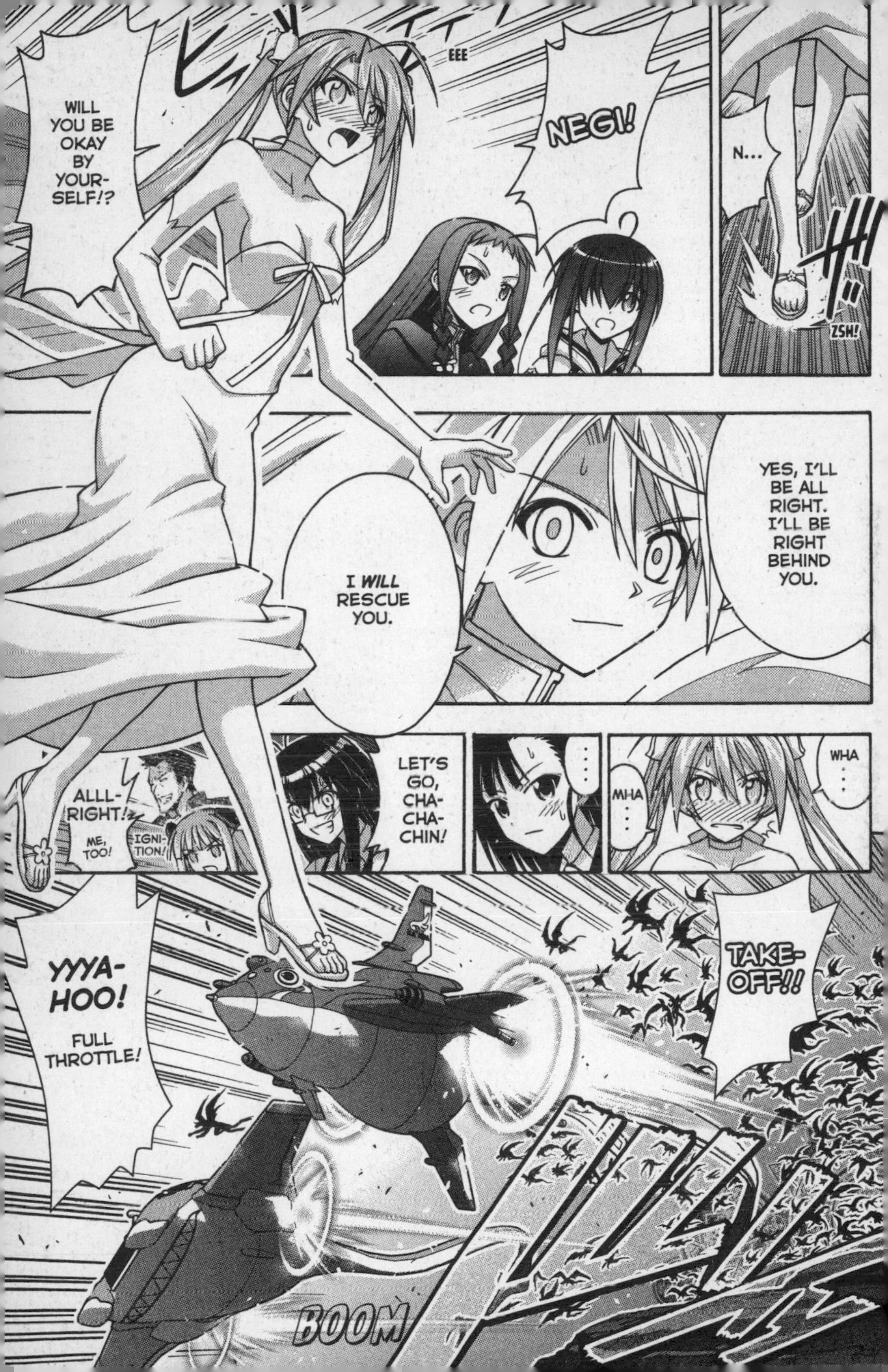
N...
ZSH!
NEGI!
EEE
WILL YOU BE OKAY BY YOURSELF!?
YES, I'LL BE ALL RIGHT. I'LL BE RIGHT BEHIND YOU.
I *WILL* RESCUE YOU.
WHA...
MHA...
...
LET'S GO, CHA-CHA-CHIN!
ALLL-RIGHT!
IGNITION!
ME, TOO!
TAKE-OFF!!
YYYA-HOO!
FULL THROTTLE!
BOOM

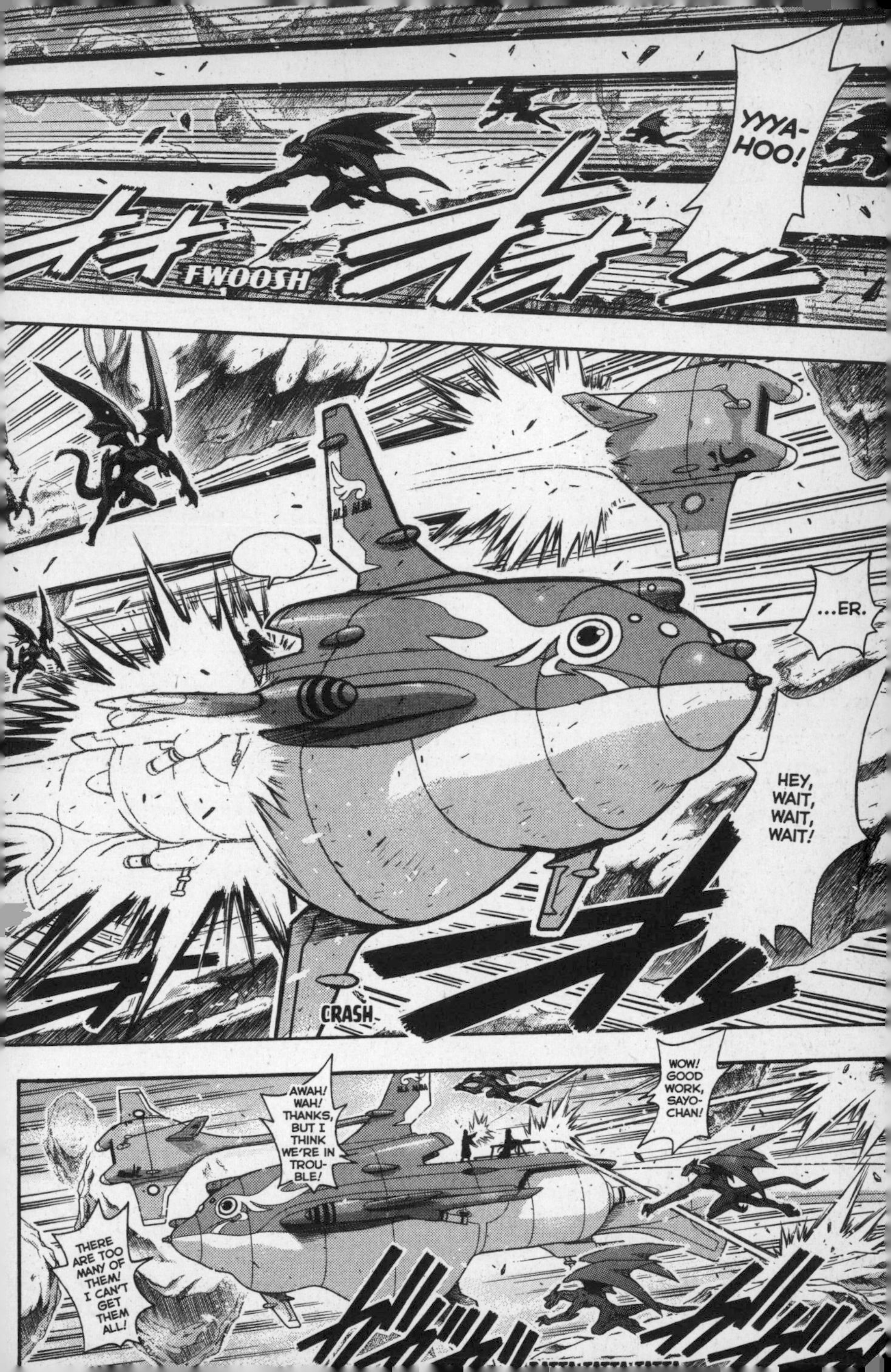
YYYA-HOO!
FWOOSH
...ER.
HEY, WAIT, WAIT, WAIT!
CRASH
WOW! GOOD WORK, SAYO-CHAN!
AWAH! WAH! THANKS, BUT I THINK WE'RE IN TROUBLE!
THERE ARE TOO MANY OF THEM! I CAN'T GET THEM ALL!

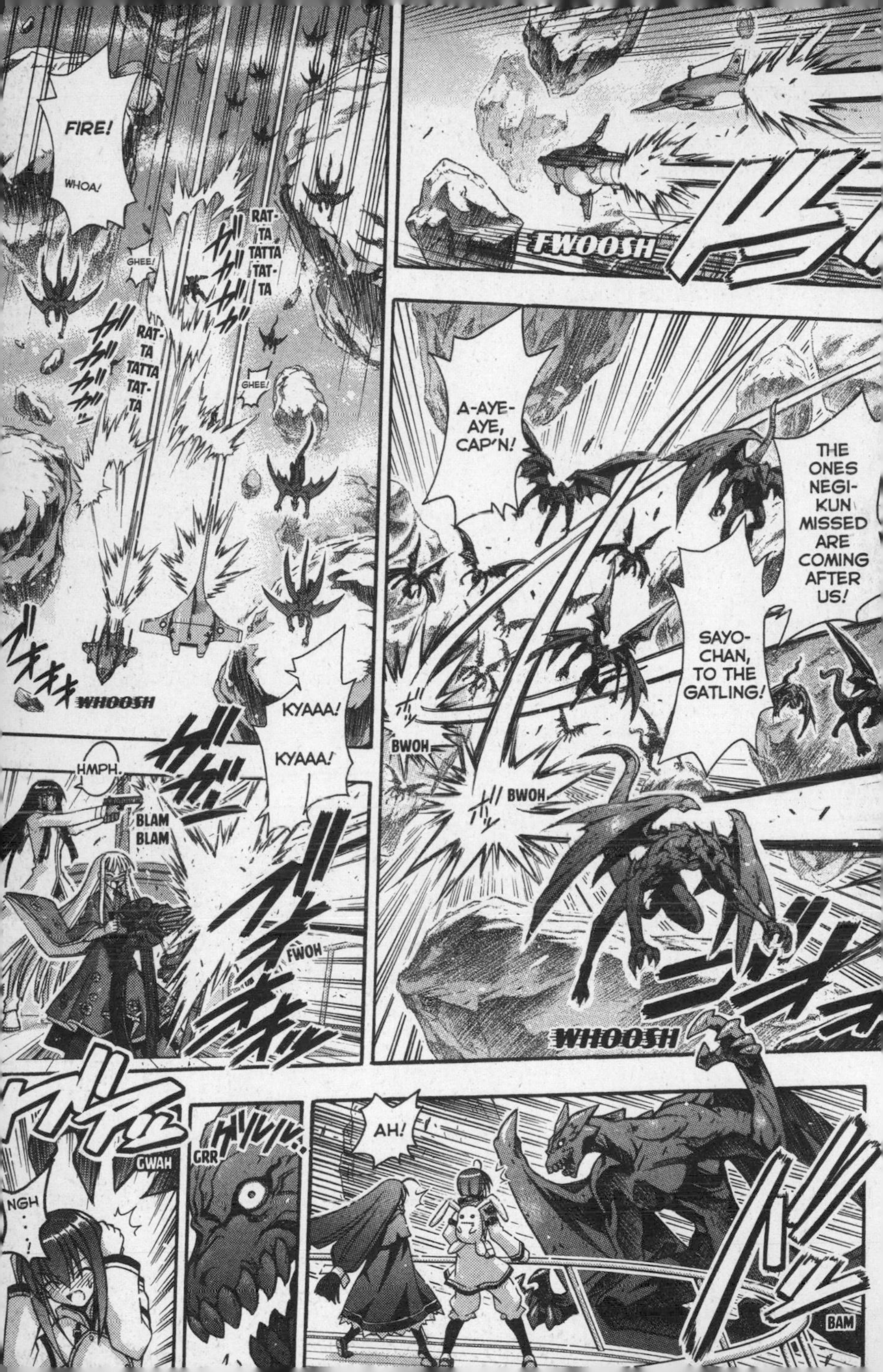
FWOOSH
THE ONES NEGI-KUN MISSED ARE COMING AFTER US!
SAYO-CHAN, TO THE GATLING!
A-AYE-AYE, CAP'N!
BWOH
BWOH
WHOOSH
FIRE!
WHOA!
RAT-TA TATTA TAT-TA
GHEE!
RAT-TA TATTA TAT-TA
GHEE!
WHOOSH
KYAAA!
KYAAA!
FWOH
BLAM BLAM
HMPH.
AH!
BAM
GRR
GWAH
NGH...!?

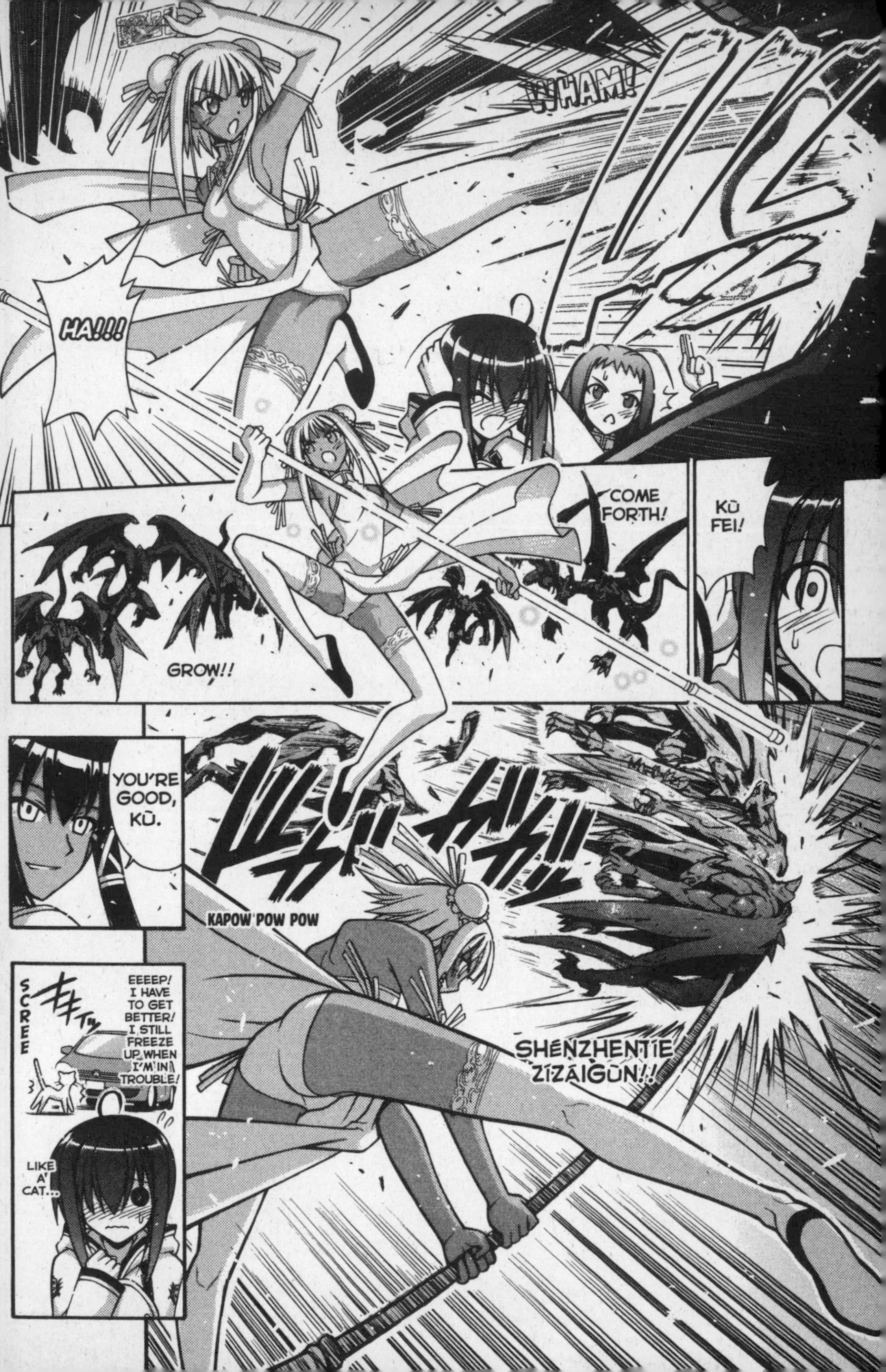
WHAM!
HA!!!
KŪ FEI!
COME FORTH!
GROW!!
KAPOW POW POW
SHÉNZHENTÍE ZÍZÁIGŪN!!
YOU'RE GOOD, KŪ.
SCREE
EEEEP! I HAVE TO GET BETTER! I STILL FREEZE UP WHEN I'M IN TROUBLE!
LIKE A CAT...

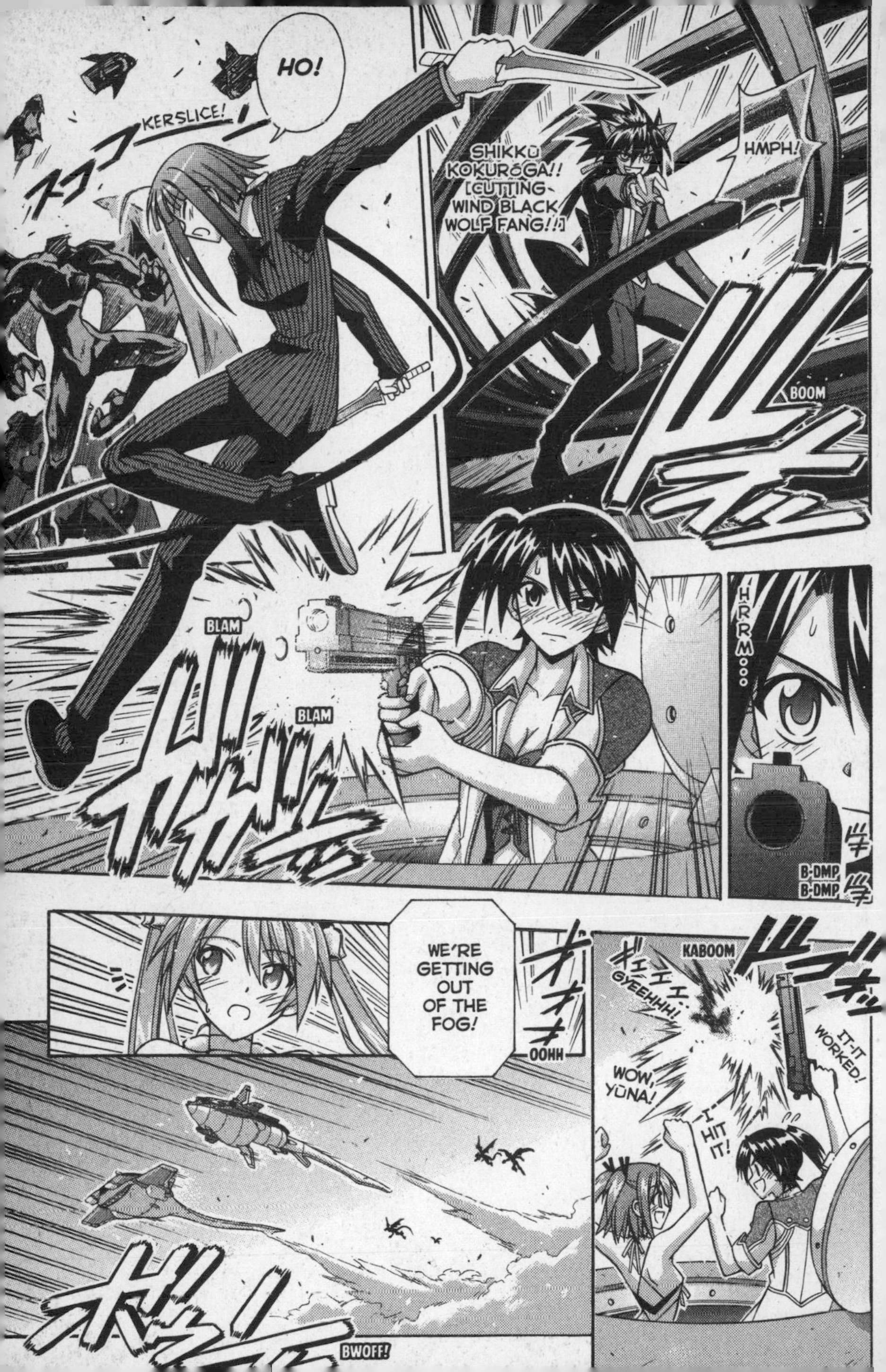
HMPH!
SHIKKŪ KOKURŌGA!! [CUTTING WIND BLACK WOLF FANG!!]
BOOM
HO!
KERSLICE!
HRRM...
B-DMP B-DMP
BLAM
BLAM
KABOOM
GYEEHHH!
IT-IT WORKED!
WOW, YŪNA!
I HIT IT!
WE'RE GETTING OUT OF THE FOG!
OOHH
BWOFF!

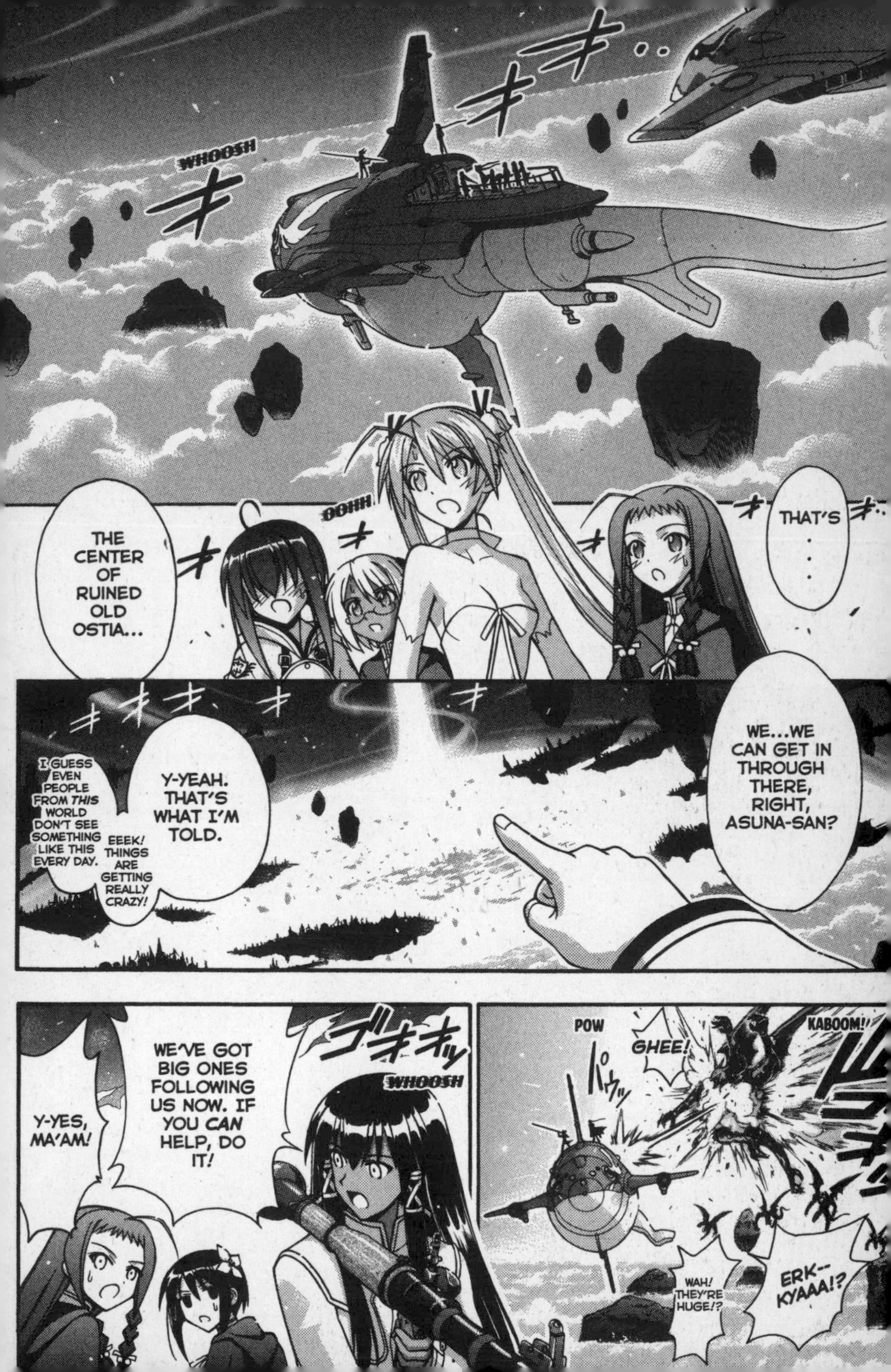
WHOOSH
THAT'S . . . .
OOHH
THE CENTER OF RUINED OLD OSTIA...
WE...WE CAN GET IN THROUGH THERE, RIGHT, ASUNA-SAN?
Y-YEAH. THAT'S WHAT I'M TOLD.
EEEK! THINGS ARE GETTING REALLY CRAZY!
I GUESS EVEN PEOPLE FROM *THIS* WORLD DON'T SEE SOMETHING LIKE THIS EVERY DAY.
KABOOM!
GHEE!
POW
ERK-- KYAAA!?
WAH! THEY'RE HUGE!?
WE'VE GOT BIG ONES FOLLOWING US NOW. IF YOU *CAN* HELP, DO IT!
WHOOSH
Y-YES, MA'AM!

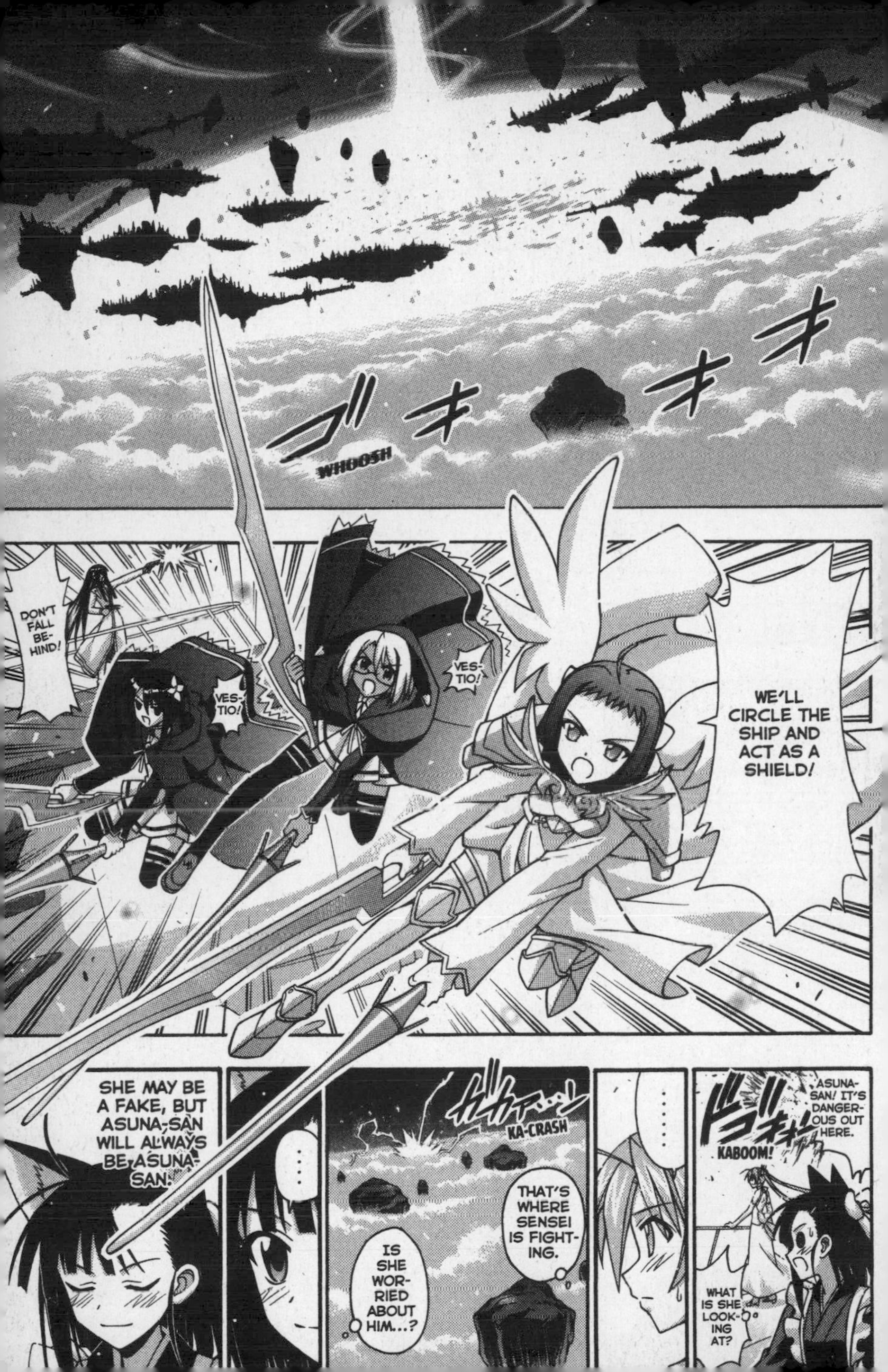
WHOOSH
WE'LL CIRCLE THE SHIP AND ACT AS A SHIELD!
VES-TIO!
VES-TIO!
DON'T FALL BE-HIND!
ASUNA-SAN! IT'S DANGER-OUS OUT HERE.
KABOOM!
WHAT IS SHE LOOK-ING AT?
......
KA-CRASH
THAT'S WHERE SENSEI IS FIGHT-ING.
IS SHE WOR-RIED ABOUT HIM...?
.....
SHE MAY BE A FAKE, BUT ASUNA-SAN WILL ALWAYS BE ASUNA-SAN.

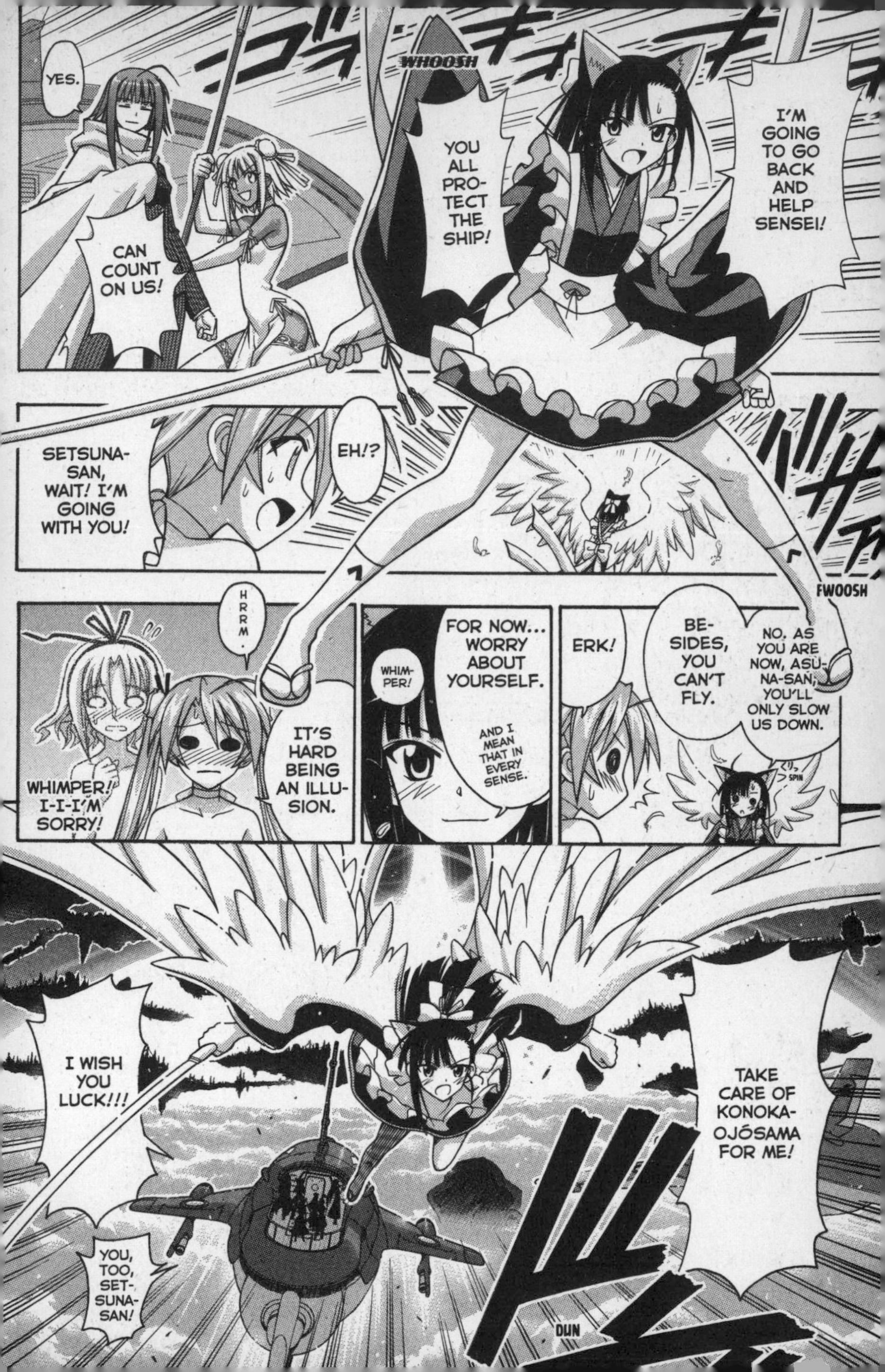
WHOOSH
I'M GOING TO GO BACK AND HELP SENSEI!
YOU ALL PROTECT THE SHIP!
YES.
CAN COUNT ON US!
FWOOSH
EH!?
SETSUNA-SAN, WAIT! I'M GOING WITH YOU!
NO. AS YOU ARE NOW, ASUNA-SAN, YOU'LL ONLY SLOW US DOWN.
BE-SIDES, YOU CAN'T FLY.
ERK!
SPIN
FOR NOW... WORRY ABOUT YOURSELF.
AND I MEAN THAT IN EVERY SENSE.
WHIMPER!
HRRM.
IT'S HARD BEING AN ILLUSION.
WHIMPER! I-I-I'M SORRY!
TAKE CARE OF KONOKA-OJŌSAMA FOR ME!
I WISH YOU LUCK!!!
YOU, TOO, SET-SUNA-SAN!
DUN

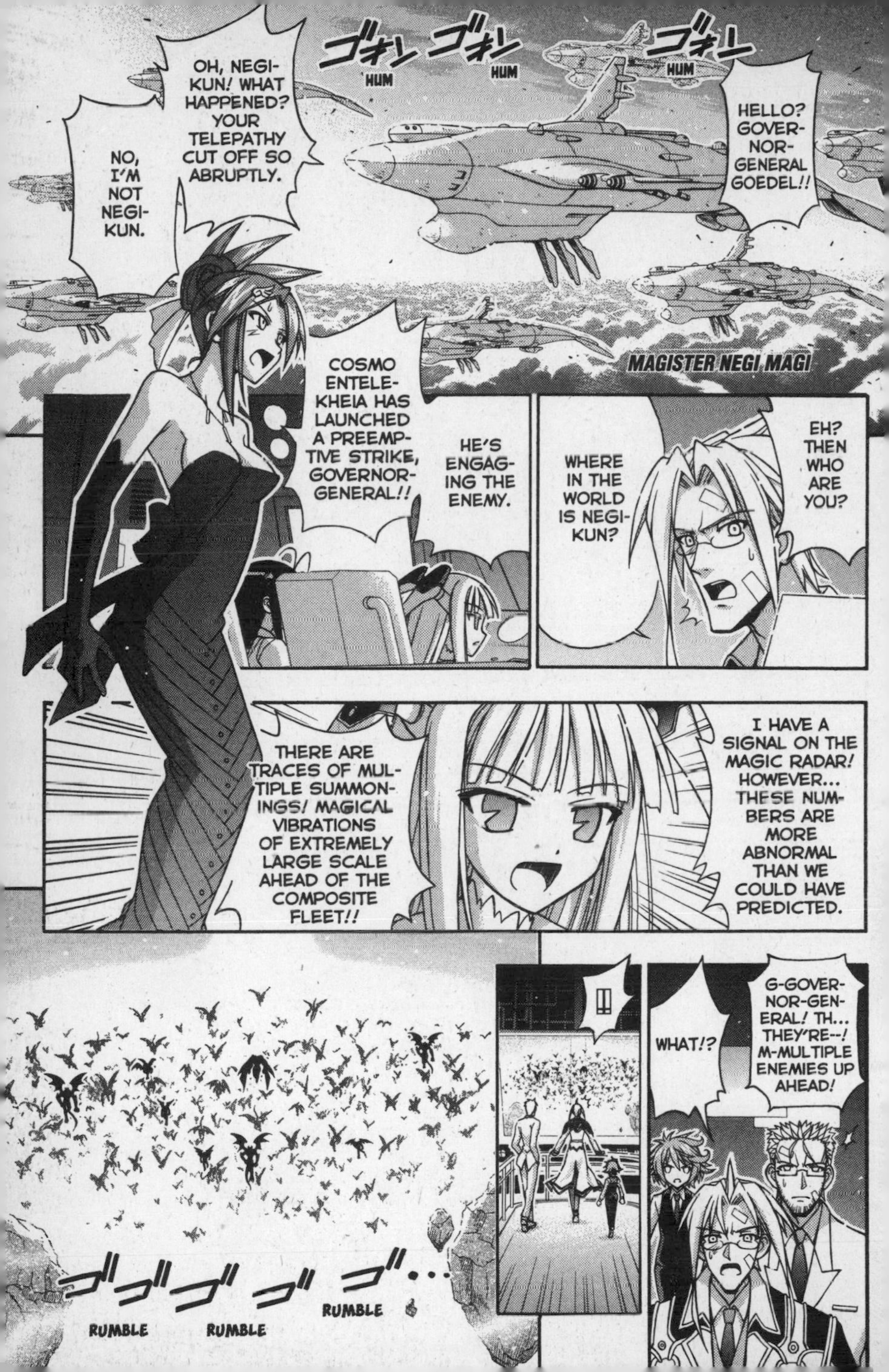

ゴォン HUM
ゴォン HUM
ゴォン HUM
HELLO? GOVERNOR-GENERAL GOEDEL!!
OH, NEGI-KUN! WHAT HAPPENED? YOUR TELEPATHY CUT OFF SO ABRUPTLY.
NO, I'M NOT NEGI-KUN.
MAGISTER NEGI MAGI
EH? THEN WHO ARE YOU?
WHERE IN THE WORLD IS NEGI-KUN?
HE'S ENGAGING THE ENEMY.
COSMO ENTELEKHEIA HAS LAUNCHED A PREEMPTIVE STRIKE, GOVERNOR-GENERAL!!
I HAVE A SIGNAL ON THE MAGIC RADAR! HOWEVER... THESE NUMBERS ARE MORE ABNORMAL THAN WE COULD HAVE PREDICTED.
THERE ARE TRACES OF MULTIPLE SUMMONINGS! MAGICAL VIBRATIONS OF EXTREMELY LARGE SCALE AHEAD OF THE COMPOSITE FLEET!!
G-GOVERNOR-GENERAL! TH... THEY'RE--! M-MULTIPLE ENEMIES UP AHEAD!
WHAT!?
!!
ゴゴゴゴゴ…
RUMBLE
RUMBLE
RUMBLE

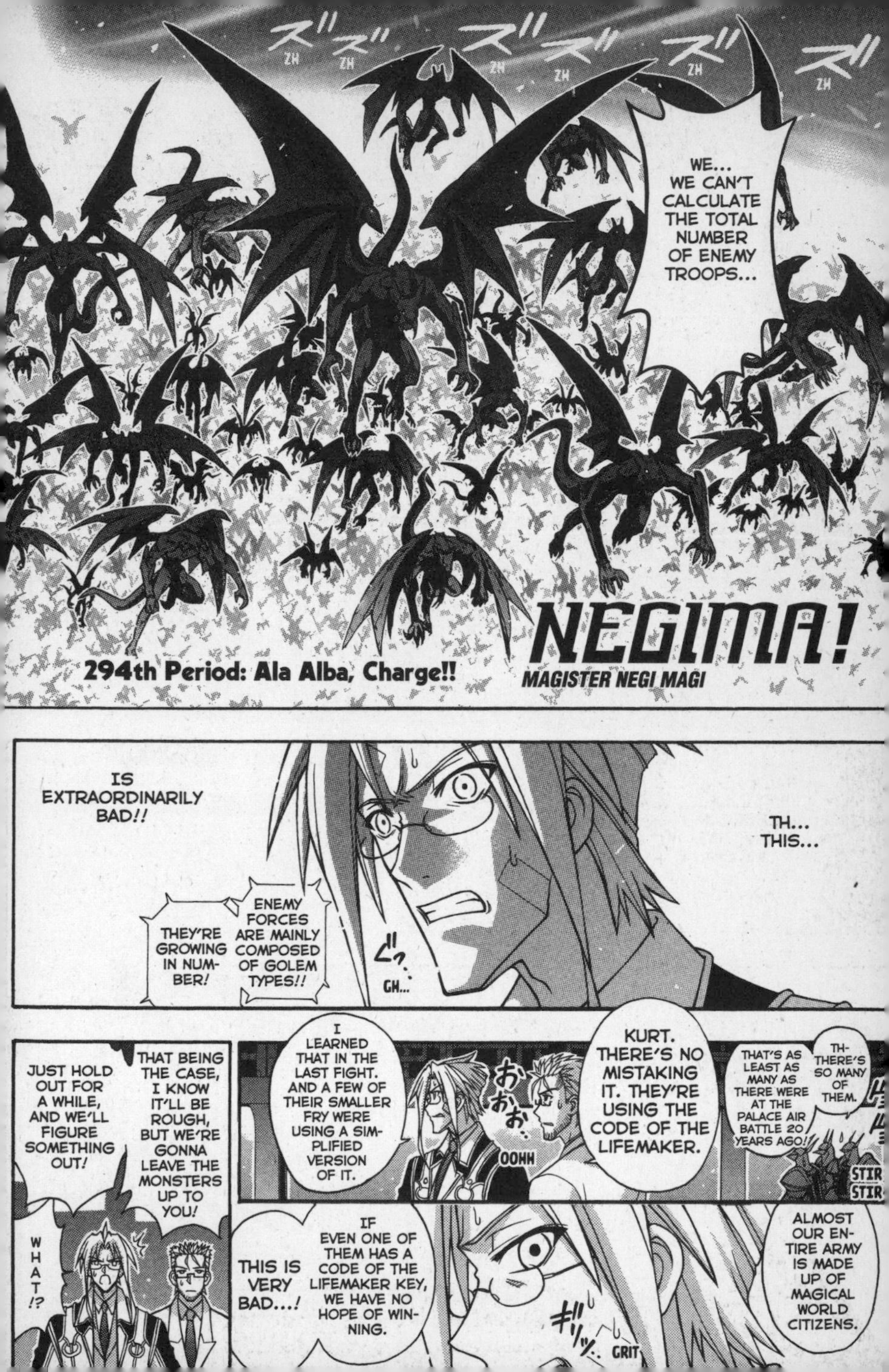
ZH ZH ZH ZH ZH ZH
WE... WE CAN'T CALCULATE THE TOTAL NUMBER OF ENEMY TROOPS...
NEGIMA!
MAGISTER NEGI MAGI
294th Period: Ala Alba, Charge!!
TH... THIS...
IS EXTRAORDINARILY BAD!!
ENEMY FORCES ARE MAINLY COMPOSED OF GOLEM TYPES!!
THEY'RE GROWING IN NUMBER!
GH...
TH- THERE'S SO MANY OF THEM.
THAT'S AS LEAST AS MANY AS THERE WERE AT THE PALACE AIR BATTLE 20 YEARS AGO!!
STIR STIR
KURT. THERE'S NO MISTAKING IT. THEY'RE USING THE CODE OF THE LIFEMAKER.
OOHH
I LEARNED THAT IN THE LAST FIGHT. AND A FEW OF THEIR SMALLER FRY WERE USING A SIMPLIFIED VERSION OF IT.
ALMOST OUR ENTIRE ARMY IS MADE UP OF MAGICAL WORLD CITIZENS.
IF EVEN ONE OF THEM HAS A CODE OF THE LIFEMAKER KEY, WE HAVE NO HOPE OF WINNING.
THIS IS VERY BAD...!
GRIT
THAT BEING THE CASE, I KNOW IT'LL BE ROUGH, BUT WE'RE GONNA LEAVE THE MONSTERS UP TO YOU!
JUST HOLD OUT FOR A WHILE, AND WE'LL FIGURE SOMETHING OUT!
WHAT!?

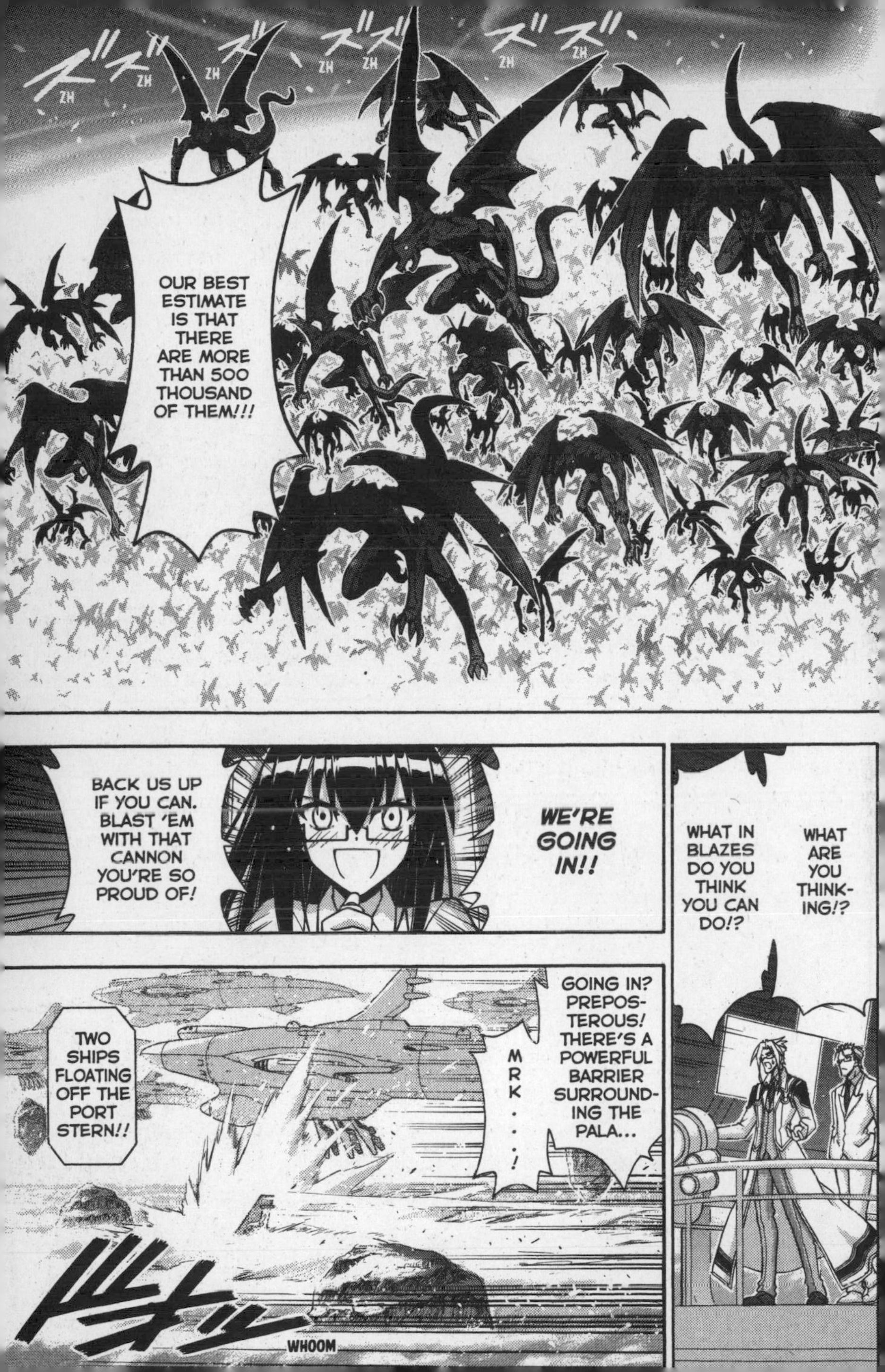
ZH
ZH
ZH
ZH
ZH
ZH
ZH
OUR BEST ESTIMATE IS THAT THERE ARE MORE THAN 500 THOUSAND OF THEM!!!
WHAT ARE YOU THINK-ING!?
WHAT IN BLAZES DO YOU THINK YOU CAN DO!?
WE'RE GOING IN!!
BACK US UP IF YOU CAN. BLAST 'EM WITH THAT CANNON YOU'RE SO PROUD OF!
GOING IN? PREPOS-TEROUS! THERE'S A POWERFUL BARRIER SURROUND-ING THE PALA...
MRK...!
TWO SHIPS FLOATING OFF THE PORT STERN!!
WHOOM

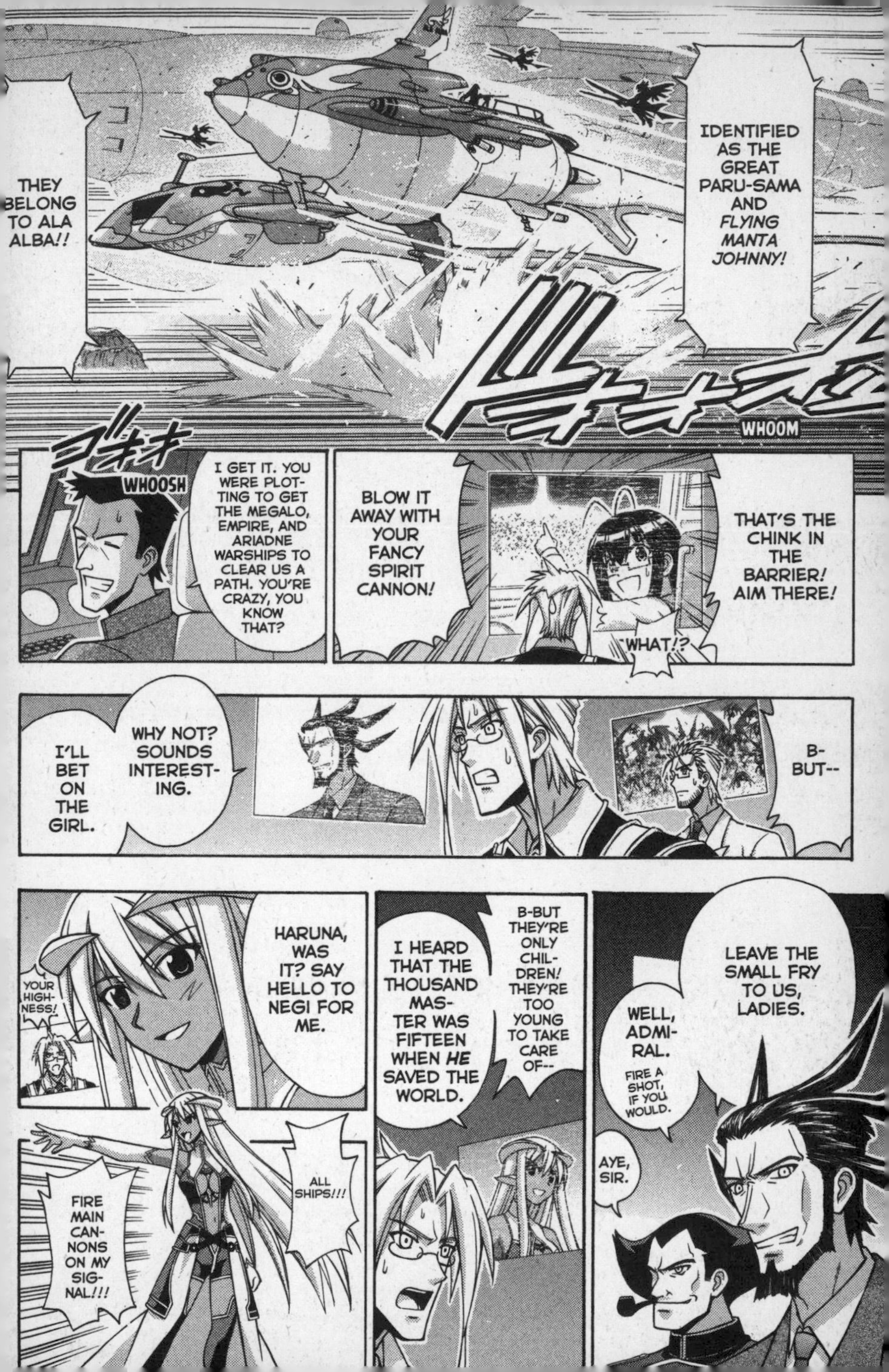
IDENTIFIED AS THE GREAT PARU-SAMA AND *FLYING MANTA JOHNNY!*
THEY BELONG TO ALA ALBA!!
WHOOM
THAT'S THE CHINK IN THE BARRIER! AIM THERE!
BLOW IT AWAY WITH YOUR FANCY SPIRIT CANNON!
WHAT!?
WHOOSH
I GET IT. YOU WERE PLOTTING TO GET THE MEGALO, EMPIRE, AND ARIADNE WARSHIPS TO CLEAR US A PATH. YOU'RE CRAZY, YOU KNOW THAT?
B-BUT--
WHY NOT? SOUNDS INTERESTING.
I'LL BET ON THE GIRL.
LEAVE THE SMALL FRY TO US, LADIES.
WELL, ADMIRAL.
FIRE A SHOT, IF YOU WOULD.
AYE, SIR.
B-BUT THEY'RE ONLY CHILDREN! THEY'RE TOO YOUNG TO TAKE CARE OF--
I HEARD THAT THE THOUSAND MASTER WAS FIFTEEN WHEN *HE* SAVED THE WORLD.
HARUNA, WAS IT? SAY HELLO TO NEGI FOR ME.
YOUR HIGHNESS!
ALL SHIPS!!!
FIRE MAIN CANNONS ON MY SIGNAL!!!

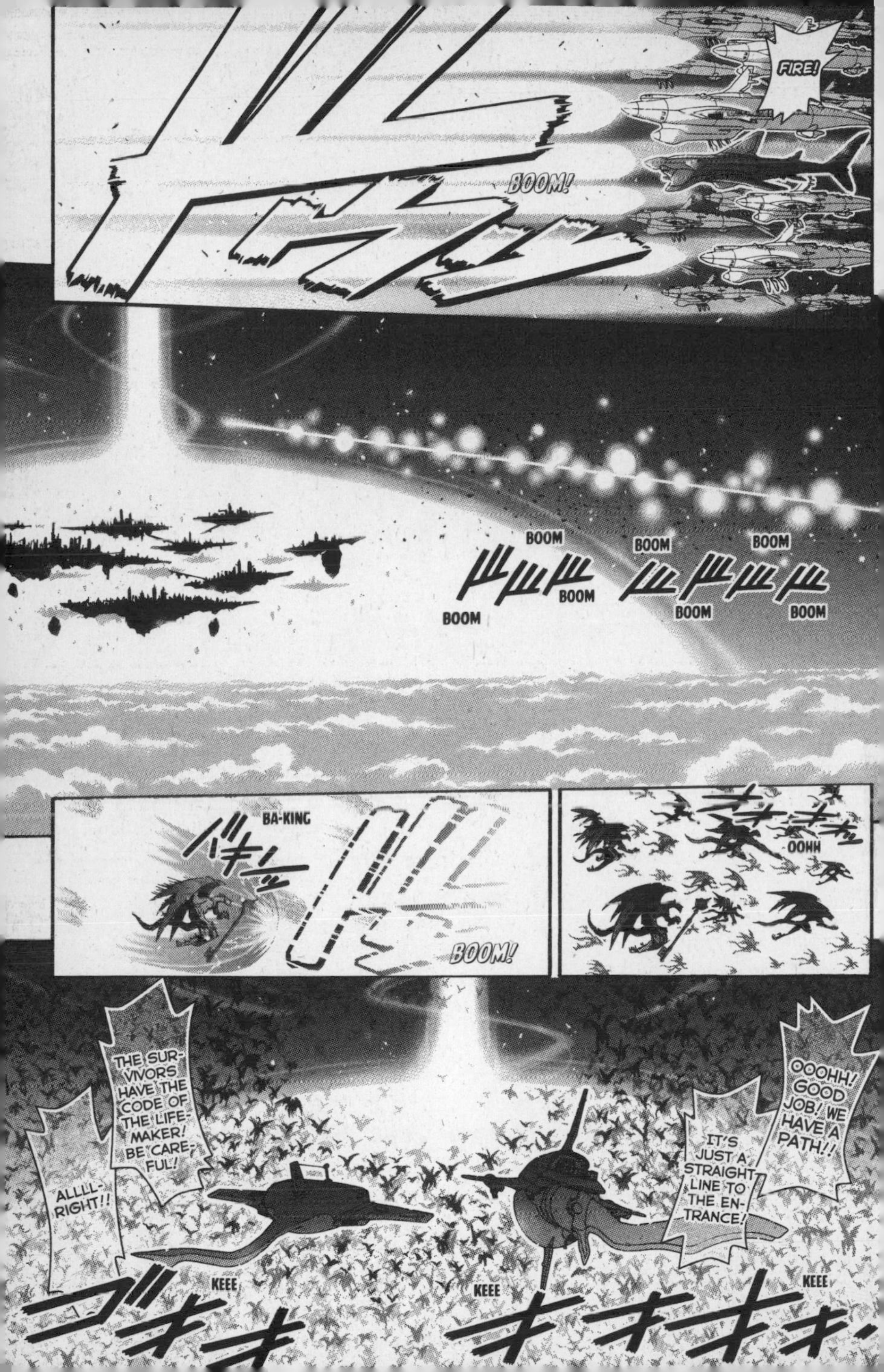

FIRE!
BOOM!
BOOM
BOOM
BOOM
BOOM
BOOM
BOOM
BOOM
OOHH
BA-KING
BOOM!
OOOHH! GOOD JOB! WE HAVE A PATH!!
IT'S JUST A STRAIGHT LINE TO THE EN-TRANCE!
THE SUR-VIVORS HAVE THE CODE OF THE LIFE-MAKER! BE CARE-FUL!
ALLLL-RIGHT!!
KEEE
KEEE
KEEE

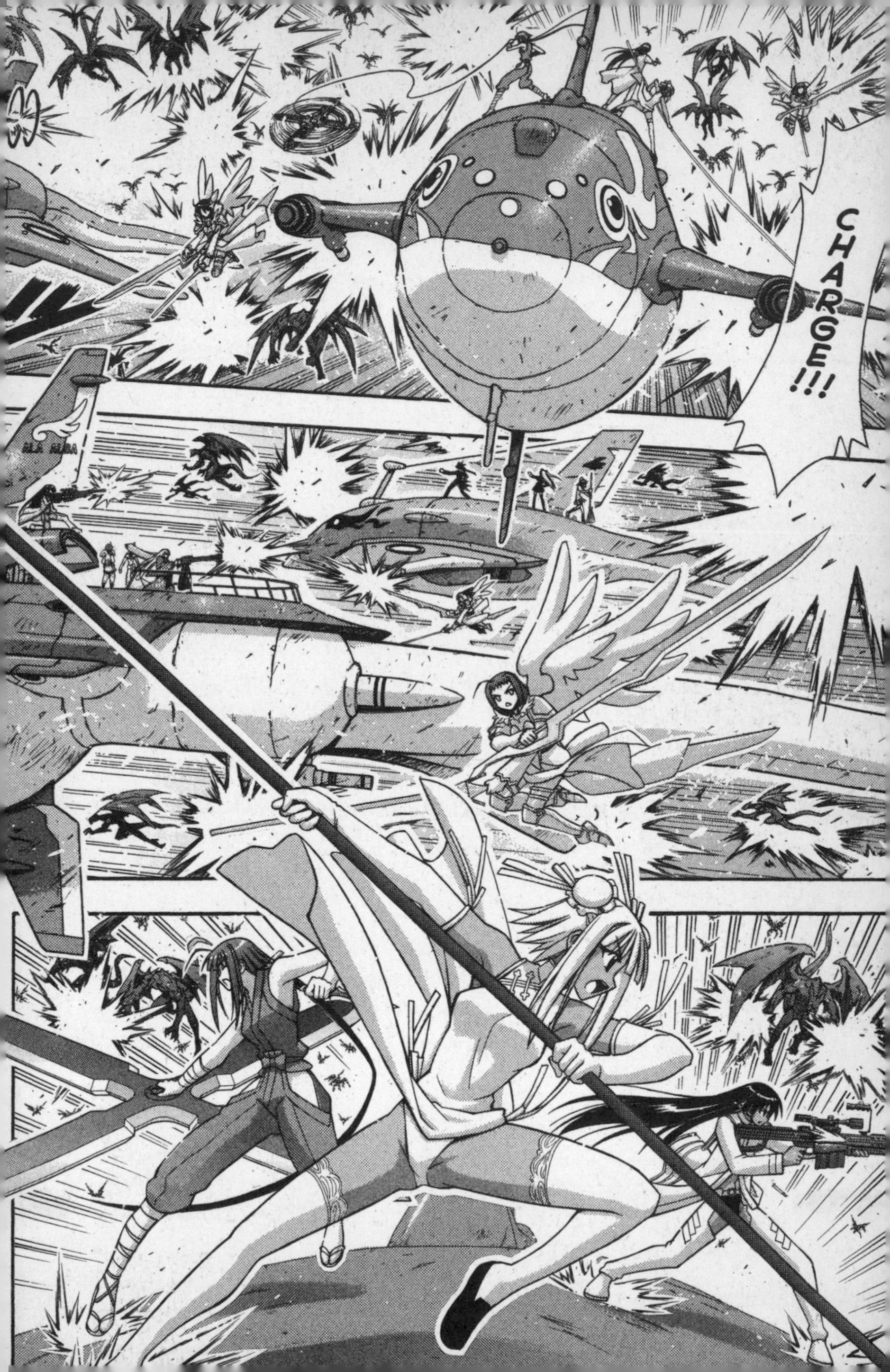
CHARGE!!!

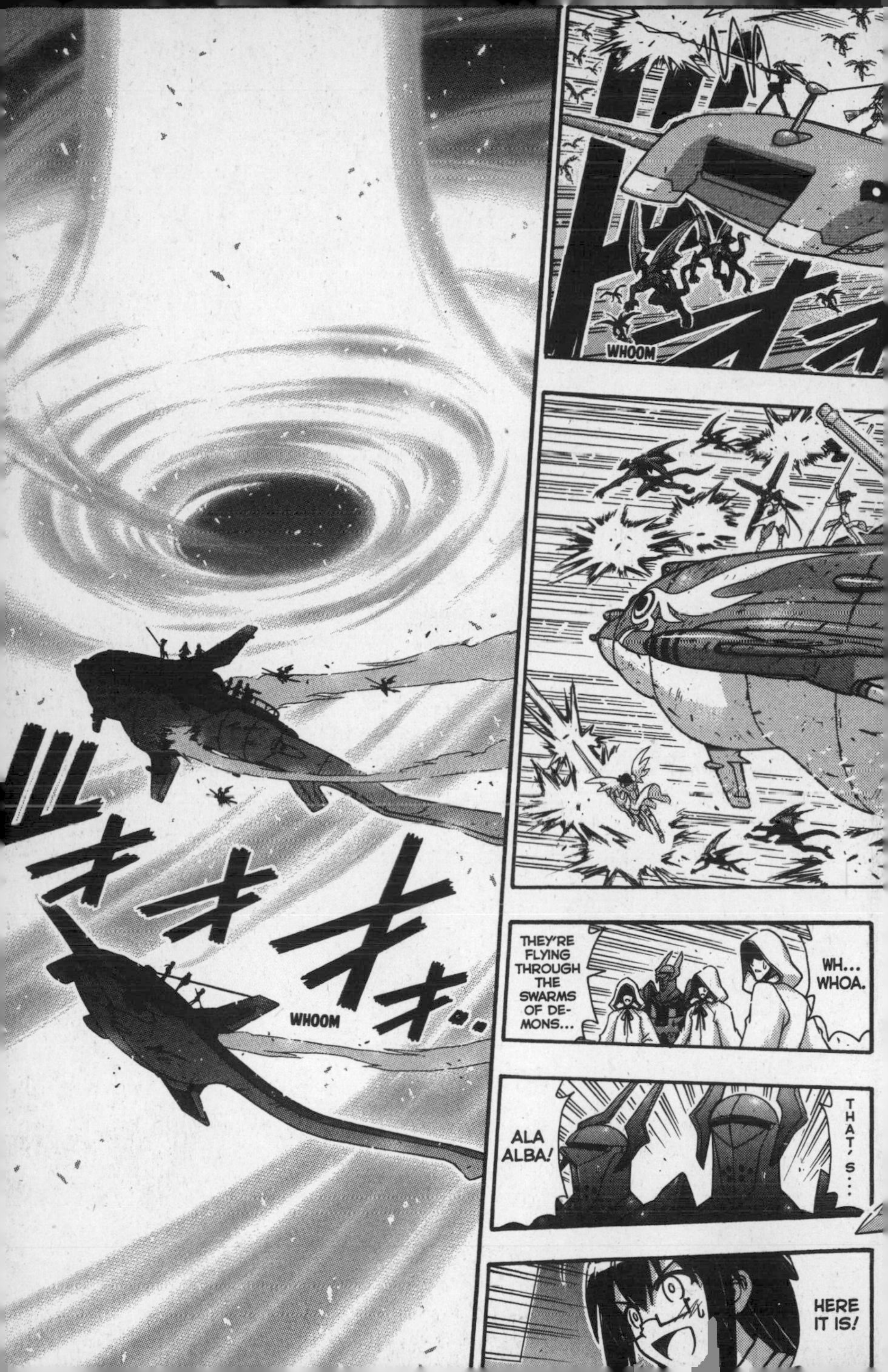
WHOOM
WH... WHOA.
THEY'RE FLYING THROUGH THE SWARMS OF DEMONS...
THAT'S...
ALA ALBA!
HERE IT IS!
WHOOM

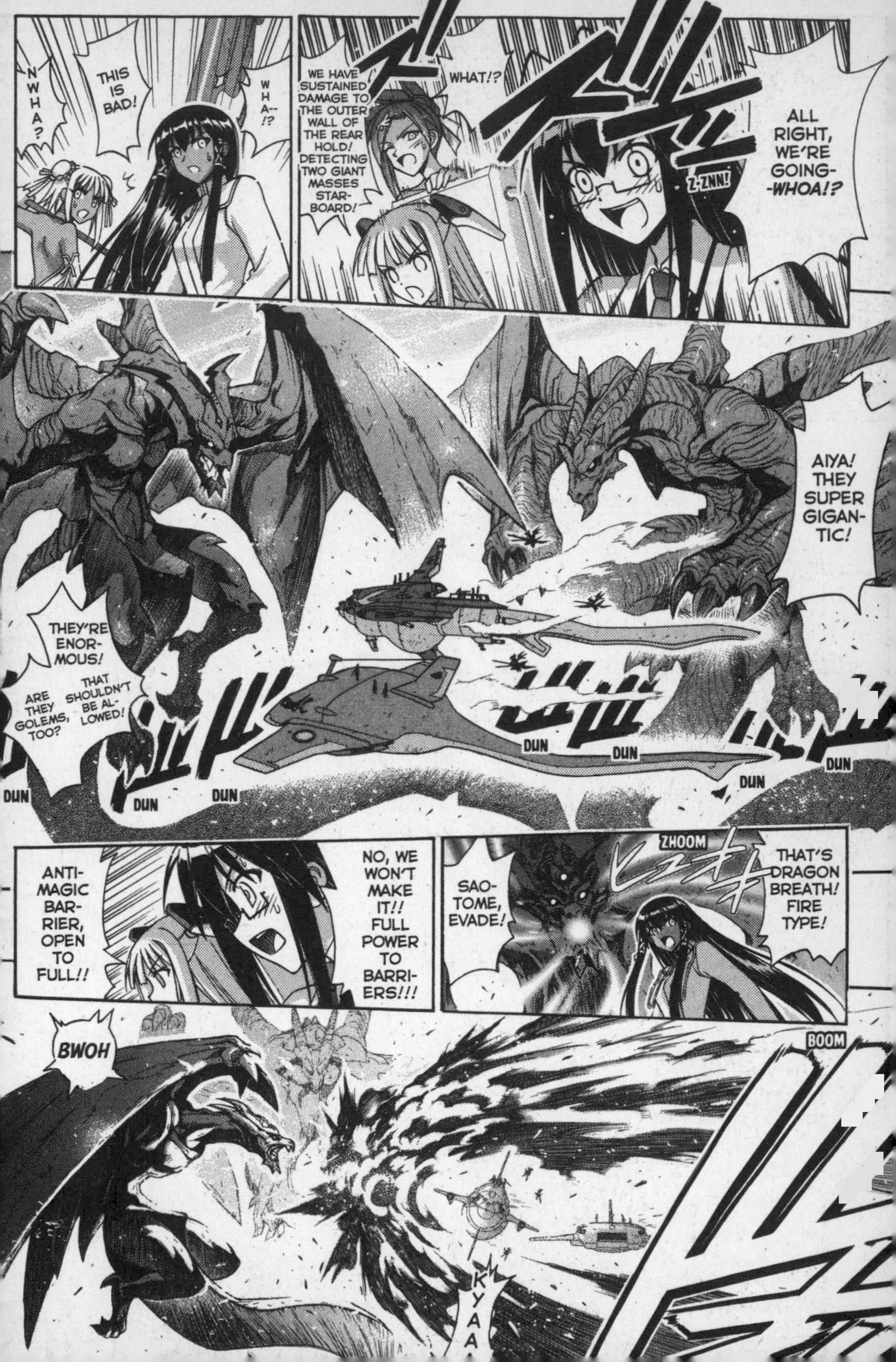

ALL RIGHT, WE'RE GOING- -WHOA!?
Z-ZNN!
WHAT!?
WE HAVE SUSTAINED DAMAGE TO THE OUTER WALL OF THE REAR HOLD! DETECTING TWO GIANT MASSES STARBOARD!
WHA--!?
THIS IS BAD!
NWHA?
AIYA! THEY SUPER GIGANTIC!
DUN
DUN
DUN
DUN
THEY'RE ENORMOUS!
THAT SHOULDN'T BE ALLOWED!
ARE THEY GOLEMS, TOO?
DUN
DUN
DUN
ZHOOM
THAT'S DRAGON BREATH! FIRE TYPE!
SAOTOME, EVADE!
NO, WE WON'T MAKE IT!! FULL POWER TO BARRIERS!!!
ANTI-MAGIC BARRIER, OPEN TO FULL!!
BOOM
BWOH
KYAA

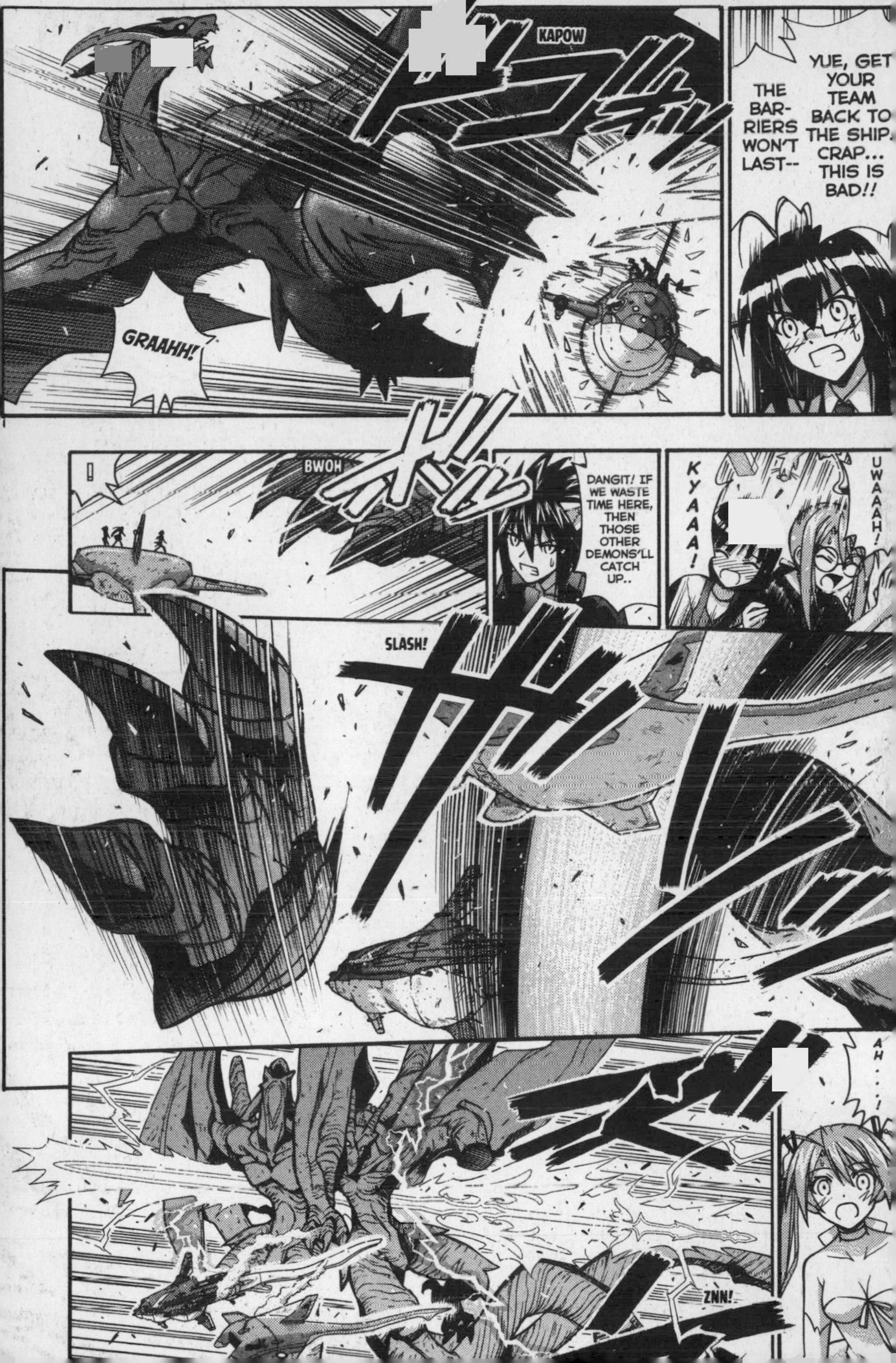
YUE, GET YOUR TEAM BACK TO THE SHIP. CRAP... THIS IS BAD!!
THE BAR-RIERS WON'T LAST--
KAPOW
GRAAHH!
UWAAAAH!
KYAAAA!
DANGIT! IF WE WASTE TIME HERE, THEN THOSE OTHER DEMONS'LL CATCH UP..
BWOH
!
SLASH!
AH...!
ZNN!

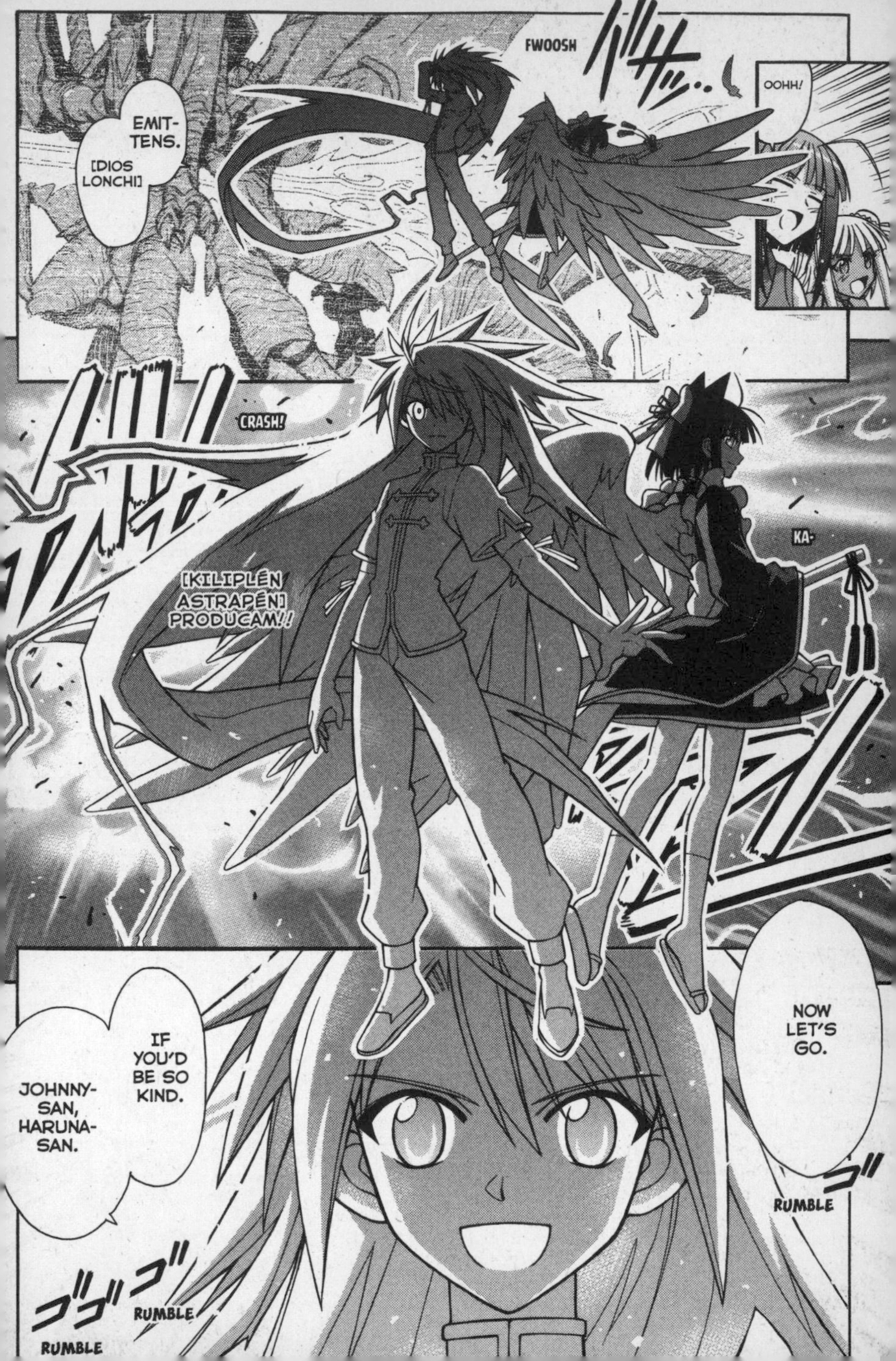
OOHH!
FWOOSH
EMIT-TENS.
[DIOS LONCHI]
CRASH!
KA-
[KILIPLÉN ASTRAPÉN] PRODUCAM!!
NOW LET'S GO.
IF YOU'D BE SO KIND.
JOHNNY-SAN, HARUNA-SAN.
RUMBLE
RUMBLE
RUMBLE

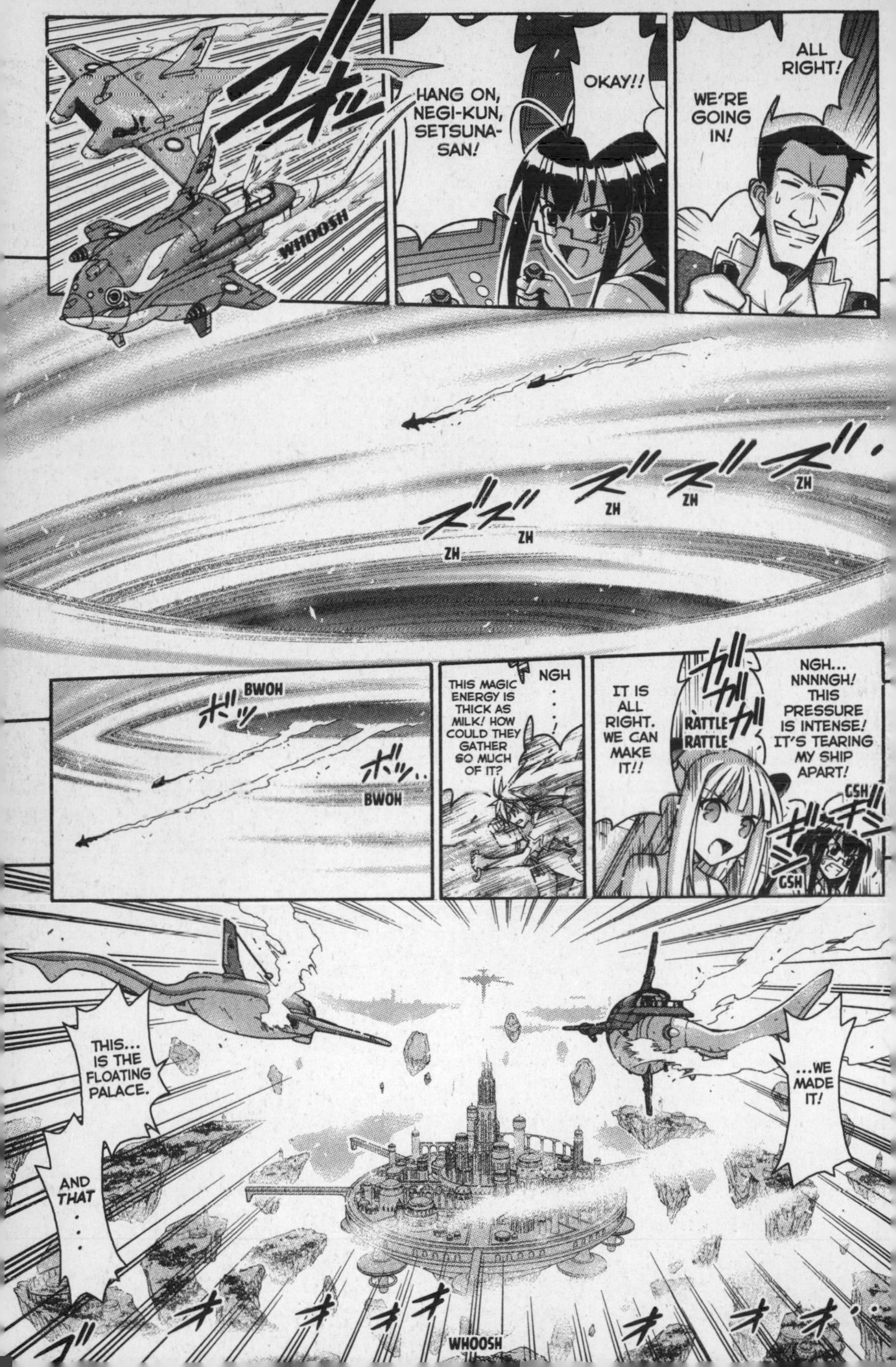
ALL RIGHT!
WE'RE GOING IN!
OKAY!!
HANG ON, NEGI-KUN, SETSUNA-SAN!
WHOOSH
ZH
ZH
ZH
ZH
ZH
NGH... NNNNGH! THIS PRESSURE IS INTENSE! IT'S TEARING MY SHIP APART!
RATTLE
RATTLE
IT IS ALL RIGHT. WE CAN MAKE IT!!
GSH
GSH
NGH . . . !
THIS MAGIC ENERGY IS THICK AS MILK! HOW COULD THEY GATHER SO MUCH OF IT?
BWOH
BWOH
...WE MADE IT!
THIS... IS THE FLOATING PALACE.
AND THAT . . .
WHOOSH

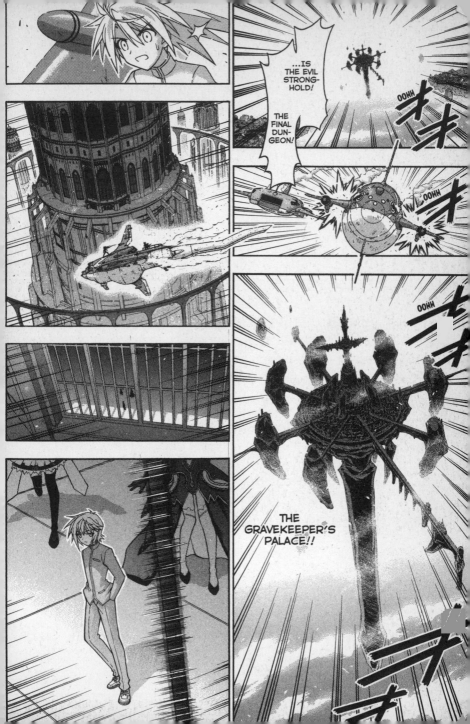

...IS THE EVIL STRONGHOLD!

THE FINAL DUNGEON!

OOHH

OOHH

OOHH

THE GRAVEKEEPER'S PALACE!!

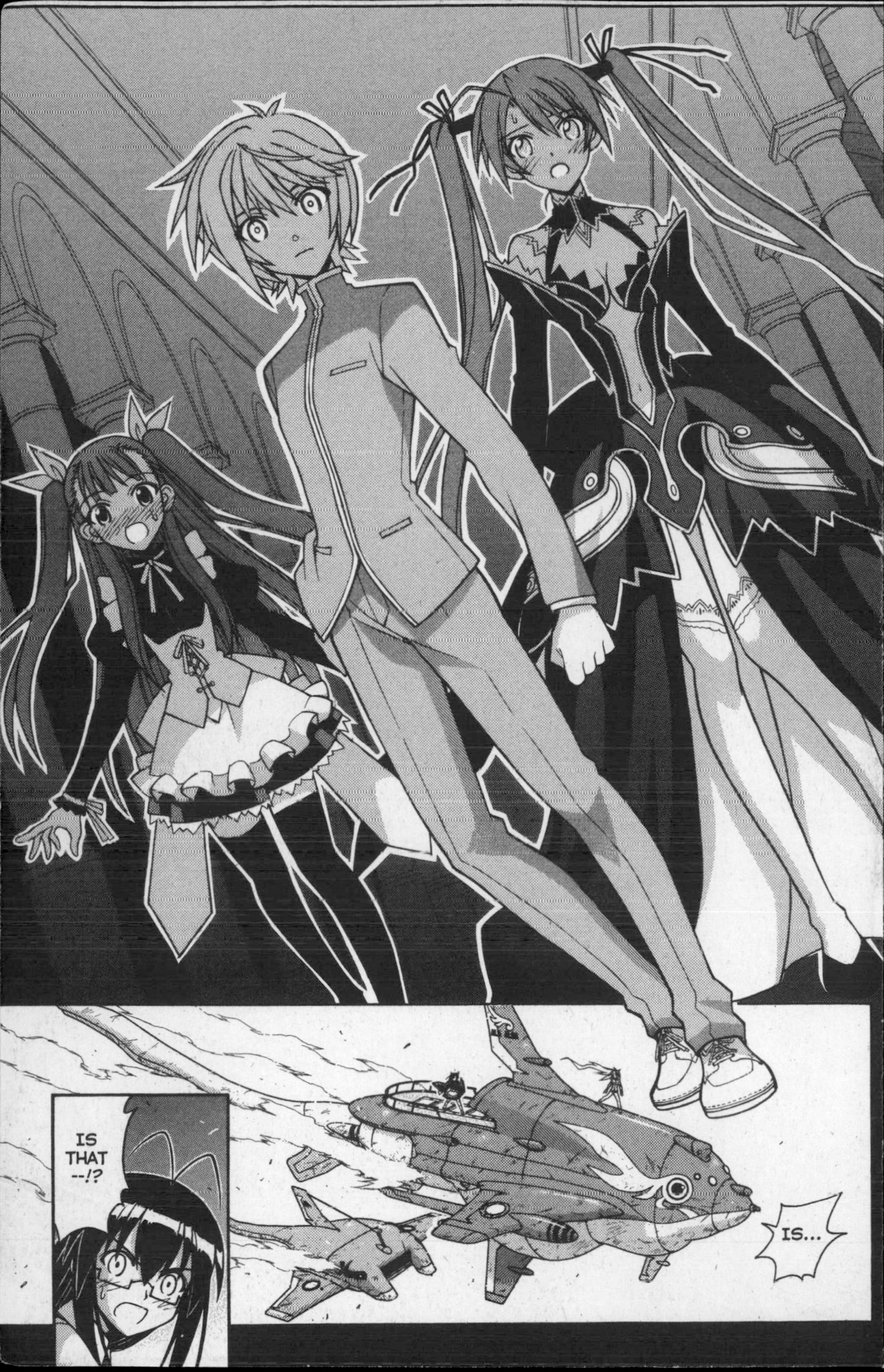
IS...
IS THAT --!?

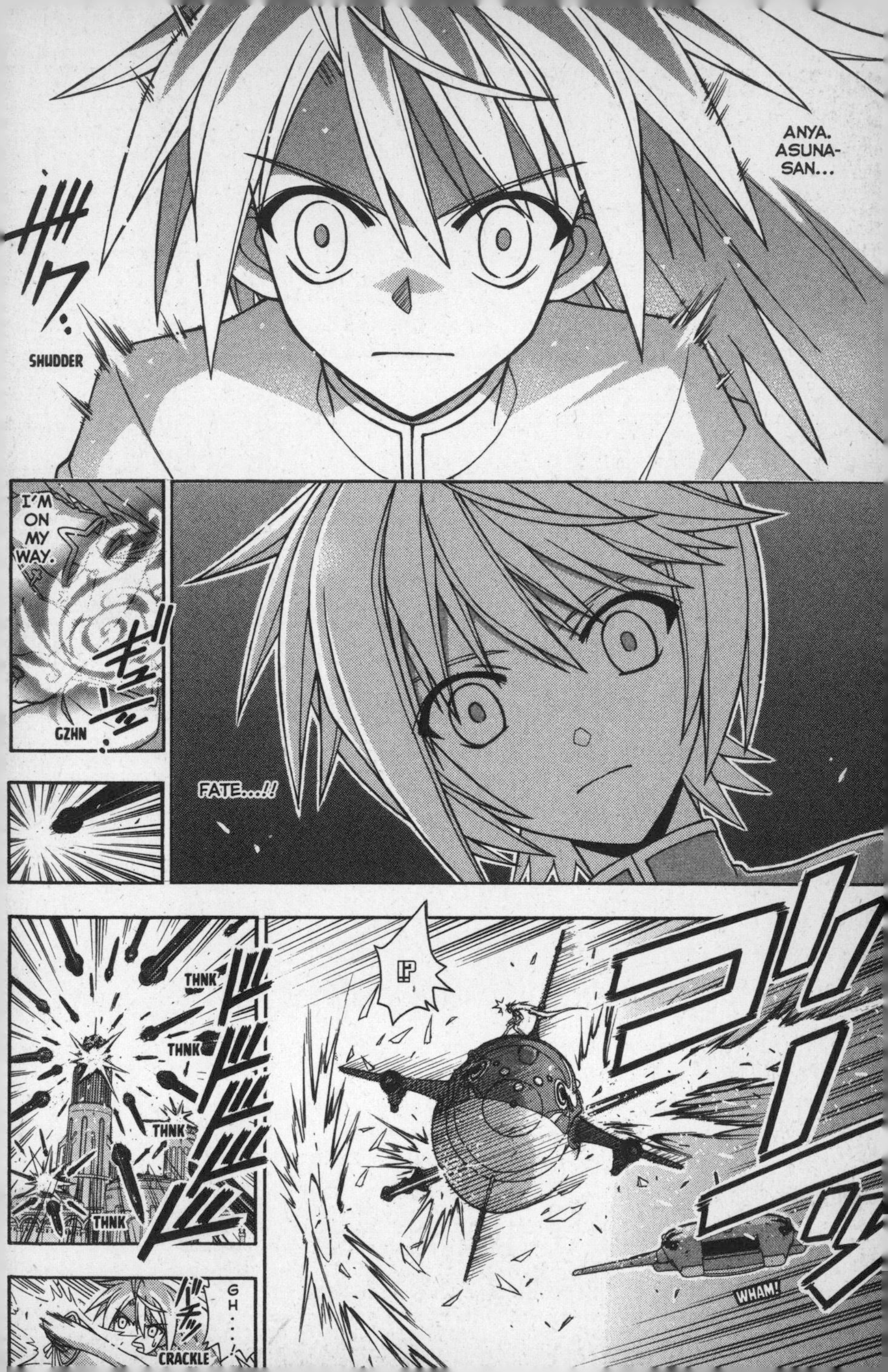

ANYA. ASUNA-SAN...
SHUDDER
FATE...!!
I'M ON MY WAY.
GZHN
!?
WHAM!
THNK
THNK
THNK
THNK
GH....
CRACKLE

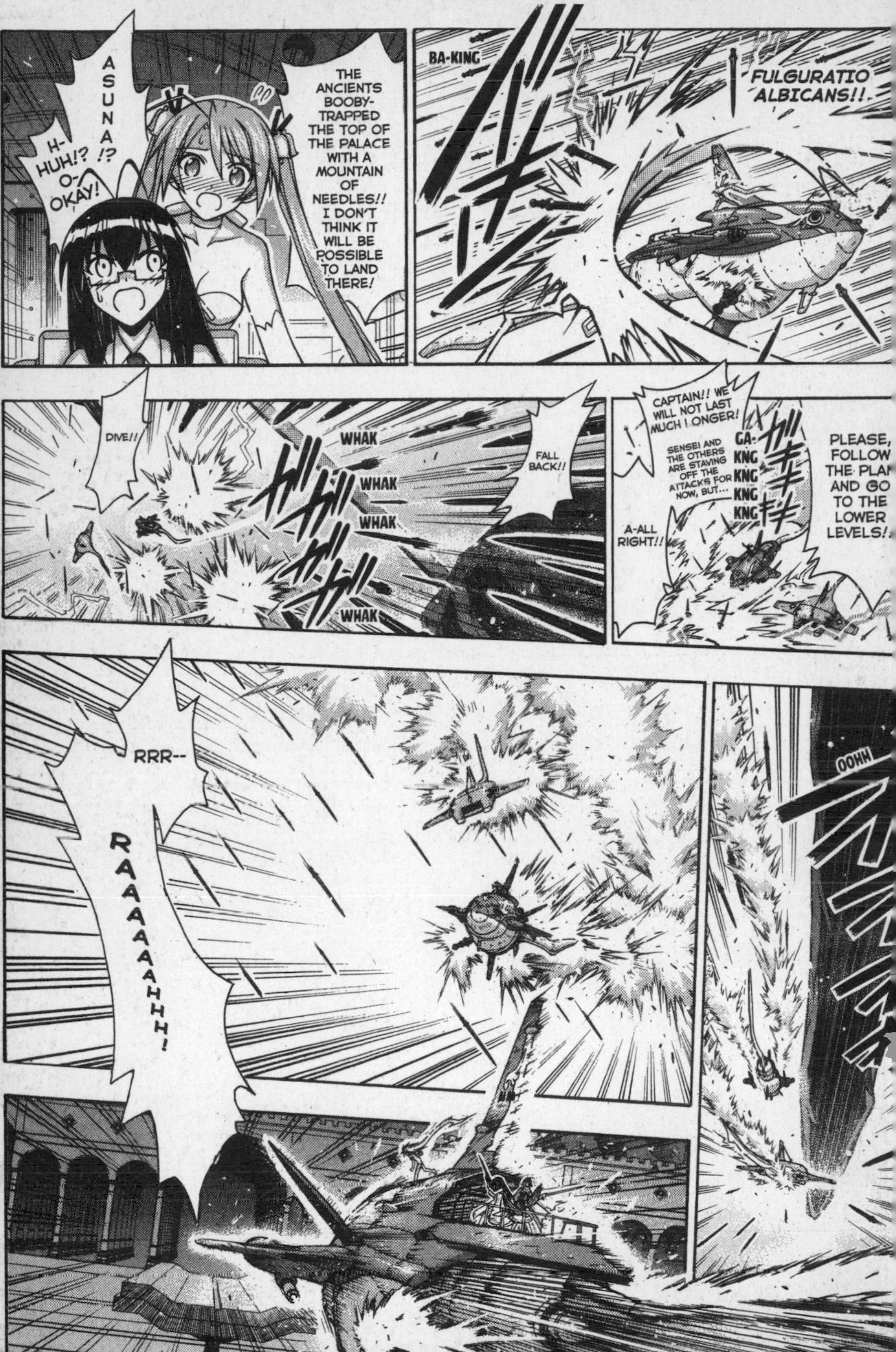
BA-KING
FULGURATIO ALBICANS!!
THE ANCIENTS BOOBY-TRAPPED THE TOP OF THE PALACE WITH A MOUNTAIN OF NEEDLES!! I DON'T THINK IT WILL BE POSSIBLE TO LAND THERE!
ASUNA!?
H-HUH!? O-OKAY!
CAPTAIN!! WE WILL NOT LAST MUCH LONGER!
PLEASE, FOLLOW THE PLA AND GO TO THE LOWER LEVELS!
SENSEI AND THE OTHERS ARE STAVING OFF THE ATTACKS FOR NOW, BUT...
GA-KNG KNG KNG KNG
A-ALL RIGHT!!
FALL BACK!!
WHAK
WHAK
WHAK
WHAK
DIVE!!
OOHH
RRR--
RAAAAAAAHHH!

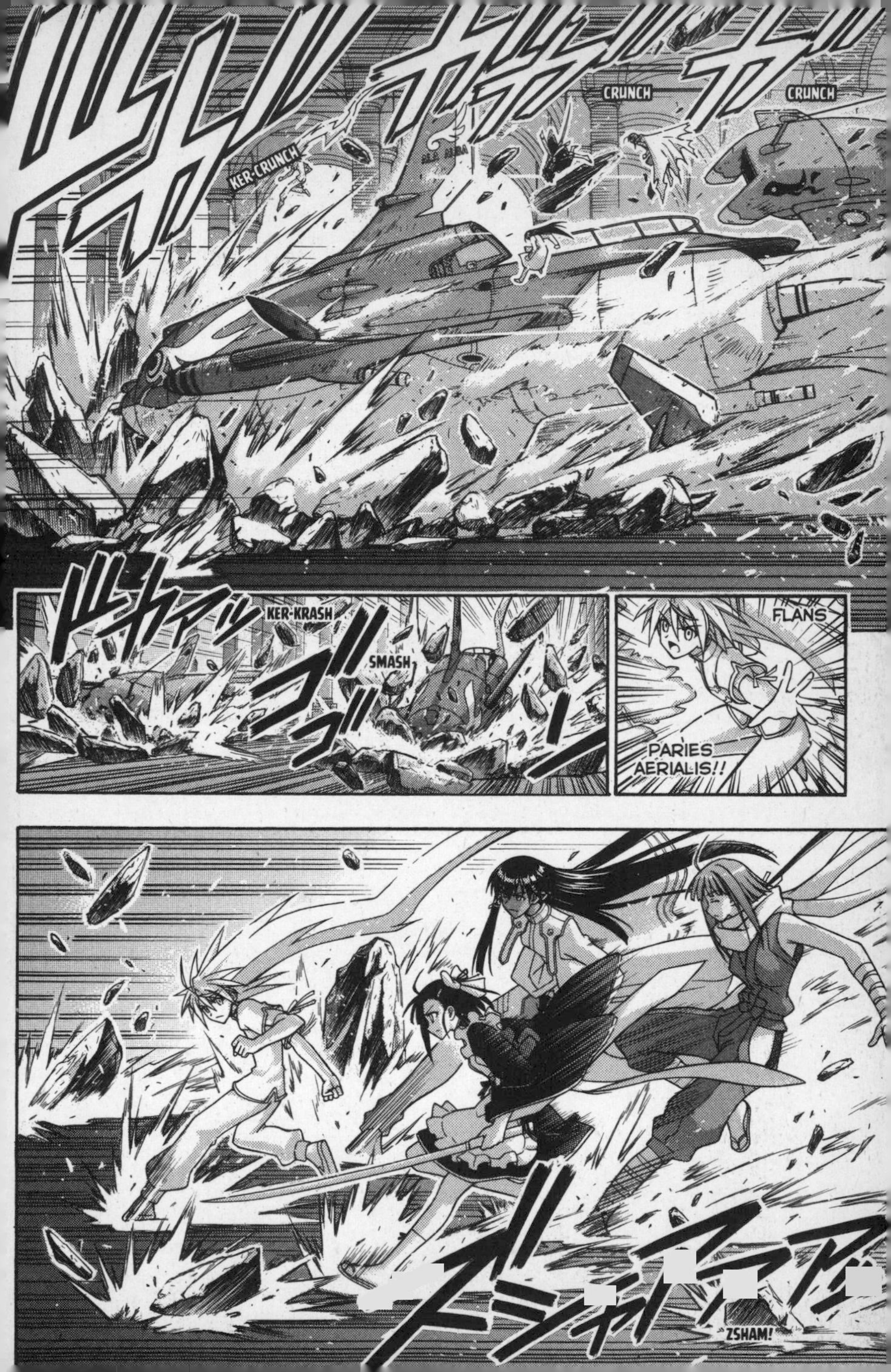
CRUNCH
CRUNCH
KER-CRUNCH
FLANS
PARIES AERIALIS!!
KER-KRASH
SMASH
ZSHAM!

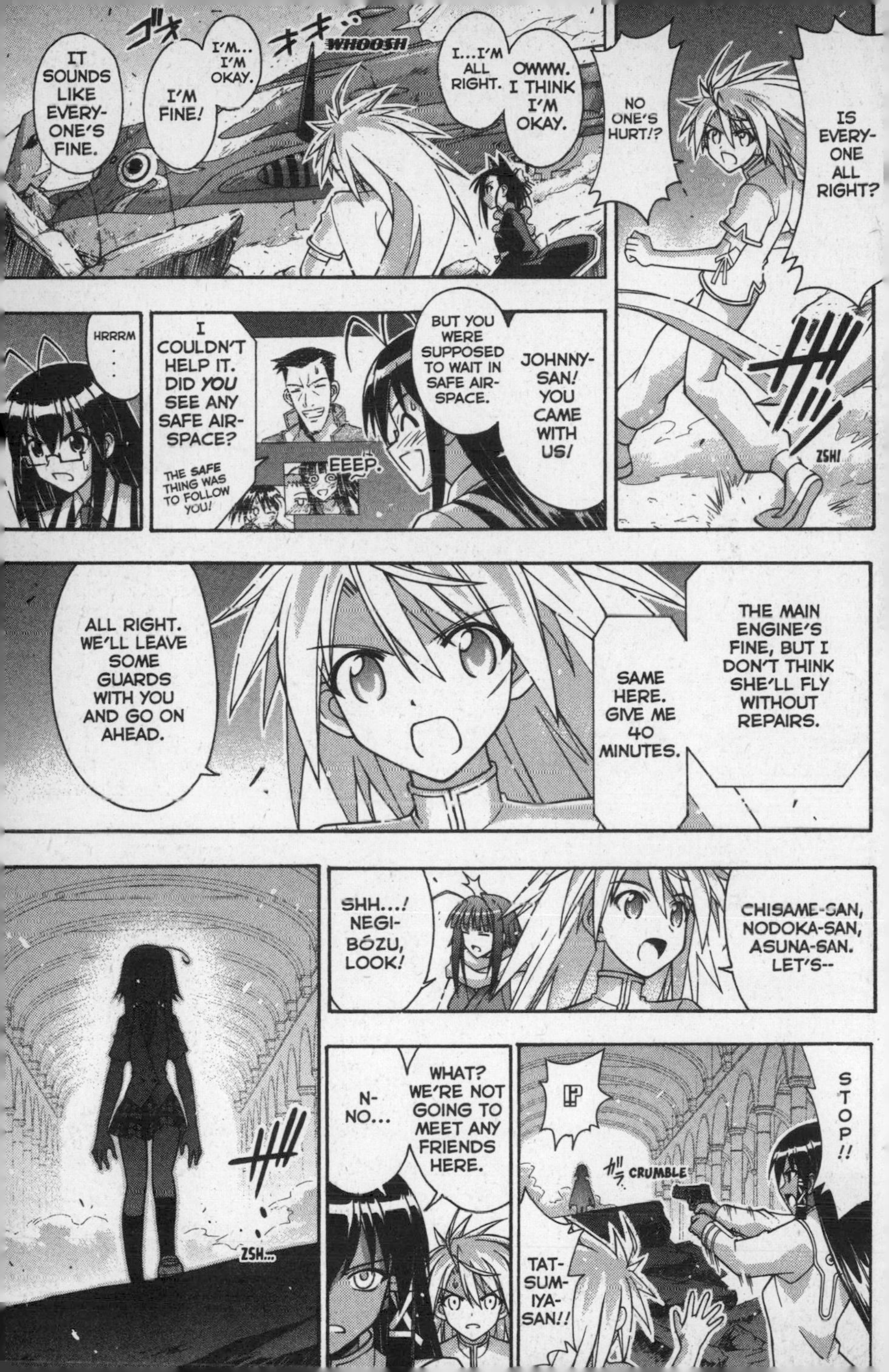
IS EVERYONE ALL RIGHT?
NO ONE'S HURT!?
ZSH!
I...I'M ALL RIGHT.
OWWW. I THINK I'M OKAY.
WHOOSH
I'M... I'M OKAY.
I'M FINE!
IT SOUNDS LIKE EVERYONE'S FINE.
JOHNNY-SAN! YOU CAME WITH US!
BUT YOU WERE SUPPOSED TO WAIT IN SAFE AIR-SPACE.
I COULDN'T HELP IT. DID *YOU* SEE ANY SAFE AIR-SPACE?
EEEP.
THE SAFE THING WAS TO FOLLOW YOU!
HRRRM...
THE MAIN ENGINE'S FINE, BUT I DON'T THINK SHE'LL FLY WITHOUT REPAIRS.
SAME HERE. GIVE ME 40 MINUTES.
ALL RIGHT. WE'LL LEAVE SOME GUARDS WITH YOU AND GO ON AHEAD.
CHISAME-SAN, NODOKA-SAN, ASUNA-SAN. LET'S--
SHH...! NEGI-BÓZU, LOOK!
STOP!!
!?
CRUMBLE
TATSUMIYA-SAN!!
WHAT? WE'RE NOT GOING TO MEET ANY FRIENDS HERE.
N-NO...
ZSH...

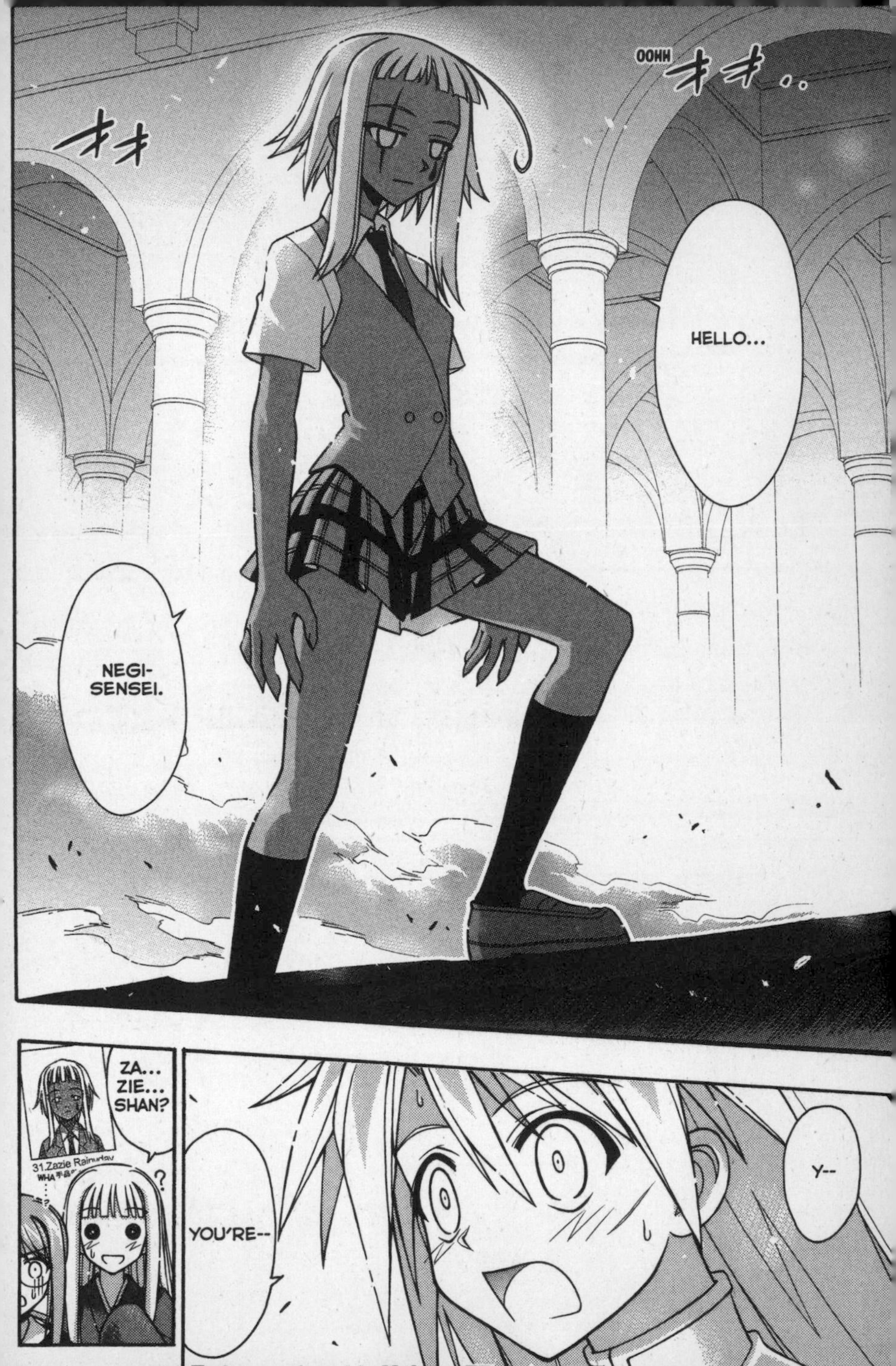
OOHH
オオ..
オオ
HELLO...
NEGI-SENSEI.
Y--
YOU'RE--
ZA... ZIE... SHAN?
31.Zazie Rainyday
WHA
?

To be continued in Volume 33

-STAFF-

Ken Akamatsu

Takashi Takemoto

Kenichi Nakamura

Keiichi Yamashita

Tohru Mitsuhashi

Yuichi Yoshida

Susumu Kuwabara

Thanks to
Ran Ayanaga

NEGI MA!

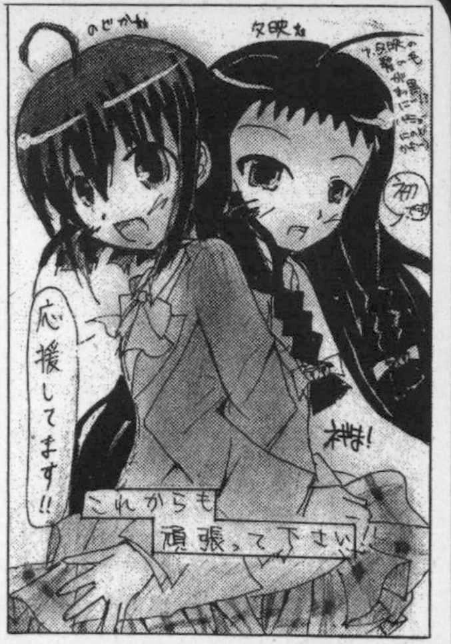
のどか
夕映
応援してます!!
これからも頑張って下さい!

NODOKA IS SO FULL OF LIFE!

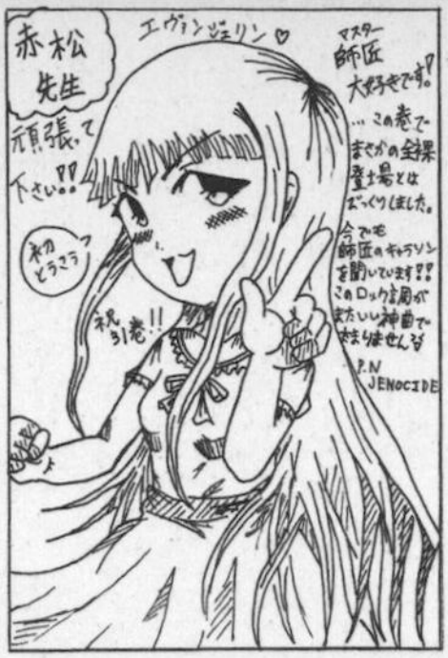
赤松先生頑張って下さい!!
エヴァンジェリン♡
マスター
師匠大好きです!
P.N. JENOCIDE

YOU'RE REALLY INTO IT, EVA ♪

JENOCIDEさん

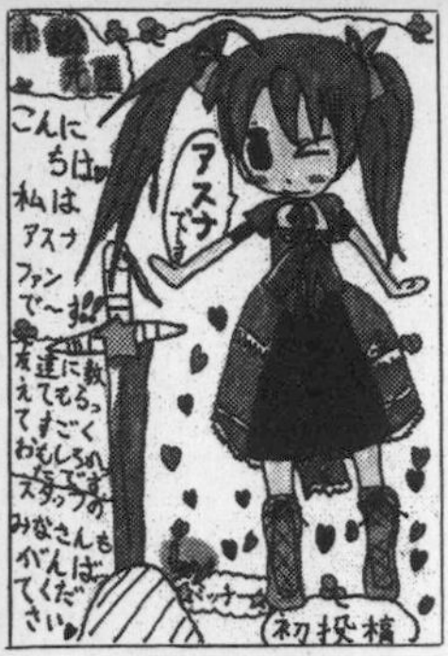
アスナです
こんにちは 私はアスナファンで〜す
みなさんもがんばってください
初投稿

SHE'S LIKE A MAGICAL GIRL ♪

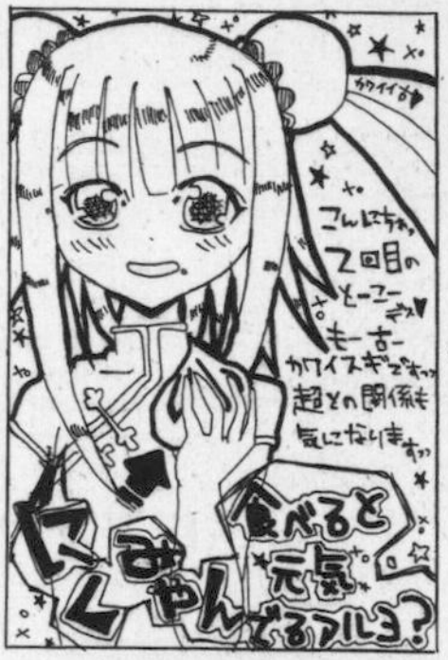
食べると元気

SUCH A CUTE KŪ!

NEGIMA!
FAN ART CORNER

AS USUAL, THANK YOU FOR ALL YOUR DRAWINGS AND LETTERS! I THINK SHIORI IS SLOWLY CLIMBING THE POPULARITY LADDER THESE DAYS. MASTER KŪ AND THE COMMANDER ARE DOING WELL, TOO ♪ PLEASE, BY ALL MEANS, SHINE LIGHT ON OTHER CHARACTERS THAT DON'T GET MUCH PAGE SPACE! (LAUGH) PLEASE SEND ART TO THE KODANSHA EDITORIAL DEPARTMENT ADDRESS AT THE END OF THE BOOK *

TEXT BY MAX

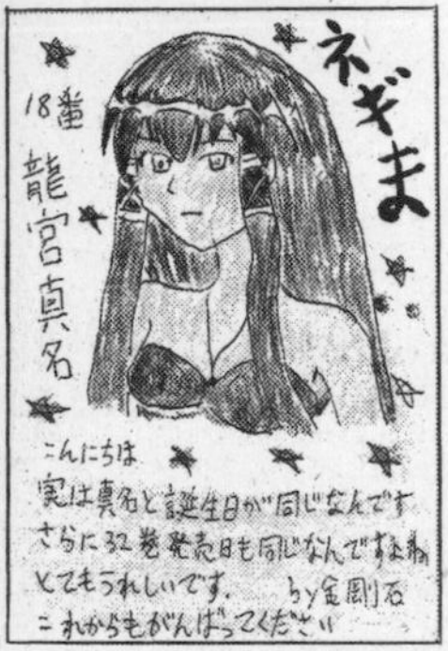
ネギま
18番
龍宮真名
こんにちは
これからもがんばってください

SEXY COMMANDER

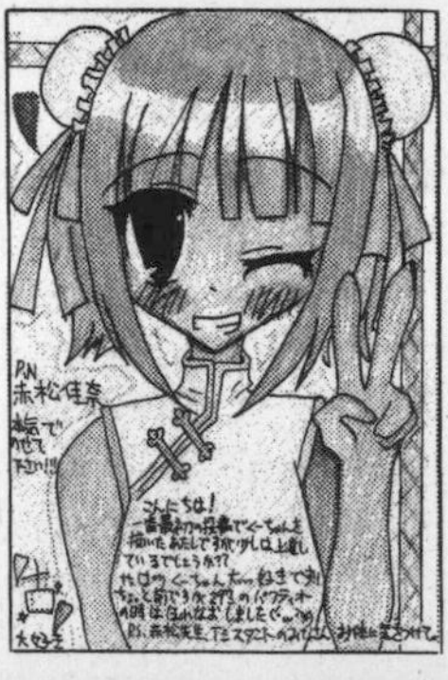
P.N.

BIG-EYED KŪ!

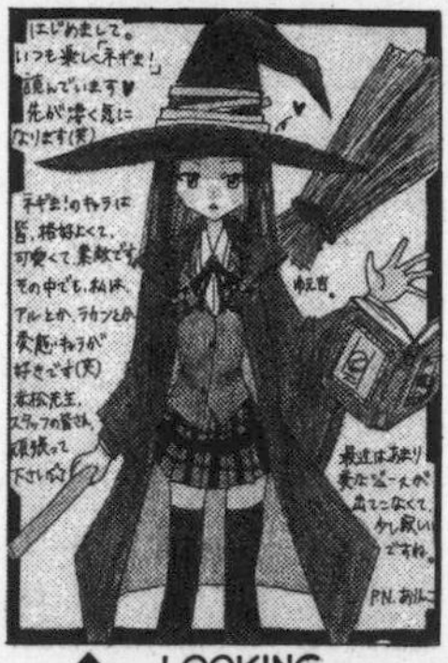
はじめまして。
P.N.

LOOKING SHARP, YUEKICHI!

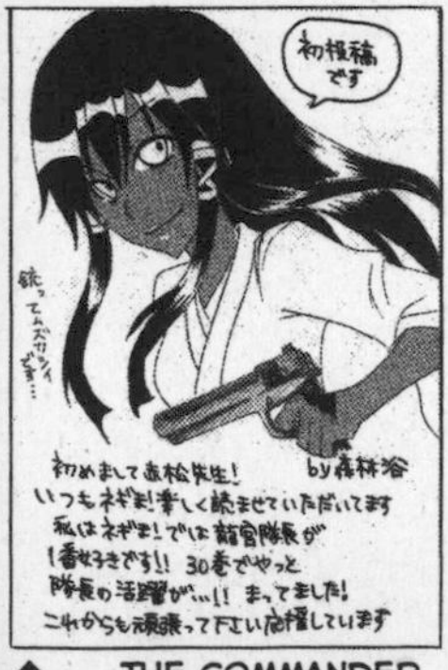
初投稿です
初めまして赤松先生!
これからも頑張って下さい

THE COMMANDER, BRIMMING WITH CONFIDENCE.

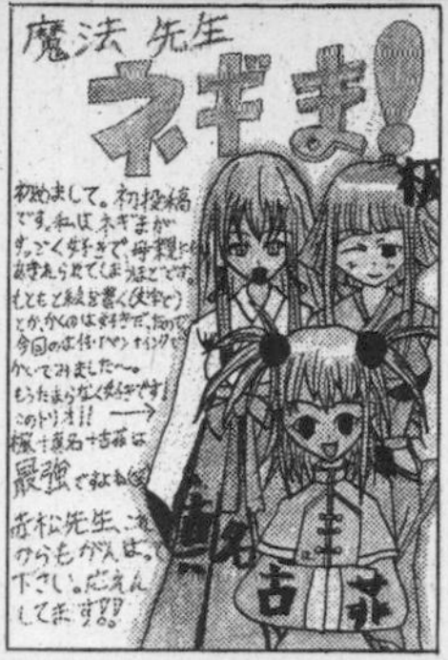
魔法先生
ネギま!

▲ AN INVINCIBLE TRIO.

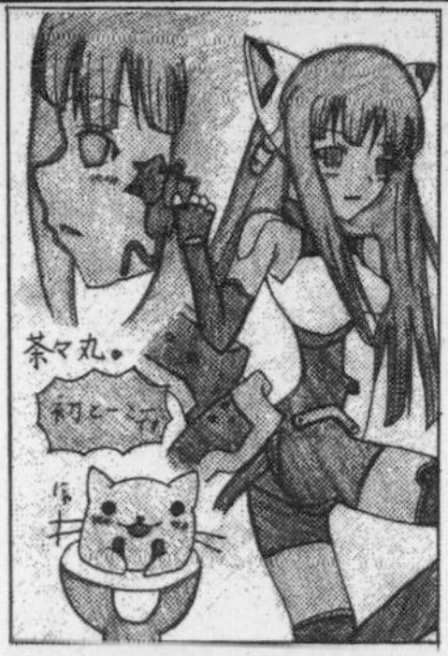
茶々丸。

▲ YOU'RE TOUGH, CHACHAMARU.

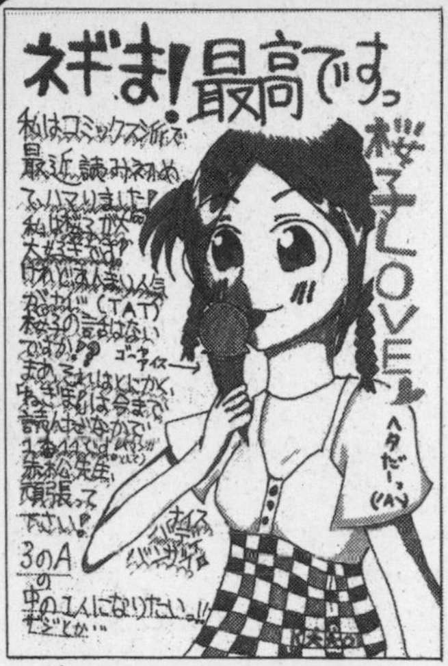
ネギま!最高です。
桜子LOVE

▲ PLEASE KEEP ROOTING FOR SAKURAKO.

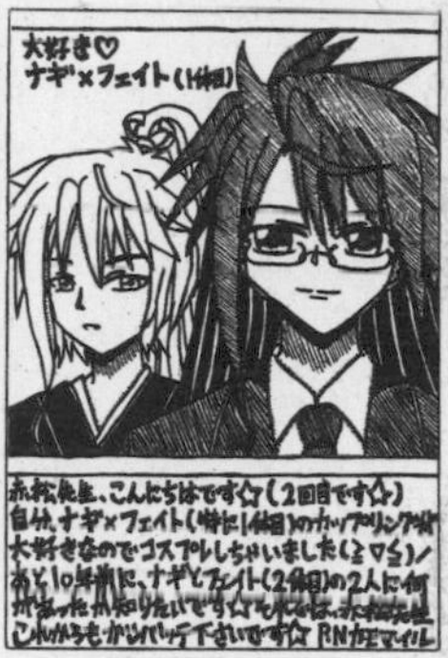

▲ THEY LOOK GOOD TOGETHER. (LAUGH)

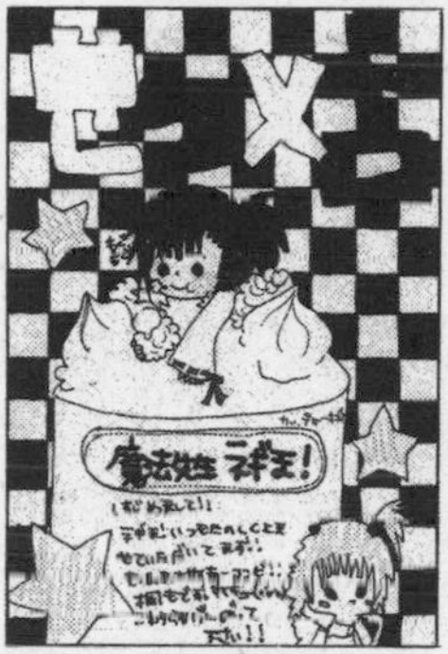
魔法先生ネギま!

▲ THEY SEEM SO STYLISH.

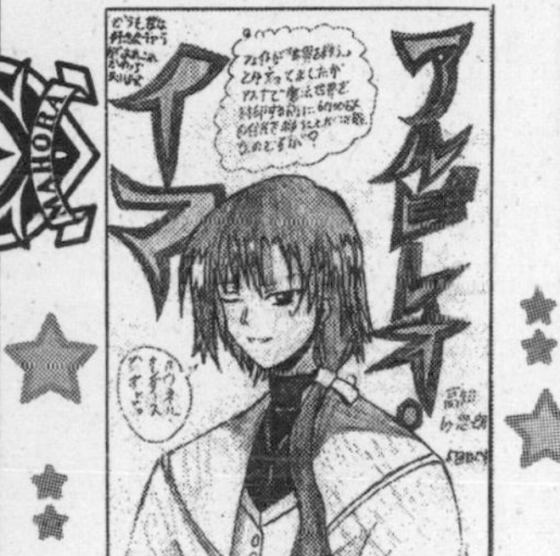

▲ A VERY NICE KŪ:NEL.

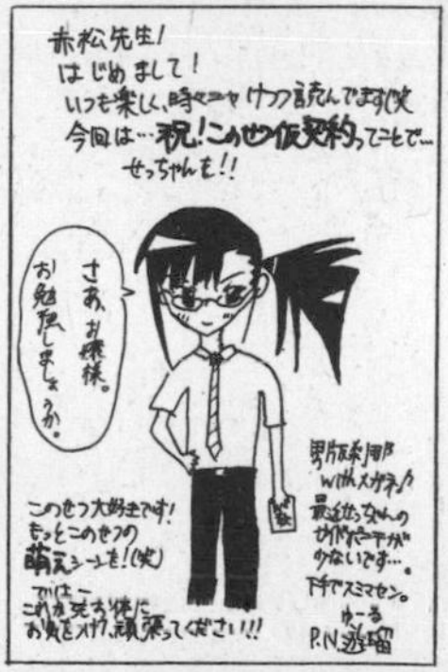
赤松先生!
はじめまして!
今回は…祝!このせつ仮契約ってことで…
せっちゃんを!!

▲ IT HAS AN UNUSUAL CHARM.

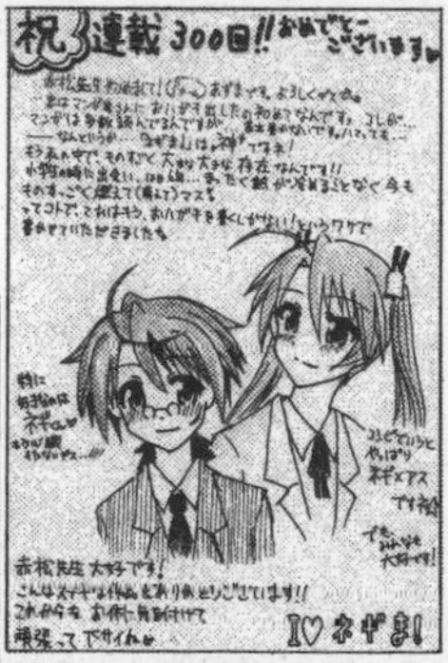
祝 連載300回!! おめでとうございます。
I♡ネギま!

▲ THE STANDARD FAVORITES.

▼ SHIORI REALLY IS ADORABLE.

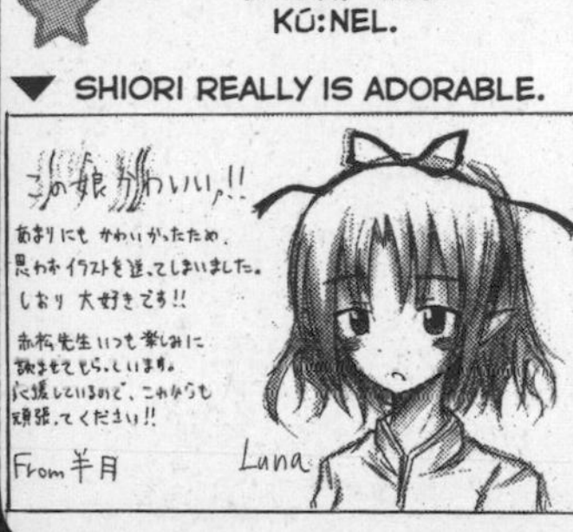
この娘かわいい!!
しおり 大好きです!!
From 半月
Luna

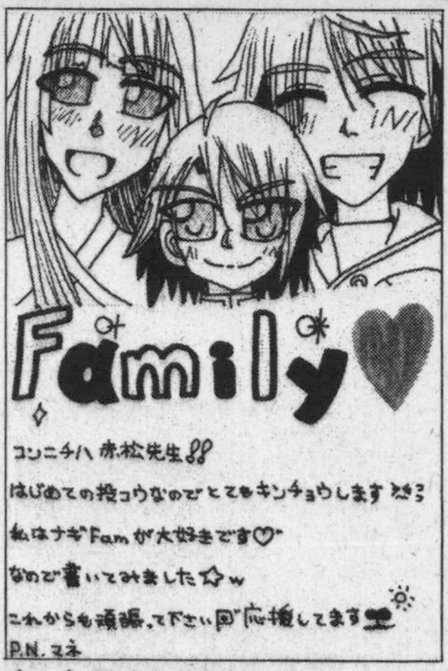
Family
コンニチハ赤松先生!!
はじめての投コウなのでとてもキンチョウします
私はネギFamが大好きです♡
なので書いてみました☆w
これからも頑張って下さい!!応援してます
P.N.マネ

▲ THEY LOOK LIKE A WARM FAMILY.

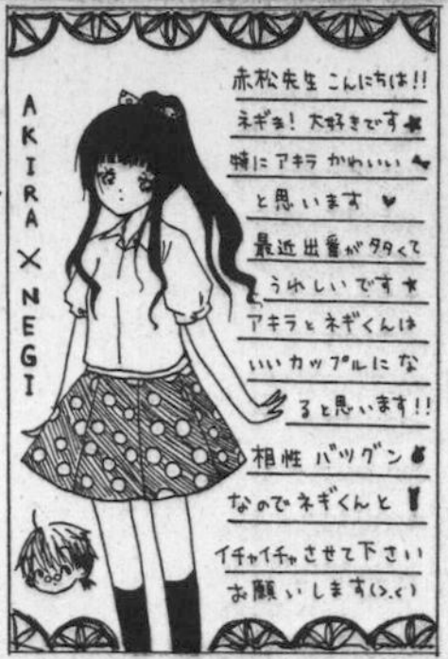
AKIRA × NEGI
赤松先生こんにちは!!
ネギま!大好きです
特にアキラかわいい
と思います♥
最近出番が多くて
うれしいです
アキラとネギくんは
いいカップルにな
ると思います!!
相性バッグン
なのでネギくんと
イチャイチャさせて下さい
お願いします(>_<)

▲ AKIRA IS SOOOOOOO CUTE ♪

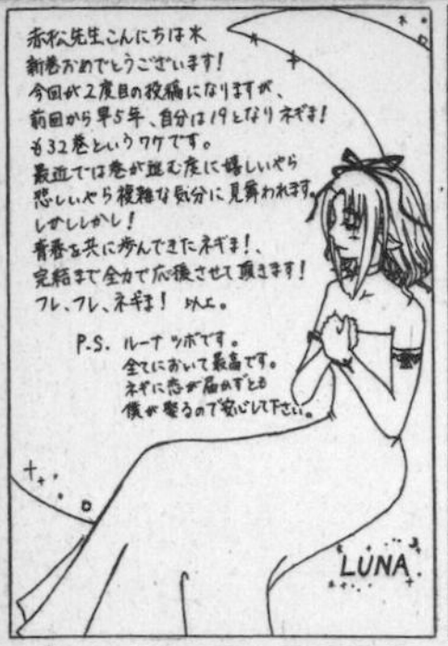
赤松先生こんにちは
新巻おめでとうございます!
今回が2度目の投稿になりますが、
前回から早5年、自分は19となりネギま!
も32巻というワケです。
最近では巻が進む度に嬉しいやら
恐しいやら複雑な気分に見舞われます。
しかししかし!
青春を共に歩んできたネギま!、
完結まで全力で応援させて頂きます!
フレ、フレ、ネギま! 以上。
P.S. ルーナツボです。
全てにおいて最高です。
ネギに恋が届かずとも
僕が養うので安心して下さい。
LUNA

▲ LUNA-SAN SURE IS POPULAR ♪

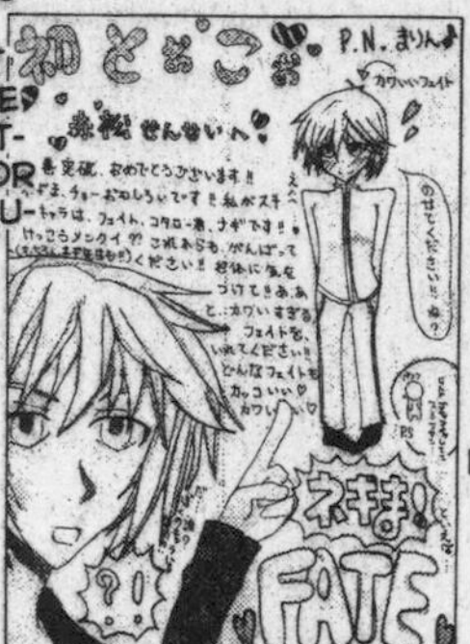
P.N.まりん
赤松せんせいへ!
ネギま!
FATE

◀ YOU'RE REALLY PUSHING FOR FATE ♪

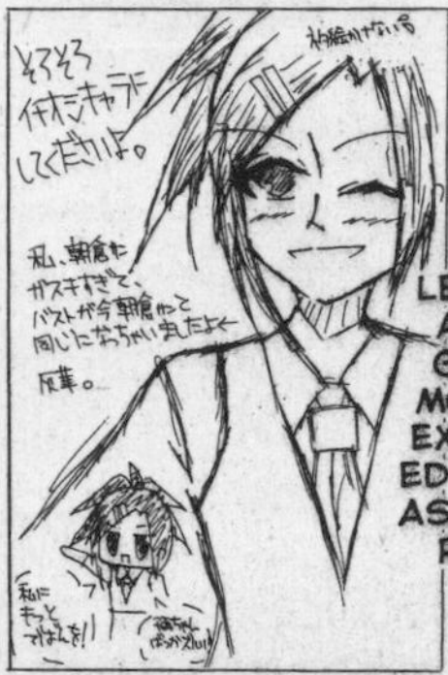

◀ LET'S ALL GET MORE EXCITED FOR ASAKURA!

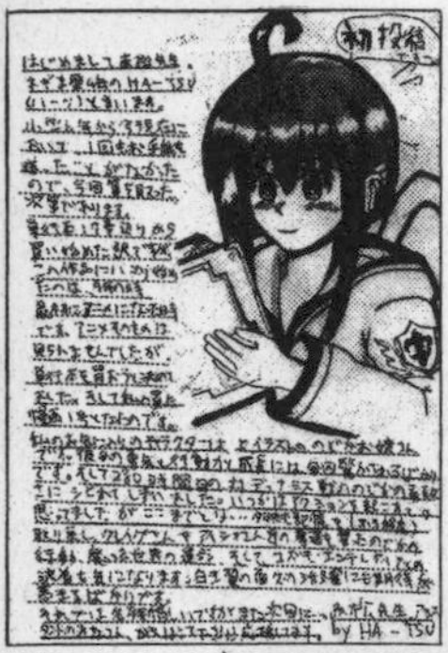
by HA-TSU

▲ NO-DOKA'S PLAYING A BIG PART, TOO.

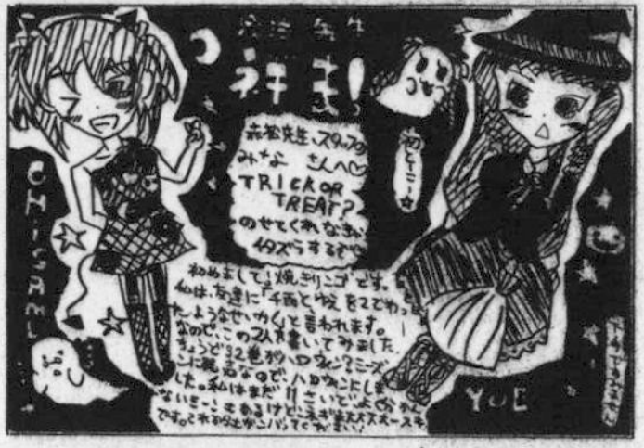
ネギま!
TRICK OR TREAT?
CHISAME
YUE

◀ THEIR COSTUMES ARE SO CUTE.

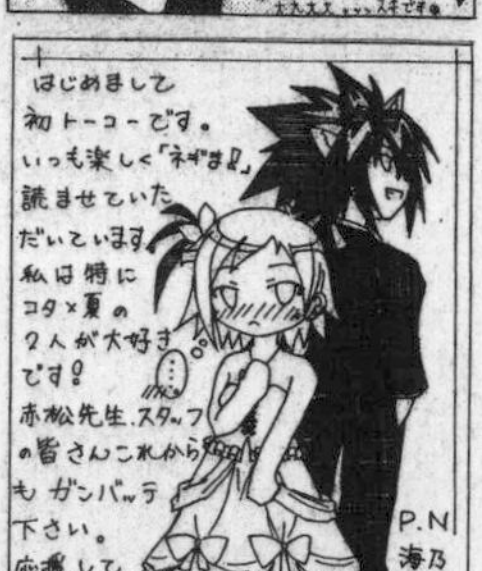
はじめまして
初トーコーです。
いつも楽しく「ネギま!」
読ませていた
だいています。
私は特に
コタ×夏の
2人が大好き
です!
赤松先生、スタッフ
の皆さんこれから
もガンバッテ
下さい。
応援して
います。
P.N
海乃
この2人今後どうなるんでしょうかねぇ?

◀ AN INCREDIBLY CUTE COUPLE.

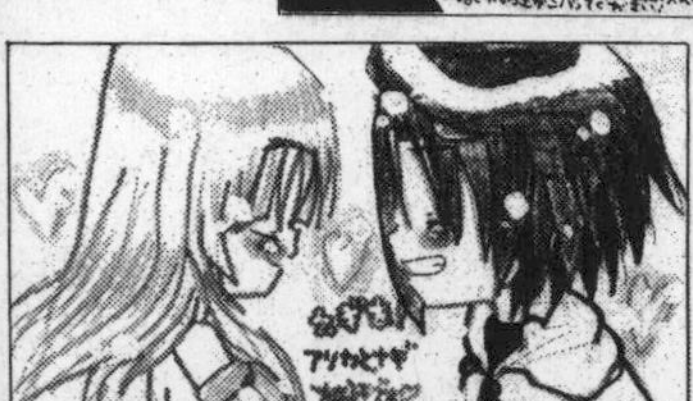

◀ SO ROMANTIC ♪

THIS VOLUME'S いち押しキャラ!

MOST DRAWN CHARACTER!

ネギ・NEGI・スプリングフィールド SPRINGFIELD

ランキング Ranking

MAGISTER NEGI MAGI

第1位

1st Place

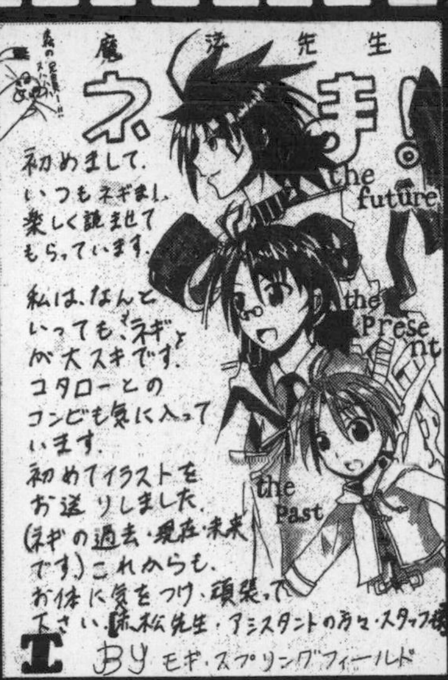

魔法先生
ネギま！
the future
the Present
the Past
初めまして。いつもネギま！楽しく読ませてもらっています。
私は、なんといっても、ネギとが大スキです。コタローとのコンビも気に入っています。
初めてイラストをお送りしました。(ネギの過去・現在・未来です。)これからも、お体に気をつけ、頑張って下さい。赤松先生・アシスタントの方々・スタッフ様
BY モギ・スプリングフィールド

DRAWING NEGI IN THE PAST, PRESENT, AND FUTURE!! IT'S SUCH AN ORIGINAL IDEA, IT WENT STRAIGHT TO FIRST PLACE. (^^)

AKAMATSU 赤松

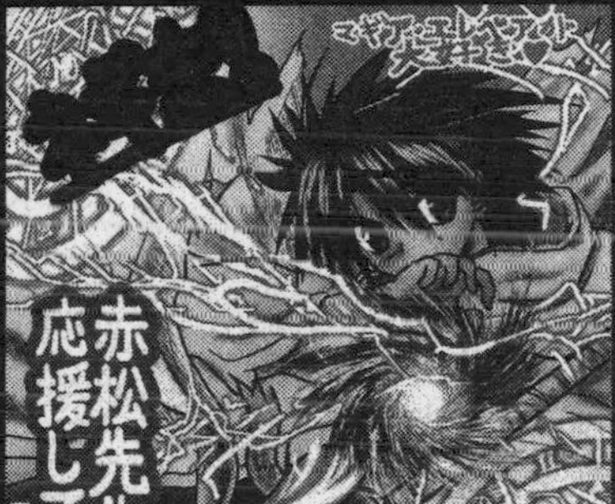

赤松先生応援してます！
negius spring fieldes

第2位

2nd Place

OOHHH! THIS IS A FAN ART POSTCARD PRINTED FROM A COMPUTER, ISN'T IT? THE COLORS ARE SO PRETTY ♥

3rd Place

第3位

ARMS AND FINGERS ARE PRETTY HARD TO DRAW. JUST LIKE MAGIC, THE ONLY THING FOR IT IS PRACTICE!!

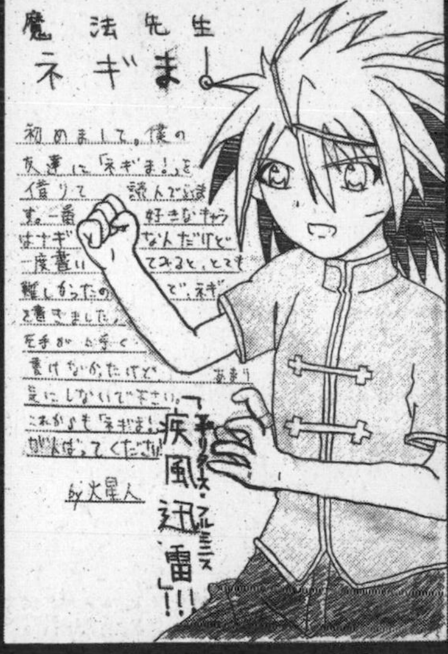

魔法先生
ネギま！
初めまして。僕の友達に「ネギま！」を借りて読んでます。一番好きなキャラはネギなんだけど一度書いてみると、とても難しかったので、ネギを書きました。
左手がうまく書けなかったけど、あまり気にしないで下さい。
これからも「ネギま！」頑張ってください。
疾風迅雷!!!
by 火星人

Misora Kasuga's
Life Counseling

HELLO! I'M THE NUN-IN-TRAINING, MISORA KASUGA. I FINALLY GOT MY VERY OWN SEGMENT. AND IT'S CALLED "MISORA KASUGA'S LIFE COUNSELING"! NOW, COCONE AND I WILL SOLVE ALL OUR CLASSMATES' PROBLEMS!

■ I'M YUE AYASE. I'M VERY PARTICULAR ABOUT THE UNDERWEAR I WEAR. HARUNA KEEPS TELLING ME I NEED TO THINK ABOUT ATTRACTING MEN, BUT I DON'T REALLY KNOW WHAT SHE MEANS.... SO WILL YOU PLEASE TELL ME WHAT "COLOR" OF UNDERWEAR WILL MAKE MEN'S HEARTS SKIP A BEAT? I WOULD LIKE TO GO BUY UNDERWEAR LIKE THAT WITH NODOKA SOMETIME. (NATSUKO KUWATANI (VOICE OF YUE), ASKING AS YUE)

★ BY MEN, YOU MEAN N-KUN, RIGHT? ER, JUST KIDDING! OUCH! IN THAT CASE, I THINK YOU'D BETTER AVOID SOMETHING TOO MATURE, LIKE BLACK. BUT WHITE IS TOO CHILDISH... MAYBE YOU SHOULD GO WITH SOMETHING INBETWEEN, LIKE SOME SHADE OF GREY. I WOULD HATE TO WEAR THAT, THOUGH (LAUGH).

"I THINK PINK WOULD BE CUTE..."

■ THIS IS NATSUMI. RECENTLY, CHIZU-NÉ'S BEEN STARING AT MY BUTT, WITH LEEKS IN HER HANDS. I'M SO SCARED I CAN'T SLEEP. WHAT SHOULD I DO...? (ADACHI, ASKING AS NATSUMI)

★ SHE'S PROBABLY LOOKING AT THE "PERSON WHO'S ALWAYS STANDING NEXT TO YOU." BUT YOU WON'T GET WHO THAT IS FROM ME!! NEE HEE HEE....

"KOTARO...?"

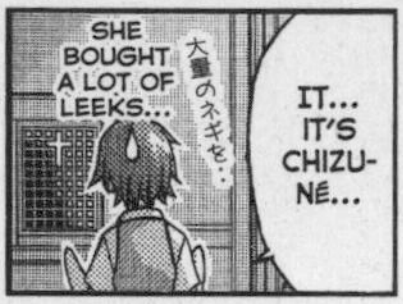
IT... IT'S CHIZU-NÉ...
大量のネギを‥
SHE BOUGHT A LOT OF LEEKS...

■ I'M AKIRA ŌKŌCHI. WILL MY STATUS AS A MEMBER OF THE SWIM TEAM EVER BE USEFUL TO THE PARTY? (HANZŌ, ASKING AS AKIRA)

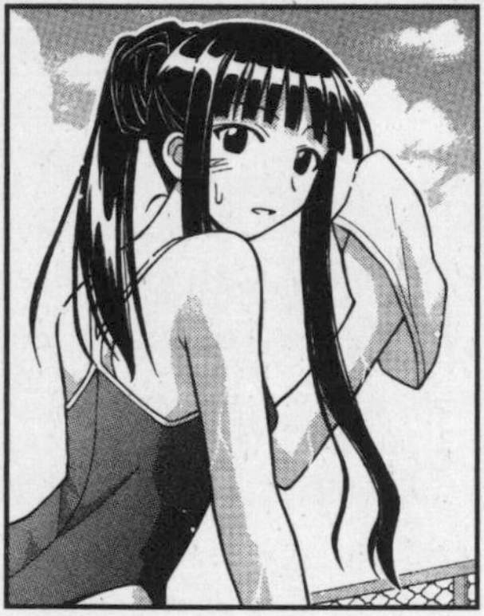

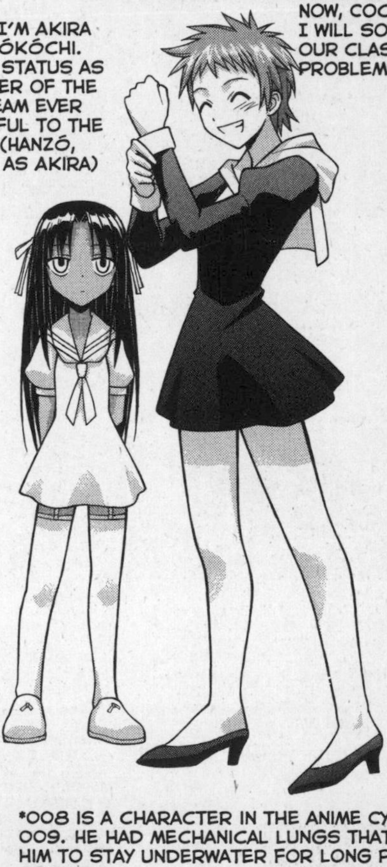

★ HMMM. I THINK THAT COULD BE DIFFICULT. 008* DIDN'T GET TO HELP MUCH EITHER. (LAUGH)

"WHAT ARE YOU TALKING ABOUT...?"

■ THE NAME'S ALBERT CHAMOMILE. LOOK AT ME. I'M FRICKIN' ADORABLE! BUT FOR SOME REASON, I HAVEN'T BEEN ON THE GRAPHIC NOVEL COVERS AT ALL LATELY! WHAT SHOULD I DO? TELL ME! (PAPI-GERI, ASKING AS CHAMO)

★ NOW THAT YOU MENTION IT, I HAVEN'T SEEN YOU AROUND ANYWHERE, CHAMOCCHI. I GUESS YOU'RE JUST NOT VERY POPULAR. NA HA HA...

"I DON'T THINK YOU'RE ONE TO TALK..."

*008 IS A CHARACTER IN THE ANIME CYBORG 009. HE HAD MECHANICAL LUNGS THAT HELPED HIM TO STAY UNDERWATER FOR LONG PERIODS OF TIME.

■ MY NAME'S ANYA. I HEARD SOMETHING THAT OPENED MY EYES: "SMALL BREASTS ARE A STATUS SYMBOL! THEY'RE A RARE COMMODITY!" EVERYONE IS BEING DECEIVED BY GIANT BREASTS! WHAT SHOULD I DO TO GET PEOPLE TO UNDERSTAND THE VALUE OF SMALL BREASTS? (TAKEFUMI, ASKING AS ANYA)

★ YEAH, SMALL BREASTS ARE GREAT! BIG ONES GET IN THE WAY WHEN YOU RUN AND STUFF. AND HEY, YOU'RE ELEVEN. STOP WORRYING ABOUT YOUR BREASTS!

"THIS ISN'T MUCH OF A CONSULTATION..."

■ THIS IS SHIORI. I GET CHILLS WHEN FATE-SAMA CALLS ME SHIORI-KUN, BUT WHEN NEGI-SAN CALLS ME LUNA-SAN, MY HEART MELTS. I'M TRYING TO DECIDE WHICH NAME SHOULD BE THE MIDDLE NAME IF I WERE TO CHANGE MY NAME TO INCLUDE BOTH. WHICH DO YOU THINK IS BETTER: LUNA SHIORI OR SHIORI LUNA? (HIRUMA, ASKING AS SHIORI)

★ LIVE STRONG.

"AND THERE IT IS..."

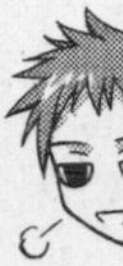

■ HARUNA SAOTOME HERE! I WANT TO BECOME WORLD FAMOUS BY DRAWING MANGA. WHAT MAGAZINE SHOULD I DEBUT WITH? SHOULD I GO WITH THE OBVIOUS CHOICE, *SHŌNEN MAGAZINE*? (KONGŌ-SEKI, ASKING AS HARUNA)

★ WELL, YOU ***HAVE*** TO GO WITH *MAGAZINE*. LOVE COMEDIES, BATTLE MANGA, GANGSTER MANGA, SPORTS MANGA--THEY'RE SO BROAD-MINDED, THEY'LL LET YOU DRAW ANYTHING! AND YOU MIGHT RUN INTO AKAMATSU-SENSEI IN THE EDITORIAL DEPARTMENT!

"...... (SWEAT DROP)"

AND NOW WE'LL SOLVE THE PERSONAL PROBLEMS OF *NEGIMA!*'S READERS.

NOW, LOST LAMBS... CONFESS YOUR SINS.

"YOU'RE CONFUSING THIS WITH A CONFESSIONAL..."

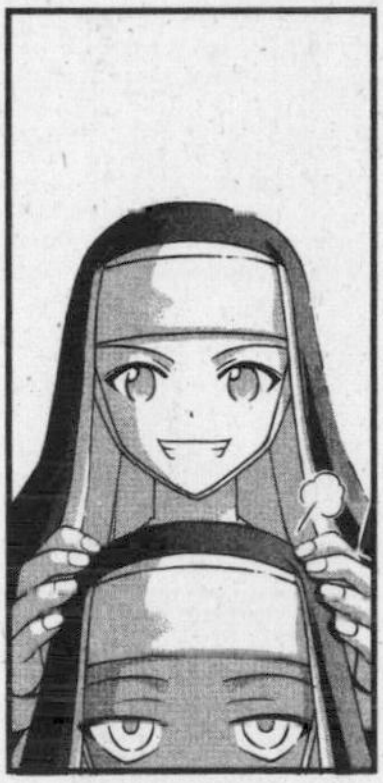

■ I DRAW MANGA WITH A VERY YOUNG GIRL AS THE MAIN CHARACTER. WHEN YOU HAVE A YOUNG GIRL AS THE MAIN CHARACTER, EVERYONE AROUND YOU TENDS TO THINK YOU'RE "INTO THAT," AND THEY ACT VERY STRANGE, TRYING NOT TO OFFEND YOU. WHAT SHOULD I DO? (KENJIRŌ HATA, AUTHOR OF *HAYATE THE COMBAT BUTLER*)

★ HMM, HMM. IF YOU WERE TO STOP DRAWING LITTLE GIRLS COLD TURKEY, THEY MIGHT BE EVEN MORE CAREFUL AROUND YOU. IT WILL LOOK LIKE YOU'RE TRYING DESPERATELY TO PROVE YOU'RE NOT INTO ANYTHING WEIRD. SO WHY NOT TRY DRAWING LOTS MORE LITTLE GIRLS? THEN THEY WON'T BE ABLE TO TELL WHAT KIND OF LITTLE GIRL YOU'RE DIRECTING YOUR LOVE AT!

"WHAT KIND OF MANGA WOULD THAT BE...? (SWEAT DROP)"

■ I LOVE FOOD. I REALLY LOVE FOOD. I LOVE IT SO MUCH, THAT I ALWAYS EAT A LOT, AND THEN I ALWAYS FEEL BAD ABOUT IT AFTERWARDS. WHAT CAN I DO TO EAT LESS? (AYANA TAKETATSU, VOICE OF EMILY SEVENSHEEP)

■ THAT'S A VERY LADYLIKE CONCERN! BUT I THINK IT'S BEST TO EAT LOTS WHILE YOU'RE STILL YOUNG! YOU CAN'T HAVE YOUR STOMACH GROWLING IN THE MIDDLE OF RECORDING SESSIONS, AFTER ALL (LAUGH). ★

"EAT A LOT OF SALAD BEFORE YOUR MEALS."

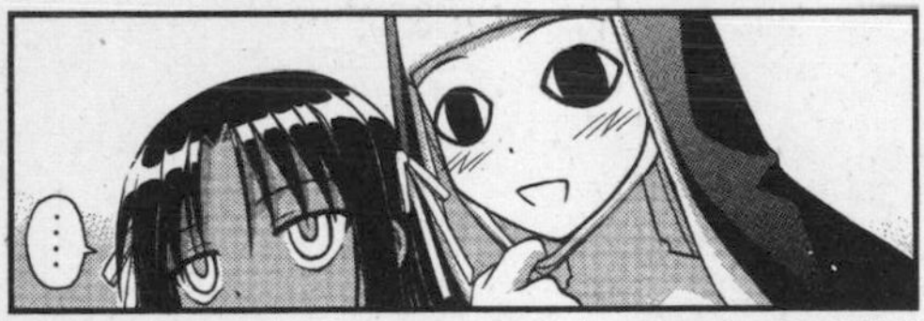
.....

PLEASED TO MEET YOU. I'M A 21-YEAR-OLD WOMAN WHO REALLY ENJOYS READING EVERY CHAPTER OF *NEGIMA!*. I HAD NEVER EXPERIENCED ROMANCE, SO LATELY I PANICKED AND STARTED DATING A GUY THAT I DON'T EVEN LIKE. I THINK IT'S POSSIBLE TO START LIKING A GUY ***WHILE*** DATING HIM, BUT THERE ARE NO SIGNS OF THAT HAPPENING, AND I'M SHY, SO IT'S REALLY HARD FOR ME TO TALK ABOUT BREAKING UP OR TO TELL HIM HOW I FEEL.... WHAT SHOULD I DO? (A A-S2)

★ HMMMM... YOU DON'T *LIKE* HIM, BUT IT SEEMS LIKE YOU DON'T REALLY *HATE* HIM, EITHER. SO MAYBE YOU SHOULD JUST TAKE IT EASY WITH THIS GUY, AND HOLD ON TO HIM WHILE LOOKING FOR ANOTHER GUY. YOU MIGHT FIND A BETTER GUY, OR START TO LIKE THE FIRST GUY. JUST BE OKAY WITH EITHER POSSIBILITY.

"I WONDER IF THE GUY LIKES YOU..."

■ I GOT A GIRLFRIEND RECENTLY, BUT I DON'T KNOW WHAT TO DO NEXT. WILL YOU PLEASE GIVE ME SOME ADVICE? (INDOMETHACIN)

★ FIRST, BUY HER EXPENSIVE GIFTS. LIKE MAYBE SOME TRACK SPIKES (LAUGH). SECOND, TELL HER YOU LOVE HER. WOMEN NEED YOU TO SAY THINGS OUT LOUD OR THEY DON'T ALWAYS KNOW HOW YOU FEEL.

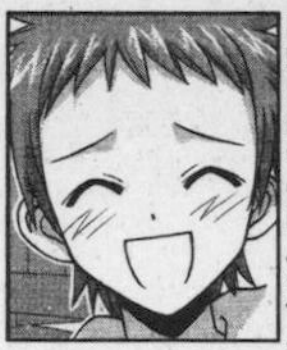

"...SHE ACTUALLY HAD SOME GOOD ADVICE FOR ONCE."

■ I'VE GRADUATED HIGH SCHOOL, AND I KEEP FAILING MY COLLEGE ENTRANCE EXAMS. WHICH WOULD MAKE A MORE EFFECTIVE GOOD-LUCK CHARM TO TAKE TO MY TESTS? *LOVE HINA* OR *NEGIMA!*? (TARŌ URASHIMA)

★ IF YOU THINK YOU'VE STUDIED HARD, *LOVE HINA*. IF YOU'RE RELYING ON LUCK, TAKE *NEGIMA!*.

"...?"

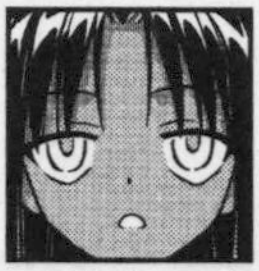

■ I'M 23 YEARS OLD, BUT I'VE NEVER HAD A GIRLFRIEND (CRY). IF THIS KEEPS UP, I'LL HAVE NO CHOICE BUT TO MAKE A TWO-DIMENSIONAL CHARACTER MY GIRLFRIEND. WHAT SHOULD I DO? (SUGACCHI)

★ NOTHING TO WORRY ABOUT! I HEAR EVEN AKAMATSU-SENSEI DIDN'T HAVE A GIRLFRIEND UNTIL HE WAS ABOUT 33! (LAUGH)

"POOR GUY..."

■ I KNOW IT'S RUDE TO PUT MYSELF ON NEGI-KUN'S LEVEL, BUT IF I HAD TO SAY ONE WAY OR THE OTHER, I'M A SUPER NEGATIVE PERSON. I TEND TO GET STUCK IN THE PAST AND STAY DEPRESSED AND PESSIMISTIC. WHAT SHOULD I DO? (KANSHI)

★ I HEAR NEGATIVITY IS PRETTY POPULAR THESE DAYS. EVERYBODY LOVES NEGI-KUN, AFTER ALL (LAUGH). POSITIVITY IS SO LAST SEASON!

"I THINK IT'S OKAY AS LONG AS YOU'RE NICE."

■ I HAVE A HABIT OF ALWAYS ACTING COOL BY LYING TO PEOPLE AND HIDING MY PREFERENCES; I'M NOT BEING MYSELF. I WANT TO STOP CONCEALING MY WEAKNESSES, MY BAD QUALITIES, MY EMBARRASSMENTS, AND LIVE TRUE TO MYSELF AS A PROUD OTAKU! HOW CAN I GET OVER MYSELF? (WA)

★ IF YOU HAVE OTAKU FRIENDS, THEN THE ANSWER IS VERY SIMPLE. I RECOMMEND YOU ALL COSPLAY OR WRITE AND SELL FAN COMICS TOGETHER. YOU CAN DO IT!

"BUT DON'T OVERDO IT..."

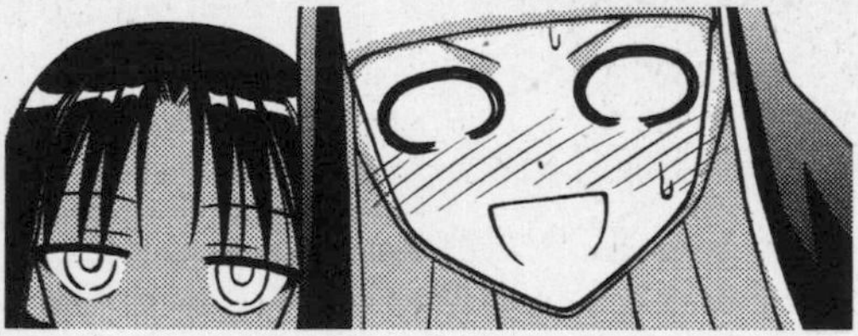

■ I WANT TO MARRY SET-CHAN, BUT WOULD SHE CHOOSE ME OVER KONOKA? (DAIFUKU)

★ LIVE STRONG.

"...THAT COULD BE TRICKY."

■ I LOVE YUE SO MUCH, I'M THINKING OF MOVING TO AYASE IN TOKYO. ...WHAT DO YOU THINK? (SWEEP GO-FER ⁘STAR⁘ KMB)

★ LIVE STRONG.

"YOU WON'T FIND YUE-SAN THERE."

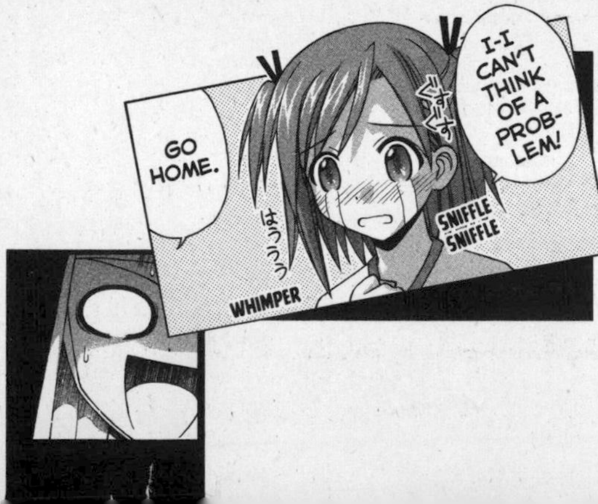
I-I CAN'T THINK OF A PROBLEM!
GO HOME.
SNIFFLE SNIFFLE
WHIMPER

3-A CLASSMATE COMPATIBILITY FORTUNES

Here we have foretold the classmates' compatibility based on their blood types and Zodiac signs. Remember that this is just fortune-telling, and fortunes aren't always accurate!

HOW IT WORKS

First, the twelve signs of the Zodiac are divided into four elements. It is said that signs of the same element are compatible, so we've put all the signs into their element groups and matched them against standard blood type compatibility fortune-telling. There is a difference in the blood type fortunes based on gender, but it wasn't a very big difference, so we didn't place anyone in male or female roles.

Zodiac element groups:

Fire -- Aries, Leo, Sagittarius
Earth -- Taurus, Virgo, Capricorn
Wind -- Gemini, Libra, Aquarius
Water -- Cancer, Scorpio, Pisces

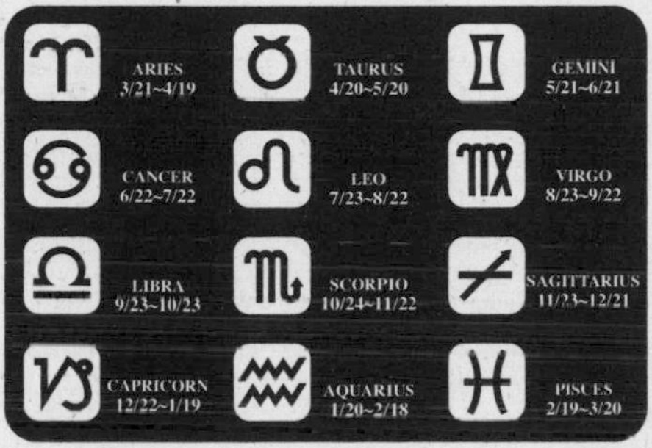

ARIES 3/21~4/19
TAURUS 4/20~5/20
GEMINI 5/21~6/21
CANCER 6/22~7/22
LEO 7/23~8/22
VIRGO 8/23~9/22
LIBRA 9/23~10/23
SCORPIO 10/24~11/22
SAGITTARIUS 11/23~12/21
CAPRICORN 12/22~1/19
AQUARIUS 1/20~2/18
PISCES 2/19~3/20

MINOR POINTS

☆ As you can tell from the chart, Virgo is the only sign with no members of class 3-A. Virgos are commonly thought to have shy, modest personalities. They have a difficult time fitting in with brash people.

It might be difficult for Virgo personalities to get along with the bold, powerful girls who keep overwhelming Negi in Class 3-A! Maybe that's why there aren't any Virgos.

☆ A, which is said to be the most common blood type in Japan, is the most common in the class, as well.
A = 11 girls, B = 6 girls, O = 7 girls, AB = 4 girls

☆ Of the elements, water has the overwhelming majority of eleven girls!
Fire = 5 girls, Earth = 6 girls, Wind = 6 girls, Water = 11 girls

3-A ZODIAC LIST

Name	Sign	Element	Blood Type
9. Misora Kasuga	Aries	Fire	A
7. Misa Kakizaki	Taurus	Earth	O
8. Asuna Kagurazaka	Taurus	Earth	B
27. Nodoka Miyazaki	Taurus	Earth	O
30. Satsuki Yotsuba	Taurus	Earth	A
6. Akira Ōkōchi	Gemini	Wind	AB
2. Yūna Akashi	Gemini	Wind	A
17. Sakurako Shiina	Gemini	Wind	B
24. Satomi Hakase	Cancer	Water	B
29. Ayaka Yukihiro	Cancer	Water	O
14. Haruna Saotome	Leo	Fire	B
28. Natsumi Murakami	Libra	Wind	A
4. Yue Ayase	Scorp.	Water	AB
5. Ako Izumi	Scorp.	Water	A
18. Mana Tatsumiya	Scorp.	Water	A
20. Kaede Nagase	Scorp.	Water	O
19. Chao Lingshen	Sag.	Fire	O
22. Fūka Narutaki	Sag.	Fire	A
23. Fumika Narutaki	Sag.	Fire	A
3. Kazumi Asakura	Cap.	Earth	O
15. Setsuna Sakurazaki	Cap.	Earth	A
21. Chizuru Naba	Aquar,	Wind	A
25. Chisame Hasegawa	Aquar.	Wind	B
11. Madoka Kugimiya	Pisces	Water	AB
12. Kū Fei	Pisces	Water	A
13. Konoka Konoe	Pisces	Water	AB
16. Makie Sasaki	Pisces	Water	O
31. Zazie	Pisces	Water	B
1. Sayo Aisaka	Unkown	Unkown	Un.
10. Chachamaru Karakuri	Unkown	Unkown	Un.
26. Eva	Unkown	Unkown	Un.

These fortunes exclude Sayo Aisaka, Evangeline, and Chachamaru, whose birthdays and blood types are unknown.

Supervision: Weekly Shōnen Magazine Editorial Department

ZODIAC ELEMENT / BLOOD TYPE CHART

■ Let's take a look at the classmates' compatibility, focusing on their element groups.

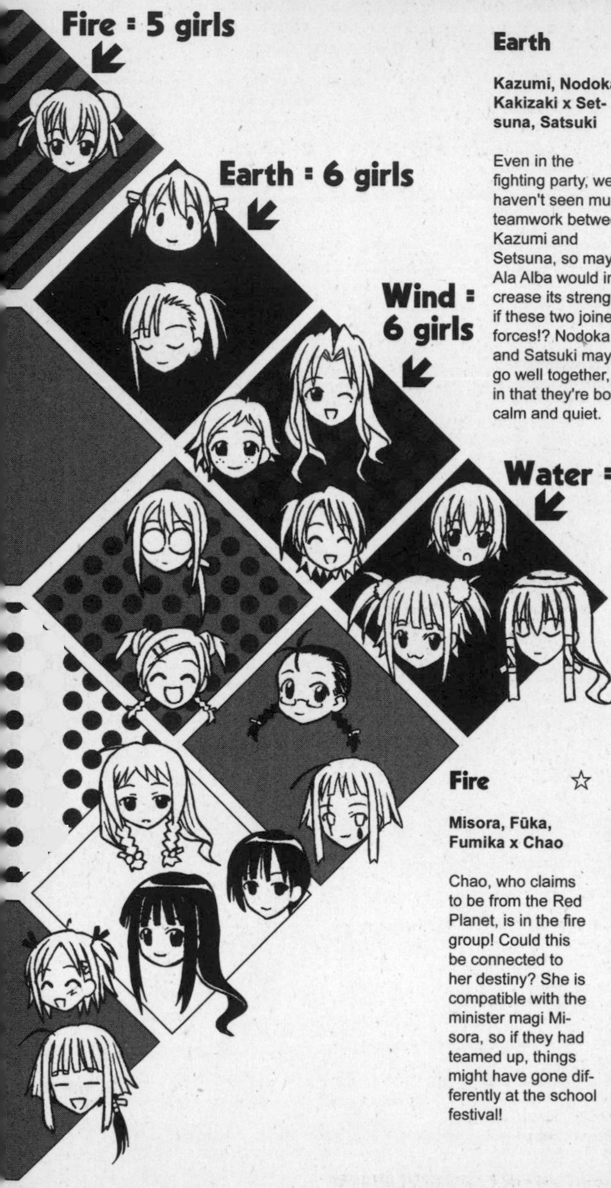

Fire : 5 girls
Earth : 6 girls
Wind : 6 girls
Water : 11 girls

Earth ☆

Kazumi, Nodoka, Kakizaki x Setsuna, Satsuki

Even in the fighting party, we haven't seen much teamwork between Kazumi and Setsuna, so maybe Ala Alba would increase its strength if these two joined forces!? Nodoka and Satsuki may go well together, in that they're both calm and quiet.

Wind ☆

Akira x Chisame, Sakurako

Akira and Chisame are both currently in Negi's Party in the Magical World. If these two practical(?) women teamed up, could a new power be born!?

Fire ☆

Misora, Fūka, Fumika x Chao

Chao, who claims to be from the Red Planet, is in the fire group! Could this be connected to her destiny? She is compatible with the minister magi Misora, so if they had teamed up, things might have gone differently at the school festival!

Water ☆

Ako, Kū Fei, Tatsumiya x Makie, Kaede, Class Rep; Hakase, Zazie x Yue, Kugimiya, Konoka

Ako and Makie share a dorm room, so they would kind of have to be friends. Tatsumiya and Kaede got in a fight in front of the movie theater during summer break, so maybe they're rivals but they respect each other's strength? Zazie(?) appeared at the end of this volume; it has been determined that she is compatible with Yue and Konoka, who are in the Magical World. We're all eager to see what happens next.

ZODIAC ELEMENT GROUPS

Fire --- Aries, Leo, Sagittarius
Earth --- Taurus, Virgo, Capricorn
Wind --- Gemini, Libra, Aquarius
Water --- Cancer, Scorpio, Pisces

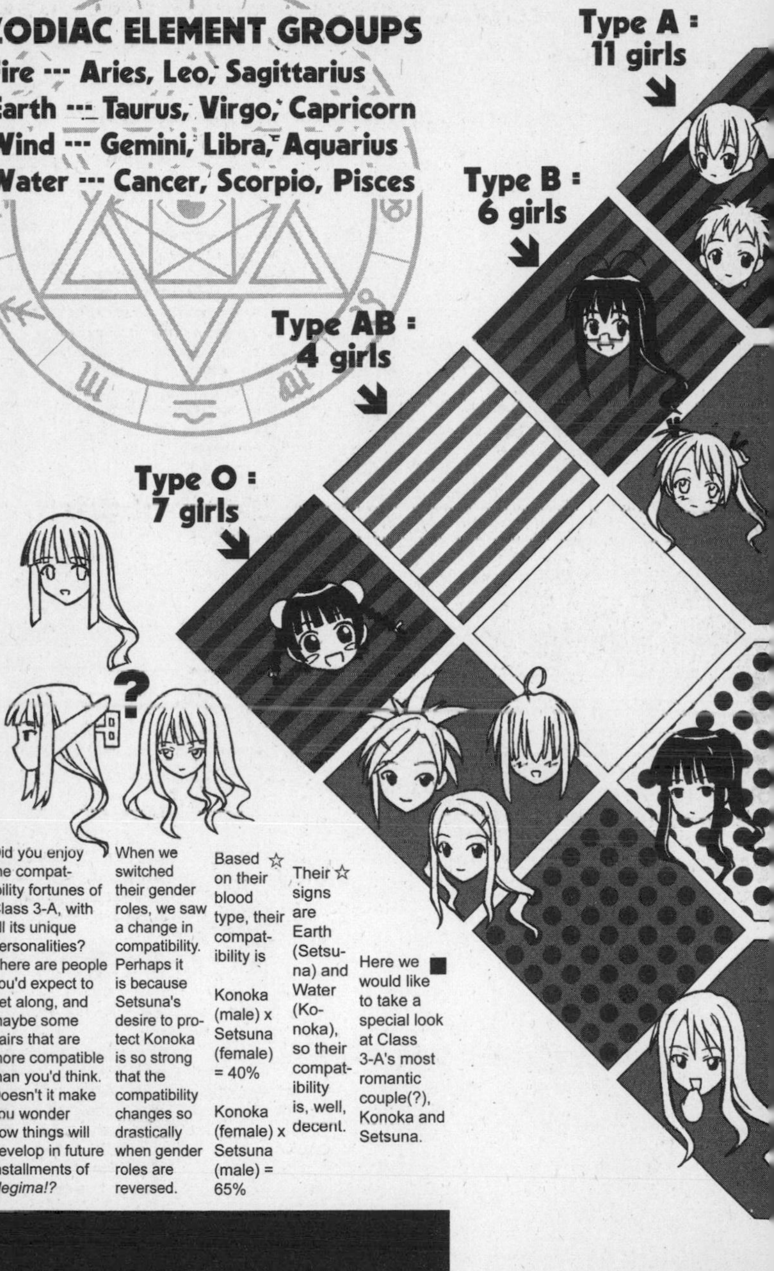
Type A : 11 girls
Type B : 6 girls
Type AB : 4 girls
Type O : 7 girls
?

Here we would like to take a special look at Class 3-A's most romantic couple(?), Konoka and Setsuna. ■

Their ☆ signs are Earth (Setsuna) and Water (Konoka), so their compatibility is, well, decent.

Based ☆ on their blood type, their compatibility is

Konoka (male) x Setsuna (female) = 40%

Konoka (female) x Setsuna (male) = 65%

When we switched their gender roles, we saw a change in compatibility. Perhaps it is because Setsuna's desire to protect Konoka is so strong that the compatibility changes so drastically when gender roles are reversed.

Did you enjoy the compatibility fortunes of Class 3-A, with all its unique personalities? There are people you'd expect to get along, and maybe some pairs that are more compatible than you'd think. Doesn't it make you wonder how things will develop in future installments of *Negima!?*

1. SAYO AISAKA
1940 ~
Don't change her seat

2. YŪNA AKASHI
Basketball team
Professor Akashi's daughter

3. KAZUMI ASAKURA
School newspaper
Mahora News (ext.B09-3780)

4. YUE AYASE
Kids' lit. club, philosophy club, library exploration club

5. AKO IZUMI
Nurse's office aide, soccer team (non-school activity)

STRONG
SUPER

6. AKIRA ŌKŌCHI
Swim team
VERY KIND

7. MISA KAKIZAKI
Cheerleader, chorus

ACTUALLY A GOOD PERSON

8. ASUNA KAGURAZAKA
AMAZING KICK

9. MISORA KASUGA
Track & field

10. CHACHAMARU KARAKURI
Tea ceremony club, go club
In case of emergency, call engineering (ext. A00-7796)

11. MADOKA KUGIMIYA
Cheerleader

12. KŪ FEI
Chinese martial arts club

Headmaster's granddaughter

13. KONOKA KONOE
Secretary, fortune-telling club, library exploration club

14. HARUNA SAOTOME
Manga club, library exploration club

15. SETSUNA SAKURAZAKI
Kendo club
Kyoto Shinmei School

16. MAKIE SASAKI
Gymnastics

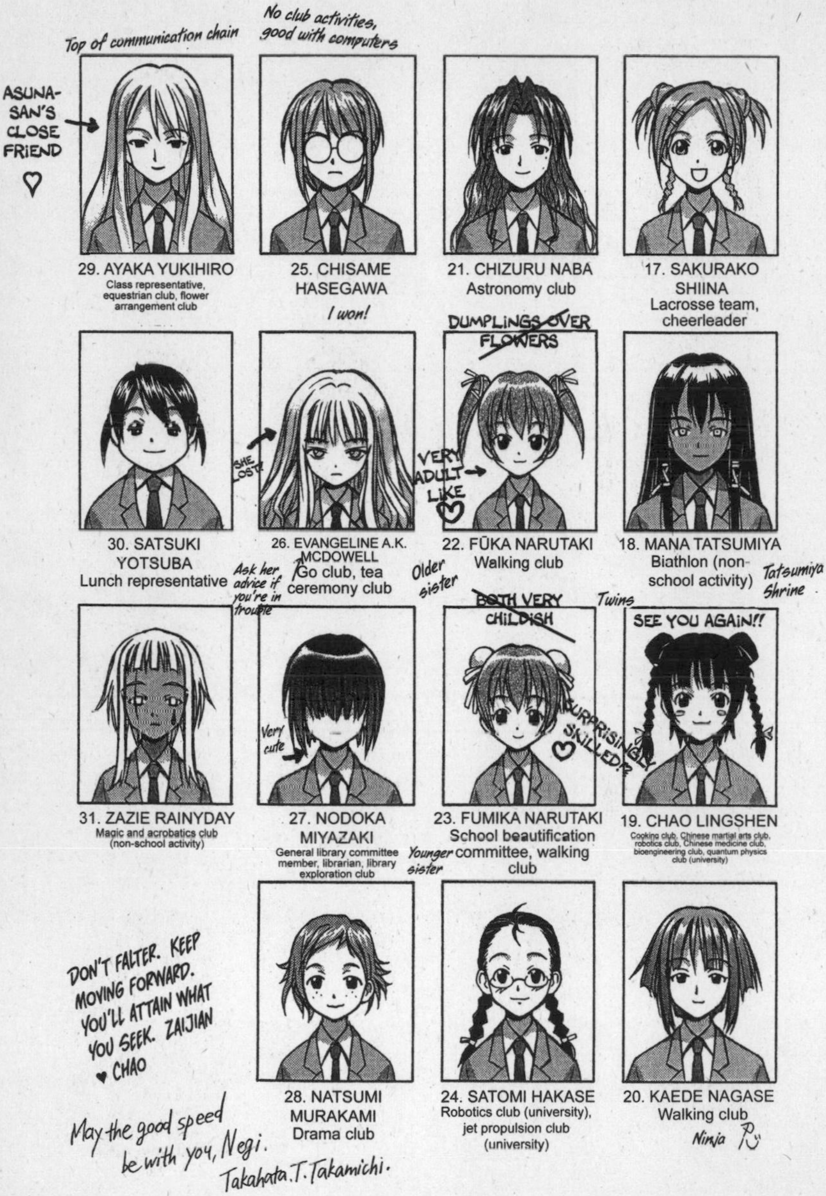

17. SAKURAKO SHIINA
Lacrosse team, cheerleader
21. CHIZURU NABA
Astronomy club
No club activities, good with computers
25. CHISAME HASEGAWA
I won!
Top of communication chain
ASUNA-SAN'S CLOSE FRIEND ♡
29. AYAKA YUKIHIRO
Class representative, equestrian club, flower arrangement club
18. MANA TATSUMIYA
Biathlon (non-school activity)
Tatsumiya Shrine
DUMPLINGS OVER FLOWERS
VERY ADULT LIKE ♡
22. FŪKA NARUTAKI
Walking club
Older sister
SHE LOST!!
26. EVANGELINE A.K. MCDOWELL
Go club, tea ceremony club
Ask her advice if you're in trouble
30. SATSUKI YOTSUBA
Lunch representative
SEE YOU AGAIN!!
19. CHAO LINGSHEN
Cooking club, Chinese martial arts club, robotics club, Chinese medicine club, bioengineering club, quantum physics club (university)
Twins
BOTH VERY CHILDISH
SURPRISINGLY SKILLED!? ♡
23. FUMIKA NARUTAKI
School beautification committee, walking club
Younger sister
Very cute
27. NODOKA MIYAZAKI
General library committee member, librarian, library exploration club
31. ZAZIE RAINYDAY
Magic and acrobatics club (non-school activity)
20. KAEDE NAGASE
Walking club
Ninja
24. SATOMI HAKASE
Robotics club (university), jet propulsion club (university)
28. NATSUMI MURAKAMI
Drama club
DON'T FALTER. KEEP MOVING FORWARD. YOU'LL ATTAIN WHAT YOU SEEK. ZAIJIAN ♥ CHAO
May the good speed be with you, Negi.
Takahata.T.Takamichi.

Zazie Rainyday

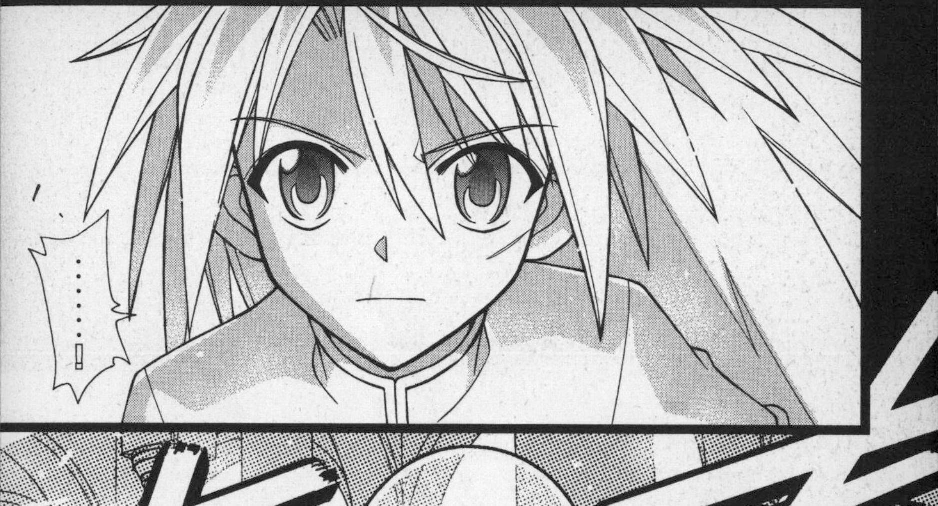
......!
WHOOSH
I'LL LET YOU MAKE THE FINAL DECISION, POYO.

he Ultimate

ion Approaches

Volume 33

On sale soon!!

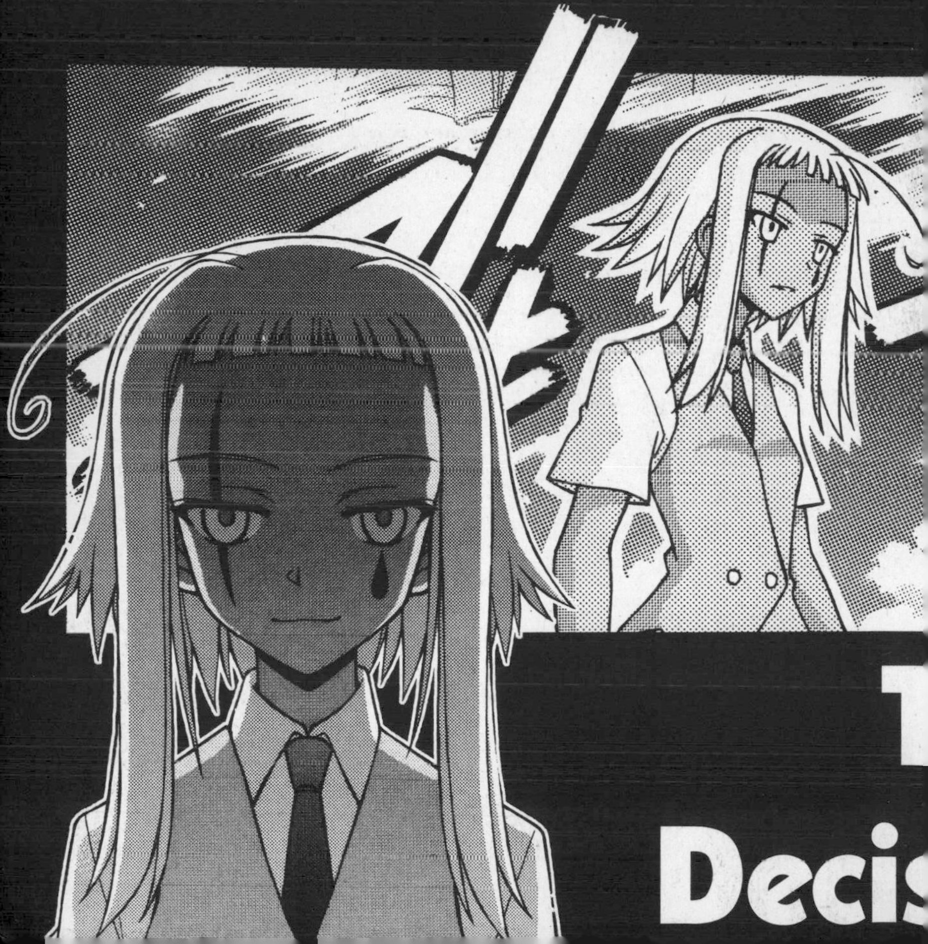

T

Decis

About the Creator

Negima! is only Ken Akamatsu's third manga, although he started working in the field in 1994 with *AI Ga Tomaranai* (released in the United States with the title *A.I. Love You*). Like all of Akamatsu's work to date, it was published in Kodansha's *Shonen Magazine*. *AI Ga Tomaranai* ran for five years before concluding in 1999. In 1998, however, Akamatsu began the work that would make him one of the most popular manga artists in Japan: *Love Hina*. *Love Hina* ran for four years, and before its conclusion in 2002, it would cause Akamatsu to be granted the prestigious Manga of the Year Award from Kodansha, as well as going on to become one of the best-selling manga in the United States.

Translation Notes

Japanese is a tricky language for most Westerners, and translation is often more art than science. For your edification and reading pleasure, here are notes on some of the places where we could have gone in a different direction with our translation of the work, or where a Japanese cultural reference is used.

Hand power, page 13

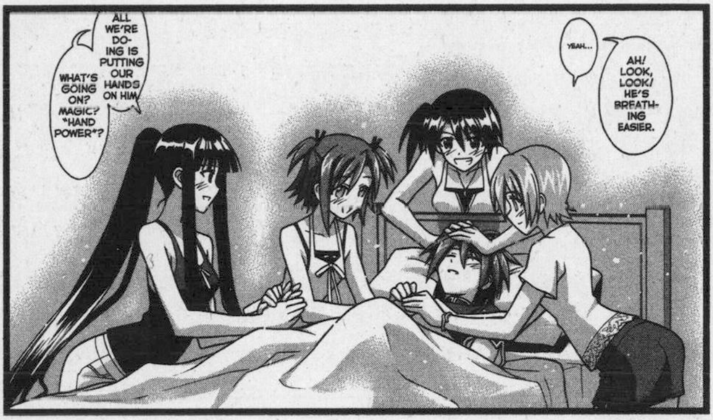
AH! LOOK, LOOK! HE'S BREATH-ING EASIER.
YEAH...
ALL WE'RE DO-ING IS PUTTING OUR HANDS ON HIM
WHAT'S GOING ON? MAGIC? "HAND POWER"?

Makie says this term in English, so she must have heard it somewhere, because she's not that good at English. Most likely, she heard it from the famous Japanese magician Mr. Maric, who claims that "hand power" is the secret to all of his magic tricks.

Tombstones, page 23

Because Japan has limited space for cemetaries, almost all of their

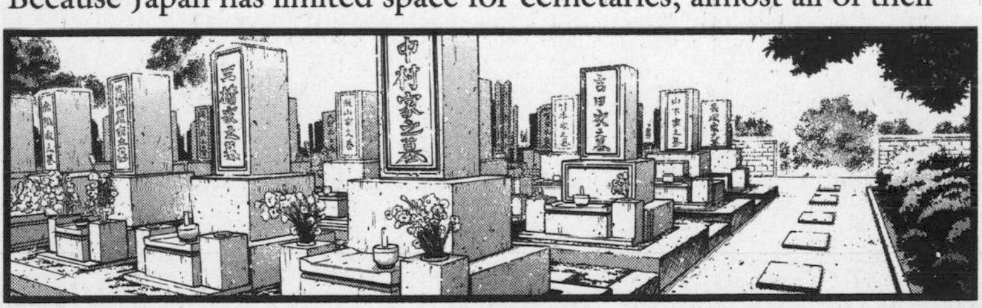

dead are cremated, and the ashes are placed in a family tomb. Ergo, a Japanese cemetary has more family tombs than individual tombs. At the Mahora cemetary, you can find the family tombs for the Yamashita family, the Yoshida family, the Nakamura family, and the Mitsuhashi family. You may recognize all of these names from the staff list at the end of the book. It's a little hard to read, but the translators believe the one on the far left is the Akamatsu family tomb.

Qualified koala bear, page 66

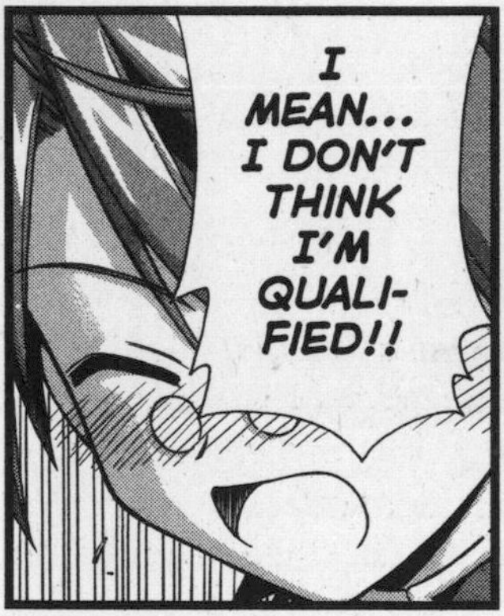
I MEAN... I DON'T THINK I'M QUALIFIED!!

For the curious, Negi says he doesn't have the *shikaku* for Makie to like him--in other words, he's not qualified. Makie is confused by the unfamiliar word, and thinks of other words that sound the same, but don't mean the same thing, including *shikaku* (blind spot), and *shikaku* (assassin). Maybe she picked them up from reading manga or something.

Jack Rakan didn't quite remember it properly, page 77

Readers with good memories (or who check their earlier volumes) will notice that in the English version, Jack Rakan does in fact say the same thing that Fate said (though the quotation marks are placed differently). This is because in Japanese, there are two words that mean almost exactly the same thing, but have subtle differences that might bring different images to the minds of Japanese readers. The one that Rakan uses is tsuchi, which refers to "earth" as in soil, or the element "earth." The word Fate uses is chi (complete with different kanji), which refers more to a "land mass," as in "land and sea" or "heaven and earth."

Game of Death and Muscle Tower, page 117

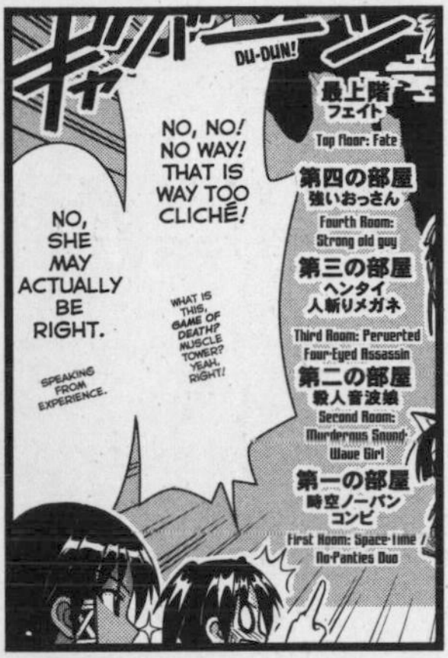
DU-DUN!
最上階
フェイト
Top floor: Fate
第四の部屋
強いおっさん
Fourth Room: Strong old guy
第三の部屋
ヘンタイ
人斬りメガネ
Third Room: Perverted Four-Eyed Assassin
第二の部屋
殺人音波娘
Second Room: Murderous Sound-Wave Girl
第一の部屋
時空ノーパン
コンビ
First Room: Space-time No-Panties Duo
NO, NO! NO WAY! THAT IS WAY TOO CLICHÉ!
WHAT IS THIS, GAME OF DEATH? MUSCLE TOWER? YEAH, RIGHT!
NO, SHE MAY ACTUALLY BE RIGHT.
SPEAKING FROM EXPERIENCE.

As you can guess from the girls' discussion, these are references to stories with towers, where the hero has to defeat an enemy (or several) in order to proceed to the next level, with the enemies getting stronger with each higher level. The Game of Death is a Bruce Lee film, and Muscle Tower is a place in Dragonball.

Okuki Yakō, page 130

Long-time readers will remember Tsukuyomi's "Hyakki Yakō" from volume 5, in which she summoned a parade of one hundred yōkai, or supernatural beings. This summon is a lot like that, except that instead of summoning hyaku (one hundred), she summons oku (one hundred million). Also, these yōkai seem to be a lot less silly.

Come forth, page 136

When Kū Fei summons her artifact, she actually uses a more old-fashioned form of Japanese to say, in effect, "adeat."

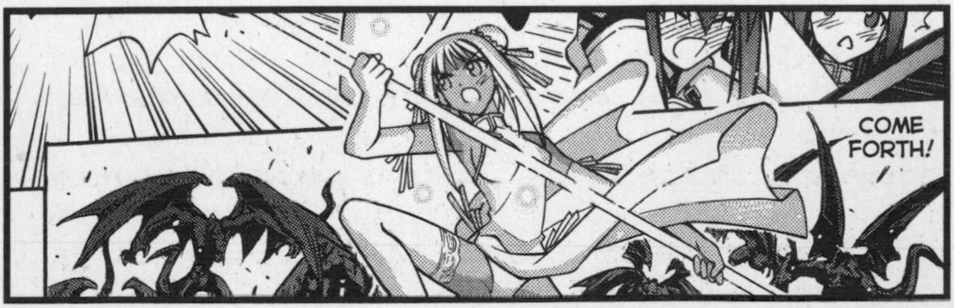
COME FORTH!

Preview of *Negima!* Volume 33

We're pleased to present you a preview from volume 33. Please check our website, www.kodanshacomics.com, to see when this volume will be available in English. For now you'll have to make do with Japanese!

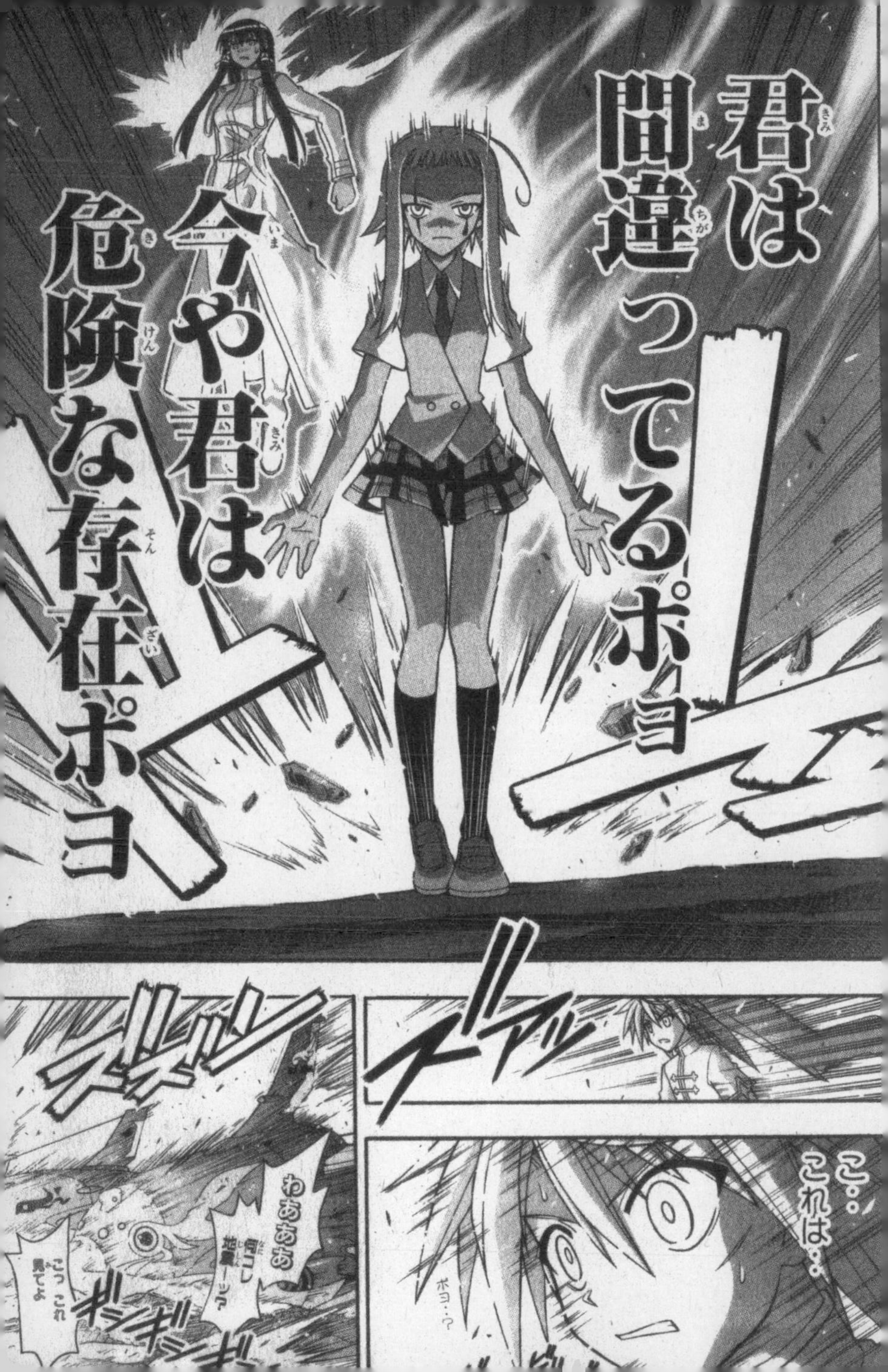
君は間違ってるポヨ
今や君は危険な存在ポヨ
ズアッ
こ・・これは・・・
ポヨ・・?
わあああ
何コレ地震ーッ?
こっこれ見てよ

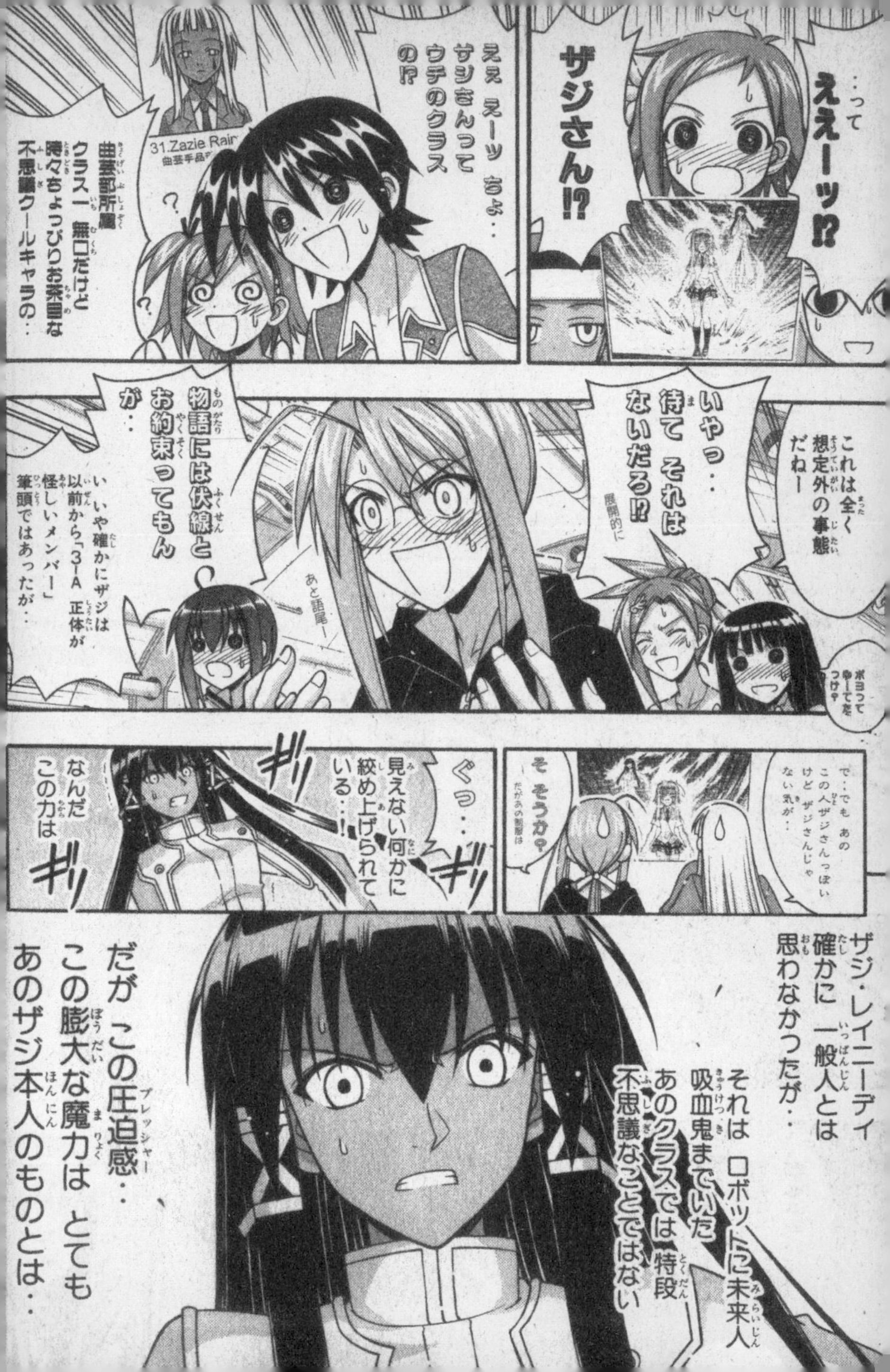

…って
ええーッ!?
ザジさん!?
ええ えーッ ちょ… ザジさんってウチのクラスの!?
31.Zazie Rain
曲芸手品部
曲芸部所属 クラス一無口だけど 時々ちょっぴりお茶目な 不思議クールキャラの…
これは全く想定外の事態だねー
ボヨってゆーてたっけ?
いやっ… 待て それはないだろ!?
展開的に
物語には伏線とお約束ってもんが…
あと語尾ー
い いや確かにザジは以前から「3-A 正体が怪しいメンバー」筆頭ではあったが…
で…でも あの この人ザジさんっぽいけど ザジさんじゃない気が…
そ そうか?
だがあの制服は
ぐっ… 見えない何かに絞め上げられている…!
ギリ
ギリ
なんだ この力は
ギリ
ザジ・レイニーデイ 確かに一般人とは思わなかったが…
それは ロボットに未来人 吸血鬼までいた あのクラスでは 特段不思議なことではない
だが この圧迫感・・ この膨大な魔力は とても あのザジ本人のものとは・・

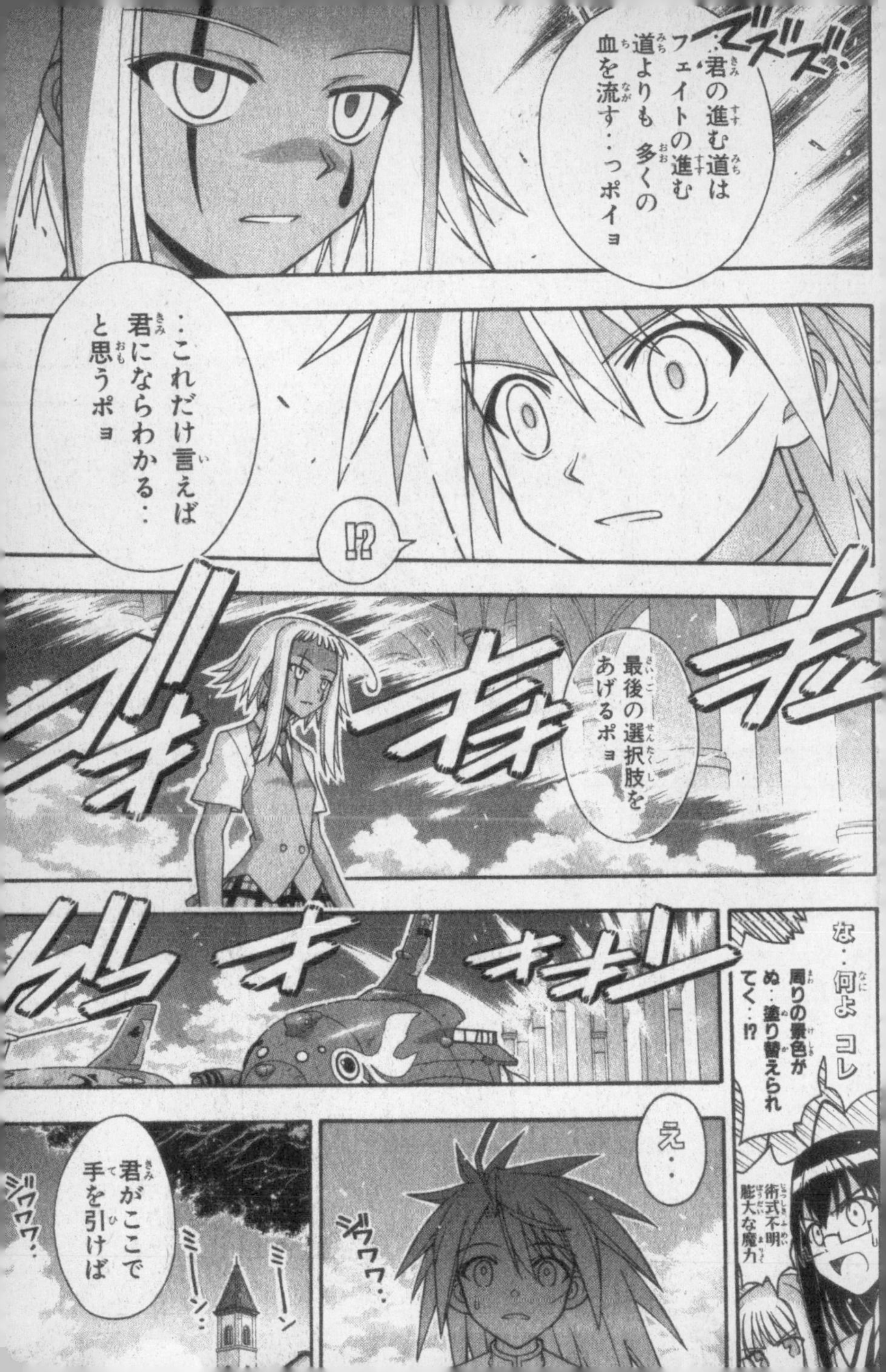
ズズズ!!
…君の進む道は フェイトの進む 道よりも 多くの 血を流す…っポイヨ
…これだけ言えば 君にならわかる… と思うポヨ
!?
最後の選択肢を あげるポヨ
な…何よ コレ
周りの景色が ぬ…塗り替えられ てく…!?
術式不明 膨大な魔力
え…
ジワワワ…
君がここで 手を引けば
ジワワワ…
ミーーン
ミーーン…

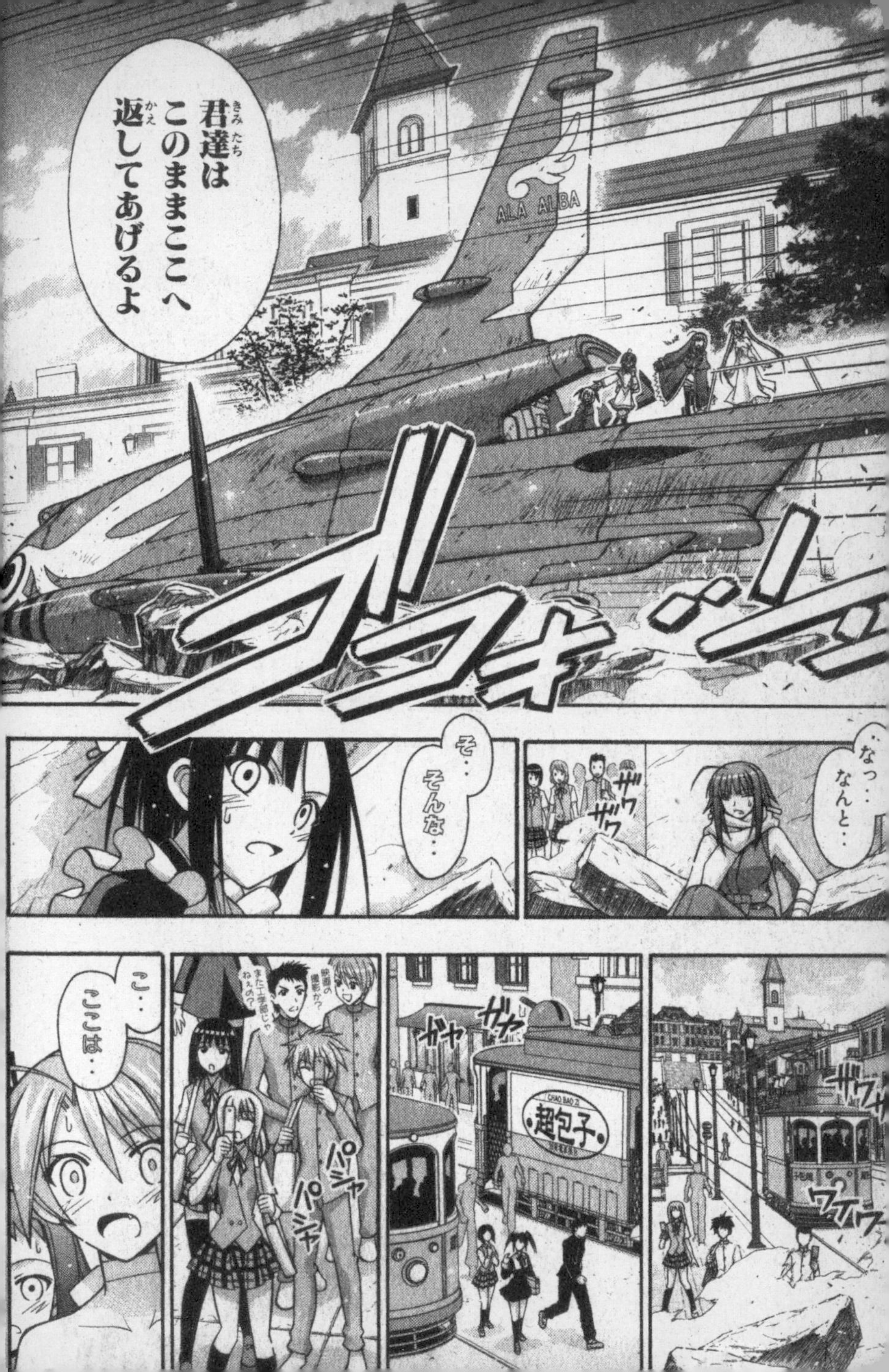
君達はこのままここへ返してあげるよ
ALA ALBA
・・なっ・・・なんと・・・
ザワ
ザワ
そ・・・そんな・・・
ザワザ
ワイワ
CHAO BAO ZI
超包子
ガヤ
ガヤ
映画の撮影か？
また工学部じゃねえの？
パシャ
パシャ
こ・・・ここは・・・

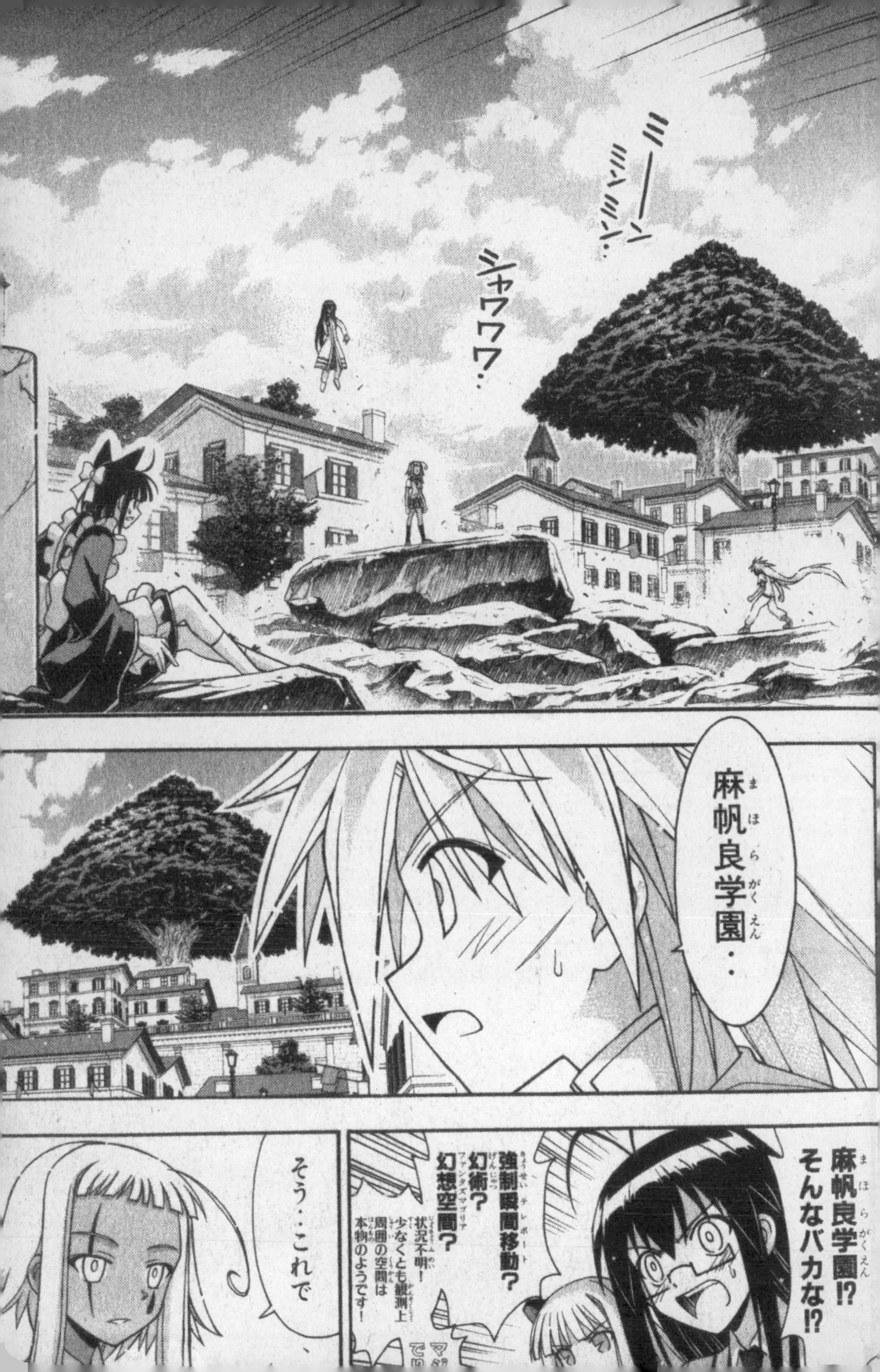
ミーーーン
ミンミン・・
シャワワワ・・
麻帆良学園・・
麻帆良学園!? そんなバカな!?
強制瞬間移動? 幻術? 幻想空間?
状況不明! 少なくとも観測上周囲の空間は本物のようです!
そう・・これで